DDC

Quick Reference Guide

Lotus 1·2·3 ™
VER. 2.2
IBM PC

Iris Blanc

Dictation Disc Company

14 East 38 Street, New York, NY 10016

INTRODUCTION

Quick Reference Guide for LOTUS 1-2-3, version 2.2, will save hours searching through technical manuals. Each function is illustrated with step-by-step key graphics to walk you through procedures. The template featured on the back cover will provide a fast reference to LOTUS 1-2-3 function keys.

An index, referencing all procedures covered in the book, appears on pages 128-133. A command index can be found on pages 125-127 while a description of functions appears on pages 107-118.

A glossary of spreadsheet terminology appears on pages 121-124.

Before You Begin

You should be familiar with the worksheet screen (illustrated on page a), basic cursor movements and highlighting procedures. Refer to page 65, "Moving the Cell Cursor," and to page 50, "Highlighting Ranges" before proceeding.

It is my hope that this booklet will help you use LOTUS 1-2-3 with ease.

Iris Blanc

Technical Editing:

David Altman

Illustration of a Lotus Spreadsheet

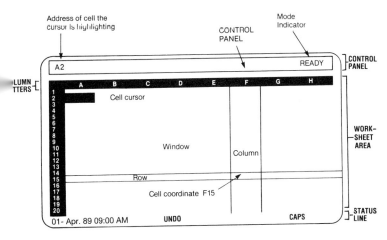

Address of cell the cursor is highlighting

CONTROL PANEL

Mode Indicator

A2   READY

CONTROL PANEL

LUMN TTERS

A   B   C   D   E   F   G   H

Cell cursor

Window

Column

Row

Cell coordinate F15

01- Apr. 89 09:00 AM   UNDO   CAPS

WORK-SHEET AREA

STATUS LINE

A

ADDING APPLICATION PROGRAMS

NOTE: • *Lotus includes two-add-in programs: Macro Library Manager and Allways.*
• *Add-in programs must be resident on the default directory.*
• *Add-in programs contain the extension .ADN.*
• *Check to determine the memory necessary to run add-in programs.*

Assigning Add-In Program to a Function Key

1. Press / (Menu) .... **/**

2. Press **A** (Add-in) .... **A**

3. Press **A** (Attach) .... **A**

4. Highlight the add-in program to be attached.

5. **ENTER** .... **↵**

6. Select a key option to invoke add-in program:

   N (No-Key)   Does not assign any key to invoke. .... **N**

   7   Assigns add-in to Alt+F7 key. **7**

   8   Assigns add-in to Alt+F8 key. **8**

(continued)

2

ADDING APPLICATION PROGRAMS (continued)

9   Assigns add-in
to Alt+F9 key. .... `9`

10   Assigns add-in
to Alt+F10 key. .... `1` `0`

7. Proceed to step 3 below to invoke add-in program.

   - OR -   OR

Press **Q** (Quit) .... `Q`
to cancel operation.

To Invoke Add-In Program

1. Press **/** (Menu) .... `/`

2. Press **A** (Add-In) .... `A`

3. Press **I** (Invoke) .... `I`

4. Highlight name of add-in program to be invoked.

5. **ENTER** .... `↵`

To Automatically Invoke Add-In Program

> *NOTE:* *Automatically invokes and attaches*
> *add-in program(s) when Lotus is*
> *started.*

1. Press **/** (Menu) .... `/`

2. Press **W** (Worksheet) .... `W`

(continue

3

ADDING APPLICATION PROGRAMS
(continued)

3. Press **G** (Global) .... **G**

4. Press **D** (Default) .... **D**

5. Press **O** (Other) .... **O**

6. Press **A** (Add-in) .... **A**

7. Press **S** (Set) .... **S**

8. Select auto-attach add-in setting option:

    1 .... **1**

    2 .... **2**

    3 .... **3**

    4 .... **4**

    5 .... **5**

    6 .... **6**

    7 .... **7**

    8 .... **8**

9. Type or highlight add-in program.

10. **ENTER** .... **←**

11. Press **Y** (Yes) .... **Y**
    to automatically invoke add-in.

12. Press **Q** (Quit) .... **Q**

13. Press **Q** (Quit) .... **Q**

(continued)

ADDING APPLICATION PROGRAMS (continued)

<u>To Detach Add-In Program</u>

> *NOTE:* *Removes **an** add-in from memory for current work session. To detach add-in from system, use /**W**orksheet **G**lobal **D**efault **O**ther **A**dd-In **C**ancel. To save setting, use /**W G D U**.*

1. Press **/** (Menu) .... | **/** |

2. Press **A** (Add-In) .... | **A** |

3. Press **D** (Detach) .... | **D** |

4. Highlight add-in to be 'detached.'

5. **ENTER**. .... | ⏎ |

<u>To Clear Add-In Program</u>

> *NOTE:* *Removes **all** add-ins from memory for current work session. To cancel add-in from system, use /**W**orksheet **G**lobal **D**efault **O**ther **A**dd-In **C**ancel. To save setting, use /**W G D U**.*

1. Press **/** (Menu) .... | **/** |

2. Press **A** (Add-In) .... | **A** |

3. Press **C** (Clear) .... | **C** |

4. Highlight add-in to be 'detached.'

5. **ENTER**. .... | ← |

CANCELLING A COMMAND

1. Press **ESC** .... Esc
    to backup one menu level or command step
    at a time.

    - OR -   OR

    Press **Ctrl + Break** .... Ctrl + Break
    to completely stop a procedure.

6

CHANGING COLUMN WIDTH

NOTE: *The column width default is 9 characters.*

For Range of Adjacent Columns

1. Press **/** (Menu) .... `/`

2. Press **W** (Worksheet) .... `W`

3. Press **C** (Column) .... `C`

4. Press **C** (Column-Range) .... `C`

5. Press **S** (Set-Width) .... `S`

6. Highlight range of columns to be modified.

7. **ENTER** . ... `↵`

8. Press right or left arrow key
   to desired column width. .... `→` or `←`

   - OR -   OR

   Type a number of desired
   column width. .... **Option**

9. **ENTER** .... `↵`

For Single Column

1. Press **/** (Menu) .... `/`

2. Press **W** (Worksheet) .... `W`

CHANGING COLUMN WIDTH (continued)

3. Press **C** (Column) .... `C`

4. Press **S** (Set-Width) .... `S`

5. Press right or left arrow key
   to desired column width. .... `→` or `←`

   - OR -   OR

   Type a number of desired
   column width ....**Option**

6. **ENTER** .... `↵`

For Global Worksheet

1. Press **/** (Menu) .... `/`

2. Press **W** (Worksheet) .... `W`

3. Press **G** (Global) .... `G`

4. Press **C** (Column-Width) .... `C`

5. Press right or left arrow key
   to desired column width .... `→` or `←`

   - OR -   OR

   Type a number of desired
   column width. ....**Option**

6. **ENTER** .... `↵`

8

CHANGING COLUMN WIDTH (continued)

Resetting Column Width

> *NOTE:* *Restores default column width to 9*
> *characters.*

For Adjacent Columns

1. Place cursor in first cell to be modified.

2. Press **/** (Menu) .... `/`

3. Press **W** (Worksheet) .... `W`

4. Press **C** (Column) .... `C`

5. Press **C** (Column-Range) .... `C`

6. Press **R** (Reset-width) .... `R`

7. Highlight range of columns to be reset.

8. **ENTER.** .... `↵`

For Single Columns

1. Place cursor in first cell to be modified.

2. Press **/** (Menu) .... `/`

3. Press **W** (Worksheet) .... `W`

4. Press **C** (Column) .... `C`

CHANGING A DIRECTORY

NOTE: *This procedure will override the*
default directory for the current
session only.

1. Press / (Menu) .... **/**

2. Press **F** (File) .... **F**

3. Press **D** (Directory) .... **D**

4. **ENTER** ....
   to accept displayed directory.

   - OR -   OR

   • Type a new directory.
   • **ENTER**. ....

10

COMBINING FILES

Copying Data

> *NOTE: Data is copied from the disk onto the current worksheet at the cursor location.*

1. Place cursor on cell where data to be copied is to begin.

2. Type **/** (Menu) .... `/`

3. Type **F** (File) .... `F`

4. Type **C** (Combine) .... `C`

5. Type **C** (Copy) .... `C`

6. • Type **E** (Entire file) .... `E`
   to copy all data in a file on disk to current worksheet.
   • Highlight file to be copied.

   - OR -   OR

   • Type **N** (Named/specified-range) .... `N`
   to copy data in a range in a file on disk to current worksheet.
   • Type range name.
   • **ENTER** .... `↵`
   • Highlight file to be copied.

7. **ENTER** .... `↵`

(continue

COMBINING FILES (continued)

Adding Data

NOTE: • *Adds numbers and the results of numeric formulas in a saved worksheet file to numbers and blank cells in the current worksheet.*
• *File/Combine Add works with numeric data only.*
• *Numbers are changed from the disk onto the current worksheet at the cursor location.*

1. Place cursor on cell where changes are to begin.

2. Type **/** (Menu) .... `/`

3. Type **F** (File) .... `F`

4. Type **C** (Combine) .... `C`

5. Type **A** (Add) .... `A`

6. • Type **E** (Entire file) .... `E`
   to add all numeric data in a file on disk to the current worksheet.
   • Highlight file to be used.

   - OR -   OR

   • Type **N** (Named/specified-range) .... `N`
   to add numeric data in a range on a saved file to the current worksheet.
   • Type range name.
   • **ENTER** .... `↵`
   • Highlight file to be used.

7. **ENTER** .... `↵`

(continued)

COMBINING FILES (continued)

Subtracting Data

NOTE: •   *Subtracts numbers and the results
of numeric formulas in a saved
worksheet file from numbers and
blank cells in the current worksheet.*
•   *File/Combine Subtract works with
numeric data only.*
•   *Numbers are changed from the
disk onto the current worksheet at the
cursor location.*

1. Place cursor on cell where subtraction is to begin.

2. Type / (Menu) .... **/**

3. Type **F** (File) .... **F**

4. Type **C** (Combine) .... **C**

5. Type **S** (Subtract) .... **S**

6. •   Type **E** (Entire file) .... **E**
     to subtract all numeric data in a file on disk
     from the current worksheet.
   •   Highlight file to be used.

     - OR -   OR

   •   Type **N** (Named/specified-range)................. **N**
     to subtract numeric data in a range in a file
     on disk from the current worksheet.
   •   Type range name.
   •   **ENTER** .... ⏎
   •   Highlight file to be used.

7. **ENTER** .... ⏎

13

COPYING

> *NOTE:* *Copies a cell, a range of cells, or a*
> *formula. See pages 20-22 to create*
> *an absolute condition.*

1. Move cursor to the first cell to be copied.

2. Type / (Menu) .... [/]

3. Type **C** (Copy) .... [C]

4. Highlight cell or range of cells to be
   copied FROM.

5. **ENTER** .... [↵]

6. Move cursor to the first cell
   to be copied TO.

7. Type . (Period) .... [.]
   to lock in the range.

8. Highlight cell or range of cells to be
   copied TO.

9. **ENTER** .... [↵]

COPYING A RANGE OF VALUES

NOTE: *Copies a range of data, replacing formulas with actual values.*

1.   Place cursor in first cell to be copied.

2.   Press / (Menu) .... **/**

3.   Press **R** (Range) .... **R**

4.   Press **V** (Value) .... **V**

5.   Highlight cell or range of cells
   to be copied FROM.

6.   **ENTER.** .... ⏎

7.   Place cursor on first cell to be copied TO.

8.   **ENTER.** .... ⏎

15

DATA PARSE

NOTE: *After a file is imported, Data/Parse will*
separate long labels into distinct text
and numeric cell entries.

1. Press **/** (Menu) .... **/**

2. Press **D** (Data) .... **D**

3. Press **P** (Parse) .... **P**

4. Press **F** (Format-Line) .... **F**

5. • Press **C** (Create) .... **C**
   to insert format line above
   the cell cursor.
   • Press **I** (Input Column) .... **I**
   • Highlight the column range that
   contains a format line and
   data to be parsed.
   • **ENTER** .... ⏎

   • Press **O** (Output Range) .... **O**
   • Highlight the address or range
   name of the first cell in a blank
   range large enough to hold rows and
   columns of parsed data.
   • **ENTER** .... ⏎

   • Press **G** (Go) .... **G**

   OR   OR

   • Press **E** (Edit) .... **E**
   to edit the format line.
   • Edit format line.
   • **ENTER** .... ⏎

DELETING A FILE

NOTE: Deletes file from disk.

1. Press / (Menu) .... `/`

2. Press **F** (File) .... `F`

3. Press **E** (Erase) .... `E`

4. Select file type to be listed:

    W lists <u>worksheet</u> files .... `W`

    P lists <u>print</u> files .... `P`

    G lists <u>graph</u> files .... `G`

    O lists <u>all other</u> files .... `O`

5. Type or highlight file name to be deleted.

6. **ENTER**. .... `⏎`

7. Press **Y** (Yes) .... `Y`
    to confirm file delete.

         - OR -   OR

    Press **N** (No) .... `N`
    to cancel operation.

DRAWING LINES

NOTE: *This procedure may be used for*
repeating any character within a cell.

Horizontal

1. Place cursor in the cell where the horizontal
    line is to begin.

2. Press \ (Backslash) .... ****
    to activate the repeat action.

3. Press - (Hyphen) or = (Equal) .... **-** or **=**
    or any other desired character.

4. **ENTER.** .... **↵**

5. To copy the line to another cell or range of cells,
    use the copy procedure (See page 13.)

Vertical

1. Adjust column to desired width (See pages 6-8.)

2. Place cursor in the cell where the vertical
    line is to begin.

3. Type ¦ (Vertical Bars) .... **¦**
    or any other desired character.

4. **ENTER** .... **↵**

5. To copy the line to another cell or range of cells,
    use the copy procedure (See page 13.)

EDITING AN ENTRY

While Typing

1. Press **Backspace**. .... `Backspace`
    to erase characters to the left
    of the cursor.

    - OR -   OR

    Press **ESC** .... `Esc`
    to cancel entire procedure.

    - OR -   OR

    *   Press **F2** (Edit) .... `F2`
    *   Use cursor keys to correct entry.
    *   **ENTER** .... `⏎`
        to place edited data into worksheet.

After Data Entry

1. Place cursor on cell to be edited.

2. Press **F2** (Edit) .... `F2`

3. Use cursor keys to correct entry.

4. **ENTER** .... `⏎`
    to place edited data into worksheet.

ENTERING DATA INTO UNPROTECTED CELLS

NOTE: • *May be used for data entry in a "fill-in-the blanks" entry form.*
• *In order for UNPROTECT to work, Global Protection must be ON.*

1. Press **/** (Menu) .... **/**

2. Press **R** (Range) .... **R**

3. Press **U** (Unprot) .... **U**

4. Highlight the cell or range of cells where data will be entered or edited.

5. **ENTER**. .... **⏎**

6. Press **/** (Menu) .... **/**

7. Press **R** (Range) .... **R**

8. Press **I** (Input) .... **I**

9. Highlight data input range.

NOTE: *Cells unprotected in step 3 constitute the "data input" range.*

10. **ENTER**. .... **⏎**

11. Enter or edit data in unprotected cells.

12. Press **ESC** .... **Esc**
to cancel operation.

ENTERING FORMULAS

Using Arithmetic Symbols

1. Place cursor in the cell where answer
    should appear.

2. Press + (Plus) .... `+`
    to put Lotus into VALUE Mode.

3. Place cursor in first cell to be calculated.

4. Type desired arithmetic symbol:

    + (addition) .... `+`

    - (subtraction) .... `-`

    * (multiplication) .... `*`

    / (division) .... `/`

5. Place cursor in next cell to be calculated.
    (Repeat steps 4 & 5 **IF** further calculations are
    necessary.)

6. **ENTER** .... `↵`

Using Arithmetic Symbols For Absolute
Conditions

1. Follow steps 1-3 above.

2. Press **F4** (Absolute) .... `F4`
    to indicate a no-change condition.

(continu

ENTERING FORMULAS (continued)

3. Type desired arithmetic symbol:

    + (addition) .... `+`

    - (subtraction) .... `-`

    * (multiplication) .... `*`

    / (division) .... `/`

4. Place cursor in next cell to be calculated.

5. Press **F4** (Absolute) .... `F4`
    (Repeat steps 4-6 if further calculations are
    necessary.)

6. **ENTER** .... `←`

Using Built-In Statistical Functions

> *NOTE: See pages 107-118 for Function*
> *Descriptions*

1. Place cursor in the cell where the answer
    should appear.

2. Type **@** ("at" symbol) .... `@`

3. Type name of desired function:

    SUM (addition) .... `S` `U` `M`

    MAX (maximum) .... `M` `A` `X`

    MIN (minimum) .... `M` `I` `N`

(continued)

ENTERING FORMULAS (continued)

COUNT (count) .... `C` `O` `U` `N` `T`

AVG (average) .... `A` `V` `G`

STD (standard deviation) .... `S` `T` `D`

VAR (variance) .... `V` `A` `R`

4. Press **(** (Open Parenthesis) .... `(`

5. Type or highlight range to be calculated.

6. Press **)** (Closed Parenthesis) .... `)`

7. **ENTER** .... `↵`

Using Built-In Statistical Functions For Absolute Conditions

1. Follow steps 1-3 on previous page.

2. Press **(** (Open Parenthesis) .... `(`

3. Type or highlight range to be calculated.

4. Press **F4** (Absolute) .... `F4`
    to indicate a no change condition.

5. Press **)** (Closed Parenthesis) .... `)`

6. **ENTER** .... `↵`

ENTERING FORMULAS (continued)

For Lookup Calculations

1. Place cursor in the cell where the answer should appear.

2. Press @ ("at" symbol) .... `@`

3. Type name of desired function:

   VLOOKUP (Vertical Lookup)
   .... `V` `L` `O` `O` `K` `U` `P`

   HLOOKUP (Horizontal Lookup)
   .... `H` `L` `O` `O` `K` `U` `P`

4. Press ((Open Parenthesis) .... `(`

5. Type cell address of search item.

   -OR-

   Place cursor on cell that contains the search item.

6. Press , (Comma) .... `,`

7. Place cursor on the first cell in the table.

8. Press . (Period) .... `.`
   to lock in the range.

9. Highlight the entire table.

(continued)

ENTERING FORMULAS (continued)

10. Type **,** (Comma) .... `,`

11. Type a number that represents the column or row
    number of the table where the data to be returned lies.
    *NOTE: First column or row in the table is
                always 0.*

12. Press **)** (Closed Parenthesis). .... `)`

13. **ENTER** .... `↵`

For IF (Logical) Functions

1. Place cursor in the cell where the answer should
    appear.

2. Press **@** ("at" symbol) .... `@`

3. Type **IF** .... `I` `F`

4. Press **(** (Open Parenthesis) .... `(`

5. Type the condition to be met.

6. Press **,** (Comma) .... `,`

7. Type the argument IF the condition is TRUE.

8. Press **,** (Comma) .... `,`

9. Type the argument IF the condition is FALSE.

10. Press **)** (Closed Parenthesis) .... `)`

11. **ENTER** .... `←`

(contin

ENTERING FORMULAS (continued)

EXAMPLE: The IF statement @IF(B3<2000, B3*.03, B*.05) applied to the problem below and entered in cell C3 will compute a 3% commission for sales less than $2,000 and compute a 5% commission when the cell contains a value greater than or equal to $2,000. (The formula should then be copied for the other salespeople.)

	A	B	C
1	SALESPERSON	SALES	COMMISSION
2			EARNED
3	ADAMS	2000	
4	PRESS	1400	
5	HARRIS	3600	
6			
7			
8			
9			
10			

ENTERING SEQUENTIAL NUMBERS IN A RANGE

1. Place cursor in cell where "start" value should begin.

2. Press **/** (Menu) .... `/`

3. Press **D** (Data) .... `D`

4. Press **F** (Fill) .... `F`

5. Highlight range where "fill" data will appear.

6. **ENTER** .... `⏎`

7. Type "start" value.

   NOTE: Lotus uses zero (0) as the start value if one is not specified.

8. **ENTER** .... `⏎`

9. Type the "step" value.
   (The increment between each of the values in the range.)

   NOTE: Lotus uses one (1) as the step value if one is not specified.

10. **ENTER** .... `⏎`

11. Type the "stop" value.
    (A value that limits the sequence.)

    NOTE: Lotus uses 8191 as the stop value if one is not specified.

12. **ENTER** .... `⏎`

ENTERING VALUES

NOTE: • *The mode indicator must say READY.*
• *The entry cannot be more than 240 characters.*
• *A value entry begins with a number or a numeric symbol: + - @ . (# $*
• *DO NOT include spaces or commas in the entry. (Commas may be included by formatting the cell for currency - See page 32.)*
• *When a value is entered, the mode indicator will display VALUE.*
• *Values will **always** right justify after entry; their alignment **cannot** be changed.*

1. Place cursor in desired cell.

2. Type value entry.

3. **ENTER** .... ←┘

    -OR-   OR

Press cursor arrow key in direction of the next entry. ....

ERASING

The Screen/Worksheet

1. Press **/** (Menu) .... `/`

2. Press **W** (Worksheet) .... `W`

3. Press **E** (Erase) .... `E`

4. Press **Y** (Yes) .... `Y`

A Cell or Range of Cells

> *NOTE: Erased cells can be recovered with*
> *UNDO. (See page 104.)*

1. Place cursor on cell to be erased.

2. Press **/** (Menu) .... `/`

3. Press **R** (Range) .... `R`

4. Press **E** (Erase) .... `E`

5. Highlight cell or range of cells to be erased.

6. **ENTER.** .... `↵`

EXITING LOTUS

To Exit Temporarily

1. Press / (Menu) .... **/**

2. Press **S** (System) .... **S**

3. Type desired DOS commands
    or program to run.

4. After running desired program,
    return to DOS.

5. Type **EXIT** .... **E** **X** **I** **T**
    to return to LOTUS.

6. ENTER. .... **⏎**

To Exit Session

1. Press / (Menu) .... **/**

2. Press **Q** (Quit) .... **Q**

3. Press **Y** .... **Y**
    to exit.

    -OR-

    Press **N** .... **N**
    to return to worksheet.

FINDING FREQUENCY OF DATA DISTRIBUTION

1. Place cursor at the top of an empty column adjacent to the last column of data.

2. Enter desired values to be used for data distribution (in ascending order).

   NOTE: This is referred to as the "bin" range.

3. Press / (Menu) .... **/**

4. Press **D** (Data) .... **D**

5. Press **D** (Distribution) .... **D**

6. Highlight range of values to be calculated in frequency distribution.

7. **ENTER** .... ⏎

8. Highlight "bin" range.

9. **ENTER** .... ⏎

   NOTE: Frequency of values will appear in the column to the right of the bin range.

FIXING/FREEZING TITLES

1. Place cursor one ROW below or one COLUMN to the right of where the freeze is to occur.

2. Press **/** (Menu) .... **/**

3. Press **W** (Worksheet) .... **W**

4. Press **T** (Titles) .... **T**

5. Select a freeze option:

    B (Both)   Freezes rows above
                      cursor and columns
                      to left of cursor .... **B**

    H (Horizontal) Freezes rows above
                      cursor .... **H**

    V (Vertical) Freezes columns to left
                      of cursor .... **V**

Clearing Title Freeze

1. Place cursor one ROW below or one COLUMN to the right of where the unfreeze is to occur.

2. Press **/** (Menu) .... **/**

3. Press **W** (Worksheet) .... **W**

4. Press **T** (Titles) .... **T**

5. Press **C** (Clear) .... **C**

32

FORMATTING

Local

> *NOTE: Will affect each cell in a range and override global cell formats.*

1. Place cursor in the first cell where the desired format should appear.

2. Press **/** (Menu) .... `/`

3. Press **R** (Range) .... `R`

4. Press **F** (Format) .... `F`

5. Select a desired format:

   F (Fixed)   Displays numbers up to 15 decimal places .... `F`

   S (Scientific) Displays numbers up to 15 decimal places in scientific notation .... `S`

   C (Currency)   Displays currency symbols: dollar signs ($) and commas (,) .... `C`

   , (Comma)   Displays numbers with commas. .... `,`

   G (General)   Displays negative numbers with a minus sign (-), without commas, & without trailing zeros .... `G`

(contin

FORMATTING (continued)

+ or -   Displays numbers as
              either a plus (+), (-), or
              (.) symbol, thus
              creating a horizontal
              bar graph .... **+** or **-**

P (Percent)   Displays numbers with
              percent symbols, up
              to 15 decimal places. ...... **P**

D (Date)   Displays serial date
              numbers and (Time)
              time in various
              formats .... **D**

T (Text)   Displays formulas
              entered rather than
              computed values .... **T**

H (Hidden)   Does not display cell
              contents. .... **H**

R (Reset)   Resets the range to
              global cell format. .... **R**

6. Type desired number of decimal places (0-15)

     - OR -

   •   Select a desired format (for Date and Time)

(continued)

FORMATTING (continued)

7. **ENTER** for single cell formatting .... ⏎

    - OR -   OR

*   Highlight the range of cells to be formatted
*   **ENTER**. .... ⏎

Global

NOTE: Will affect the entire worksheet.

1. Place cursor anywhere on the worksheet.

2. Press **/** (Menu) .... **/**

3. Press **W** (Worksheet) .... **W**

4. Press **G** (Global) .... **G**

5. Press **F** (Format) .... **F**

6. Follow steps 5 - 6 on previous pages.

7. **ENTER**. .... ⏎

GRAPHING

Creating a Graph

NOTE: The X axis is the horizontal scale.
The Y axis is the vertical scale.

1.   Retrieve worksheet from which graph is to be created.

2.   Press / (Menu) .... `/`

3.   Press **G** (Graph) .... `G`

4.   Press **T** (Type) .... `T`

5.   Select desired graph type:

L   (Line) .... `L`

B   (Bar) .... `B`

S   (Stacked-Bar) .... `S`

P   (Pie). .... `P`

6.   Press **X** .... `X`
to set X-axis **label** range.

7.   Highlight range to be scaled.

8.   **ENTER**. .... `⏎`

9.   Press **A** .... `A`
to set Y-axis data range.

NOTE: A is the only data range used in a pie chart.

10.   Highlight range to be scaled.

11.   **ENTER**. .... `⏎`

(continued)

GRAPHING (continued)

To set additional data ranges:

12. • Press **B**
    to set second Y-axis data range
    or to set pie chart shading values .... `B`

   • Press **C**
    to set third Y-axis data range .... `C`

   • Press **D**
    to set fourth data range .... `D`

   • Press **E**
    to set fifth data range .... `E`

   • Press **F**
    to set sixth data range .... `F`

13. Highlight range to be scaled.

14. **ENTER** .... `↵`

(contin

GRAPHING OPTIONS

Creating a Legend

> *NOTE:* *If already working in the graphing*
> *submenu, steps 1 and 2 below need*
> *not be repeated.*

1. Press **/** (Menu) .... `/`

2. Press **G** (Graph) .... `G`

3. Press **O** (Options) .... `O`

4. Press **L** (Legend) .... `L`

5. Press **A** .... `A`
   to name first Y-axis legend.

6. Type name for first legend.

7. **ENTER.** .... `↵`

8. Repeat steps 4-7 until all legend names have
   been entered.

Creating Titles

> *NOTE:* *If already working in the graphing*
> *submenu, steps 1 and 2 below need*
> *not be repeated.*

1. Press **/** (Menu) .... `/`

2. Press **G** (Graph) .... `G`

3. Press **O** (Options) .... `O`

(continued)

GRAPHING OPTIONS (continued)

4. Press **T** (Titles) .... T

5. Press **F** (First) .... F

6. Type a title or heading.

7. **ENTER** .... ↵

If a subtitle is desired:

8. Repeat steps 4-7. At step 5, Press S (Second).

Creating Data Labels

> *NOTE:*   • *If already working in the graphing submenu, steps 1 and 2 below need not be repeated.*
>   • *A data label indicates values plotted on a bar or line graph and usually appears at the top of each bar or at the plotted point on a line graph.*

1. Press **/** (Menu) .... /

2. Press **G** (Graph) .... G

3. Press **O** (Options) .... O

4. Press **D** (Data-Labels) .... D

5. Highlight range to receive labels.

(continu

GRAPHING OPTIONS (continued)

6. Select a range to be labeled:
   A .... 🅰
   B .... 🅱
   C .... 🅲
   D .... 🅳
   E .... 🅴
   F .... 🅵

      - OR -   OR

   G (Group) Enters all ranges .... 🅶

      - OR -   OR

   Q (Quit) Cancels operation .... 🆀

7. Highlight range containing the labels.

8. **ENTER.** .... ⏎

9. Select a label alignment option:
   C (Center) .... 🅲
   L (Left). .... 🅻
   A (Above) .... 🅰
   R (Right) .... 🆁
   B (Below) .... 🅱

10. Press **Q** (Quit) .... 🆀
    to return to worksheet.

(continued)

GRAPHING OPTIONS (continued)

Cancelling Graph Settings

1. Press **/** (Menu) .... `/`

2. Press **G** (Graph) .... `G`

3. Press **R** (Reset) .... `R`

4. Select a reset option:

    G (Graph)   Resets all graph settings .. `G`

    X   Resets X-data range .... `X`
    A - F   Resets A - F data
                      range(s) .... `A` - `F`
    R (Range)   Resets all data range
                      settings .... `R`
    O (Options)   Resets all options
                      settings .... `O`
    Q (Quit)   To return to graph
                      menu. .... `Q`

Viewing Graphs

> *NOTE: If already working in the graphing
> submenu, steps 1 and 2 below need
> not be repeated.*

Procedure I

1. Press **/** (Menu) .... `/`

2. Press **G** (Graph) .... `G`

3. Press **V** (View) .... `V`

(continu

GRAPHING OPTIONS (continued)

Procedure II

While in READY MODE:

- Press **F10** (Graph Key) ....

<u>Saving Graphs (for printing)</u>

> *NOTE:* • *If already working in the graphing submenu, steps 1 and 2 below need not be repeated.*
> • *Graph image will be saved for printing only.*
> • *Graphs will automatically be assigned a .PIC extension and cannot be retrieved by LOTUS. To save graph settings for later recall, see section on next page.*

1. Press / (Menu) .... ⬛ **/**

2. Press **G** (Graph) .... ⬛ **G**

3. Press **S** (Save) .... ⬛ **S**

4. Type name of graph to be saved.

5. **ENTER**. .... ⬛

(continued)

GRAPHING OPTIONS (continued)

Saving Graphs (for recall)

> *NOTE:* • *If already working in the graphing submenu, steps 1 and 2 below need not be repeated.*

1. Press **/** (Menu) .... `/`

2. Press **G** (Graph) .... `G`

3. Press **N** (Name) .... `N`

4. Press **C** (Create) .... `C`

5. **ENTER** .... `⏎`

6. Type a graph name.

7. **ENTER** .... `⏎`

Listing Graphs (Graph / Name Table)

> *NOTE:* *Will create an alphabetical list of created graphs, graph types and titles.*

1. Place cursor in a cell in an available section of the worksheet.

2. Press **/** (Menu) .... `/`

3. Press **G** (Graph) .... `G`

4. Press **N** (Name) .... `N`

5. Press **T** (Table) .... `T`

(continu

GRAPHING OPTIONS (continued)

6. Highlight cell to begin list.

7. **ENTER** .... ◄┘

Printing

> *NOTE:* • *PrintGraph must be installed to proceed.*
> • *The graph must be saved as a graph (.PIC) file.*

1. Return to READY MODE.

2. Press **/** (Menu) .... **/**

3. Press **Q** (Quit). .... **Q**
   to exit system.

4. Press **Y** (Yes) .... **Y**
   to confirm exit.

5. Press **P** (PrintGraph) .... **P**

6. Press **I** (Image-Select) .... **I**

7. Highlight graph to be printed.

8. Press **spacebar** to mark graph for printing.
   (A symbol will be entered next to the selected
   graph). .... **Space**

9. Repeat steps 7 & 8 for each graph selection.

10. **ENTER**. .... ◄┘

(continued)

GRAPHING OPTIONS (continued)

11. Press **A** (Align) .... `A`

12. Press **G** (Go) .... `G`

13. Press **Q** (Quit) .... `Q`

14. Press **E** (Exit) .... `E`
    to exit PrintGraph and return to Access system.

Printing Graphs with Appearance Changes

NOTE: • *Will allow changes in graph's size, typeface, color, angle of rotation, width and height and top and left margins.*
• *PrintGraph uses only its own fonts; your printer's fonts cannot be used.*

Changing Fonts

NOTE: • *If already working in the PrintGraph submenu, steps 1-5 need not be repeated.*

1. Return to READY Mode.

2. Press **/** (Menu) .... `/`

3. Press **Q** (Quit) .... `Q`
   to exit system.

4. Press **Y** (Yes) .... `Y`
   to confirm exit.

(continu

GRAPHING OPTIONS (continued)

5. Press **P** (PrintGraph) .... P

6. Press **S** (Settings) .... S

7. Press **I** (Image) I

8. Press **F** (Font) .... F

9. Select a font option:

   1 Indicates font to be used
      for first line of graph's title 1

   2 Indicates font to be used
      for all other alphanumeric
      characters 2

10. Using up and down cursor keys,
    highlight desired font. .... ↑ ↓

11. Press **Spacebar** .... Space
    to mark selection.

    *NOTE: To de-select, highlight selection and
            press Spacebar again.*

12. **ENTER** .... ↵

(continued)

GRAPHING OPTIONS (continued)

Changing Graph Size

> *NOTE:* *If already working in the PrintGraph*
> *submenu, steps 1-5 need not be*
> *repeated.*

1. Return to READY Mode.

2. Press **/** (Menu) .... **/**

3. Press **Q** (Quit) .... **Q**
    to exit system.

4. Press **Y** (Yes) .... **Y**
    to confirm exit.

5. Press **P** (Print Graph) .... **P**

6. Press **S** (Settings) .... **S**

7. Press **I** (Image) .... **I**

8. Press **S** (Size) .... **S**

9. Select a sizing option:

    F (Full)   Sets rotation to 90° to
                     print sideways .... **F**

    H (Half)   Sets rotation to 0°
                     allowing printing of
                     two graphs per page .... **H**

    M (Manual)   Allows for **custom**
                     height, width, margins
                     and rotation .... **M**

(continu

GRAPHING OPTIONS (continued)

• Select a **custom** option:

T (Top)   to set top margin ..... ⊞

L (Left)   to set left margin ..... ⊞

W (Width)   to set width. .... ⊞

H (Height)   to set height. .... ⊞

R (Rotation) to set rotation. .... ⊞

Q (Quit)   to cancel operation.. ⊞

• Type desired number of
inches for each option
selected ....**Option**

• **ENTER** .... ⊞

Q (Quit)   To return to Image
menu .... ⊞

48

HELP

HIDING COLUMNS

NOTE: *Hides selected columns without erasing data. Formulas in hidden columns continue to work correctly.*

1. Press / (Menu) .... **/**

2. Press **W** (Worksheet) .... **W**

3. Press **C** (Column) .... **C**

4. Press **H** (Hide) .... **H**

5. Highlight range of columns to be hidden.

6. **ENTER** .... ⏎

Redisplaying Hidden Columns

1. Press / (Menu) .... **/**

2. Press **W** (Worksheet) .... **W**

3. Press **C** (Column) .... **C**

4. Press **D** (Display) .... **D**

5. Highlight range of columns to be redisplayed.

6. **ENTER** .... ⏎

HIGHLIGHTING RANGES

1. Place cursor in first cell in the range
   to be highlighted.

2. **ENTER** .... ⏎
   to highlight individual cell.

   - OR -   OR

   • Press . (Period) . ... ▪
     to lock in range.
   • Use cursor keys to
     highlight range. .... ↑ ↓ ← →

3. **ENTER** .... ⏎

51

IMPORTING A FILE

1. Place cursor in cell where imported data is to begin.

2. Press / (Menu) .... **/**

3. Press **F** (File) .... **F**

4. Press **I** (Import) .... **I**

5. Press **T** (Text) .... **T**
   to import labels and numbers from a nondelimited text flle.

   NOTE: Do Not use with a delimited text file.

   - OR -   OR

   Press **N** (Numbers) .... **N**
   to import only numbers from a nondelimited text file or to import numbers and labels from a delimited text file.

6. Type name of file to be imported.

7. **ENTER**. .... ⏎

   NOTE: To calculate imported data, it is necessry to use the Data/Parse procedure to place data in cells. (See page 15.)

INSERTING / DELETING COLUMNS AND ROWS

1. Place cursor in the column where the insertion or deletion is to occur.

2. Press **/** (Menu) .... **/**

3. Press **W** (Worksheet) .... **W**

4. Press **I** (Insert) .... **I**

   - OR -   OR

   Press **D** (Delete) .... **D**

5. Press **C** (Column) .... **C**

   - OR -   OR

   Press **R** (Row) .... **R**

6. **ENTER** .... ⏎
   to insert or delete **one** column or row.

   - OR -   OR

   • Highlight across (for column) or down (for row) for desired number of columns or rows to be inserted or deleted.
   • **ENTER** .... ⏎

INSERTING PAGE BREAK

NOTE: • *Will insert desired page breaks in printed worksheets.*
• *DO NOT enter data in the row where page break marker (: :) appears.*

1. Place cursor in row where page break is desired.

2. Press **/** (Menu) .... `/`

3. Press **W** (Worksheet) .... `W`

4. Press **P** (Page) .... `P`

To Remove Page Break

1. Place cursor in any cell in the row where page break markerappears.

2. Press **/** (Menu) .... `/`

3. Press **W** (Worksheet) .... `W`

4. Press **D** (Delete) .... `D`

5. Press **R** (Row) .... `R`

6. **ENTER**. .... `←`

JUSTIFYING LABELS
(In a Range)

> *NOTE:* • *Paragraphs may be created from columns of labels to fit into a specific width.*
> • *Continuous text will justify until a non-label entry is reached.*

1. Press / (Menu) .... `/`

2. Press **R** (Range) .... `R`

3. Press **J** (Justify) .... `J`

4. Highlight the range to receive justified text.

5. **ENTER** .... `←`

LABELS

ENTERING LABELS

NOTE: • *The mode indicator must say READY.*

• *The entry cannot be more than 240 characters.*

• *When a label is longer than the cell's column width, the text will continue into the next cell if it is blank; otherwise, the entry will be truncated.*

Alphabetic

NOTE: Alphabetic labels will automatically left justify after entry. To center, right justify, or fill the cell with a character, see ALIGNING LABELS section on next page.

1. Place cursor in desired cell.

2. Type label text.

3. **ENTER** .... ↵

  -OR-   OR

  Press cursor arrow key in direction
  of next entry .... ↓ → ↑ ←

(continued)

LABELS (continued)

<u>Numeric</u>

> *NOTE: Numeric labels **will not** calculate.*

1. Place cursor in desired cell.

2. Type an **apostrophe** (label prefix) .... `'`

> *NOTE: Using an apostrophe as a label prefix
> will left justify the numeric label and
> will indicate that the entry is <u>not</u> a
> value.*

3. Type label text.

4. **ENTER** .... `↵`

      -OR-   OR

   Press cursor arrow key in direction
   of the next entry. .... `↓` `→` `↑` `←`

<u>Aligning Labels</u>
(right, center or fill the cell)

Before cell entry

1. Place cursor in desired cell.

2. Type a label prefix option:

   " (quote)   to right justify .... `"`

   ^ (caret)   to center .... `^`

   **** (backslash)   to repeat a character
                           to fill the cell .... `\`

                                                    (contir

LABELS (continued)

3. Type label text.

4. **ENTER** .... ↵

    -OR-   OR

    Press a cursor arrow key in the
    direction of the next entry .... ↓ → ↑ ←

After cell entry

1. Place cursor in desired cell.

2. Type **/** (Menu) .... /

3. Type **R** (Range) .... R

4. Type **L** (Label) L

5. Select desired alignment option:

    L (Left) L

    R (Right) .... R

    C (Center) C

6. **ENTER** (for single-cell alignment) .... ↵

    -OR-

    • Highlight range of cells to be aligned.
    • **ENTER**. .... ↵

LISTING FILES

NOTE: *Lists files in the current directory*

1.   Press **/** (Menu) .... `/`

2.   Press **F** (File) .... `F`

3.   Press **L** (List) .... `L`

4.   Select a file type option:

   W   lists <u>worksheet</u> files. .... `W`

   P   lists <u>print</u> files. .... `P`

   G   lists <u>graph</u> files .... `G`

   O   lists <u>all</u> files .... `O`

   L   lists all files linked to
   current worksheet by formula
   references. .... `L`

<u>Listing Files in a Different Drive/Directory:</u>

5.   Press **ESC** .... `Esc`

6.   Press **ESC** .... `Esc`

7.   Type new drive and/or directory.

8.   Type a filename (with extension) to list.

9.   **ENTER**. .... `⏎`

59

MACROS

NOTE: • *Macros are saved keystroke instructions which may be played back at a later time to perform a particular task.*
• *Macros may be saved on an individual worksheet or in a macro library with other macros.*
• *Macros may be created through the Learn Feature by performing the task to be automated.*
• *The "Learn Range" indicates where the keystrokes will be recorded on the worksheet.*
• *The "Learn Range" must be specified before the macro is created.*

Specifying The Learn Range

1. Place cursor in a cell in an empty part of the worksheet.

2. Press **/** (Menu) .... **/**

3. Press **W** (Worksheet) .... **W**

4. Press **L** (Learn) .... **L**

5. Press **R** (Range) .... **R**

6. Highlight a long single column range.

7. **ENTER**. .... ⏎

(continued)

MACROS (continued)

Clearing the Learn Range

1. Press **/** (Menu) .... /

2. Press **W** (Worksheet) .... W

3. Press **L** (Learn) L

4. Press **E** (Erase) .... E

5. Press **Y** (Yes) .... Y
    to clear learn range.

    -OR-   OR

    Press **N** (No) .... N
    to return to READY mode.

Cancelling the Learn Range

   NOTE: Cancels the specified learn range.

1. Press **/** (Menu) .... /

2. Press **W** (Worksheet) .... W

3. Press **L** (Learn) L

4. Press **C** (Cancel) C

(continue

MACROS (continued)

Recording a Macro

> *NOTE: Lotus records keystrokes in macro
> instruction format.*

1. Place cursor in the first cell in the "Learn Range".

2. Press **ALT + F5** .... `Alt` + `F5`
    to turn on recording feature.

3. Type keystrokes to be recorded.

4. Press **ALT + F5** .... `Alt` + `F5`
    to turn off recording feature.

Naming a Macro

1. Press **/** (Menu) .... `/`

2. Press **R** (Range) .... `R`

3. Press **N** (Name) .... `N`

4. Press **C** (Create) .... `C`

5. Type macro name (as the range name).

> *NOTE: A macro may be named with a \
> (backslash) followed by a letter, e.g.: W*

6. Highlight first cell of the macro as the
    range to name.

(continued)

MACROS (continued)

Running a Macro

If macro was named with a \ (backslash) and a single letter:

1. Press **ALT + Letter** .... **Alt** + letter

If macro was named with characters:

1. Press **ALT + F3** (Run) .... **Alt** + **F3**
    to display a menu of range names.

2. Type or highlight macro range name or address.

3. **ENTER**. .... ⏎

4. Press **ESC** .... **Esc**
    to change to POINT mode.

5. Move cursor to the first cell of the macro.

6. **ENTER**. .... ⏎

Debugging a Macro

1. Press **ALT + F2** (Step) .... **Alt** + **F2**
    to turn STEP mode on.

2. Depending how macro was named:
    Press **ALT + Letter** .... **Alt** + letter

    - OR -   OR

    Press **ALT + F3** .... **Alt** + **F3**
    to start runing the macro.

(continued

MACROS (continued)

3. Press **SPACEBAR** .... Space
   to execute the first macro instruction.

   NOTE: Repeat step 3 as many times as necessary to find macro error.

4. Press **CTRL + BREAK** .... Ctrl + Break
   to end the macro.

5. Press **ALT + F2** .... Alt + F2
   to turn STEP mode off.

To Edit the Macro:

6. Place cursor in macro range.

7. Press **F2** (edit) F2

8. Edit macro.

9. **ENTER** .... ⏎

10. Run the macro again.

Saving a Macro

1. Press **/** (Menu) .... /

2. Press **F** (File) .... F

3. Press **S** (Save) .... S

4. Type file name.

   NOTE: The macro will be saved as part of the worksheet.

5. **ENTER**. .... ⏎

MOVING

> *NOTE:* *Moves a cell or range of cells (including Columns and Rows) to a blank area.*

1. Place cursor on first cell to be moved.

2. Press **/** (Menu) .... `/`

3. Press **M** (Move) .... `M`

4. Highlight cell or range of cells to be moved FROM.

5. **ENTER**. .... `↵`

6. Place cursor on first cell in the range to be moved TO.

7. **ENTER**. .... `↵`

MOVING THE CELL CURSOR

*NOTE: The actions below may be used in the
READY and POINT modes.*

To Move:

Right (one cell) .... ➡️

Left (one cell) .... ⬅️

Down (one row) .... ⬇️

Up (onc row) .... ⬆️

Screen Page Down .... PgDn

Screen Page Up .... PgUp

Screen Page Right
(in READY and POINT modes) . Ctrl + ➡️ or Tab

Screen Page Left
(in READY and POINT modes) . Ctrl + ⬅️ or Tab

Directly to a Cell
  1. Press **F5** (GOTO) F5

  2. Type cell address.

  3. **ENTER** .... ⏎

Home (A1) Position .... Home

Bottom Right Edge of Worksheet ..... End + Home

(continued)

MOVING THE CELL CURSOR (continued)

Left Edge of a List .... `End` + `←`

Right Edge of a List .... `End` + `→`

Top of a List .... `End` + `↑`

Bottom of a List .... `End` + `↓`

PRINTING

A Worksheet / Range to the Printer

1. Place cursor on first cell to be printed.

2. Press **/** (Menu) .... `/`

3. Press **P** (Print) .... `P`

4. Press **P** (Printer) .... `P`

5. Press **R** (Range) .... `R`

6. Press **.** (period) to lock in the range .... `.`

7. Highlight range to be printed.

8. **ENTER** .... `⏎`

9. Press **A** (Align) .... `A`

10. Press **G** (Go) .... `G`

11. Press **Q** (Quit) .... `Q`

A Worksheet (or Selected Range) to a Text File on Disk

> *NOTE:* *Creates an ASCII file which may be used in word processing. (See page 73 to create an ASCII file to be used with a database program.)*

1. Place cursor on first cell to be printed.

2. Press **/** (Menu) .... `/`

3. Press **P** (Print) .... `P`

(continued)

PRINTING (continued)

4. Press **F** (File) .... `F`

5. Type name of text file to be created.

   *NOTE: A .PRN extension will automatically
            be assigned to the file.*

6. **ENTER** .... `⏎`

7. Press **R** (Range) .... `R`

8. Highlight range to be printed to disk.

9. **ENTER** .... `⏎`

10. Press **O** (Options) .... `O`

11. Press **M** (Margins) .... `M`

12. Press **N** (None) .... `N`
    to reset margins to 0.

13. Press **O** (Other). .... `O`

14. Press **U** (Unformatted) .... `U`
    to delete headers, footers, and page breaks.

15. Press **ESC**. .... `Esc`

16. Press **A** (Align) .... `A`

17. Press **G** (Go) .... `G`

18. Press **Q** (Quit) .... `Q`

(continu

PRINTING (continued)

A Worksheet in Compressed Print

1. Place cursor on first cell to be printed.

2. Press **/** (Menu) .... `/`

3. Press **P** (Print) .... `P`

4. Press **P** (Printer) .... `P`

5. Press **R** (Range) .... `R`

6. Press **.** (period) to lock in the range .... `.`

7. Highlight range to be printed.

8. **ENTER** .... `⏎`

9. Press **0** (Options) .... `O`

10. Press **M** (Margins) .... `M`

11. Press **R** (Right) .... `R`

12. Type 132 (for standard 80-column printer)

    - OR -

    Type 240 (for a wide-column printer)

13. **ENTER**. .... `⏎`

14. Press **S** (Setup). .... `S`

15. Press **** (Backslash) .... `\`

(continued)

PRINTING (continued)

16. Type Setup String (refer to printer manual for appropriate code) .... **Option**

   NOTE: \015 may be used for EPSON printers.

17. **ENTER.** .... ⏎

18. Press **ESC** .... Esc

19. Press **A** (Align) .... A

20. Press **G** (Go) .... G

21. Press **Q** (Quit) .... Q

<u>A Worksheet with Borders</u>

   NOTE: •   Will print selected rows or columns on every page.
   •   Border rows and columns must correspond to a print range.
   •   Do not include rows and columns as borders that were included in the print range.

1. Place cursor on first cell to be included in the border.

2. Press **/** (Menu) .... /

3. Press **P** (Print) .... P

4. Press **P** (Printer) .... P

5. Press **O** (Options) .... O

(continu

PRINTING (continued)

6. Press **B** (Borders). .... `B`

7. Select a border option:

    C (Columns) Prints vertical headings
    on left side of each page .. `C`

    R (Rows) Prints horizontal headings
    across top of each page ... `R`

8. Highlight column or row to be used as border.

9. **ENTER**.. .... `←`

10. Press **ESC**. .... `Esc`

11. Press **A** (Align) .... `A`

12. Press **G** (Go) .... `G`

13. Press **Q** (Quit) .... `Q`

A Worksheet with Adjusted Margins

> *NOTE: Overrides default margins and sets
> left, right, top and bottom margins.*

1. Press **/** (Menu) .... `/`

2. Press **P** (Print) .... `P`

3. Press **P** (Printer) .... `P`

4. Press **O** (Options) .... `O`

(continued)

PRINTING (continued)

5. Press **M** (Margins) .... **M**

6. Select a margin option:

L (Left)	Sets margins from left edge from 0-240 characters	**L**
R (Right)	Sets margins from left edge (to right) from 0-240 characters.	**R**
B (Bottom)	Sets margins from bottom edge from 0-32 lines	**B**
T (Top)	Sets margins from top edge from 0-32 lines	**T**
N (None)	Clears current margins settings, resets top, left and bottom margins to 0, and right margin to 240 ...	**N**

7. **ENTER** .... ⏎
   to accept margin setting.

      - OR-   OR

   - Type desired left, right, bottom or top margin number ....**Option**
   - **ENTER**. .... ⏎

8. Repeat steps 5-7 for each change to be made.

(continu

73

PRINTING (continued)

9. Press **ESC** .... Esc

10. Press **A** (Align) .... A

11. Press **G** (Go) .... G

12. Press **Q** (Quit) .... Q

A Worksheet (or Selected Range) to an ASCII text file (for Database)

Note: Creates an ASCII file which may be used in database.

1. Press **/** (Menu) .... /

2. Press **R** (Range) .... R

3. Press **F** (Format) .... F

4. Press **G** (General) .... G

5. Press **/** (Menu) .... /

6. Highlight range to be formatted.

7. Press **P** (Print) .... P

8. Press **F** (File) .... F

9. Type name of text file to be created.

10. **ENTER** .... Ctrl

11. Press **R** (Range) .... R

12. Highlight range to be printed to disk.
DO NOT include field names or titles.

13. Follow steps 9-18 on page 68.

(continued)

74

PRINTING (continued)

A Worksheet with Headers and/or Footers

NOTE: • *Header and footer text may be centered, left or right-justified by preceding the header/footer entry with vertical bars as follows:*
 centered: ¦ (one vertical bar)
 right-justified: ¦¦ (two vertical bars)
 left-justified: None
 • *Lotus will not print a footer on last page of print run unless / P P P is entered <u>after print job.</u>*

1. Place cursor on first cell of the range to be printed.

2. Press **/** (Menu) .... `/`

3. Press **P** (Print) .... `P`

4. Press **P** (Printer) .... `P`

5. Press **O** (Options) .... `O`

6. Press **H** (Header) .... `H`

 - OR -   OR

 Press **F** (Footer) .... `F`

7. • Type header or footer text.

 - OR -

 • Type \ (backslash) followed by cell address containing header or footer text.

(continued)

PRINTING (continued)

8. **ENTER.** .... ⏎

9. Press **ESC** .... Esc

10. Press **R** (Range) .... R

11. Highlight range to be printed.

12. **ENTER.** .... ⏎

13. Press **A** (Align) .... A

14. Press **G** (Go) .... G

15. Press **Q** (Quit) .... Q

> *NOTE:* - *To print the date automatically:*
>   • *Type an @ symbol as part of header/footer text.*
> - *To print a page number automatically:*
>   • *Type a # symbol as part of header/footer text.*

EXAMPLES:

Entry: @¦JANUARY SALES¦¦Page #
Resulting Header:

| 6/30/91 | JANUARY SALES | Page 1 |

Entry: JANUARY SALES¦¦Page #
Resulting Header:

| JANUARY SALES | Page 1 |

PROTECTING THE WORKSHEET

NOTE: *Will protect worksheet from changes.*

1. Press **/** (Menu) .... /

2. Press **W** (Worksheet) .... W

3. Press **G** (Global) .... G

4. Press **P** (Protection) .... P

5. Press **E** (Enable) .... E

   - OR -   OR

   Press **D** (Disable) .... D

QUERYING A DATABASE/FINDING EXTRACTING RECORDS

NOTE: *The "input", "criteria" and "output"*
ranges must be created before Data
Query/FIND, EXTRACT, UNIQUE, or
DELETE functions can be used.

Creating the Input Range
(The range containing database records to be queried.)

1. Press / (Menu) .... `/`

2. Press **D** (Data) .... `D`

3. Press **Q** (Query) .... `Q`

4. Press **I** (Input) .... `I`

5. Type or highlight "input" range.

   NOTE: *The first row of the range must*
   include the field names.

6. **ENTER** .... `↵`

7. **ESC** three times to return
   to READY mode. .... `Esc` `Esc` `Esc`

(continued)

QUERYING A DATABASE/FINDING EXTRACTING RECORDS (continued)

Creating the Criteria Range

8. • Place cursor in a cell in an available area of the worksheet.
   • Type the <u>exact</u> field names used in the input range.

   - OR -

   • Copy field names from input range to an available area of the worksheet.

9. Place cursor in a cell below field to be searched (in criteria range.)

10. Type search criteria. (Data to be searched FOR.)

11. **ENTER**. .... ⏎

   NOTE: Repeat steps 9-11 for each field to be searched.

12. Press **/** (Menu) .... `/`

13. Press **D** (Data) .... `D`

14. Press **Q** (Query) .... `Q`

15. Press **C** (Criteria) .... `C`

16. Type or highlight "criteria" range.

   NOTE: The first row of the range must include the field names.

17. **ENTER** .... ⏎

18. PRESS **ESC** three times to return to READY mode. .... `Esc` `Esc` `Esc`

(continued)

QUERYING A DATABASE/FINDING
EXTRACTING RECORDS (continued)

Creating the Output Range

1. • Place cursor in a cell in an available area of the
        worksheet.
    • Type the <u>exact</u> field names used in the input range.

      - OR -

    • Copy field names from input range to an available
      area of the worksheet.

2. Press / (Menu) .... **/**

3. Press **D** (Data) .... **D**

4. Press **Q** (Query) .... **Q**

5. Press **O** (Output) .... **O**

6. Type or highlight "output" range.

    *NOTE: The first row of the range must
            include field names that match field
            names in input and criteria ranges.
            However, output range field names
            may be in any order.*

7. **ENTER** .... **↵**

(continued)

QUERYING A DATABASE/FINDING EXTRACTING RECORDS (continued)

Extracting (Copying) Records In The Database to Output Range

8.. • Press **E** (Extract) .... E
to obtain records that meet the
criteria and copy them to the output range.

> NOTE: If the output range does not contain
> enough room for the data, an error
> message will appear; it will then be
> necessary to create a larger output
> range.

   -OR-   OR

• Press **U** (Unique) to obtain **unique** records. .... U
(Duplicate records will not be copied to the
output range.)

9. Press **Q** (Quit) .... Q
to view output.

Finding Records In The Database

> NOTE: Highlights records in input range that
> match specified criteria.

1. Press **/** (Menu) .... /

2. Press **D** (Data) .... D

3. Press **Q** (Query) .... Q

4. Press **F** (Find) .... F
(The cursor highlights the first record that
meets the criteria.)

(continued

QUERYING A DATABASE/FINDING EXTRACTING RECORDS (continued)

5. Use cursor Up and Down arrow keys .... **⬆ ⬇**
   to highlight next record(s) that
   meets the criteria.

6. **ESC** four times to return
   to READY mode. .... **Esc Esc Esc Esc**

Deleting Records In the Database

1. Press / (Menu) .... **/**

2. Press **D** (Data) .... **D**

3. Press **Q** (Query) .... **Q**

4. Press **I** (Input) .... **I**

5. Highlight record(s) in input range to be deleted.

6. Type **D** (Delete) .... **D**

   -OR-   OR

   Type **C** (Cancel) .... **C**

QUITTING

1. Press / (Menu) .... `/`

2. Press **Q** (Quit) .... `Q`

3. Type **Y** to quit .... `Y`
   if worksheet is already saved.

   -OR-   OR

   • Type **Y** to quit .... `Y`

   • Type **Y** to confirm .... `Y`
     if worksheet is not saved.

   - OR -   OR

   • Type **N** (to return to worksheet) .... `N`

OPTION:

4. Type **E** (Exit) .... `E`

RETRIEVING A FILE

NOTE: *The retrieved worksheet will replace the worksheet currently on the screen.*

1. Type / (Menu) .... **/**

2. Type **F** (File) .... **F**

3. Type **R** (Retrieve) .... **R**

4. Type filename to be retrieved.

   - OR -

   Highlight filename to be retrieved using cursor arrow keys.

5. **ENTER** .... **←**

Retrieving Files in a Different Drive/Directory

1. Follow steps 1-3 above.

2. Press **ESC** twice .... **Esc** **Esc**

3. Type new drive and/or directory.

4. **ENTER** .... **←**

5. Highlight filename to be retrieved using cursor arrow keys.

6. **ENTER** .... **←**

SAVING A FILE

84

SAVING A FILE

> *NOTE:* *When a file is saved, Lotus assigns a*
> *.WK1 extension to the filename unless*
> *a different extension is specified.*

Saving a New Worksheet

1. Press / (Menu) .... **/**

2. Press **F** (File) .... **F**

3. Press **S** (Save) .... **S**

4. Type a filename
    to save into the current directory.

    - OR -

    To save into a different directory:

    - Press **ESC**
      three times .... **Esc** **Esc** **Esc**
    - Type new drive
      and / or directory.
    - Type a filename.

5. **ENTER**. .... **←**

Re-Saving/Overwriting a Worksheet

1. Press / (Menu) .... **/**

2. Press **F** (File) .... **F**

3. Press **S** (Save) .... **S**

(contin

SAVING A FILE (continued)

4. **ENTER** .... ⏎

5. Press **R** (Replace) .... R
   to replace an existing file with the new file.

   - OR -   OR

Press **B** (Backup) .... B
to create a backup file with the extension .BAK while
maintaining the existing file with the extension .WK1

   - OR -   OR

Press **C** (Cancel) C
to cancel the operation.

Saving a Portion of Current Worksheet as a New File

1. Press **/** (Menu) .... /

2. Press **F** (File) .... F

3. Press **X** (Xtract) X

4. Select a saving option:

   F To save formulas and cell
       contents from current
       worksheet to new worksheet .... F

   V To save results of formulas and
       labels as a new worksheet V

  . Type a new filename.

(continued)

SAVING A FILE (continued)

6.   Highlight range of worksheet to be saved as a
     separate file.

7.   **ENTER.** .... ⏎

Saving a File with a Password

   NOTE: Password names are case sensitive.

1.   Press **/** (Menu) .... /

2.   Press **F** (File) .... F

3.   Press **S** (Save) .... S

4.   Type a filename.

5.   Press **SPACEBAR** once. .... Space

6.   Press **P** (Password). .... P

7.   **ENTER.** .... ⏎

8.   Type a password.

9.   **ENTER.** .... ⏎

10. Type password again (at 'Verify' prompt).

11. **ENTER** .... ⏎

     If Updating the File:

12. Press **R** (Replace) .... R

SAVING A FILE (continued)

Changing a Password

1. Press / (Menu) .... **/**

2. Press **F** (File) .... **F**

3. Press **S** (Save) .... **S**

4. Press **BACKSPACE** once. .... **Backspace**
   to clear 'Password Protected' prompt.

5. Follow steps 4-12 beginning on previous page.

Deleting a Password

1. Type / (Menu) .... **/**

2. Type **F** (File) .... **F**

3. Type **S** (Save) .... **S**

4. Press **BACKSPACE** once .... **Backspace**
   to clear 'Password Protected' prompt.

5. **ENTER** .... **↵**

6. Type **R** (Replace) .... **R**
   to update file without a password.

(continued)

SEARCHING A RANGE
for Character Strings

NOTE: Searches for character strings in labels and / or formulas within a specified range.

1. Press **/** (Menu) .... **/**

2. Press **R** (Range) .... **R**

3. Press **S** (Search) .... **S**

4. Highlight the range to be searched.

5. **ENTER** .... ⏎

6. Type the string to be searched FOR.

7. **ENTER** .... ⏎

8. Select a desired option:

    F Searches for formulas .... **F**

    L Searches for labels .... **L**

    B Searches for both labels and formulas **B**

9. Press **F** (Find) .... **F**
   to highlight first occurrence of search string.

10. Press **N** (Next) .... **N**
    to search for next occurrence.

    - OR -   OR

    Press **Q** (Quit) .... **Q**
    to cancel operation.

(contir

SEARCHING A RANGE (continued)

Replacing a Character String

1. Press / (Menu) .... **/**

2. Press **R** (Range) .... **R**

3. Press **S** (Search) .... **S**

4. Highlight the range to be searched.

5. **ENTER**. .... **⏎**

6. Type the string to be searched FOR.

7. **ENTER**. .... **⏎**

8. Select a desired option:

    F Searches for formulas .... **F**

    L Searches for labels .... **L**

    B Searches for both labels and formulas ..... **B**

9. Press **R** (Replace) .... **R**

10. Type the replacement string.

11. **ENTER** .... **⏎**

(continued)

SEARCHING A RANGE (continued)

12. Select a desired option when first occurrence
    is highlighted:

    R Replaces current string
           with replacement string .... 🔲R

    A Replaces ALL remaining occurrences
           with replacement string .... 🔲A

    N Finds the next occurrence .... 🔲N

    Q Stops search .... 🔲Q

13. **ENTER** . ... 🔲↵
    to return to READY mode.

SETTING DEFAULTS

NOTE: • *Settings apply globally during the current work session. If current settings are desired for future work sessions, they may be saved through / Worksheet Global Default Update in a file called 123.CNF.*
• *The current status of settings should be reviewed before changes are made.*

Viewing Default Setting Status

1. Press **/** (Menu) .... **/**

2. Press **W** (Worksheet) .... **W**

3. Press **G** (Global) .... **G**
   to display first page of global settings.

4. Press **D** (Default) .... **D**
   to display second page of global settings.

Changing Default Settings

1. Press **/** (Menu) .... **/**

2. Press **W** (Worksheet) .... **W**

3. Press **G** (Global) .... **G**

4. Press **D** (Default) .... **D**

(continued)

SETTING DEFAULTS (continued)

5. Select a default setting option:

A (Autoexec) .... A
Directs Lotus whether or not to run an
autoexec macro
- Press **Y** (Yes) ..... Y
to automatically
execute a macro.

- OR -

- Press **N** (No) ...... N
not to auto-
matically execute a
macro.

D (Directory) .... D
Sets drive and diretory names
- Type desired
directory .... **Option**
- **ENTER** .... ↵

P (Printer) .... P
- Press **A** .... A
to control printer
signal at each line of
output.
- Press **Y** (Yes) ..... Y
not to send line
feeds.

- OR -   OR

- Press **N** (No) ...... N
to send line feeds.

(continu

SETTING DEFAULTS (continued)

- OR -

- Press **B** .... **B**
  to set bottom page
  default.
- Type number of
  desired lines for
  bottom margin. **Option**
- **ENTER** .... ⏎

- OR -

- Press **I** .... **I**
  to identify
  interface or port.
- Type desired option.

- OR -

- Press **L** .... **L**
  to set left margin
  default.
- Type desired left
  margin .... **Option**
- **ENTER** .... ⏎

- OR -

- Press **N** .... **N**
  to name
  additional printer(s)
  being used.
- Highlight printer to be
  used.

(continued)

SETTING DEFAULTS (continued)

- OR -

- Press **P** .... P
  to set page length.
- Type number of
  desired page
  length .... **Option**

- **ENTER** .... ⏎

  - OR -

- Press **R** .... R
  to set right margin
  default.
- Type desired right
  margin .... **Option**

- **ENTER**. .... ⏎

  - OR -

- Press **S**. .... S
  to indicate printer
  setup string.
- Type desired
  setup string ..... **Option**

- **ENTER** .... ⏎

  - OR -

(continu

SETTING DEFAULTS (continued)

- Press **T** .... 🆃
  to set top margin.
- Type number of
  desired lines for
  top margin. ...... **Option**

- **ENTER** .... ⏎

  - OR -

- Press **W** .... 🆆
  to pause after each
  printed page.
- Press **Y** (Yes) ..... 🆈
  to pause after
  each page.

  - OR -

- Press **N** (No) ...... 🅽
  not to pause after
  each page.

O (Other) .... 🅾
  Sets clock formats, help access method,
  beep, sets attach add-ins and undo feature.

(continued)

SETTING DEFAULTS (continued)

Select an "Other" option:

A (Add-In) .... A

- Press **S** .... S
  to set an
  auto-attach add-in.
- Type desired number
  (1-8) of auto-attach
  add-in .... **Option**
- Type or highlight
  file name of add-in
- **ENTER**. .... ⏎

  - OR -

  . Press **C** C
    to detach add-in.

B (Beep) .... B

- Press **Y** (Yes) ..... Y
  to turn beep on.

  - OR -

  . Press **N** (No) ..... N
    to turn beep off.

C (Clock) C

- Press **S** .... S
  to set standard
  date & time format

(continue

SETTING DEFAULTS (continued)

- OR -

- Press I .... ▐█▌.
  to set inter-
  national date & time
  format

  - OR -

- Press **N** .... ▐N▌
  to display nothing.

  - OR -

- Press **C** .... ▐C▌
  to display date &
  time in format se-
  lected.

  - OR -

- Press **F**. .... ▐F▌
  to display current
  worksheet filename in
  left corner.

(continued)

SETTING DEFAULTS (continued)

H (Help) .... **H**

- Press **I** .... **I**
  to keep Help open
  during work session.

  -OR-

- Press **R** .... **R**
  to open and close
  Help for each work
  session.

I (International) .... **I**

- Press **P** .... **P**
  to set punctuation
  symbols.
- Press **A-F** .... **A**
  to select desired
  punctuation format.

  - OR -

- Press **C** .... **C**
  to set currency
  symbols.
- Type desired currency
  symbol ....**Option**

- **ENTER**. .... **⏎**

- Press **P** .... **P**
  to precede currency
  value with symbol.

(continue

SETTING DEFAULTS (continued)

- OR -

- Press **S** .... $\boxed{S}$
to follow value
with currency symbol.

- OR -

- Press **D** .... $\boxed{D}$
to set date
format.
- Press **A-D**
.... $\boxed{A}$ - $\boxed{D}$

- OR -

Press **T** .... $\boxed{T}$
to set time
format. -
- Press **A-D**
.... $\boxed{A}$ - $\boxed{D}$

-OR -

- Press **N** .... $\boxed{N}$
to use parentheses
or minus sign for
negative values.
- Press **P**
(Parenthesis) ...... $\boxed{P}$

- OR -

- Press **S** (Sign) .... $\boxed{S}$

(continued)

SETTING DEFAULTS (continued)

U (Undo) .... U

* Press **E** .... E
  to enable Undo
  feature.

  - OR -

* Press **D** .... D
  to disable Undo
  feature.

<u>To Update Default Settings</u>

1. Press **/** (Menu) .... /

2. Press **W** (Worksheet) .... W

3. Press **G** (Global) .... G

4. Press **D** (Default) .... D

5. Press **U** (Update) .... U

SORTING DATA

> *NOTE:* Sorting may be accomplished on one or two columns (fields) in ascending or descending order.

1. Press **/** (Menu) .... **/**

2. Press **D** (Data) .... **D**

3. Press **S** (Sort) .... **S**

4. Press **D** (Data-Range) .... **D**

5. Type or highlight* data range to be sorted.

> **NOTE:* Labels at the top of the database *SHOULD NOT* be included when highlighting since they will be sorted along with the data.

6. **ENTER** .... ⏎

7. Press **P** (Primary-Key) .... **P**

8. Place cursor in column to be primary sorted.

9. **ENTER** .... ⏎

10. Type **A** (Ascending) .... **A**

    - OR -   OR

    Type **D** (Descending) .... **D**

11. **ENTER**.. .... ⏎

(continued)

SORTING DATA (continued)

OPTIONAL
<u>To Sort on Seconday Field:</u>

- Press **S** (Secondary-Key) .... `S`

- Place cursor in column to be
  secondary sorted.

- **ENTER** .... `←`

- Type **A** (Ascending) .... `A`

  - OR -   OR

- Type **D** (Descending) .... `D`

- **ENTER** .... `←`

12. Press **G** (Go) .... `G`

TRANSPOSING DATA

*NOTE: Transposes data from horizontal to
vertical arrangement and vice versa.
Formulas are replaced by values.*

1. Press / (Menu) .... **/**

2. Press **R** (Range) .... **R**

3. Press **T** (Trans) .... **T**

4. Highlight range to be transposed.

5. **ENTER**. .... ⏎

6. Place cursor on first available cell to
    receive transposed data.

7. **ENTER** .... ⏎

104

UNDO
(Previous Command)

NOTE: • *Lotus must be in READY mode.*
• *UNDO cannot be used while working in PRINTGRAPH, INSTALL, TRANSLATE, ACCESS MACRO, LIBRARY MANAGER and ALLWAYS Programs.*

1. Press **Alt + F4** (Undo) ....  **Alt** + **F4**

WINDOWS

1. Place cursor one ROW below or one COLUMN to the right of where split is to occur.

2. Press / (Menu) .... **/**

3. Press **W** (Worksheet) .... **W**

4. Press **W** (Window) .... **W**

5. Select a screen split option:

   H (Horizontal) .... **H**

   V (Vertical) .... **V**

To Select A Scrolling Option:

6. Repeat steps 2-4 above.

7. Press **S** (Sync) .... **S**
   to synchronize scrolling

   -OR-   OR

   Press **U** (Unsync) .... **U**
   to unsynchronize scrolling

   *NOTE: Press F6 to move from one window
            to another.*

Clearing the Window

1. Follow steps 2-4 above.

2. Press **C** (Clear) .... **C**

WORKSHEET STATUS

NOTE: *Will display the current global worksheet settings status.*

1. Press / (Menu) .... `/`

2. Press **W** (Worksheet) .... `W`

3. Press **S** (Status) .... `S`

4. Press any key to return to worksheet.

FUNCTION DESCRIPTIONS

@ABS

Calculates the absolute (positive value) of x.

@ACOS

Calculates the arc cosine of a value.

@ASIN

Calculates the arc sine of a value.

@ATAN

Calculates the arc tangent of a value.

@ATAN2

Calculates the four-quadrant arc tangent of y/x.

@AVG

Averages values in a list.

@CELL

Produces information about an **attribute** for the first cell in a range.

@CELLPOINTER

Produces information about an **attribute** for the current cell.

(continued)

FUNCTION DESCRIPTIONS (continued)

@CHAR

Indicates the Lotus International Character Set equivalent which code x produces.

@CHOOSE

Finds the value or string in a list that is specified by the offset number.

@CLEAN

Eliminates non-printable characters such as ASCII codes from character string.

@CODE

Indicates the Lotus International Character Set code which corresponds to first character in a string.

@COLS

Counts the number of columns in a range.

@COS

Calculates the cosine of x angle which is measured in radians. The answer results in a value from -1 to 1.

@COUNT

Counts and indicates the nonblank cells in a list. Cells containing values as well as labels are counted.

(continued)

FUNCTION DESCRIPTIONS (continued)

@CTERM

Computes the number of periods required for an investment
(present value) to increase to a **future value**, earning a fixed
interest rate per period.

@DATE

Calculates the date number for the specified year, month
and day.

@DATEVALUE

Calculates the date number for a string entered as a date.

@DAVG

A database function that averages values in a field of the
input range that meets criteria in the criteria range.

@DAY

Calculates the day of the month in date number.

@DCOUNT

A database function that counts and indicates nonblank
cells in a field of the input range that meet criteria in the
criteria range.

@DDB

Using the double-declining balance method, calculates the
depreciation allowance of an asset for a specified period.

(continued)

110

FUNCTION DESCRIPTIONS (continued)

@DMAX

A database function that finds and indicates the largest value in a field of the input range that meets the criteria in the criteria range.

@DMIN

A database function that finds and indicates the smallest value in a field of the input range that meets the criteria in the criteria range.

@DSTD

A database function that calculates the standard deviation of the values in a field of an input range that meets the criteria in the criteria range.

@DSUM

A database function that sums the values in a field of an input range that meet the criteria in the criteria range.

@DVAR

A database function that calculates the variance of values in a field of an input range that meet the criteria in the criteria range.

@ERR

Indicates an error message (ERR) if a wrong value is entered. This function is usually used with @IF to indicate an error value.

(continued)

FUNCTION DESCRIPTIONS (continued)

@EXACT

Compares string1 with string1 and indicates 1 if true (they are the same), 0 if false (they are not the same).

@EXP

Calculates the value of e raised to the power x.

@FALSE

Produces a 0 (false) as a logical value.

@FIND

Calculates the position in a string in which the first occurrence of a seach-string is found.

@FV

Calculates the future value of an investment at the end of each period which is compounded at a periodic interest rate.

@HLOOKUP

Finds the contents of a cell in the highlighted row of a horizontal lookup table.

@HOUR

Calculates the hour in integer form.

(continued)

FUNCTION DESCRIPTIONS (continued)

@IF

Answers a true/false question and calculates data according to the answer.

@INDEX

Locates the value from within a range.

@INT

Produces the integer part of a value.

@IRR

Calculates the rate of return expected from a series of cash flows generated by an investment.

@ISERR

Tests x for the an ERRor value and returns 1 if true, 0 if false.

@ISNA

Tests x for an NA value and returns 1 if true, 0 if false.

@ISNUMBER

Tests x for a value and returns 1 (true) if x is a value or a blank cell and returns 0 (false) if x is a string.

(continued

FUNCTION DESCRIPTIONS (continued)

@ISSTRING

Tests x for a string and returns 1 (true) if x is a literal string containing a label or string formula and returns 0 (false) if x is a value or blank cell.

@LEFT

Indicates the first n characters in string.

@LENGTH

Counts the number of characters in a string.

@LN

Calculates the natural logarithm of x.

@LOG

Calculates the common logarithm (base 10) of x.

@LOWER

Converts uppercase letters in a string to lowercase letters.

@MAX

Finds and indicates the largest value in a list.

@MID

Indicates n characters from string beginning with the character at start-number. The first start number in a string is 0.

(continued)

FUNCTION DESCRIPTIONS (continued)

@MIN

Finds and indicates the lowest value in a list.

@MINUTE

Calculates minutes in integer form in time-number.

@N

Indicates the entry in the first cell in a range as a value and returns the value if the cell contains a value and returns a 0 if the cell does not contain a value.

@NA

Produces an NA (not available) value.

@NOW

Produces the current date and time.

@NPV

Calculates the net present value of a series of future cash flows discounted at a fixed, interest rate.

@PI

Returns the value . is the ratio of the circumference of a circle to its diameter.

(continued

FUNCTION DESCRIPTIONS (continued)

@PMT

Calculates the amount of the periodic payment needed to pay off a loan using a specified periodic interest rate and number of payment periods.

@PROPER

Converts the letters in a string to inital caps for the first letter of each word and lower case for remaining letters.

@PV

Calculates the present value of an investment based on a series of payments discounted at a periodic interest rate over the number of periods in term.

@RAND

Indicates a random value between 0 and 1.

@RATE

Calculates periodic interest rate necessary for payments (present value) to grow to a future value in a specified term.

@REPEAT

Repeats characters in a cell which is not limited to the cell width. The label prefix \ (backslash) followed by a character will repeat labels to fill one cell. @REPEAT is not limited to the column width.

(continued)

FUNCTION DESCRIPTIONS (continued)

@REPLACE

Replaces n characters in the original string with the new string beginning at the start number.

@RIGHT

Indicates the last n characters in a string

@ROUND

Rounds a value to a specified number of places.

@ROWS

Counts the number of rows in a range.

@S

Indicates the entry in the first cell in a range as a label and returns the label if the cell contains a label and returns a 0 if the cell does not contain a label.

@SECOND

Calculates the seconds in integer form in time-number.

@SIN

Calculates the sine of an x angle measured in radians.

@SLN

Calculates the straight-line depreciation allowance of an asset for one period.

(continued)

FUNCTION DESCRIPTIONS (continued)

@SQRT

Calculates the positive square root of a value or 0.

@STD

Calculates the standard deviation of values in a list.

@STRING

Converts the x value into a string with specified decimal places.

@SUM

Adds values in a list.

@SYD

Calculates the sum-of-the-years' digits depreciation allowance of an asset for a specified period.

@TAN

Calculates the tanget of x angle measured in radians.

@TERM

Calculates the number of payment periods necessary to reach future value, when the investment earns a periodic interest rate.

@TIME

Calculates the time number for the specified hour, minutes and seconds.

(continued)

FUNCTION DESCRIPTIONS (continued)

@TIMEVALUE

Calculates the time number for a sting that looks like a time

@TRIM

Removes leading, trailing and consecutive spaces from a string.

@TRUE

Produces a 1 (true) as a logical value.

@UPPER

Converts lowercase letters in a string to uppercase letters.

@VALUE

Converts a number entered as a string to its corresponding value.

@VAR

Calculates variance of values in a list.

@VLOOKUP

Finds the contents of a cell in the highlighted column of a horizontal lookup table.

@YEAR

Calculates the year in integer form in date-number.

FUNCTION KEYS

KEY	KEY NAME	FUNCTION PERFORMED
F1	HELP	Accesses Help menu.
F2	EDIT	In READY mode, puts Lotus in EDIT mode to enable cell contents to be edited.
F3	NAME	In POINT mode, displays a list of named ranges.
F4	ABS(olute)	Changes a cell or range of cells from relative to absolute to mixed values.
F5	GOTO	In READY mode, moves cursor directly to new cell location specified.
F6	WINDOW	Moves cursor between windows during screen split.
F7	QUERY	In READY mode, repeats last DATA/QUERY specified.
F8	TABLE	In READY mode, repeats last DATA/TABLE specified.
F9	CALC	In READY mode, recalculates formulas in a worksheet; In VALUE and EDIT modes, converts a formula to its current value.
F10	GRAPH	Displays graph with current settings.

(continued)

120

FUNCTION KEYS (continued)

KEY	KEY NAME	FUNCTION PERFORMED
Alt + F1	COMPOSE	In READY, EDIT and LABEL modes, creates international characters that cannot be entered directly from keyboard.
Alt + F2	STEP	Accesses STEP mode to execute macros one step at a time.
Alt + F3	RUN	In READY mode, displays list of macro names for selecting a macro to run.
Alt + F4	UNDO	In READY mode, cancels any changes made to worksheet. Pressing Alt+F4 again will restore changes.
Alt + F5	LEARN	Accesses Learn feature to capture keystrokes for macros. Pressing Alt+F5 again will turn feature off.
Alt + F7	APP1	In READY mode, accesses add-in program assigned to key.
Alt + F8	APP2	In READY mode, accesses add-in program assigned to key.
Alt + F9	APP3	In READY mode, accesses add-in program assigned to key.
Alt + F10	APP4	In READY mode, displays add-in menu and accesses add-in program assigned to key.

GLOSSARY

Absolute Value
A term used in the copying process to indicate reproduction of a cell without change. Sometimes referred to as "no change."

Add-Ins
Special programs that can be used with LOTUS to extend its capabilities.

Cell
A single location on a worksheet.

Cell Address
A column letter and row number, e.g., A1 or F12.

Column
The vertical portions of the worksheet, e.g., A,B,C, etc. There are 256 columns in a worksheet.

Column Width
A term used to refer to the size of a cell. A cell may be made wider or narrower from its default size of 9 characters.

Cursor
The cell pointer.

Copying
Reproducing data from one location to another.

Data Range
The range of values used to create a graph.

Default
The preset conditions of LOTUS which may be modified. For example: column width settings.

(continued)

GLOSSARY (continued)

Editing
Changing the contents of a cell.

Field Names
Column headings (labels) that appear in the first row of a database which identify the content of each column.

File
A saved worksheet.

File Name
The name given to a saved worksheet.

Font
Characters available in a typeface in varying sizes and/or styles which may be used in ALLWAYS or PRINTGRAPH to change the appearance of the printed worksheet or graph.

Formatting
Using special commands to display worksheet data.

Function
A built-in formula that performs calculations or special operations.

Global
A command affecting the entire worksheet.

Graphing
Preparing a visual interpretation of data in the form of bar, line, stacked bar graph or pie chart.

Label
The column and row headings or titles that begin with a letter or label prefix.

Label Prefix
Characters that precede the label to control label alignment.

(continued)

GLOSSARY (continued)

Learn
A LOTUS feature used to create macros.

Local
A command that changes a specific portion of the worksheet.

Logical Function
An @function that answers a true/false question and calculates data according to the answer.

Logical Operator
Symbols such as > <, #AND#, and #OR# used in logical formulas to evaluate equality and inequality.

Macro
A series of recorded keystrokes that automates a LOTUS task.

PrintGraph
The LOTUS program that prints graph files.

Range
A cell or a rectangular group of adjacent cells in the worksheet.

Range Address
The location of a range in the worksheet: A3.D5.

Range Name
A name given to identify a range on the worksheet.

Relative
A term used in the copy process to indicate the automatic change of the cell references in the formula to adapt to the new location.

(continued)

GLOSSARY (continued)

Retrieve
The process of accessing a saved file.

Row
The horizontal portion of the worksheet. e.g. 1, 2, 3, etc.
There are 8,192 rows in a worksheet.

Save
Stores a copy of the worksheet on disk.

Setup String
Characters preceded by a \ that directs the printer to print in
a certain way.

Scroll
A vertical or horizontal cursor movement which will display
portions of the spreadsheet that exist beyond the limits of
the screen.

Sort
The process of arranging records in a database in a particular order according to the contents of one field.

Value
A numerical or formula entry on the worksheet used in
calculations.

Window
A software command to split the spreadsheet horizontally or
vertically into separate scrollable worksheets.

Worksheet
A columnar spreadsheet containing 256 columns and 8,192
rows used to calculate or analyze data.

COMMAND INDEX

COMMAND INDEX (CONTINUED)

GRAPH COMMANDS

MOVE COMMAND

PRINT COMMANDS

QUIT COMMAND

COMMAND INDEX (CONTINUED)

128

INDEX

(continued

129

INDEX (continued)

(continued)

INDEX (continued)

(continued)

131

INDEX (continued)

(continued)

INDEX (continued)

(continued)

INDEX (continued)

At your local bookstore, or directly from us.

Did we make one for you?

	CAT. NO.		CAT. NO.
AppleWorks (Ver. 2)	A-17	Microsoft Word 5.5	C-28
AppleWorks (Ver. 3)	H-17	Microsoft Works	K-17
dBase III Plus	B-17	Multimate Adv II & Ver 4	G-17
dBase IV	B-18	PC & MS DOS	X-17
DisplayWrite 4	D-4	Professional Write	P-17
DOS 5	J-17	Quattro Pro	Q-17
First Publisher 3.0	F-17	SuperCalc 3	S-17
Lotus 1-2-3	L-17	WordPerfect 4.2	W-17
Lotus 1-2-3 (Ver 2.2)	L2-17	WordPerfect 5.0	W-5.0
Microsoft Windows 3	N-17	WordPerfect 5.1	W-5.1
Microsoft Word 5.0	C-17	WordStar 6.0	R-17

----------------ORDER FORM----

 Dictation Disc Company
14 East 38 Street, New York, NY 10016

Accept my order for the following titles at $7.95 each.

QTY.	CAT. NO.	DESCRIPTION

( ) I enclose check.   Add $2 for postage and handling.

Name

Address

City, State, Zip

BATTLEFIELD AND DISASTER NURSING
POCKET GUIDE

Editor

Elizabeth Bridges, Col US Air Force Reserve Nurse Corps

Dedication

*To US military nurses and medics who care for
those in harm's way*

JONES AND BARTLETT PUBLISHERS

Sudbury, Massachusetts

BOSTON   TORONTO   LONDON   SINGAPORE

World Headquarters

Jones and Bartlett	Jones and Bartlett	Jones and Bartlett
Publishers	Publishers Canada	Publishers International
40 Tall Pine Drive	6339 Ormindale Way	Barb House, Barb Mews
Sudbury, MA 01776	Mississauga, Ontario	London W6 7PA
978-443-5000	L5V 1J2	United Kingdom
info@jbpub.com	Canada	
www.jbpub.com		

Jones and Bartlett's books and products are available through most book-
stores and online booksellers. To contact Jones and Bartlett Publishers directly,
call 800-832-0034, fax 978-443-8000, or visit our website www.jbpub.com.

Substantial discounts on bulk quantities of Jones and Bartlett's publications
are available to corporations, professional associations, and other qualified
organizations. For details and specific discount information, contact the special
sales department at Jones and Bartlett via the above contact information or
send an email to specialsales@jbpub.com.

Production Credits

Publisher: Kimberly Brophy
Acquisitions Editor–EMS: Christine Emerton
V.P., Manufacturing and Inventory Control: Therese Connell
Text Design: Anne Spencer
Director of Marketing: Alisha Weisman
Production Manager: Jenny L. Corriveau
Production Assistant: Tina Chen
Photo Research Manager and Photographer: Kimberly Potvin
Cover design: Kristin E. Ohlin
Cover Images (left to right): Courtesy of Lance Cpl. Daniel Lowndes/U.S. Marines;
Courtesy of Master Sgt. Lance Cheung/U.S. Air Force; Courtesy of Cpl. Zachary
Dyer/U.S. Marines
Chapter opener image: © AbleStock
Composition: diacriTech, Chennai, India
Printing and Binding: Transcontinental Metrolitho
Cover Printing: Transcontinental Metrolitho

6048

Printed in Canada
13 12 11 10 9 8 7 6 5 4 3

Contents

■ Acknowledgments

Editor
Elizabeth Bridges, Col US Air Force Reserve Nurse Corps
IMA - Director, Clinical Investigations Facility, Travis AFB, CA
Assistant Professor University of Washington School of Nursing, Seattle, WA
Clinical Nurse Researcher University of Washington Medical Center, Seattle, WA

Contributors
Elizabeth Bridges, Col US Air Force Reserve Nurse Corps
Paula Mondloh, Col US Air Force Reserve Nurse Corps (ret)
Chester 'Trip' Buckenmaier III, COL, US Army Medical Corps
E. Tina Cuellar, Maj US Air Force Reserve Nurse Corps
Kathryn Gaylord, COL US Army Nurse Corps
Won Kim, MAJ US Army Medical Corps
Eddie Lopez, LCDR US Navy Nurse Corps
Jean Lord, CDR US Navy Nurse Corps
Darcy Mortimer, Capt US Air Force Nurse Corps
Louis Stout, LTC US Army Nurse Corps

Reviewers
A special thanks to the individuals who provided expert content review.

Catherine Carr, PhD, RN University of Washington School of Nursing
Helen Crouch, Ltc US Air Force Reserve, Basic Science Corps
JoAnn Danner, Maj US Air Force Reserve Nurse Corps
Marla DeJong, Ltc US Air Force Nurse Corps
Mark Gosling, Capt US Air Force Nurse Corps
Duane Hospenthal, Col US Air Force Medical Corps
Donald Jenkins, Col US Air Force Medical Corps
Elizabeth Mann, MAJ US Army Nurse Corps
Clinton Murray, MAJ US Army Medical Corps
Gautam Nayak, LCDR US Navy Medical Corps
Nurses of the 28th Combat Support Hospital, Iraq
W. Brian Perry, Col US Air Force Medical Corps
Rebecca Phillips, PhD, RN University of Oklahoma College of Nursing
Catherine "Kit" Ryan, LTC US Army Nurse Corps
Jacqueline Rychnovsky, CAPT(s) US Navy Nurse Corps
Kim Smith, COL US Army Nurse Corps
Janice Stinson, CAPT US Navy Nurse Corps

Zsolt Stockinger, CDR US Navy Medical Corps
Angela Stone, MAJ US Army Nurse Corps
Karen Thomas, PhD, RN University of Washington School of Nursing
Lauren Thorngate, MN, RN University of Washington Medical Center
David Zumbro, Ltc USAF Medical Corps

This pocket guide was supported by a grant to The Geneva Foundation
from the TriService Nursing Research Program Resource Center for
Excellence in Nursing (MDA-905-02-1-T816 [N02-P19] Research to
Practice in the Military Health Care System—PI CAPT Patricia Watts
Kelley, NC, USN)

Special thanks to Patricia Watts Kelley, CAPT US Navy Nurse Corps,
Ms Maria Burcroff, and Deborah Kenny, LTC US Army Nurse Corps from
the TriService Nursing Research Program for their unending support
of this project and to Col Paula Mondloh USAFR NC (ret), for her
extraordinary contributions to this guide.

■ Disclaimer

This project was sponsored by the TriService Nursing Research Program, Uniformed Services University of the Health Sciences; however, the information or content and conclusions do not necessarily represent the official position or policy of, nor should any official endorsement be inferred by The Geneva Foundation, the TriService Nursing Research Program, Uniformed Services University of the Health Sciences, the Department of Defense, or the U.S. Government.

Dosage Selection

The authors and publisher have made every effort to ensure the accuracy of dosages cited herein. However, it is the responsibility of every practitioner to consult appropriate information sources to ascertain correct dosages for each clinical situation, especially for new or unfamiliar drugs and procedures. The authors, editors, publisher, The Geneva Foundation, TriService Nursing Research Program, Uniformed University of the Health Sciences, and the Department of Defense cannot be held responsible for any errors found in this book.

Use of Trade or Brand Names

Use of trade or brand names in this publication is for illustrative purposes only and does not imply endorsement by The Geneva Foundation, the TriService Nursing Research Program, Uniformed University of the Health Sciences, or the Department of Defense.

For Informational Use Only

This document is designed to be a reference, but it does not replace DoD policies, instructions, or guidelines. USAF AE/CCATT will follow AF/AMC directives. USAF medical personnel will only perform care within the scope of their practice.

■ **Primary/Secondary Assessment**

Primary Assessment
- **A**ssess scene safety
- **A**ssess mechanism of injury
- **A**irway with C-spine immobilization
- **B**reathing
- **C**irculation
- **D**isability (Neurological Status)
- **E**xpose/Environment control

Secondary Assessment
- **F**ull set of vitals/Focused adjuncts/Family
- **G**ive comfort measures/pain medication
- **H**istory; Head-to-toe assessment
- **I**nspect posterior surfaces
- **J**ot it down
- Reassess! Reassess!

FIGURE 1

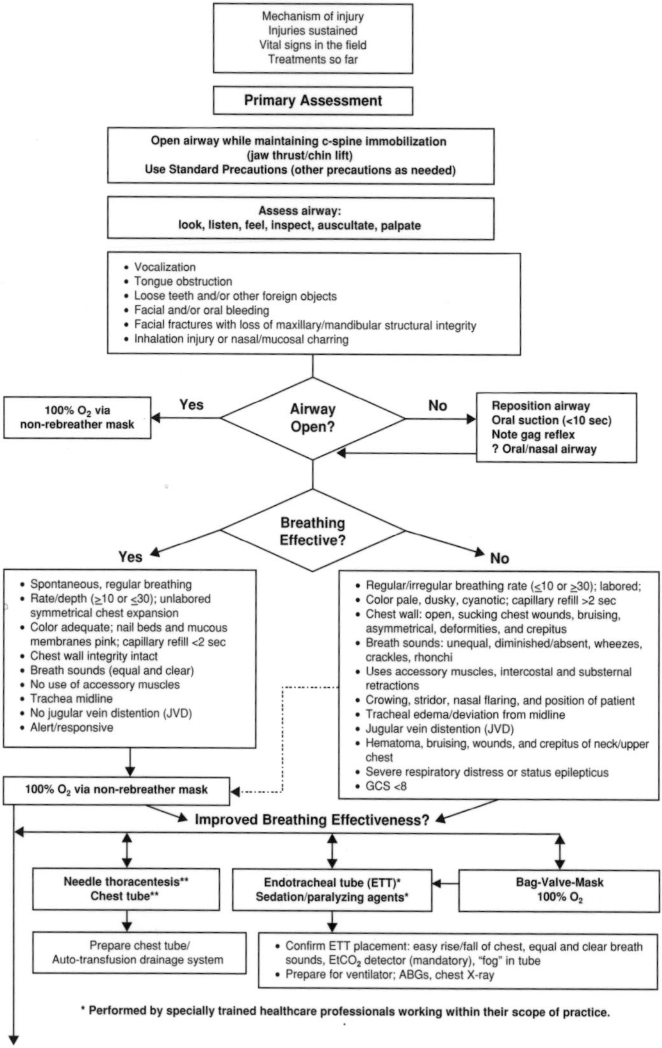

```
┌─────────────────────────────┐
│    Mechanism of injury      │
│    Injuries sustained       │
│    Vital signs in the field │
│    Treatments so far        │
└─────────────────────────────┘

┌─────────────────────────────┐
│    Primary Assessment       │
└─────────────────────────────┘

┌────────────────────────────────────────────────────┐
│ Open airway while maintaining c-spine immobilization │
│              (jaw thrust/chin lift)                  │
│ Use Standard Precautions (other precautions as needed)│
└────────────────────────────────────────────────────┘

┌────────────────────────────────────────────────────┐
│              Assess airway:                          │
│   look, listen, feel, inspect, auscultate, palpate   │
└────────────────────────────────────────────────────┘
```

- Vocalization
- Tongue obstruction
- Loose teeth and/or other foreign objects
- Facial and/or oral bleeding
- Facial fractures with loss of maxillary/mandibular structural integrity
- Inhalation injury or nasal/mucosal charring

	Airway Open?	
Yes ←		→ **No**

100% O₂ via non-rebreather mask (Yes)

No: Reposition airway / Oral suction (<10 sec) / Note gag reflex / ? Oral/nasal airway

Breathing Effective?

Yes ← → **No**

Yes:
- Spontaneous, regular breathing
- Rate/depth (≥10 or ≤30); unlabored symmetrical chest expansion
- Color adequate; nail beds and mucous membranes pink; capillary refill <2 sec
- Chest wall integrity intact
- Breath sounds (equal and clear)
- No use of accessory muscles
- Trachea midline
- No jugular vein distention (JVD)
- Alert/responsive

No:
- Regular/irregular breathing rate (≤10 or ≥30); labored; capillary refill >2 sec
- Color pale, dusky, cyanotic; capillary refill >2 sec
- Chest wall: open, sucking chest wounds, bruising, asymmetrical, deformities, and crepitus
- Breath sounds: unequal, diminished/absent, wheezes, crackles, rhonchi
- Uses accessory muscles, intercostal and substernal retractions
- Crowing, stridor, nasal flaring, and position of patient
- Tracheal edema/deviation from midline
- Jugular vein distention (JVD)
- Hematoma, bruising, wounds, and crepitus of neck/upper chest
- Severe respiratory distress or status epilepticus
- GCS <8

100% O₂ via non-rebreather mask

Improved Breathing Effectiveness?

Needle thoracentesis** / Chest tube**	Endotracheal tube (ETT)* / Sedation/paralyzing agents*	Bag-Valve-Mask 100% O₂

Prepare chest tube/ Auto-transfusion drainage system

- Confirm ETT placement: easy rise/fall of chest, equal and clear breath sounds, EtCO₂ detector (mandatory), "fog" in tube
- Prepare for ventilator; ABGs, chest X-ray

* Performed by specially trained healthcare professionals working within their scope of practice.

FIGURE 1 *(Continued)*

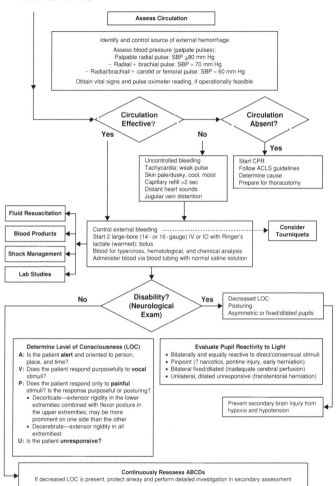

Assess Circulation

Identify and control source of external hemorrhage

Assess blood pressure (palpate pulses):
Palpable radial pulse: SBP ≥80 mm Hg
– Radial/+ brachial pulse: SBP ≈ 70 mm Hg
– Radial/brachial/+ carotid or femoral pulse: SBP ≈ 60 mm Hg

Obtain vital signs and pulse oximeter reading, if operationally feasible

Circulation Effective?

Yes **No**

Circulation Absent?

Yes

Uncontrolled bleeding
Tachycardia; weak pulse
Skin pale/dusky, cool, moist
Capillary refill >2 sec
Distant heart sounds
Jugular vein distention

Start CPR
Follow ACLS guidelines
Determine cause
Prepare for thoracotomy

Fluid Resuscitation

Blood Products

Shock Management

Lab Studies

Control external bleeding
Start 2 large-bore (14- or 16-gauge) IV or IO with Ringer's lactate (warmed); bolus
Blood for type/cross, hematological, and chemical analysis
Administer blood via blood tubing with normal saline solution

Consider Tourniquets

No **Disability? (Neurological Exam)** **Yes**

Decreased LOC
Posturing
Asymmetric or fixed/dilated pupils

Determine Level of Consciousness (LOC)
A: Is the patient **alert** and oriented to person, place, and time?
V: Does the patient respond purposefully to **vocal** stimuli?
P: Does the patient respond only to **painful** stimuli? Is the response purposeful or posturing?
  • Decorticate—extensor rigidity in the lower extremities combined with flexor posture in the upper extremities; may be more prominent on one side than the other
  • Decerebrate—extensor rigidity in all extremitiest
U: Is the patient **unresponsive**?

Evaluate Pupil Reactivity to Light
• Bilaterally and equally reactive to direct/consensual stimuli
• Pinpoint (? narcotics, pontine injury, early herniation)
• Bilateral fixed/dilated (inadequate cerebral perfusion)
• Unilateral, dilated unresponsive (transtentorial herniation)

Prevent secondary brain injury from hypoxia and hypotension

Continuously Reassess ABCDs
If decreased LOC is present, protect airway and perform detailed investigation in secondary assessment

FIGURE 1 *(Continued)*

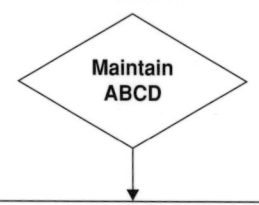

Secondary Assessment

Expose/Environment Control
- Remove all clothing; secure weapons
- Avoid loss of body heat: maintain increased ambient temperature, cover with baffled space blanket (Blizzard) or active warming

---

Full Set of Vital Signs/Focused Interventions/Family Presence
- Vital signs, temperature, pulse oximetry
- ECG monitor, lab studies, blood typing
- Nasogastric/oral gastric tube, if not contraindicated
- Urinary catheter, if not contraindicated
- DPL, FAST exam, X-ray
- Family/unit member presence

Give Comfort Measures
Reassurance, pain management

FIGURE 1 *(Continued)*

History: AMPLET

> **A:** Allergies
> **M:** Medication/ETOH/drugs/smoker
> **P:** Past medical history
> **L:** Last meal/drink; females: last menstrual period
> **E:** Events preceding injury
> **T:** Tetanus immunization

Head-to-Toe Assessment
Inspect Posterior Surface
Systematic identification of all injuries: DCAPBTLS

> **D**eformity
> **C**ontusion
> **A**brasion
> **P**uncture/penetrating injury
> **B**urns
> **T**enderness
> **L**aceration
> **S**welling

Source: Used with permission of the Emergency Nurses Association. *Trauma Nursing Core Course Provider Manual*, Sixth edition, © ENA, 2007.

Trauma/Medical

■ Blast Injury

TIP Key for care: Focus not only on the primary symptoms or injury, but also on the mechanism so as to identify possible hidden injuries.

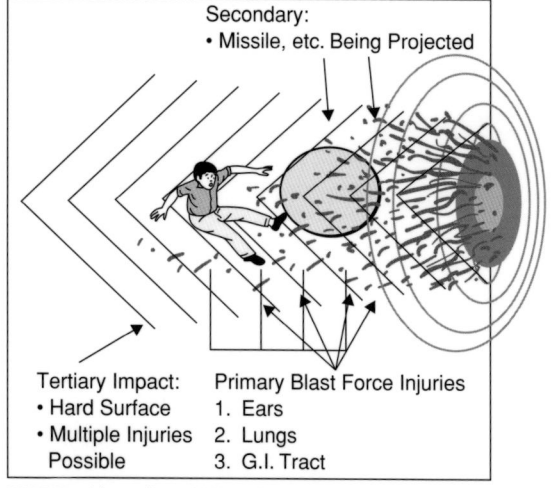

Secondary:
• Missile, etc. Being Projected

Tertiary Impact:
• Hard Surface
• Multiple Injuries Possible

Primary Blast Force Injuries
1. Ears
2. Lungs
3. G.I. Tract

FIGURE 2A Injury patterns: (A) Open-air explosion.

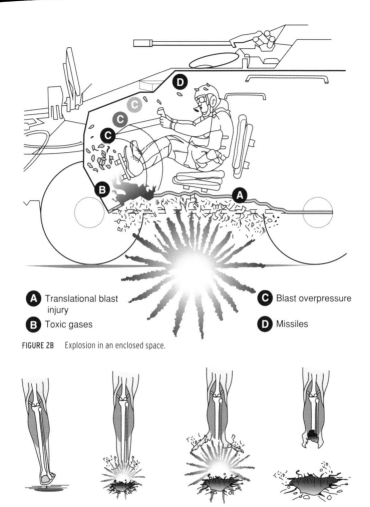

A Translational blast injury

B Toxic gases

C Blast overpressure

D Missiles

FIGURE 2B   Explosion in an enclosed space.

FIGURE 2C   Landmine injury.
Source (for parts A–C): U.S. Department of Defense. *Emergency War Surgery Handbook.* The Borden Institute, Washington, D.C. (2006).

Risk Factors

The following factors increase the risk of a blast injury:

- **Victim's location:** Inside versus outside. The highest risk occurs in a confined space (vehicle) or enclosed space (building) versus an open space; blast waves reflect off walls/corners.
- **Medium:** Increased risk if the blast is transmitted through water.
- **Body position:** Open air—increased risk if standing versus lying; water—treading water.
- **Type of explosion:** Pure fuel explosion.
- Increased severity of injury should be suspected if other individuals were killed by the explosion.

TABLE 2-1 Types of Blast Injuries

Primary Blast Injury: caused by barotrauma; primarily affects gas-filled organs

Body Area Affected	Signs and Symptoms
Ears (otologic)	• Tympanic membrane rupture • Hearing loss • Tinnitus • Otalgia (ear pain) • Foreign material in ear • Vertigo (middle ear damage) • Bleeding of cerebrospinal fluid from external canal (rule out basilar skull fracture)
Lungs (pulmonary contusion, pneumothorax, pneumomediastinum, pulmonary hemorrhage, alveolar rupture, pulmonary edema, arterial gas embolism)	• Generally acute presentation or rapid deterioration (may occur with/without external thoracic trauma) • Nonspecific (common to all types): cyanosis, tachypnea, dyspnea, chest pain • Contusion: crackles, decreased breath sounds, dullness, hemoptysis • Pneumothorax/pneumomediastinum, hemopneumothorax: decreased breath sounds, resonance, retrosternal crunch, subcutaneous crepitus, tracheal deviation, hemoptysis • Chest X-ray: • Butterfly pattern: infiltration spreading from hilum with sparing of lung margins • Zebra pattern (rib markings): underlying pulmonary contusion • Pulmonary trauma (hemo/pneumothorax, hemo/pneumomediastinum)
Gastrointestinal (hematoma/perforation of bowel wall; hematoma/tear of mesentery artery, rupture of hollow abdominal viscera)	• May not manifest for 24-48 hours • Abdominal or rectal pain • Peritoneal signs • Nausea/vomiting • Bloody diarrhea • Hematemesis • Constant feeling of needing to empty bowel • Testicular pain • Unexplained hypotension/hypoperfusion/fever
Ocular (corneal/scleral perforation, cuts/lacerations of eyelid, conjunctival hemorrhage, open globe injury, foreign body, globe rupture)	• Vision defects • Eye pain • Facial trauma • Eyelid trauma Concurrent injuries: • Maxillary/mandibular fracture • Blowout orbit • Teeth fracture • High incidence of penetrating brain injuries with open globe injuries

(Continued)

TABLE 2-1 Types of Blast Injuries *(Continued)*	
Primary Blast Injury: caused by barotrauma; primarily affects gas-filled organs	
Body Area Affected	Signs and Symptoms
Extremity (traumatic amputation)	Caused by blast wave, not fragment injury; indicates very close proximity to explosion; high mortality
Neurological (traumatic brain injury, cerebral air embolism)	Acute: concussion, loss of consciousness, amnesia Delayed: traumatic brain injury; post-traumatic stress disorder

Secondary Blast Injury: penetrating/nonpenetrating fragmentation wounds

- Soft-tissue trauma
- Fragmentation wounds (most common injury in explosion)
- Impalement
- Ocular penetration
- Traumatic amputations
- Biological fragments (bone): rule out infectious disease transmission (e.g., hepatitis B, HIV)

To date, there have been two reported cases of infectious disease transmission from suicide bomber to victim.

Tertiary Blast Injury: displacement of the person and impact, resulting in blunt trauma

- Blunt trauma
- Fractures
- Closed head trauma
- Solid-organ (spleen/liver/kidney) contusions/fractures
- Closed/open brain injuries

History is important to detect hidden injuries. For example, a fall of more than 20 feet is likely to cause thoracolumbar vertebral injuries and visceral injuries; shipboard accidents may cause primary/tertiary trauma due to transmission of the blast wave through the water and hull of the ship.

Quaternary Blast Injury

- Thermal: flash burns unless victim is trapped inside a burning structure or clothing caught fire
- Chemical burns
- Smoke/toxic inhalation: burning Teflon (found in AFVs) releases phosgene
- Psychological (rule out TBI): may affect individuals not directly exposed to the blast
- Crush injuries: increased morbidity/mortality if a building collapses
- Exacerbation of underlying medical condition (cardiac, pulmonary)
- Radiological contamination ("dirty bomb") or chemical agents

Primary Blast Lung Injury

Blast lung injury (BLI) is the primary cause of early death after a blast. The underlying pathology of BLI consists of alveolar overdistention and rupture, as well as multifocal subpleural, intra-alveolar, and perivascular hemorrhages. Larger blast impulses may cause hemopneumothoraces, traumatic emphysema (subcutaneous emphysema), and bronchopleural fistulas. Most casualties who have a clinically significant BLI show signs and symptoms of acute respiratory failure within minutes of the explosion, making a chest radiograph or other diagnostic test unnecessary. *The following concurrent blast injuries indicate a high risk for BLI:*

- Skull fracture
- Burns > 10% body surface area (BSA)
- Penetrating injury to head or torso
- Injury to four or more body areas

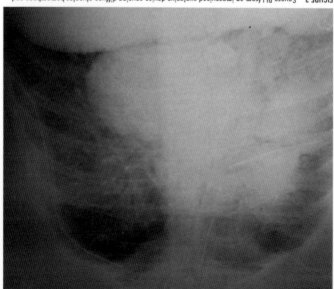

FIGURE 3 Severe BLI from an improvised explosive device causing diffuse alveolar hemorrhage and massive hemoptysis. The blast appears to have struck from the right, as evidenced by the greater injury in the right lung fields. Note the relative sparing of the lung margins (butterfly pattern) and the presence of rib markings reflecting underlying tissue damage.

Source: Reprinted from *Crit Care Nurs Clin North Am,* vol. 18, E. J. Bridges, "Blast Injuries: From Triage to Critical Care," pp. 333-348, Copyright 2006, with permission from Elsevier. [http://www.sciencedirect.com/science/journals/08959885]

Care of BLI:

ABCs

Chest tube for pneumothorax

• If blast lung injury is suspected, a prophylactic chest tube should be considered if patient is to be transported by air

Judicious volume resuscitation if not contraindicated due to other injuries/hemorrhage

Oxygen

Mechanical ventilation

• Avoid high pressures; use lung-protective ventilation
• Limit peak inspiratory/plateau pressure
• Avoid positive end expiratory pressure (PEEP) if possible

Ventilatory modes

- SIMV/pressure support
- Volume-controlled ventilation: inverse ratio (I:E = 2:1)

Permissive hypercapnia (do not use if concurrent head injury)

Treat the patient, not the X-ray

Arterial Gas Embolism

There is an increased risk of arterial gas embolism with positive-pressure ventilation. This complication is manifested as follows:

- Coronary circulation: arrhythmias, ischemia
- Cerebral circulation: headache, vertigo, ataxia, seizures, loss of consciousness (LOC), sensory loss
- Retinal vessels: retinal artery air emboli

Care of arterial gas embolism:

- 100% oxygen (or hyperbaric oxygen if available)
- Positioning: flat, supine

Gastrointestinal Injury

Intestinal/gastric perforation may lead to peritonitis and hemorrhage. There may be delayed perforation due to transmural contusion with subsequent ischemia and necrosis. There is an increased risk of solid-organ injury with underwater blasts. (See the "Abdominal/Gastrointestinal" section.)

The key to treatment of gastrointestinal (GI) injury is early detection. There is an increased risk for GI injury if multiple detonations occur in a complex environment (i.e., inside a structure).

Diagnosis is made as follows:

- Signs and symptoms include nausea/vomiting, abdominal pain, peritonitis, rectum, testes, and tenesmus (painful anal sphincter spasm and urgent urge to defecate or urinate).
- Standard diagnostic tests—radiograph, computerized tomography (CT), diagnostic peritoneal lavage, and ultrasound—may be useful in detecting solid-organ damage, hemorrhage, and perforation but are not sensitive or specific for bowel wall injuries. Thus a negative exam does not rule out GI injury.
- Repeat the abdominal assessment.
- A high index of suspicion is necessary for early detection of occult injury with clinical deterioration (e.g., hemodynamic instability, increased fluid requirements, unresolved acidosis).

Ocular Injury Assessment

See the "Ocular" section.

Otologic Injury

Injuries may include tympanic membrane rupture, foreign material in ear, inner ear damage, and hearing loss. It is important to rule out basilar skull fracture. Signs and symptoms include deafness, tinnitus, otalgia (ear pain), and vertigo. Rule out other primary blast injuries (pulmonary, neurological).

Care of otologic injury:

- **If isolated auditory injury:** Monitor for 4 hours, then discharge. (See the "Neurological" section for additional evaluation guidelines.)

Discharge instructions: Return for medical care in case of pulmonary symptoms (e.g., shortness of breath, hemoptysis), GI symptoms (e.g., abdominal pain, nausea/vomiting, bloody diarrhea), or change in level of consciousness or other neurological signs/symptoms.

- No urgent care required if isolated auditory injury.
- Gently remove debris/blood from ear: No irrigation!
- Keep ear clean and dry.
- Antibiotics—prophylactic not indicated unless there is possibility of basilar skull fracture. In that case, use second-generation cephalosporins; treat infection.
- Consultation for audiology assessment.
- May require alternate method of communication.

Psychological Trauma
See the "Mental Health" section.

Soft-Tissue/Musculoskeletal Injury
See the "Soft-Tissue Trauma" or "Orthopedic-Musculoskeletal" section.

Thermal Injuries
See the "Burns" section.

Traumatic Brain Injury
See the "Neurological" section.

References

Cave KM, Cornish EM, Chandler DW. Blast injury of the ear: Clinical update from the Global War on Terror. Mil Med 2007;172:726-730.

Centers for Disease Control and Prevention. Explosions and blast injuries: A primer for clinicians. http://emergency.cdc.gov/masscasualties/explosions.asp (accessed November 2007).

Injuries from explosives. In Salome JP, Pons PT (Eds.), Prehospital Trauma Life Support: Military Version (6th ed., pp. 564-581). St. Louis: Mosby, 2007.

Leibovici D, Gorfit ON, Shapira SC. Eardrum perforation in explosion survivors: Is it a marker of pulmonary blast injury? Ann Emerg Med 1999;34:168-172.

Mallonee S, Sharat S, Stennies G, et al. Physical injuries and fatalities resulting from the Oklahoma City bombing. JAMA 1996;276:382-387.

Nelson TJ, Clark T, Stedje-Larsen ET, et al. Close proximity blast injury patterns from improvised explosive devices in Iraq: A report of 18 cases. J Trauma 2007;62(5).

Pizov R, Oppenheim-Eden A, Matot I, et al. Blast lung injury from an explosion on a civilian bus. Chest 1999;115:165-172.

Sasser SM, Sattin RW, Hunt RC, et al. Blast lung injury. *Prehosp Emerg Care* 2006;10(2):165-172.

Thompson D, Brown S, Mallonee S, et al. Fatal and nonfatal injuries among U.S Air Force personnel resulting from the terrorist bombing of the Khobar Towers. *J Trauma* 2004;57:208-215.

Warden D. Military TBI during the Iraq and Afghanistan wars. *J Head Trauma Rehab* 2006;21(5):398-402.

Wong JML, Marsh D, Abu-Sitta G, et al. Biological foreign body implantation in victims of the London July 7th suicide bombings. *J Trauma* 2006;60(2):402-404.

■ Burns

TABLE 2-2	Establish A BURN PLAN
Airway	• 100% O_2 via non-rebreather mask • Rule out inhalation injury and CO poisoning • Intubate sooner than later
Breathing	• Chest wall intact or circumferential torso burn? • Assist breathing
Urine plan	• Urine output (UOP): 30-50 mL/h • Electrical burn: UOP 75-100 mL/h
Resuscitation	• Will have ↑ blood pressure and heart rate; no hypotension; normotensive ≠ adequate resuscitation • Two large-bore IVs: can place in burned or unburned skin (fluid = Ringer's Lactate) • Estimate total body surface area (TBSA) and fluid requirements • Electrical: cardiac arrest, ECG, cardiac enzymes
Nasogastric tube	• For burns covering > 20% TBSA • Other injuries
Pulses and pH	• Pulses present? • Circumferential burns? • Electrical injury • ABGs; resolution of base deficit
Lines, IV	• Two large-bore IVs, arterial line, CVP • Sutured in place
Accurate I&O	• Use JTTS Burn Resuscitation Flow Sheet
Notify burn unit	• IAW local directives • Prepare for transport: send copies of medical records, labs, X-ray

BURNS

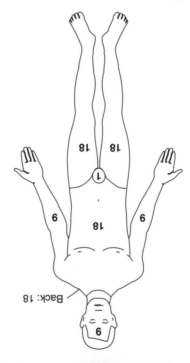

Back: 18

FIGURE 4 Adult Rule of Nines.

- Patient's hand + fingers = 1%
- Add all second- and third-degree burns to calculate total body surface area (TBSA) burned

Rule of 10

- Estimate burn size to the nearest 10.
- %TBSA × 10 = initial fluid rate in mL/h (for adult patients weighing 40 kg to 80 kg).
- For every 10 kg above 80 kg, increase the rate by 100 mL/h.

  Example: Patient with 27% TBSA burn
- 27 × 10 = 270 mL/h
- Monitor urine output

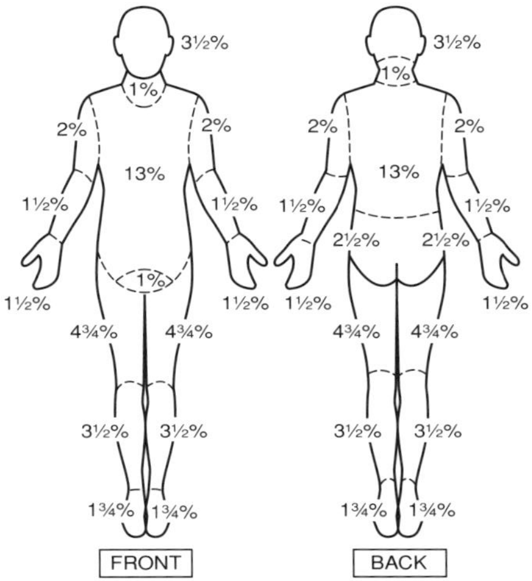

AREA	Birth-1 yr	1-4 years	5-9 years	10-14 years	15 years	ADULT	2'	3'	TOTAL
Head	19	17	13	11	9	7			
Neck	2	2	2	2	2	2			
Ant. Trunk	13	13	13	13	13	13			
Post. Trunk	13	13	13	13	13	13			
R. Buttock	2½	2½	2½	2½	2½	2½			
L. Buttock	2½	2½	2½	2½	2½	2½			
Genitalia	1	1	1	1	1	1			
R.U. Arm	4	4	4	4	4	4			
L.U. Arm	4	4	4	4	4	4			
R.L. Arm	3	3	3	3	3	3			
L.L. Arm	3	3	3	3	3	3			
R. Hand	2½	2½	2½	2½	2½	2½			
L. Hand	2½	2½	2½	2½	2½	2½			
R. Thigh	5½	6½	8	8½	9	9½			
L. Thigh	5½	6½	8	8½	9	9½			
R. Leg	5	5	5½	6	6½	7			
L. Leg	5	5	5½	6	6½	7			
R. Foot	3½	3½	3½	3½	3½	3½			
L. Foot	3½	3½	3½	3½	3½	3½			
						TOTAL			

FIGURE 5   Adult Lund-Browder TBSA calculation. Add all second- and third-degree burns for TBSA burned.

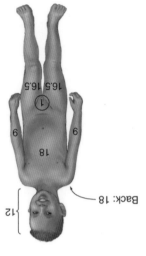

FIGURE 7   Child Lund-Browder TBSA calculation.

Back: 18

12

16.5 16.5

1

9   9

18

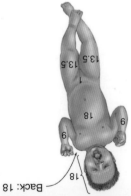

FIGURE 6   Infant Lund-Browder TBSA calculation.

Back: 18

18

13.5 13.5

1

18

9   9

TABLE 2-3 Burn Severity Determination		
Burn	Characteristics	Course
1° (first degree)	Superficial. Involves only the epidermis. Skin intact, red in color, dry surface, no blisters; painful; hypersensitive. (Note: Not included when estimating % TBSA.)	Heals in 3-6 days; palliative care
2° (second degree): superficial partial thickness	Involves epidermis and part of the dermis. Skin intact with blisters, red in color; capillary refill present, painful; moist/weeps fluid.	• Heals in 10-14 days without surgery; minimal scarring • May go to OR for debridement and cleaning with Hibiclens
2° (second degree): deep partial thickness	Involves epidermis and deep into the dermis. Decreased moistness; skin is ivory/white/mottled; absent or prolonged blanching.	Some healing in 21-28 days. Requires grafting
3° (third degree): full thickness	Dermis destroyed; skin is translucent, parchment-like or leathery appearance, or charred. Dry, thrombosed blood vessels, painless, nonblanching.	Requires debridement and grafting
4° (fourth degree)	Extends into deep structures: muscle, tendon, bone.	Requires extensive debridement or amputation

Fluid Resuscitation in Case of Adult Burns

Determine pre-burn "dry" weight.

< 20% TBSA: oral hydration with electrolyte-containing fluids unless contraindicated.

20% TBSA: first 24 hours (note that the clock starts at the time of burn injury. not the arrival at the MTF):

- IV Ringer's lactate (RL)
- Formula: 2-4 mL/kg/% BSA burned
- Give half of the total calculated amount over the first 8 hours
- Give the remaining half over the next 16 hours
- Maintain UOP of 30-50 mL/h; increase or decrease IV rate by 20% q 2 h to reach target UOP (30-50 mL)

Example: 80-kg patient with 30% BSA (assumes no other trauma)

$$2 \text{ mL} \times 80 \text{ kg} \times 30\% \text{ BSA} = 4800 \text{ mL RL for the first}$$
$$24 \text{ hours (estimated)}$$

Sources: U.S. Army Institute of Surgical Research, Burn facts poster. American Burn Association, *Advanced Burn Life Support Course Instructor Manual* (Chapter 3), 2005. Reproduced with permission.

Pediatric Burn Fluid Resuscitation

A child is defined as weighing less than 30 kg. Note that children have greater surface-to-weight ratios and greater fluid requirements.

First 24 hours (note that the clock starts at the time of burn injury, not the arrival at the MTF):

- Resuscitation: RL at 3-4 mL/kg/% BSA burned
- Give half of the total calculated amount over the first 8 hours
- Give the remaining half over the next 16 hours

PLUS:

Maintenance fluids: D_5 ½ NS (Rate is constant; do not titrate)
- First 10 kg of body weight: 100 mL/kg over 24 hours
- Second 10 kg of body weight: 50 mL/kg over 24 hours
- For each 1 kg of body weight above 20 kg: 20 mL/kg over 24 hours

Maintain UOP of 1 mL/kg/h

Example: 23-kg child with 20% burn

Resuscitative Fluids (RL) 3 mL/kg/% BSA burned	Maintenance Fluid (D_5 ½ NS)
(3 mL) × (23 kg) × (20% BSA) = 1,380 mL	100 mL × 10 kg = 1,000 mL 50 mL × 10 kg = 500 mL 20 mL × 3 kg = 60 mL 1,560 mL
Estimated total fluids in first 24 hours = Resuscitate (1,380 mL) + Maintenance (1,560 mL) = 2,940 mL	

Source: American Burn Association, Advanced Burn Life Support Course Instructor Manual (Chapter 7), 2005. Reproduced with permission.

Burn Resuscitation Goals

Recommendations for hypotension (assumes no other injuries)

Optimal blood pressure should be individualized. If MAP is not adequate (generally < 55 mm Hg) to maintain UOP goal of at least 30 mL/h, the following steps are recommended:
- Vasopressin 0.02-0.04 units/min IV drip (DO NOT TITRATE)
- Monitor CVP (Goal 8-10 cm H_2O)
  ○ If CVP not at goal, increase fluid rate
  ○ If CVP at goal, add norepinephrine 2-20 mcg/min IV
- If additional pressors are needed, reevaluate the patient. These patients may be volume depleted but also suspect a missed injury. Consider dobutamine drip at 5 mcg/kg/min (max dose 20 mcg/kg/min). If hypotension persists, look for a missed injury. Consider adding epinephrine or neosynephrine as a last resort. If in catecholamine-resistant shock and no ongoing blood loss, consider IAW physician order:
- Acidemia: pH < 7.20: ventilator adjusted to target $PaCO_2$ 30-35 mm Hg
  ○ If unresponsive, consider sodium bicarbonate IV 2-5 mEq over 4-8 h; do not exceed 50 mEq/h
- Adrenal insufficiency: Check cortisol level; hydrocortisone 100 mg IV q 8 h considered
- Hypocalcemia: maintain calcium > 1.1 mmol/L
  ○ Monitor for ECG changes, especially during IV replacement
  ○ Calcium chloride 500-1000 mg IV (<1 mL/min); repeat q 4-6 h
  ○ Calcium gluconate 500-2000 mg IV (0.5 mL/min)

Source: JTTS Clinical Practice Guidelines for Burn Care, November, 2008.

JTTS Burn Resuscitation Flow Sheet

Date:	Initial Treatment Facility:

Name	SSN	Pre-burn Est. Wt (kg)	%TBSA	Estimated fluid vol. pat. should receive		
				1st 8 hrs	2nd 16th hrs	Est. Total 24 hrs

Date & Time of Injury	BAMC/ISR Burn Team DSN 312-429-2876

Tx Site/Team	HR from burn	Local Time	Crystalloid	Colloid	TOTAL	UOP	Base Deficit	BP	MAP (>55 %)	CVP	Pressors (Vasopressin 0.04 µ/min)
1st											
2nd											
3rd											
4th											
5th											
6th											
7th											
8th											
Total Fluids 1st 8 hrs:											
9th											
10th											
11th											
12th											
13th											
14th											
15th											
16th											
17th											
18th											
19th											
20th											
21st											
22nd											
23rd											
24th											
24 hr Total Fluids:											

FIGURE 8   JTTS Burn Resuscitation Flowsheet.
Source: Reproduced from J. L. Ennis, et al., The Journal of TRAUMA© Injury, Infection, and Critical Care 64 (2008); S146–S151. Used with permission of Lippincott Williams & Wilkins. [http://lww.com]

- Annotate appropriate blocks (not shown): name, estimated "dry" weight, % TBSA, calculated IV fluids for 8, 16, and 24 hours
- HR from burn = time of injury, *not* arrival to MTF
- IV fluids and UOP carry over from lower levels of care
  Example: Patient arrives at MTF 3 hours post-burn. MTF will start its charting for "4th" hour. IVF and UOP totals from echelon I and II care, prior to arrival at the MTF, should be placed in "3rd" hour row.

TABLE 2-4   First 72 Hours Post-Burn Resuscitation

Maintain strict I&O. Avoid oliguria, over-resuscitation, IV bolus therapy, and UOP > 60 mL/r. Count IV medications/drips when calculating the hourly input.

Time Post-Burn	Crystalloids RL, D₅ ¼ NS, D₅ W, NS	Colloids, Albumin, Blood Products, Hespan
1-24 hours	RL: • Per adult/pediatric formula (reevaluated after 8-12 hours) D₅ ¼ NS: • Per pediatric maintenance formula	If: • ≥ 12 hours for large burn • Resuscitation: ≥ 6 mL/kg/% TBSA • Start albumin as described below • Known blood loss: give blood products
25-48 hours	RL, D₅ ¼ NS, or D₅W: • Adult maintenance: half of first 24-hour intake; titrate to UOP and Na⁺	Give 5% albumin: mL × % TBSA × kg < 30% TBSA = not required Add to IV NS 30-49% TBSA = 0.3 mL 50-69% TBSA = 0.4 mL > 70% TBSA = 0.5 mL If albumin is not available, fresh frozen plasma or synthetic colloid can be used at the same dose.
49-72 hours	• Continue maintenance fluids • Calculate insensible water losses mL/day = 1 mL/kg/% burn/24 h	Stop albumin

Example

Albumin Administration	Insensible Water Loss Replacement/24 Hours
40% TBSA in a 70-kg patient: 0.3 mL × 70 kg × 40% 0.3 × 2800 = 840 mL/24 h = 35 mL/h	1 mL × 70 kg × 50% BSA = 3500 mL 3500 mL/24 h = 146 mL/h

Conditions Requiring Additional Fluid Resuscitation

Electrical injury:
- Maintain UOP 75-100 mL/h
- Consider IV mannitol and sodium bicarbonate for pigmenturia

Inhalation injury
Delayed resuscitation
Preexisting dehydration (caffeine, operational mission, ETOH)
Concomitant trauma/multisystem trauma: soft-tissue injury secondary to blunt, penetrating, and blast injuries

Sources: JTTS Clinical Practice Guidelines for Burn Care, November 2008; *Emergency War Surgery Handbook* (Chapter 28), 2004; U.S. Army Institute of Surgical Research, Burn facts poster.

TABLE 2-5 Burn Wound Management

Burn Location	Treatment	Comments
Scalp, trunk, neck, extremities	Wrap in 5% Sulfamylon solution soaked dressings TID and prn to keep dressings moist	• There is less mess as opposed to Sulfamylon or Silvadene cream • Easier for receiving institution to clean up upon arrival • Keep dressings moist rather than saturated
Ears	Sulfamylon cream BID	Do not use a pillow under the head
Eyelids	Apply bacitracin ophthalmic ointment to eyelids QID Apply erythromycin ophthalmic ointment in the eyes QID	• Consult Ophthalmology for all patients with deep facial burns or corneal injury

Note: Elevate head and injured extremities 30-45 degrees. Do not use pillows if ears are burned. Dress wounds in the position of function.

Source: U.S. Army Institute of Surgical Research. Emergency War Surgery Handbook (Chapter 28: JTTS Clinical Practice Guidelines for Burn Care). October, 2006.

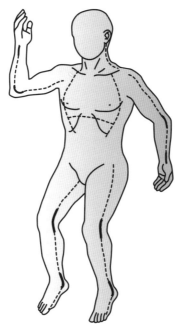

FIGURE 9 Escharotomy. The dashed lines show incision sites and the bold lines denote major joints.
Source: U.S. Department of Defense. Emergency War Surgery Handbook. The Borden Institute, Washington, D.C. (2006).

TABLE 2-6 Emergent Burn Syndromes

Warning: Assure adequate UOP and blood pressure.

Condition	Description	Management
Eschar syndrome • Restriction of blood flow to unburned skin due to edema and inelastic eschar • Usually occurs within first 24 hours post burn	• Extensive and/or circumferential burns of the chest/abdomen (i.e., difficult ventilation, abdominal compartment syndrome) • Circumferential/constricting burn of the extremities with diminished or absent pulses • Pressures < 30 mm Hg	Escharotomy • Beside cautery or scalpel incision through constricting eschar to improve circulation; includes unburned skin at both ends of the incision • Monitor pulses and control excessive bleeding post procedure
Compartment syndrome • Usually occurs within first 24 hours post burn • In severe burns, may also have eschar syndrome	• Circumferential burns • Usually follows eschar syndrome • Edema in a closed facial space of both burned and unburned extremities • ≥ 6 mL/kg/TBSA resuscitation • Causes extensive tissue, vessel, and nerve damage	Fasciotomy • To the OR • Wounds open; delayed closure • Monitor pulses and control excessive bleeding post procedure
Abdominal compartment syndrome • Delayed or inadequate escharotomy	• ≥ 6 mL/kg/TBSA resuscitation • Bladder/abdominal pressure • Increased ventilator pressures (check q 4 h) to OR < 25 mm Hg • Low UOP • Hypotension	To OR for decompression; laparotomy may be needed if pressure > 25 mm Hg

Source: U.S. Army Institute of Surgical Research, Emergency War Surgery Handbook (Chapter 28 (2004): JTTS Clinical Practice Guidelines for Burn Care), November, 2008.

TABLE 2-7 Inhalation Burns

Suspected victims include persons who were present during a closed-space incident or explosion; who were elderly or young; or who had loss of consciousness, exposure to noxious fumes, facial burns, carbonaceous sputum, or large burns. Note that fluid resuscitation needs increase dramatically with inhalation injury.

Level	Cause	Signs and Symptoms	Treatment
Above glottis	Thermal	• Pharyngeal burns and soot • Hoarseness • Strider • Rapid airway obstruction; onset may be delayed until fluid resuscitation is adequate	• Give 100% cool, humidified O₂ via non-rebreathing mask or ETT; elevate HOB > 30° • Intubate early rather than later; use size-8 ETT to facilitate bronchoscopy
Below glottis	Chemical/steam	• Depends on type and amount of substance • Bronchospasm • Bronchorrhea • Low SaO₂	• Give 100% cool, humidified O₂ via non-rebreathing mask or ETT; elevate HOB > 30° • Intubate early rather than later; use size-8 ETT to facilitate bronchoscopy • Decontaminate PRN; protect providers • May receive aerosolized heparin 5000 units with albuterol 2.5 mg q 4 h • Observe for 24 hours

Source: U.S. Army Institute of Surgical Research, Emergency War Surgery Handbook (Chapter 28 (2004): JTTS Clinical Practice Guidelines for Burn Care), November, 2008.

TABLE 2-8	Carboxyhemoglobin (COHgb) Levels	
Draw blood for this test at the same time blood is drawn for ABG.		
Exposure	Blood COHgb	Signs and Symptoms
Mild	< 15%	None; normal level for smokers/truckers
Moderate	15-39%	Headache, confusion, nausea, visual changes, lethargy
Severe	40-60%	Mental status changes (hallucinations, combativeness, delirium, coma), cardiovascular collapse, death (COHgb > 50%)

In Case of Suspected/Actual Carbon Monoxide Poisoning:
- CO has a 200 times greater affinity to bond to hemoglobin than O_2, so SaO_2 is unreliable.
- Cherry-red complexion is a late sign.
- Give 100% O_2 via non-rebreathing mask or ETT until COHgb < 15-20%.
- Half-life of COHgb = 250 minutes on room air; with 100% FiO_2 = 45 minutes.

Source: American Burn Association, *Advanced Burn Life Support Course Instructor Manual* (Chapter 2), 2005.

Chemical Burns (Acids/Alkali)
A key consideration in cases involving chemical burns is to protect healthcare workers. Note that alkali burns may yield deep tissue damage.
Care of chemical burns:
- Brush dry materials off the skin surface before starting water/saline irrigation.
- Remove all clothing.
- Immediately irrigate the affected area with *copious amounts of water/saline*.
- Implement fluid resuscitation/management as with a thermal burn.
- Irrigation may be required for several hours.
- Irrigate eyes until the patient is seen by an ophthalmologist.

Petroleum Injuries (Not Flame Burns)
- Delipidation; full-thickness skin necrosis is common—may not be initially evident
- Hydrocarbon absorption: becomes evident in 6-24 hours; may lead to hepatic and renal failure, lead toxicity

White Phosphorus Burns
Metal fragments that contain white phosphorus ignite when exposed to air. They may be found on clothing or embedded in soft-tissue. Treat thermal burns from burning clothing as a thermal injury:
- *Copious water/saline irrigation*, and saline-soaked dressings—keep wet.
- Hypocalcemia and hyperphosphatemia may occur.
  - Monitor QTc (normal < 48 msec)
  - Calcium gluconate IV 1-2 gm (90-180 mg elemental calcium) over 10-20 min)

- Rapid surgical removal of metal is often required.
- Apply topical burn antimicrobial agents to burns.

Sources: *Emergency War Surgery Handbook* (Chapter 28), October 2006; American Burn Association, *Advanced Burn Life Support Course Instructor Manual* (Chapter 6), 2005.

TABLE 2-9   Burn Pain Management

Obtain vital signs and continuous pulse oximetry before and after administration of any medications. Rule out hypoxia, hypovolemia, and compartment syndrome.

Pain varies in the acute and healing phases and with burn depth; it may be described as "burning," "aching," or "sharp" after dressing changes. Neuropathic pain may be described as "burning," "tingling," "shooting," or "numbing." Pain is managed best when medications are given continuously rather than as needed using the most effective drug for the patient.

Drug	Dose/Notes

Morphine	IV is preferred route in acute and early phases:
	• Moderate to severe and/or anticipated or procedural pain (wound care)
	• Respiratory rate >12/min (adult)
	IM/SC absorption during resuscitation is unreliable; avoid during hospitalization.
	Dose: IV route onset 5–10 min; peaks in 20 min; $t_{\frac{1}{2}}$ = 2–4 h
	• Load: up to 5 mg IVP
	• 2–10 mg IVP over 5 min q 10–12 min to effect
	Procedure:
	  ○ Premedicate 30 min prior to start
	  ○ 1- to 2-mg increments over 30 sec, q 5–10 min
	  ○ Taper down toward the end of procedure/painful stimuli to limit post-procedure respiratory depression
	• Continuous IV drip: 5 mg/h; may be given in combination with IV bolus for break-through pain
	Treatment of overdose: naloxone 0.4mg IVP.

Fentanyl	IV is preferred route in acute and early phases. IV dose: 1–2 min; peaks 3–5 min; $t_{\frac{1}{2}}$ = 3.6 h • Load: up to 50 mcg IVP • 25–75 mcg q 1–2 h • Continuous IV drip: 250 mcg/h Oralet (oral transmucosal): onset 5–15 min; peak 20–30 min; $t_{\frac{1}{2}}$ = 6.6 h. • Lozenges on a stick (200–1600 mcg) • To dissolve, move around mouth and under tongue Treatment of overdose: naloxone 0.4mg IVP.
Midazolam	Loading dose: 2–5 mg IVP over 2–5 min for intubated patients. Treatment of overdose: flumazenil IVP 0.2 mg (2 mL) over 15 sec; repeat q 1 min until effect; most patients respond to 0.6 to 1 mg. Maximum dose: 1 mg.
Lorazepam	Dose: IV: 44 mcg/kg or 2.0 mg total.
Propofol	Anesthetic: avoid in burn patients due to fatty lipid content; dramatically increases CO_2 production.

Transfer/Transport of Burn Injuries

- Use burn pads; send extra for re-enforcement of dressings.
- Do not pack post-escharotomy incisions with dry gauze.
- ≥ 20% TBSA: NG/OG tube for potential ileus; HOB ↑ 30°
- Vital signs, circulation checks, UOP q 1 h
- Send all medical records/fluid resuscitation documentation.

Stresses of Flight

- Decreased partial pressure: exacerbates cardiopulmonary compromise due to decreased oxygenation (burn injury, CO poisoning, anemia, concurrent pulmonary blast injury). Treat with increased flow O_2.
- Barometric pressure changes: increased gas expansion leads to gastric distention and risk of aspiration and discomfort, ocular trauma, and cardiopulmonary compromise.
- Decreased humidity: exacerbates fluid loss.
- Vibration: may increase pain; give IV analgesics.
- Thermal stress: loss of natural insulation and skin integrity may increase hypothermia and pain. The severity of the burn affects the autonomic temperature regulatory functions and may increase O_2 demand.

Source: AFI 41-307, Aeromedical Evacuation Patient Considerations and Standards of Care (Chapter 28), August 2003.

Additional Burn Care Considerations

Avoid tape; it will not adhere to burned skin.

- Use suture or staple IVs instead.
- Secure ETT and NG with cloth tape using a nonslip knot.

Diuretics are never indicated except if gross pigmenturia is present and the patient is unresponsive to IV fluids. In such a case, give IV mannitol. Glycosuria is common following severe thermal injury and may cause hypovolemia secondary to osmotic diuresis. In such a case, follow these steps:

- Monitor the patient's urine for glucose.
- Give IV insulin as needed.

Sources: U.S. Army Institute of Surgical Research, Burn facts poster; *Emergency War Surgery Handbook* (Chapter 28), 2004.

References

AFI 41-307, Aeromedical Evacuation Patient Considerations and Standards of Care, August 2003. http://www.e-publishing.af.mil/shared/media/epubs/AFI41-307.pdf

American Burn Association, *Advanced Burn Life Support Course Instructor Manual,* 2005.

Emergency War Surgery Handbook (Chapter 28, Burns), 2004. http://www.brooksidepress.org/Products/ Emergency_War_Surgery/index.htm

JTTS Clinical Practice Guidelines for Burn Care, November 2008.

Micromedex, PDR Electronic Library, 2007.

U.S. Army Institute of Surgical Research, Burn facts poster.

■ Cardiac

Pulseless Cardiac Arrest: Adult Patient

Source: Adapted from AHA guidelines for cardiopulmonary resuscitation and emergency cardiovascular care. Part 7.2: Management of cardiac arrest. *Circulation* 2005;112(24):IV58-IV66.

ACLS should be performed only by qualified providers. Refer to the ACLS guidelines and medical orders.

Cardiopulmonary Resuscitation

Start CPR, the key is to avoid interruption in compressions.

- Begin compressions: 100/min; 1 cycle = 30 compressions, then 2 breaths (5 cycles = 2 minutes).
- Administer oxygen when available.
- Attach a monitor/defibrillator when available.
- Secure the airway (this should not interfere with defibrillation): ventilate at a rate of 8-10 breaths/min once the airway is stabilized.

Ventricular Tachycardia/Fibrillation

- 1 shock (if unwitnessed arrest, perform 5 cycles of CPR before defibrillation).
  - Biphasic (120-200 J)
  - Monophasic (360 J)
- 5 cycles of CPR (1 cycle = 30 compressions, then 2 breaths).
- Check rhythm and then give shock (continue CPR until ready to shock; do not stop while defibrillator is charging).
  - Biphasic (same as first shock or higher)
  - Monophasic (360 J)
- Resume CPR immediately after every shock.
- Medications (IV or IO): give during CPR and before or after shock.
  - Epinephrine 1 mg IV/IO (repeat q 3-5 min) or
  - Vasopressin 40 units IV/IO to replace first or second epinephrine dose
- Give 5 cycles of CPR.
- Check rhythm/pulse every 2 minutes and before each shock.
- Give shock if needed.
  - Biphasic (same as first shock or higher)
  - Monophasic (360 J)
- Resume CPR.
- Consider antiarrhythmics (give during CPR and before or after shock).
  - Amiodarone 300 mg IV/IO; repeat dose 150 mg IV/IO over 10 min; then 0.5 mg/min × 18 h or
  - Lidocaine 1-1.5 mg/kg first dose; repeat dose at 0.5-0.75 mg/kg IV/ IO up to maximum 3 doses; or 3 mg/kg infusion; 1-4 mg/min
- Consider magnesium: 1-2 gm IV/IO for torsades de pointes.
- Treat underlying cause.
- Give 5 cycles of CPR; continue assessment of rhythm q 2 min; give shocks and medications as indicated above.

Asystole/Pulseless Electrical Activity

Source: Adapted from AHA guidelines for cardiopulmonary resuscitation and emergency cardio-vascular care. Part 7.2: Management of cardiac arrest. *Circulation* 2005; 112(24):IV58-IV66.

Do not shock patients with asystole or pulseless electrical activity (PEA). The key is to give them uninterrupted/high-quality CPR and to treat reversible causes.

- Give 5 cycles of CPR.
- Give the following medications:
  - Epinephrine 1 mg IV/IO repeat q 3-5 min *or*
  - Vasopressin 40 U IV/IO to replace first or second dose of epinephrine
  - Atropine 1 mg IV/IO for asystole/slow PEA; repeat q 3-5 min (up to 3 doses)
- Give 5 cycles of CPR.
- Check the rhythm every 2 minutes.
- Treat the underlying cause.

Possible Causes of Pulseless Arrest, Bradycardia, and Tachycardia
Six H's
- Hypovolemia
- Hypoxia
- Hydrogen ion (acidosis)
- Hypokalemia/hyperkalemia
- Hypoglycemia
- Hypothermia

Five T's
- Toxins
- Tamponade (cardiac)
- Tension pneumothorax
- Thrombosis (coronary/pulmonary)
- Trauma (TBI, hypovolemic shock)

Bradycardia
Source: Adapted from AHA guidelines for cardiopulmonary resuscitation and emergency cardiovascular care. Part 7.3: Management of symptomatic bradycardia and tachycardia. *Circulation* 2005;112(24): IV67-IV77.

Bradycardia is defined as heart rate < 60 bpm or heart rate that is inadequate for the patient's clinical condition. The key measures in its management are:

- Airway
- Breathing
- Oxygen
- ECG
- Blood pressure
- Pulse oximetry
- Treat reversible causes
- IV

In case of bradycardia, proceed as follows:

- Assess for signs/symptoms of poor perfusion (altered mental status, chest pain, hypotension, heart failure, syncope, seizures).
- If adequate perfusion is present, monitor the patient.
- If inadequate perfusion is present:
  ◦ Transcutaneous pacing (Type II second-degree heart block or third-degree heart block)
  ◦ Atropine 0.5 mg IV q 3–5 min (maximum dose 3 mg); useful for symptomatic bradycardia and any type of symptomatic nodal AV block
- Begin pacing if patient remains unresponsive to medications.
- Give vasopressors via continuous drip (while waiting for pacer or if pacing is ineffective):
  ◦ Epinephrine 2–10 mcg/min
  ◦ Dopamine 2–10 mcg/kg/min
- Prepare for placement of a transvenous pacemaker.
- Treat the underlying cause.

Tachycardia with Pulse: Stable Patient

Source: Adapted from AHA guidelines for cardiopulmonary resuscitation and emergency cardio-vascular care. Part 7.2: Management of cardiac arrest. *Circulation* 2005;112(24):IV58–IV66.

The key measures in management of tachycardia in a patient who has a pulse are as follows:

- Airway
- Breathing
- Oxygen
- ECG
- Blood pressure
- Pulse oximetry
- Treat reversible causes
- IV

Narrow QRS: Stable Patient

The key measures in management of a stable patient with narrow QRS are as follows:
Perform vagal maneuvers (Valsalva maneuver or carotid sinus massage).
If regular rhythm (sinus tachycardia, reentry SVT):

- Adenosine 6 mg rapid IV push; 12 mg rapid IV push (may repeat 12 mg dose); total dose 30 mg
- Adenosine will not convert atrial fibrillation/flutter, ectopic atrial tachycardia, junctional tachycardia, or VT

Evaluate the rhythm response. If it is converted, observe for recurrence. Treat recurrence with adenosine, diltiazem, or a beta blocker. For rate control consider the following:

- Diltiazem 0.25 mg/kg over 2 min; repeat in 15 min with 0.35 mg/kg
- Verapamil 2.5-5 mg IV over 2 min (3 min in an older person); repeat 5-10 mg q 15-30 min; total 20 mg
- Beta blocker (use with caution in a setting of congestive heart failure or pulmonary disease):
  - Atenolol 5 mg slow IV (over 5 min); repeat dose after 10 min if rhythm persists or is stable (IV medication not currently in joint formulary)
  - Metoprolol 5 mg IV/IO slow push at 5-min intervals; total 15 mg (only IV beta blocker in joint formulary)

Treat the underlying cause.

Consult a cardiologist.

In case of irregular rhythm (atrial fibrillation, atrial flutter, multifocal atrial tachycardia):

- Consult a cardiologist.
- Control the heart rate with diltiazem or a beta blocker.

Wide QRS: Stable Patient

The key measures in management of a stable patient with wide QRS are as follows:

In case of a regular rhythm (ventricular tachycardia or uncertain rhythm):

- Give amiodarone 150 mg IV over 10 min; repeat as needed to maximum dose of 2.2 gm/24 h. Maintenance infusion is 540 mg × 18 h (0.5 mg/min).
- Prepare for elective synchronized cardioversion, if patient is unresponsive to medication.
- If SVT with aberrancy, treat with adenosine (6 mg rapid IV push, 12 mg rapid IV push—repeat × 1).

In case of an irregular rhythm (atrial fibrillation with aberrancy), consult a cardiologist.

In case of atrial fibrillation with WPW:

- Avoid AV nodal blocking agents—adenosine, digoxin, verapamil, diltiazem.
- Give antiarrhythmics: amiodarone 150 mg IV over 10 min.

In case of recurrent polymorphic VT, consult a cardiologist.

In case of torsades de pointes, give magnesium 1-2 gm diluted in D_5W (50-100 mL) over 5-60 min, then infusion 0.5-1 gm/h.

Tachycardia with Pulse: Unstable Patient

Source: Adapted from AHA guidelines for cardiopulmonary resuscitation and emergency cardio-vascular care. Part 7.2: Management of cardiac arrest. *Circulation* 2005;112(24):IV58-IV66.

Patients with this condition may demonstrate mental status changes, hypotension, and chest pain. Serious signs and symptoms are uncommon with a heart rate < 150 bpm in a patient without impaired cardiac function. The key measures in management of an unstable patient with tachycardia and a pulse are as follows:

- Airway
- Breathing
- Oxygen
- ECG
- Blood pressure
- Pulse oximetry
- Treat reversible causes
- IV

Proceed with management as follows:

Provide sedation.

If there is unstable narrow-complex reentry tachycardia, give adenosine 6 mg rapid IV push; 12 mg rapid IV push; repeat × 1 while preparing for cardioversion.

Provide synchronized cardioversion (unstable SVT due to reentry, unstable atrial fibrillation/flutter, unstable monomorphic VT):

- Monophasic: 100-200 J; escalate second shock as needed (for VT, use shocks of 100 J, 200 J, 300 J, and 360 J)
- Biphasic: 100-120 J; escalate second shock as needed

If there is unstable polymorphic VT, -treat the rhythm as ventricular fibrillation.

If there is any question whether the rhythm is monomorphic or polymorphic in an unstable patient, treat it as ventricular fibrillation with unsynchronized defibrillation.

TABLE 2-10 Emergency Cardiac Medications

This table is intended as a guideline only. Refer to the physician's orders for specific instructions.

Drug	Indications	Dose	Precautions
Adenosine	• Stable, narrow-complex AV nodal or sinus nodal reentry tachycardias • Unstable reentry SVT (while awaiting cardioversion) • Undefined stable narrow-complex tachycardia as a diagnostic maneuver • Stable, wide-complex tachycardia in patients with known reentry	• 6 mg IV over 1-2 sec followed by 20 mL saline flush • If no response at 1-2 min, 12 mg IV push (may repeat total of 2 doses)	• Brief asystole after dose • Flushing, dyspnea, transient chest pain • Not effective for Afib, Aflutter, or VTach

(Continued)

TABLE 2-10   Emergency Cardiac Medications (Continued)

This table is intended as a guideline only. Refer to the physician's orders for specific instructions.

Drug	Indications	Dose	Precautions
Amiodarone	• Narrow-complex tachycardia from reentry if rhythm uncontrolled by adenosine, vagal maneuvers, and AV nodal blockade • Hemodynamically stable VT, polymorphic VT with normal QT, wide-complex tachycardia of uncertain origin • Preferred over lidocaine	• **VFib/pulseless VT unresponsive to CPR, shock, vasopressor:** 300 mg IV/IO in 30 mL; may repeat 150 mg IV/IO push in 3-5 min • **Tachyarrhythmias:** loading dose (IV): 150 mg (150 mg in 100 mL D_5W; 1.5 mg/mL) over 10 min (15 mg/min); followed by 360 mg (900 mg in 500 mL D_5W; 1.8 mg/mL) over 6 h (1 mg/min); then 0.5 mg/min IV for 18 h; maximum initial infusion rate is 30 mg/min • Supplemental doses for recurrent or resistant arrhythmias: 150 mg q 10 min to maximum daily IV dose 2.2 gm • Maintenance dose after 24 h: 0.5 mg/min (720 mg/24 h)	• Concentrations greater than 2 mg/mL should be administered via central line • Contraindications: cardiogenic shock, acute MI, acute heart block
Aspirin	Acute coronary syndrome	160- to 325-mg tables (chewing is preferable)	Contraindications: acute GI ulcer disease, ASA sensitivity, asthma
Atropine	• Symptomatic bradycardia • Asystole	• **Bradycardia:** 0.5 mg IV q 3-5 min up to 3 doses or 3 mg • **Aystole/slow PEA:** 1 mg IV/IO q 3-5 min up to 3 mg • Endotracheal dose 2-2.5 × IV dose	• Do not push slowly: dose < 0.5 mg leads to paradoxical bradycardia • Increases myocardial O_2 demand
Beta blockers	• Narrow-complex tachycardia (reentry or automatic foci) uncontrolled by adenosine and vagal maneuvers • Rate control in AFib/AFlutter • Angina	Atenolol: 2.5 to 5 mg IV over 5 min (slow). If arrhythmia persists after 10 min and dose is tolerated, give second dose 5 mg IV over 5 min. Total 10 mg in 10-15 min. Metoprolol: • Arrhythmia: 2.5 to 5 mg IV/IO at 5-min intervals to 15 mg • AMI: initial 3 IV boluses of 5 mg each at 2-min intervals; 15 min after full IV dose, 50 mg PO q 6 h for 48 h	• Only recommended for use in patients with preserved ventricular function • Monitor for bradycardia, AV conduction delays, hypotension • Contraindications: second/third-degree heart block, hypotension, congestive heart failure, reactive airway disease, AFib/Flutter with WPW • Usual dose is 50-200 mcg/kg/min

(Continued)

TABLE 2-10   Emergency Cardiac Medications (Continued)

This table is intended as a guideline only. Refer to the physician's orders for specific instructions.

Drug	Indications	Dose	Precautions
		Propranolol: 0.1 mg/kg slow IV push in 3 equal doses at 2- to 3-min intervals Esmolol: loading dose, 500 mcg/kg/min (0.5 mg/kg) × 1 min, followed by 4-min infusion at 50 mcg/kg/min, for total of 200 mcg/kg. If inadequate response, give second bolus 0.5 mg/kg over 1 min and increase infusion to 100 mcg/kg/min to maximum infusion rate of 300 mcg/kg/min	
Calcium	· Not routinely used for cardiac arrest · Hyperkalemia · Calcium-channel blocker toxicity	Calcium chloride (10%) 5-10 mL (8-16 mg/kg); repeat as necessary	10% solution contains 27.2 mg calcium per mL
Clopidogrel	· STEMI · Unstable angina · Non-STEMI	Loading dose: 300 mg PO	· Hold if CABG is anticipated in next 7 days · Use in patients up to age 75 · Use in conjunction with ASA, heparin, and fibrinolysis
Digoxin	· AFib/AFlutter · SVT · Heart failure	· **Atrial arrhythmias**: loading dose, 0.25 mg IV/PO every 2 h up to maximum of 1.5 mg; maintenance dose, 0.125 to 0.375 mg PO daily or 0.125-0.25 mg IV daily · **Heart failure**: loading dose, 0.4-0.6 mg IV/PO, additional doses of 0.1-0.3 mg IV/PO q 6-8 h prn; maintenance dose, 0.1-0.4 mg PO daily	Use with caution with AMI, AV block, hypokalemia, hypocalcemia, hypercalcemia, hypomagnesemia, WPW, severe bradycardia
Diltiazem	· Stable, narrow-complex, reentry-mechanism tachycardias if uncontrolled or unconverted by adenosine or vagal maneuvers · Stable narrow complex, from automaticity mechanism, uncontrolled or unconverted by adenosine of vagal maneuvers · Control rate of ventricular response in AFib/AFlutter	· Atrial arrhythmias: initial dose, 0.25 mg/kg (~20 mg) IV over 2 min; if inadequate response after 15 min, may give second bolus of 0.35 mg/kg (25 mg) over 2 min · Continuous infusion: initial dose, 5-10 mg/h; increase in 5 mg/h increments up to 15 mg/h, maintained for up to 24 h; titrate to heart rate	· Contraindications: acute MI with pulmonary edema, administration of IV beta blockers in past few hours, cardiogenic shock, second/third-degree heart block without functioning ventricular pacemaker, symptomatic hypotension, VTach

(Continued)

TABLE 2-10   Emergency Cardiac Medications *(Continued)*

This table is intended as a guideline only. Refer to the physician's orders for specific instructions.

Drug	Indications	Dose	Precautions
Dobutamine	Severe systolic heart failure	• Admixture 250 mg/250 mL D$_5$W or NS • 2-20 mcg/kg/min (doses up to 40 mcg/kg/min have been used)	Doses > 20 mcg/kg/min associated with increased heart rate
Dopamine	• Hypotension, especially if associated with symptomatic bradycardia • Post-resuscitation hypotension	• Range 2-20 mcg/kg/min • 1-4 mcg/kg/min–dopaminergic • 2-10 mcg/kg/min–beta • > 10 mcg/kg/min alpha	No benefit from low-dose dopamine to protect the kidneys or increase renal blood flow
Epinephrine	• Cardiac arrest (VFib, pulseless VT, asystole, PEA (IV push) • Symptomatic bradycardia (IV infusion) if atropine and transcutaneous pacing fails or is not available • Vasopressor • Anaphylactic shock	• **Cardiac arrest**: 1 mg IV/IO (10 mL of 1:10,000); repeat q 3-5 min (may replace one dose with vasopressin) • Endotracheal dose: 2-2.5 mg (dilute in 10 mL NS or sterile water) if IV/IO not available • **Symptomatic bradycardia with hypotension**: mix 1 mL of 1:1000 solution/500 mL NS or D$_5$W); initial dose, 1 mcg/min; typical dose, 2-10 mcg/min	Higher doses may be beneficial for beta blocker and calcium-channel blocker overdose
Furosemide	Pulmonary congestion if associated volume overload	Acute-onset pulmonary edema without hypovolemia • 0.5 mg/kg IV Chronic fluid overload • 1 mg/kg IV	Use with caution in patients who have not received volume expansion
Heparin	Adjunct use in acute coronary syndrome	Unfractionated heparin • Bolus: 60 units/kg • Infusion: 12 units/kg • Goal aPTT: 50-70 sec Enoxaparin (LMWH) • Initial dose: a single IV bolus dose of 30 mg and 1 mg/kg SUBQ; maintenance dose: 1 mg/kg SUBQ every 12 h; maximum dose: 100 mg for the first 2 doses only	• UFH recommended for patients > 75 years • LMWH is an alternative to UFH for patients < 75 years who are receiving fibrinolysis

(Continued)

TABLE 2-10   Emergency Cardiac Medications (Continued)

This table is intended as a guideline only. Refer to the physician's orders for specific instructions.

Drug	Indications	Dose	Precautions
Ibutilide	• Acute conversion of AFib (with or without WPW) < 48 h duration • Rate control in AFib/AFlutter	• Weight ≥ 60 kg: IV diluted or undiluted 1 mg over 10 min; may repeat 1-mg dose after 10 min if unsuccessful • Weight < 60 kg: initial dose of 0.01 mg/kg • 0.1 mg/mL in 10-mL vial = 1 mg	• Only administer in patients with preserved ventricular function • High risk for ventricular arrhythmias (polymorphic VT, torsades de pointes) • Correct ↓K+ and ↓Mg+ before initiation • Monitor continuously for arrhythmia at the time of administration and at least 4-6 h after dose • Contraindicated if baseline QTc > 440 msec
Lidocaine	• Alternative to amiodarone • Stable monomorphic VT with preserved ventricular function • Polymorphic VT with normal baseline QT interval after treatment of ischemia and correction of electrolyte imbalances • Polymorphic VT (torsades de pointes)	• Initial dose: 1-1.5 mg/kg; repeat 0.5-0.75 mg/kg every 5-10 min to maximum of 3 mg/kg • Maintenance infusion: 1-4 mg/min	• If ventricular function is impaired, use amiodarone instead of lidocaine • Monitor for CNS toxicity (slurred speech, altered consciousness, muscle twitching, seizures) • Monitor for bradycardia
Magnesium	• VF/pulseless VT associated with torsades de pointes • Polymorphic VT with electrolyte imbalances • Hypomagnesemia	• Cardiac arrest due to torsades de pointes or VF/VTach due to ↓Mg+: 1-2 gm in 50-100 mL D₅W at over 30-60 min; maximum infusion rate: 150 mg/min • Infusion: 0.5-1 gm/h	• Prophylactic use in MI no longer recommended • Decrease dose with impaired liver function or LV dysfunction • Do not exceed infusion rate of 2 gm/h (leads to hypotension)
Morphine	• Continued ischemic pain unresponsive to nitrates • Primary pulmonary congestion	• 2-4 mg IV with additional doses of 2-8 mg IV q 5-15 min	• Avoid with hypovolemia
Nitroglycerin	• Initial treatment of choice for ischemic pain • IV NTG for heart failure/pulmonary congestion, persistent ischemia • Pulmonary congestion	• Admixture: 50-100 mL in 250 mL D₅W or NS at 10-20 mcg/min; increase by 5-10 mcg/min until desired clinical effect is achieved • Low dose (30-40 mcg/min) produces venodilation • High dose (> 150 mcg/min) produces arterial dilation	• Blunted effect with hypovolemia • Monitor for hypotension • Contraindicated SBP < 90 mm Hg or > 30 mm Hg below baseline; extreme bradycardia (< 50 bpm) or tachycardia (> 100 bpm) or if patient has received phosphodiesterase inhibitor for erectile dysfunction in past 24 h • Use with caution with inferior or right ventricular MI

(Continued)

TABLE 2-10 Emergency Cardiac Medications (Continued)

This table is intended as a guideline only. Refer to the physician's orders for specific instructions.

Drug	Indications	Dose	Precautions
Nitroprusside	• Severe heart failure • Hypertensive emergencies	• Admixture 50-100 mg/250 mL D_5W • Dose 0.1-5 mcg/kg/min, up to 10 mcg/kg/min	• Monitor for hypotension • Risk for cyanide toxicity with infusion > 3 mcg/kg/min for > 72 h in patients with renal or hepatic failure
Norepineph-rine	• Severe hypotension • Septic shock	• Admixture: 4-8 mg/ 250 D_5W or D_5 NS (16-32 mcg/mL) • Initial dose: 0.5-1 mcg/min; titrate to effect • Range: 2-12 mcg/min; maximum dose: 30 mcg/min	• Relative contraindication: hypovolemia • Increases myocardial O_2 requirements • May lead to extravasation
Oxygen	• Acute chest pain • Suspected hypoxemia • Cardiopulmonary arrest	• Nasal cannula 2-6 L/min in case of chest pain/mild distress • Non-rebreather mask: 10-15 L/min; minimum: 6 L/min • Bag/valve mask or ETT: 100%	
Procainamide	• Stable monomorphic VT • Control of heart rate in AFib/AFlutter (with or without WPW) • AV reentrant narrow com-plex tachycardias that are uncontrolled by adenosine and vagal maneuvers	• Non-VFib/VTach arrest: 20 mg/min IV infusion until: ○ Arrhythmia is suppressed ○ Hypotension develops ○ QRS widens > 50% ○ PR or QT interval length-ens > 50% ○ Total 17 mg/kg is given (1.2 gm for 70-kg patient) • May give up to 50 mg/min in emergency • Infusion: 1-4 mg/min (D_5W or NS) ○ Reduce dose with renal failure	• Only use in patients with preserved ventricular function • Use caution with prolonged QT • Monitor ECG/BP continu-ously during administration
Sodium bicar-bonate	• Not a first-line drug in CPR • May be beneficial if preex-isting metabolic acidosis, hyperkalemia, or tricyclic antidepressant overdose	Initial dose: 1 mEq/kg	• Use only under special circumstances • Dosing is based on the bicarbonate or base deficit
Vasopressin	• Pulseless VTach/VFib refractory to defibrillation • Septic shock	40 U IV/IO may replace either first or second dose of epinephrine in treatment of pulseless cardiac arrest	

(Continued)

TABLE 2-10   Emergency Cardiac Medications *(Continued)*

This table is intended as a guideline only. Refer to the physician's orders for specific instructions.

Drug	Indications	Dose	Precautions
Verapamil	· Stable, narrow-complex, reentry mechanism tachycardias if uncontrolled or unconverted by adenosine or vagal maneuvers · Stable, narrow complex, from automaticity mechanism uncontrolled or unconverted by adenosine or vagal maneuvers · Control rate of ventricular response in AFib/AFlutter	· Atrial arrhythmias: 2.5-5 mg IV over 2 min; may give additional 5- to 10-mg dose if no response after 30 min; total dose: 20 mg · Alternative dosing: 5 mg IV q 15 min, to a total dose of 30 mg	· For elderly patients, administer over 3 min · Administer loading dose under continuous ECG and BP monitoring · Give 20-50% of normal dose in patients with liver disease · Only for narrow-complex reentry tachycardias that are atrial in origin · Contraindication: heart failure

Electrocardiogram

TABLE 2-11   Leads for Bedside Monitoring

Monitoring Purpose	Lead Recommendation
Arrhythmia detection	Three-lead system: MCL-1 (select Lead I on monitor) Five-lead system: · Aberrancy versus ectopy: V1 (V6) · AFib/AFlutter: II, III, aVF (whichever lead allows best visualization of fibrillation/flutter waves)
ST-segment monitoring	· Right coronary artery: III or aVF · Left anterior descending/circumflex: V3 · Activity-induced ischemia (no specific vessel identified): V5 · Best lead combinations: (1) III and V3 or (2) III, V3, and V5 (or select leads based on ECG changes during previous ischemic event)
QTc	Identify 12-lead with most well-defined T wave: V3, V4, II
Axis deviation	I, aVF (detection of new-onset/progressing bundle branch block)
Best Lead Combinations	
One lead	V1 or V6 (MCL-1 or MCL-6)
Two leads	Arrhythmia: V1 and III ST Segment: V3 and III Arrhythmia + ST segment: V1 or V6 + aVF or III

Basic Arrhythmias

Rate (bpm)	Rhythm	P wave	PR (sec)	QRS (sec)	Conduction
60-100	Regular	Before every QRS	0.12-0.20	0.04-0.01	Normal

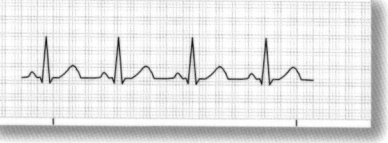

FIGURE 10   Normal sinus rhythm.
Source: Reproduced from *Arrhythmia Recognition: The Art of Interpretation,* courtesy of Tomas B. Garcia, MD.

Rate (bpm)	Rhythm	P wave	PR (sec)	QRS (sec)	Conduction
< 60	Regular	Before every QRS	0.12–0.20	0.04–0.10	Normal

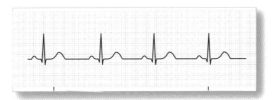

FIGURE 11 Sinus bradycardia.
Source: Reproduced from *Arrhythmia Recognition: The Art of Interpretation*, courtesy of Tomas B. Garcia, MD.

Rate (bpm)	Rhythm	P wave	PR (sec)	QRS (sec)	Conduction
> 100	Regular	Before every QRS	0.12–0.20	0.04–0.10	Normal

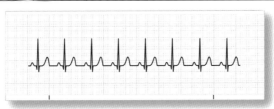

FIGURE 12 Sinus tachycardia.
Source: Reproduced from *Arrhythmia Recognition: The Art of Interpretation*, courtesy of Tomas B. Garcia, MD.

Rate (bpm)	Rhythm	P wave	PR (sec)	QRS (sec)	Conduction
Dependent on underlying rhythm	Regular except for PAC	Premature P wave different from sinus P wave			

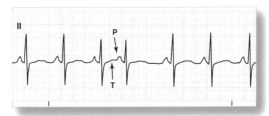

FIGURE 13 Premature atrial complexes.
Source: Reproduced from *Arrhythmia Recognition: The Art of Interpretation*, courtesy of Tomas B. Garcia, MD.

Rate (bpm)	Rhythm	P wave	PR (sec)	QRS (sec)	Conduction
Variable 250-450	Atrial-regular Ventricular-regular or irregular	Flutter (F) waves (sawtooth)	Variable	Normal unless aberrant conduction	Variable 2:1, 3:1, 4:1

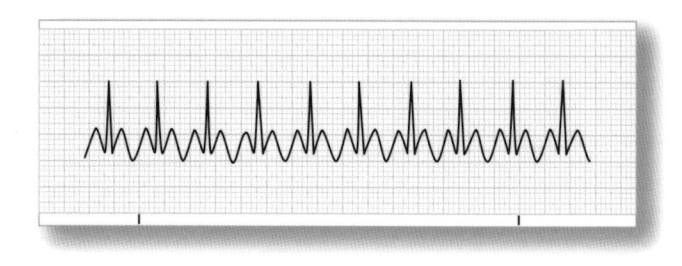

FIGURE 14   Atrial flutter.
Source: Reproduced from *Arrhythmia Recognition: The Art of Interpretation,* courtesy of Tomas B. Garcia, MD.

Rate (bpm)	Rhythm	P wave	PR (sec)	QRS (sec)	Conduction
Atrial-uncountable (400-600) Ventricular-uncontrolled > 100; controlled < 100	Irregularly irregular	Fibrillation waves	Unmeasurable	Normal	Intermittent; may cause aberrant conduction

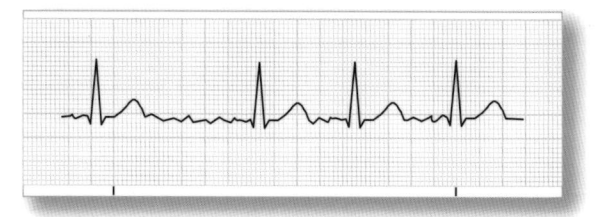

FIGURE 15   Atrial fibrillation.
Source: Reproduced from *Arrhythmia Recognition: The Art of Interpretation,* courtesy of Tomas B. Garcia, MD.

Rate (bpm)	Rhythm	P wave	PR (sec)	QRS (sec)	Conduction
100-280	Regular	Not identifiable	Not measurable	Normal	Varies depending on cause

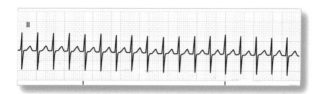

FIGURE 16 Supraventricular tachycardia.
Source: Reproduced from *Arrhythmia Recognition: The Art of Interpretation*, courtesy of Tomas B. Garcia, MD.

Rate (bpm)	Rhythm	P wave	PR (sec)	QRS (sec)	Conduction
Depends on underlying rhythm	Irregular	Occur before, during, after QRS	Variable	Normal, may be aberrant	Retrograde (junction to atria and ventricles)

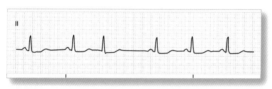

FIGURE 17 Premature junctional complexes.
Source: Reproduced from *Arrhythmia Recognition: The Art of Interpretation*, courtesy of Tomas B. Garcia, MD.

Rate (bpm)	Rhythm	P wave	PR (sec)	QRS (sec)	Conduction
40-60	Regular	Occur before, during, after QRS	Variable	Usually normal	Retrograde through the atria; normal through ventricles

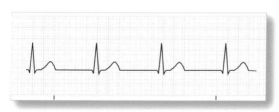

FIGURE 18 Junctional rhythm.
Source: Reproduced from *Arrhythmia Recognition: The Art of Interpretation*, courtesy of Tomas B. Garcia, MD.

Rate (bpm)	Rhythm	P wave	PR (sec)	QRS (sec)	Conduction
Depends on underlying rhythm	Regular except for PVCs	P wave not associated with PVC	Variable	Wide and bizarre. Variable morphology depending on foci	Complex initiates in ventricle

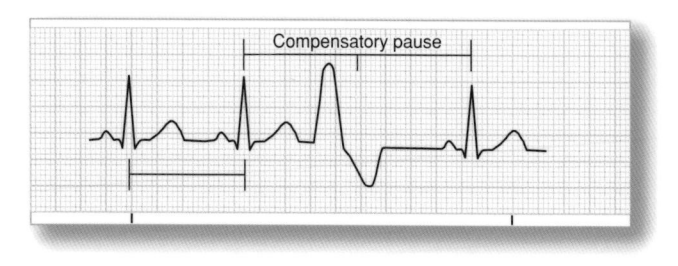

FIGURE 19 Premature ventricular complexes.
Source: Reproduced from *Arrhythmia Recognition: The Art of Interpretation,* courtesy of Tomas B. Garcia, MD.

Rate (bpm)	Rhythm	P wave	PR (sec)	QRS (sec)	Conduction
100-220	Regular or slightly irregular	Not present or disassociated from QRS	N/A	> 0.12	Impulse originates in ventricles; may be retrograde fusion or disassociated

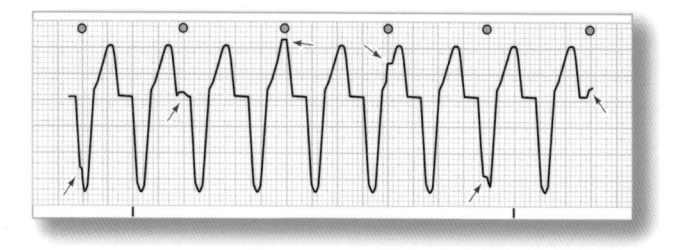

FIGURE 20 Ventricular tachycardia/flutter.
Source: Reproduced from *Arrhythmia Recognition: The Art of Interpretation,* courtesy of Tomas B. Garcia, MD.

Rate (bpm)	Rhythm	P wave	PR (sec)	QRS (sec)	Conduction
	Chaotic	Not present	Not present	Twist around baseline	Impulse originates in ventricles; may be retrograde fusion or disassociated

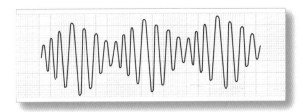

FIGURE 21 Torsades de pointes (polymorphic ventricular tachycardia).

Rate (bpm)	Rhythm	P wave	PR (sec)	QRS (sec)	Conduction
Rapid	Chaotic	None seen	N/A	No QRS complex	Random, irregular

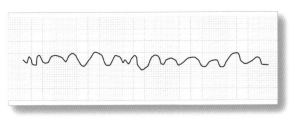

FIGURE 22 Ventricular fibrillation.

Rate (bpm)	Rhythm	P wave	PR (sec)	QRS (sec)	Conduction
None	None	May be present if atrial activity	None	None	No ventricular conduction

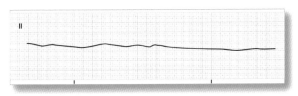

FIGURE 23 Ventricular asystole.
Source: Reproduced from *Arrhythmia Recognition: The Art of Interpretation*, courtesy of Tomas B. Garcia, MD.

Rate (bpm)	Rhythm	P wave	PR (sec)	QRS (sec)	Conduction
60-100	Regular	Normal precede each QRS	> 0.20	0.04-0.10 may be abnormal; bundle branch block	Normal through atria, delayed through AV node, normal through ventricle

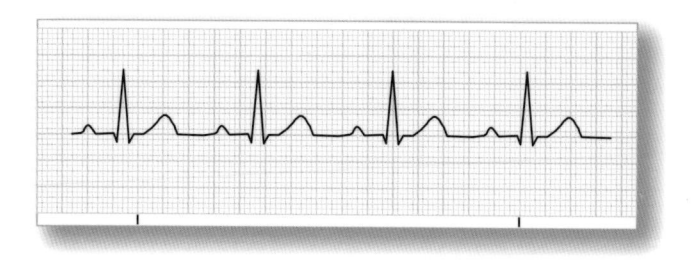

FIGURE 24   First-degree AV block.
Source: Reproduced from *Arrhythmia Recognition: The Art of Interpretation*, courtesy of Tomas B. Garcia, MD.

Rate (bpm)	Rhythm	P wave	PR (sec)	QRS (sec)	Conduction
Variable depending on underlying rhythm	Irregular; group beating	Normal	Gradually lengthens and then a beat is dropped	Normal	Some P waves not conducted

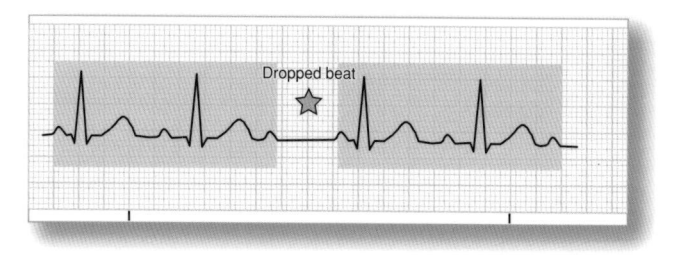

FIGURE 25   Second-degree AV block type I (Wenchkbach).
Source: Reproduced from *Arrhythmia Recognition: The Art of Interpretation*, courtesy of Tomas B. Garcia, MD.

Rate (bpm)	Rhythm	P wave	PR (sec)	QRS (sec)	Conduction
Depends on underlying rhythm	Irregular d/t blocked beats	Usually regular	Constant for all conducted beats	Usually wide d/t conduction defect	P before each QRS; periodic nonconducted P wave (bundle branch block)

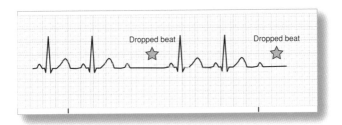

FIGURE 26   Second-degree AV block type II.
Source: Reproduced from *Arrhythmia Recognition: The Art of Interpretation*, courtesy of Tomas B. Garcia, MD.

Rate (bpm)	Rhythm	P wave	PR (sec)	QRS (sec)	Conduction
Atrial-normal Ventricular- < 45	Regular	Normal; dissociated from QRS	No consistent PR	Normal if pacemaker in junction; abnormal if ventricular pacemaker	Dissociated; normal conduction within atria and ventricles

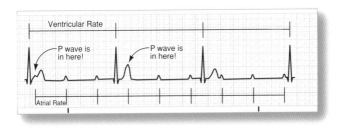

FIGURE 27   Third-degree AV block (complete block).
Source: Reproduced from *Arrhythmia Recognition: The Art of Interpretation*, courtesy of Tomas B. Garcia, MD.

TABLE 2-12 Wide-Complex Tachycardia: Aberrancy versus Ectopy

If patient is unstable, treat the condition as ventricular tachycardia and consult with a cardiologist as soon as possible.

	Aberrancy (10–15%)	Ectopy (80%)
Hemodynamic stability	Not diagnostic (if patient is unstable, go to ACLS protocol immediately)	
Rate	Not diagnostic	
Rhythm	Marked irregularity: atrial fibrillation with aberrancy	Slight irregularity; Marked irregularity: polymorphic VT
P wave	Precedes QRS	Dissociated from QRS or may be retrograde after QRS
QRS — Bundle branch morphology: RBBB (QRS + polarity V1-V2); LBBB (QRS, polarity V1-V2)	RBBB pattern: Triphasic rsR' (V1; rabbit); qRs (V6); Rs (V6). LBBB pattern: absence of initial R wave or small initial r (< 0.4 sec)	RBBB pattern: Monophasic R or qR in V1; Triphasic RsR' (left rabbit ear taller in V1); rS (V6). LBBB pattern: Broad r wave (> 0.4 sec) in V1-V2; Slurring or notching of down-stroke of S wave in V1; Delayed nadir of S wave (> 0.06 sec) in V1; Any q wave in V6
Width: QRS > 160 msec helpful if Class I antiarrhythmic used	< 0.14 sec unless preexisting bundle branch block	RBBB WCT > 0.14 sec; LBBB WCT > 0.16 sec
Axis	Often normal	Extreme right axis deviation (−90° to ±180°); RBBB (like WCT) left of −30°; LBBB (like WCT) right of +90°; Axis shift > 40° from NSR
Concordance: QRS complexes in V1-V6 are monophasic and all in the same direction	Positive concordance may occur with WPW	Negative concordance; Positive concordance
Fusion beats: QRS intermediate morphology between sinus beat and ventricular beat		Favors VT

Brugada Criteria for VT versus SVT

If there is any doubt about the patient's condition, treat it as ventricular tachycardia. Otherwise, follow these steps:

• Evaluate V1-V6 for concordance. If concordance, = VT.
• If RS complex is present in precordial lead, measure the interval between the onset of the r wave and the nadir of the S wave.
  ○ Is rS interval in one precordial lead > 100 msec? If yes, = VT.
  ○ Is rS interval < 100 msec? If no, assess for AV dissociation.
    ◦ If AV dissociation present, = VT.
    ◦ If AV dissociation absent, evaluate QRS morphology.
• QRS morphology for VT must be present in V1 or V2 and V6. If not, = SVT with aberrancy.

QTc Monitoring

Indications for monitoring are as follows:

Patients receiving antiarrhythmic agents known to increase QT interval or risk for torsades de pointes:

- Medications in formulary: amiodarone (prolongs QT interval but does not increase risk for torsades de pointes), procainamide, quinidine, erythromycin, droperidol, chloroquine, haloperidol
- See University of Arizona Center for Education and Research on Therapeutics, comprehensive list: www.torsades.org

New-onset bradycardia (heart block)

Severe hypokalemia and/or hypomagnesemia

Acute neurological event (subarachnoid hemorrhage, trauma)

Findings are interpreted as follows:

- The QT interval must be corrected for heart rate.
- A bedside monitor may overestimate the QTc, but generally does not underestimate it. Always validate any abnormal QTc with a 12-lead ECG.
- Select the bedside monitoring lead based on the lead with the most prominent T wave on 12-lead ECG. Usual leads are V3, V4, II, and V2.
- Measure from the beginning of the QRS complex to the end of the T wave.
- If a U wave is present, measure from the onset of QRS to the lowest point between the T and U waves.
- If a biphasic T wave is present, measure from the onset of the QRS to the point of final return to baseline.

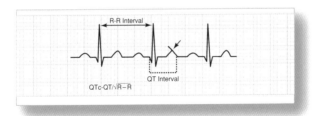

FIGURE 28A Example of QT interval measurement.

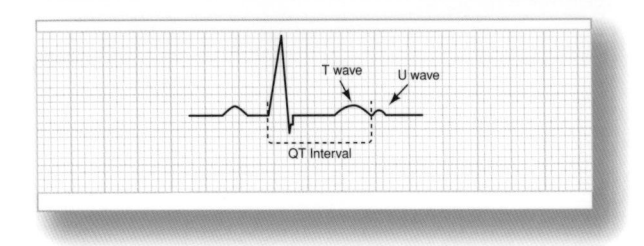

FIGURE 28B   Example of QT interval measurement when a U wave is present.

QTc = QT observed/√Preceding R-R (sec)
Or
QTc = QT + 0.00175 (ventricular rate-60) Note: This equation is correct for low/high HR.
Normal: women ≤ 0.48 sec, men ≤ 0.47 sec
Risk for torsades de pointes: QTc > 50 msec

Source: Drew BJ, Califf RM, Funk M, et al. Practice standards for electrocardiographic monitoring in hospital settings: An American Heart Association scientific statement from the Councils on Cardiovascular Nursing, Clinical Cardiology, and Cardiovascular Disease in the Young: Endorsed by the International Society of Computerized Electrocardiology and the American Association of Critical-Care Nurses. *Circulation* 2004;110(17):2721-2746.

12-Lead Electrocardiogram

TABLE 2-13   Correct Position for Precordial Leads

Correct lead position is essential; incorrect lead placement may lead to a missed or erroneous diagnosis.

Lead	Standard Placement	Right-Sided ECG	
V1	Fourth ICS, right sternal border	V1R	Fourth ICS, left sternal border
V2	Fourth ICS, left sternal border	V2R	Fourth ICS, right sternal border
V3	Halfway between V2 and V4	V3R	Halfway between V2R and V4R
V4	Fifth ICS, left midclavicular line	V4R	Fifth ICS, right midclavicular line
V5	Halfway between V4 and V6 horizontal with V4 (at the anterior axillary line)	V5R	Halfway between V4R and V6R, horizontal with V4R (at the anterior axillary line)
V6	Horizontal to V4 at the midaxillary line	V6R	Horizontal to V4R at the midaxillary line

ICS = Intercostal Space

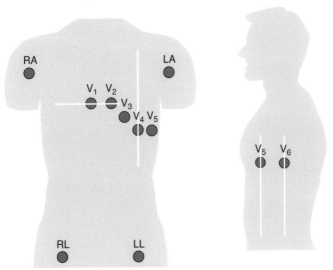

FIGURE 29   Standard precordial ECG lead placement.
Source: Modified from *Arrhythmia Recognition: The Art of Interpretation,* courtesy of Tomas B. Garcia, MD.

When interpreting the results of a 12-lead ECG, consider the following issues:
- Is the ECG technically good?
- What is the heart rate (atrial and ventricular)?
- Intervals (PR, QRS, QTc)?
- Heart rhythm?

- Axis determination? (See Table 2-14.)
- Abnormalities in the P wave, PR interval/interval, QRS complex/interval, ST segment, or T wave?
- Does the patient have atrial/ventricular enlargement, conduction defects, myocardial ischemia/infarction, pericarditis, pericardial effusion, drug effects, or electrolyte effects?

TABLE 2-14 Axis Determination

Look at Lead I and II or a VF to determine the axis.

Possible Causes	I	II or aVF
Normal	Positive	Positive
Left axis deviation	Positive	Negative
Right axis devia-tion	Negative	Positive
Indeterminant	Negative	Negative

Possible Causes	
Normal	–
Left axis deviation	Normal variant (diaphragm elevation), left ventricular enlargement, inferior myocardial infarction, right-sided tension pneumothorax, ventricular pacemaker, left anterior hemiblock, left bundle branch block, ventricular tachycardia
Right axis devia-tion	Normal variant (children), right ventricular enlargement, lateral myocardial infarction, left-sided tension pneumothorax, pulmonary embolism, left posterior hemiblock, right bundle branch block
Indeterminant	Ventricular tachycardia

TABLE 2-15 Overview of ECG Changes

Conduction Abnormalities	
Right bundle branch block	• QRS ≥ 0.12 • V1 upright (rsR')
Left bundle branch block	• QRS ≥ 0.12 sec • V1 negative
Left anterior hemiblock	• Left axis deviation > –30° (no inferior MI or LVH) • q wave in Lead I, s wave in Lead III (qI/sIII)
Left posterior hemiblock	• Right axis deviation > +110° (no RVH) • s wave in I, q wave in Lead III (sI/qIII)
Wolff-Parkinson-White syndrome	• PR < 0.11 sec • Delta wave • Wide QRS • SVT

Chamber Enlargement and Hypertrophy (Adult)	
Right atrial enlargement	• Positive in II, III, aVF > 2.5 mm high • Positive component of the P wave in V1 > 1 mm
Left atrial enlargement	• P wave in II, III, aVF > 0.11 sec in duration • Negative component of the P wave in V1 > 1 mm
Right ventricular enlargement	• R wave in V1 or V2 + S wave in V5 or V6 ≥ 10 mm
Left ventricular enlargement	• S wave in V1 or V2 + R wave in V5 or V6 ≥ 35 mm

Other	
Subarachnoid hemorrhage	• ST-segment elevation or depression • T-wave changes (diffuse) • Long QT intervals • U wave • Arrhythmia

(Continued)

TABLE 2-15	Overview of ECG Changes *(Continued)*
Cerebral hemorrhage, subdural hematoma	• U wave (camel's hump) • Wide, inverted T waves
Hypothermia	• Sinus bradycardia • Long QT interval • Osborne waves (J waves): extra positive deflection between the terminal portion of the QRS complex and the beginning of the ST segment
Pericarditis	• ST-segment elevation (local or diffuse)
Other	
Pericardial effusion	• Decreased voltage • Electrical alternans
Pulmonary embolism	• Looks like MI/anterior ischemia • RBBB • RAE • Right axis deviation • Atrial arrhythmias
Hypokalemia (< 3 mEq/L)	• Depressed ST segment • Flat T waves • Prominent U waves
Hyperkalemia (> 5.5 mEq/L)	• Tall, peaked T waves with narrow base (tented) • Shortened QT • Severe hyperkalemia: wide QRS/ST elevation
Hypocalcemia (< 6.1 mg/dL)	• Prolonged ST and QT
Hypercalcemia (> 12 mg/dL)	• Shortened QT; ST segment disappears

Acute Myocardial Infarction

Source: Based on the AHA guidelines for unstable angina/non-ST myocardial infarction (MI) and ST myocardial infarction.

Obtain history. There is a high likelihood that the signs and symptoms represent acute coronary syndrome if the patient has any of the following:

• Known history of coronary artery disease
• Typical chest pain (chest or left arm pain or discomfort as chief symptom reproducing previous angina)
• Hemodynamic changes (hypotension, diaphoresis, pulmonary crackles/edema, transient mitral regurgitation murmur)
• New (or presumably new) ST-segment deviation (ST elevation or depression > 1 mm) or T-wave inversion in multiple precordial leads
• Elevated cardiac enzymes (troponin I or CK-MB)

TABLE 2-16 Signs and Symptoms Consistent with Acute Coronary Syndrome (Angina/Myocardial Infarction): OPQRST Mnemonic.

	Key Questions	Characteristics	Atypical (Generally Not Consistent with Ischemia) or Not a Sensitive Indicator of Ischemia
Onset	When did the symptoms begin?	Gradual; intensity may wax and wane (can also be caused by esophageal disease)	Acute onset (rule out pneumothorax, acute aortic dissection, pulmonary embolism)
Provocation and palliation	What makes the pain/discomfort worse? (position, deep breath, palpation)	Exertional and/or stops with cessation of activity; relief with use of nitroglycerin or a GI cocktail does not differentiate between esophageal pain and ischemic pain	Reproducible with palpation or occurs with eating (not postprandial); non-exertional; positional (worse when lying down)
Quality	What does the pain or discomfort feel like?	May be discomfort instead of pain (pressure, squeezing, tightness, fullness; associated with diaphoresis, nausea/vomiting	Pleuritic (sharp or knife-like pain related to respiratory movements or cough)
Radiation	Does the pain travel to another part of the body?	Often diffuse, radiation to right or left arms and/or shoulders; pain to the right arm is a more sensitive indicator of ischemia than pain to the left arm	Levine's sign (fist in center of chest); radiation between scapula (rule out acute aortic dissection); primary or sole location in the mid/lower abdominal region or lower extremities; localized with one finger; Pain above the nose or below navel is rarely cardiac.
Severity	Use a 1-10 scale	Worse than previous angina or similar to previous MI	–
Time	Is the pain intermittent or continuous?	Angina: usually lasts for 2-5 min and is relieved by rest or NTG. ACS pain: may occur at rest and generally lasts longer than 30 min.	Fleeting pain lasting a few seconds; constant pain that lasts for days

Differential Diagnosis for Chest Pain

Chest pain may be a sign of a potentially life-threatening condition:

- Acute coronary syndrome
- Dissecting aortic aneurysm
- Pulmonary embolism
- Pneumothorax
- Pericardial tamponade
- Pericarditis

TABLE 2-17 Cardiac Enzyme Panel*

Obtain baseline levels of CK-MB and troponin I, and then take these measurements q 8 h × 3 or until the levels begin declining.

Marker	Normal	Onset	Peak	Return to Normal
CK-MB	0-5 ng/mL	3-12 h	24 h	48-72 h
Troponin I**	0-0.2 ng/mL	3-12 h	24 h	5-10 d
Troponin T†	0-0.03 ng/mL	3-12 h	12 h-2 d	5-14 d

*Diagnose STEMI from ECG. Use biomarkers to aid in diagnosis of non-STEMI and to confirm STEMI. Also, use biomarkers if their serial measurement will aid in evaluating the effectiveness of fibrinolytic therapy.

**Troponin I is not usually elevated after acute or chronic severe muscle trauma despite an increase in CK-MB, which makes it useful in diagnosing myocardial infarction.

†Troponin T may be elevated with muscle damage and may be falsely increased in renal failure.

12 Lead ECG

A normal ECG does not rule out an MI (only 40-50% of patients will have ST elevation).

Use the following criteria to diagnose MI:

- Transient ST-segment changes (> 1 mV) in at least two contiguous leads (ST-segment changes that develop during a symptomatic episode at rest and resolve when the patient is asymptomatic suggest acute ischemia.)
- New-onset Q waves
- New-onset bundle branch block

TABLE 2-18 ECG Characteristics of Ischemia, Injury, and Infarction

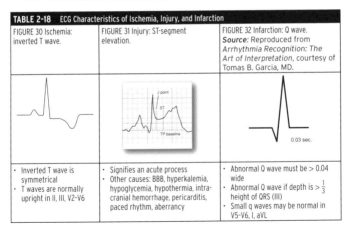

FIGURE 30 Ischemia: inverted T wave.	FIGURE 31 Injury: ST-segment elevation.	FIGURE 32 Infarction: Q wave. *Source:* Reproduced from *Arrhythmia Recognition: The Art of Interpretation,* courtesy of Tomas B. Garcia, MD.
· Inverted T wave is symmetrical · T waves are normally upright in II, III, V2-V6	· Signifies an acute process · Other causes: BBB, hyperkalemia, hypoglycemia, hypothermia, intracranial hemorrhage, pericarditis, paced rhythm, aberrancy	· Abnormal Q wave must be > 0.04 wide · Abnormal Q wave if depth is > $\frac{1}{3}$ height of QRS (III) · Small q waves may be normal in V5-V6, I, aVL

TABLE 2-19 ECG Changes Associated with MI Location*

Location of MI	Indicative Changes (T-Wave Inversion, ST-Segment Elevation, Q Waves)	Reciprocal Changes (ST-Segment Depression)	Complications
Anterior	V1-V4 Loss of normal R-wave progression	I, aVL, II, III, aVF	LV failure, LBBB, RBBB, hemiblocks, Type II second-degree AV blocks, atrial arrhythmias
Lateral	I, aVL, V5, V6	II, III, aVF, V1, V2	
Anterolateral	I, aVL, V3-V6	II, III, aVF	
Septal	V1, V2		BBB, hemiblocks
Inferior	II, III, aVF	I, aVL, V1-V4	Bradycardia (sinus, junctional), first-degree AV block, Type I second-degree AV block, third-degree AV block, LBBB, arrhythmias
Inferolateral	II, III, aVF, V5-V6		
Posterior	None	V1-V2, sometimes V4 Taller R wave than normal ST-segment depression Upright, tall T waves	Similar to inferior
Right ventricle	V1, V3R-V6R (V4R most sensitive)	II, III, aVF (if inferior MI)	Right ventricular failure, similar to inferior
Non-Q wave MI	Loss of R-wave amplitude rather than Q waves in leads facing infarcted area		

*A normal ECG does not rule out an MI.

Acute Medical Management

The following are general guidelines. Refer to specific medical orders as well.

- ABCs and MONA (morphine, oxygen, nitroglycerine, aspirin)
  - Oxygen: maintain SaO$_2$ > 90%
  - Administer to all patients with unstable angina/non-STEMI/STEMI.
    - Absolute indications: SpO$_2$ < 90%, respiratory distress or other signs/symptoms of hypoxemia
- Obtain intravenous access.
- Obtain initial labwork (cardiac enzymes, electrolytes).
- Aspirin: 162 mg PO (nonenteric), chewed
  - Contraindications: history of anaphylaxis or if aspirin was taken before presentation
  - Alternative (if unable to take ASA): clopidogrel (loading dose: 300 mg; followed by 75 mg daily)
- 12-lead ECG (repeat in 5-10 min if not diagnostic)

Nitroglycerin (NTG):
- Sublingual: 0.4 mg SL or spray q 5 min (maximum 3 doses) for ongoing ischemic discomfort
- Intravenous for persistent ischemia, heart failure, or hypertension:
  - Start infusion at 10 mcg/min and increase by 10-20 mcg/min q 5-10 min (maximum dose: 200 mcg/min).
  - Titrate to effect: SBP < 110 mm Hg (previously normotensive patient) or 25% below the starting mean arterial blood pressure if hypertension was present.
- Contraindications:
  - SBP < 90 mm Hg or > 30 mm Hg below baseline
  - Severe bradycardia (< 50 bpm)
  - Tachycardia (> 100 bpm) in absence of symptomatic heart failure
  - Use with caution with right ventricular or inferior MI.
  - Within 24 hours of sildenafil or 48 hours of tadalafil use (erectile dysfunction)

Morphine:
- Give for uncontrolled ischemic discomfort despite NTG.
- Dose: 2-4 mg IV, with 2- to 8-mg increments IV q 5-15 min

Beta blocker:
- Metoprolol: 5 mg IV over 1-2 min; repeat q 5 min for total of 15 mg; start oral dose 15 min after last IV dose (25-50 mg PO q 6 h × 48 h)
- Esmolol: 50 mcg/kg/min, increasing to a maximum dose of 200-300 mcg/kg/min (ultrashort acting)
- Contraindications to beta blockers (relative)
  - First-degree AV block (PR > 0.24 sec)
  - Second/third-degree heart block in absence of functioning pace-maker
  - Heart failure (crackles, S_3)
  - Low-output state (oliguria, hypotension, tachycardia)
  - High risk for cardiogenic shock (tachycardia, Killip Class II or III)
  - Active asthma or reactive airway disease

Electrolytes
- Maintain serum potassium > 4 mEq/L
- Maintain serum magnesium > 2 mEq/L

Acute Heart Failure/Cardiogenic Shock Related to ACS (additional care)
- Furosemide: pulmonary edema; dose, 0.5-1 mg/kg
- Rule out hypovolemia (right ventricular/inferior MI)
- Dopamine: SBP 70-100 mm Hg with signs/symptoms of shock: dose, 5-15 mcg/kg/min

- Norepinephrine: SBP < 70 mm Hg with signs/symptoms of shock; dose, 0.5-30 mcg/min
- Dobutamine: SBP 70-100 mm Hg and no signs/symptoms of shock; dose, 2-20 mcg/kg/min

For arrhythmia management (either bradycardia or tachycardia), refer to the ACLS guidelines and medical orders.

Fibrinolytics

Indications (rule out all contraindications):

- ST elevation MI (STEMI) with symptom onset with past 12 hours and ST elevation > 1 mm (0.1 mV) in at least two contiguous precordial leads or at least 2 adjacent limb leads
- Posterior MI
- STEMI within past 12 hours and new or presumably new left bundle branch block

Absolute contraindications:

- STEMI with symptoms more than 24 hours old
- ST-segment depression (except true posterior MI)
- History of any intracranial hemorrhage
- History of ischemic stroke in the past 3 months
- Presence of cerebral vascular malformation or primary or metastatic intracranial malignancy
- Signs or symptoms of aortic dissection
- Bleeding diathesis or severe bleeding (with exception of menses)
- Significant closed-head or facial trauma in past 3 months

Relative contraindications:

- History of chronic, severely controlled hypertension or uncontrolled hypertension on presentation (SBP > 180 mm Hg or DBP > 110 mm Hg)
- History of ischemic stroke more than 3 months previously
- Dementia
- Any known intracranial disease that is not an absolute contraindication
- Traumatic or prolonged (> 10 min) CPR
- Major surgery within the preceding 3 weeks
- Internal bleeding within the preceding 2-4 weeks or an active peptic ulcer
- Noncompressible vascular punctures
- Pregnancy
- Current use of anticoagulants

TABLE 2-20	Fibrinolytic Agents
Generic Name	Dose
Alteplase (t-PA)	Accelerate • 15 mg IV bolus, then 0.75 mg/kg over 30 min (maximum dose: 50 mg) • 0.5 mg/kg over next 60 min (maximum dose: 35 mg)
Reteplase	• 10-unit IV bolus over 2 min • 30 min later, give 10-unit IV bolus over 2 min
Streptokinase	1.5 million units IV with 50 cc NS or D_5W over 60 min
Tenecteplase	Single bolus (based on patient's weight)

Patient Weight (kg)	Dose (mg)
< 60	30
≥ 60 to < 70	35
≥ 70 to < 80	40
≥ 80 to < 90	45
≥ 90	50

References

ACC/AHA 2007 guidelines for the management of patients with unstable angina/non ST-elevation myocardial infarction: A report of the American College of Cardiology/American Heart Association Task Force on Practice Guidelines. *Circulation* 2007;116(7):e148-e304.

Antman EM, et al. ACC/AHA guidelines for the management of patients with ST-segment elevation myocardial infarction. *Circulation* 2004;110(9):e82-e293.

Swap C, Nagurney J. Value and limitations of chest pain history in the evaluation of patients with suspected acute coronary syndromes. *JAMA* 2005;294:2623.

■ Hemodynamic Monitoring

TABLE 2-21	Hemodynamic Indices/Equations	
Indices	Equation	Normal
Systolic blood pressure (SBP)		Normal < 120 mm Hg
Diastolic blood pressure (DBP)		Normal < 80 mm Hg
Mean arterial pressure (MAP)	(SBP + 2DBP)/3	70-100 mm Hg Goal: > 65 mm Hg
Pulse pressure (PP)	SBP − DBP	~40 mm Hg
Central venous pressure (CVP) or right atrial pressure (RAP)		2-6 mm Hg
Cardiac output (CO)	HR × SV/1000	4-6 L/min
Cardiac index (CI)	CO/BSA	2.5-4 L/min/m²
Stroke volume (SV)	CO/HR × 1000	60-180 mL/beat
Stroke volume index (SVI)	CI/HR × 1000	33-47 mL/beat/m²
Systemic vascular resistance (SVR)	(MAP − RAP)/CO × 80	800-1200 dynes/sec/cm⁻⁵
Systemic vascular resistance index (SVRI)	(MAP − RAP)/CI × 80	1900-2400 dynes/sec/cm⁻⁵/m²
Systolic pressure variation (SPV)	SBP_{max} (vent inspiration) − SBP_{min} (vent expiration)	> 10 mm Hg indicates fluid responsiveness

(Continued)

TABLE 2-21 Hemodynamic Indices/Equations (Continued)

Indices	Equation	Normal
Systolic pressure variation (SPV%)	$SBP + \dfrac{(SPV_{max}/2)}{SBP - SBP_{min}} \times 100$	> 10% indicates fluid responsiveness
Pulse pressure variation (PPV%)	$\dfrac{(pp_{max} - pp_{min})}{(pp_{max} + pp_{min}/2)} \times 100$	> 8% (Vt > 8 mL/kg); < 12% (Vt < 8 mL/kg) indicates fluid responsiveness
Stroke volume variation	$SVV\% = \dfrac{(SV_{max} - SV_{min})}{(SV_{max}/2)} \times 100$	> 9.5% indicates fluid responsiveness

TABLE 2-22 Oxygenation Indices

Indices	Equation	Normal
Arterial O_2 content	$(Hgb \times 1.36 \times SaO_2) + (0.003 \times PaO_2)$	20 mL/dL
Alveolar O_2 tension	$(Pb - PH_2O)FiO_2 - PaCO_2/0.8$	Adjust for altitude
$ScvO_2$	Obtain from vena cava	< 70%
SvO_2	Obtain from distal port of PA catheter	60-80%
O_2 delivery (DO_2)	$CO \times (SaO_2 \times Hgb \times 1.36) \times 10$	1000 mL/min
O_2 delivery index (DO_2I)	$CI \times (SaO_2 \times Hgb \times 1.36) \times 10$	600 mL/min/m²
O_2 consumption (VO_2)	$CO \times (SaO_2 - SvO_2) \times Hgb \times 1.36$	250 mL/min
O_2 consumption index (VO_2I)	$CI \times (SaO_2 - SvO_2) \times Hgb \times 1.36$	125 mL/min/m²
O_2 extraction ratio (O_2ER)	DO_2/VO_2	25%
PaO_2/FiO_2 ratio	Interpret relative to FiO_2	100 mm Hg/0.21 = 475

Blood Pressure Measurement

- If you can palpate a radial pulse: SBP is at least 80 mm Hg (MAP > 60 mm Hg).
- If you cannot palpate a radial pulse but you can palpate a brachial pulse: SBP ≈ 70 mm Hg.
- If you cannot palpate a brachial pulse but you can palpate a femoral/carotid: SBP ≈ 60 mm Hg.

For hypotensive resuscitation, the goal is a barely palpable radial pulse (MAP > 60 mm Hg).

TABLE 2-23 Blood Pressure Classification

	SBP (mm Hg)	DBP (mm Hg)
Normal	< 120	< 80
Prehypertension	120-139	80-89
Stage 1 hypertension	140-159	90-99
Stage 2 hypertension	≥ 160	≥ 100

Source: Chobanian A, et al. Seventh report of the joint national committee on prevention, detection, evaluation, and treatment of high blood pressure. Hypertension 2003;42:1206.

The arm should be supported horizontal to the level of the heart. If the arm is in the dependent position or is supported on an armrest, it may cause a 10-20 mm Hg overestimation of SBP. If the patient is in lateral position, blood pressure from the "up" arm may be higher than central pressure or pressure from the lower arm by 10 mm Hg.

Use the correct cuff size. A too-small cuff may lead to overestimation of BP; a too-large cuff may lead to underestimation of BP.

TABLE 2-24 Recommendations for Correct BP Cuff Size Based on Arm Circumference	
Arm Circumference (cm)	Cuff Size
22-26	Small adult (12 × 22 cm)
27-34	Adult (16 × 30 cm)
35-44	Large adult (16 × 36 cm)
45-52	Adult-thigh (16 × 42 cm)

Arm circumference is measured at ½ the distance from the acromion process to the elbow.

Source: Pickering, T, et al. Recommendations for blood pressure measurement in humans and experimental animals. *Hypertension* 2005;45:142.

Forearm vs Upper Arm: On average, forearm SBP exceeds upper arm (brachial) SBP by 10 mm Hg.
Arterial Line vs Oscillometric Cuff:
There is no basis for comparing blood pressure taken by arterial line versus oscillometric cuff. This comparison does not provide any indication of the accuracy of either method. The difference between the two methods depends on the location of arterial line insertion and the patient's vascular tone.

TABLE 2-25   Invasive Hemodynamic Monitoring Setup

Prepare the Equipment
- Perform hand hygiene.
- Use IV normal saline only.
- Label the bag and tubing: solution/additive, monitoring line location, date/time in ZULU format.
- Note the IV bag fluid level every shift and/or at patient care hand-off.

Validated Protocol for Invasive Pressure Line Preparation (also for AE/CCATT)
1. Perform hand hygiene.
2. Gather supplies (NS IV bag, pressure monitoring kit, 10-cc syringe, pressure bag). Ensure compatible transducer/tubing during patient care hand-offs (i.e., CCATT).
3. Prime the pressure monitoring system to remove all air.
- Remove the pressure monitoring kit from the package, open the blood salvage reservoir, tighten the connections, close the roller clamp, turn the stopcock off to the patient (off toward the distal end), and remove the vented stopcock cap.
- Invert the IV bag. Using sterile technique, insert the spike into the IV bag.
- Leave the spiked bag upside down, open the roller clamp, and simultaneously activate the fast-flush device continuously while gently squeezing to apply pressure to the IV bag to slowly clear air from the IV bag and drip chamber. Completely fill the drip chamber with IV fluid.
- Turn bag upright once fluid is advanced sufficiently past the drip chamber.
- Apply gentle pressure (50 mm Hg) to the IV bag (or hang the bag approximately 30 inches above the distal end of the tubing) and activate the fast-flush device. Advance fluid, priming the stopcock.
- Orient the blood reservoir so that air will be completely removed by the advancing fluid (tilt the distal end upright at 45°) and continue flushing to prime the entire line.
- Close the reservoir and flush this line to move any residual air bubbles from the reservoir.
- Perform rocket flush. (*Never perform when the line is attached to the patient.*)
  - Turn the stopcock off to the distal end of the catheter ("off to patient").
  - Attach a 10-cc syringe to the stopcock near the transducer using sterile technique. Slowly withdraw enough IV fluid to fill the syringe.
  - Turn the stopcock off to the transducer.
  - Flush the line quickly with 10 cc NS from the syringe to remove any remaining air bubbles.
  - Turn the stopcock off.
  - Inspect the line, remove any remaining air by fast-flushing the line, and rocket flush prn.
  - Remove the syringe and cap the stopcock with a closed cap using sterile technique.
4. Place the IV line into a pressure bag and inflate the bag to 250-300 mm Hg. Check for air in the line.
5. Evaluate dynamic response characteristics (goal: adequate or optimal).

Level Stopcock at Transducer (Using a Leveling Device)
- Supine (0-45° HOB): phlebostatic axis (fourth ICS, half of anterior-posterior chest)
- 30° lateral: half the vertical distance from surface of bed to left sternal border
- 90° left lateral: fourth ICS/left parasternal border
- 90° right lateral: fourth ICS/midsternum
Mark the location on the patient's chest for future measurements.

Zeroing
Follow the manufacturer's guidelines.
- Turn the stopcock nearest to the transducer *off to the patient* and *open to the air.*
- Push and release the zeroing button on the monitor; note when zero is reached.
- Cap and turn the stopcock to open.
Relevel at the same reference level and zero every shift and/or at patient care hand-off, and whenever the position changes.

ICS = intercostal space.

Source: E.J. Bridges and K. Evers. *Hemodynamic Monitoring at Altitude.* TriService Nursing Research Program.

| TABLE 2-26 | Invasive Hemodynamic Monitoring Management |

Insertion Site Care
- Catheter should be sutured in place.
- Use sterile gauze or a semi-permeable transparent dressing.
- Secure and immobilize the extremity in the position of function.
- Dressing change:
  - Gauze: q 48 h
  - Transparent: q 7 d
  - After site inspection or if loose, wet, or damp
  - Change dressing before transport or if dressing will expire during transport period
- Monitor circulatory and neurological status of the extremity distal to the insertion site.

Drawing Blood from an Arterial Line
Perform hand hygiene; use aseptic technique and Standard Precautions.

Tubing Without Aspiration Chamber
- Attach the syringe to the proximal stopcock.
- Open the stopcock to the syringe and catheter, and aspirate an amount equal to 5-7 times the dead-space (tip of catheter to port). Discard this fluid.
- Close the stopcock to the halfway position; remove the syringe.
- Attach the blood-sampling syringe; open the stopcock to the syringe and catheter.
- Withdraw the minimum amount needed for testing.
- Close the stopcock to the halfway position; remove the syringe.
- If ABGs are needed, immediately remove any air bubbles, and cap, label, and send the syringe immediately for analysis.
- Open the stopcock to the syringe and inline flush; activate the flush until all blood is removed from the stopcock and port.
- Open the stopcock to the inline flush and catheter, and clear all blood.
- Evaluate the dynamic response characteristics of the system.
- Reference and rezero the system.

Tubing with Aspiration Chamber (e.g., Edwards LifeSciences VAMP)
Always follow the manufacturer's guidelines.
- With the system open, slowly aspirate blood into the inline reservoir to the prescribed level.
- Close the stopcock to the reservoir.
- Swab the needleless sample access site.
- Insert the needleless vacuum tube holder into the access site.
- Withdraw blood.
- Remove the syringe or vacuum tube holder (pull straight out); swab the site of blood.
- Open the stopcock to the reservoir.
- Using the inline plunger, re-infuse the collected blood until the reservoir is in the starting position.
- Flush the system by activating the fast-flush device to clear the tubing.
- Evaluate the dynamic response characteristics of the system.
- Reference and rezero the system.

Discontinuing an Arterial Line
- Perform hand hygiene; don gloves.
- Close the stopcock to the catheter.
- Remove the dressing and sutures; gently remove the catheter and quickly place sterile gauze over the site.
- Apply continuous direct pressure for 5 minutes and until bleeding stops.
- Apply a dry sterile circumferential compression dressing.
- Observe for rebleeding, infection, and compromised circulation distal to the insertion site.

Functional Hemodynamics

Functional hemodynamics is defined as mechanical ventilator-induced changes in arterial BP (systolic pressure variation [SPV], pulse pressure variation [PPV]) or stroke volume variation (SVV). These measurements are used for two purposes:

- To predict a patient's responsiveness to a fluid bolus (SV increase > 10%)
- They may be an earlier indicator of hemorrhage than changes in HR or BP (identified by a decrease in SPV > 4 mm Hg without any change in medications that would change vascular tone)

Assess functional hemodynamics when the patient has signs of hypoperfusion and fluid bolus is being considered. The following consider-ations apply:

- Being fluid responsive does not mean that the patient should always receive fluids—only that the patient will most likely respond to a bolus with an increased SV. The decision to administer fluids must be balanced against the risk for pulmonary compromise, particularly in patients who may have underlying pulmonary injury (e.g., blast lung injury, ARDS).
- Having a relatively low CVP or PAOP does not mean that a patient will respond to fluids. The CVP and PAOP are only predictive of fluid responsiveness in approximately 50% of cases.

The patient must meet the following conditions for performance of functional measures:

- Arterial line (undamped—adequate or optimal)
- Mechanically ventilated—no spontaneous breaths or variable tidal volume (pressure support)
- Stable cardiac rhythm—no ectopy during period of data collection
- No cor pulmonale (acute RV dysfunction)
- Closed chest

Follow this procedure to assess functional hemodynamics:

- Ensure adequate dynamic response characteristics of the arterial line.
- Ensure that the arterial pressure line is correctly referenced to the phlebostatic axis.
- Turn the monitor sweep speed to 6.25 mm/sec (this will compress the arterial waveform).
- Monitor the arterial line/respiratory tracing.
- Identify the inspiratory/expiratory phases.
- Using the stop cursor, exactly measure the maximum SBP/DBP during inspiration and the minimum SBP/DBP during expiration. Exact measurement of pressures is imperative to avoid introducing an error into the calculations.

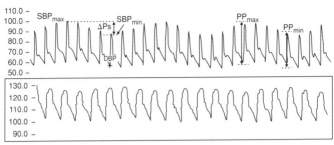

FIGURE 33 Example of SPV and PPV. Top: A fluid responder (SPV = 13 mm Hg). Bottom: A fluid non-responder (SPV = 4 mm Hg). Tidal volume = 8 mL/kg.

Systolic Pressure Variation. Obtain the SPV directly from the arterial line or a proprietary monitor.

$$SPV = SBP_{max} - SBP_{min}$$

$$SPV(\%) = SBP_{max} - SBP_{min}/(SPV_{max} + SPV_{min}/2) \times 100$$

Note that SPV(%) may be a more sensitive indicator when the patient is hemodynamically unstable.

Pulse Pressure Variation. Obtain the PPV directly from the arterial line or a proprietary monitor.

$$PPV = [(PP_{max} - PP_{min})/(PP_{max} + PP_{min}/2)] \times 100$$

Non-invasive Stroke Volume. Measurement of noninvasive stroke volume/stroke volume variation requires a proprietary transducer/bedside monitor attached to an arterial line with automatic calculation of SV/SVV. Currently only Flotrac/Vigileo (Edwards LifeSciences) is available for use in AOR.

$$SVV\% = [(SV_{max} - SV_{min})/(SV_{max} + SV_{min}/2)] \times 100$$

TABLE 2-27	**Threshold Values to Predict If a Patient Will Respond to a Fluid Bolus (↑SV or CI > 10%)**	
Index	Vt	Threshold Value
SPV	8-11 mL/kg	10 mm Hg
SPV	8-11 mL/kg	10%
PPV	< 8 mL/kg > 8 mL/kg	8% 12%
SVV	10 mL/kg	9.5%

Limited research has been performed for threshold values for Vt < 10 mL/kg. Functional indices may not be good predictors of fluid responsiveness if Vt < 8 mL/kg.

The absolute values and threshold values for all function indices are affected by factors other than fluid responsiveness.

Tidal volume: ↑ absolute values with ↑Vt; must have a stable Vt for comparison of values across time.

Ejection fraction: limited research in patients with decreased ejection fraction (< 40%).

Vascular resistance: acute changes (titration of vasoactive medications/compensatory response) affect absolute values:

- Vasodilation increases BP and SV variability. If the patient is hemodynamically unstable with functional indicators indicating fluid responsiveness, first reevaluate the patient's tolerance to titration of the vasoactive medication.
- Vasopressor-induced vasoconstriction decreases absolute values but does not mean that the underlying intravascular volume deficit has been resolved.

Spontaneously Breathing Patients

Perform the following tests.

Passive Leg Raising (PLR)

- Acutely elevate the legs to 30-45°.
- Monitor the change in aortic flow or SV/CO (use Doppler) from baseline to 1 minute after PLR.
- Thresholds: ↑Aortic flow > 10% or ↑SV/CO > 12%.

Do not perform the PLR test in patients with depressed right heart function.

Right Atrial Pressure Variation (RAPV)

- The patient must take a breath of adequate depth.
- ΔRAP (RAP_{insp} - RAP_{exp}) < 1 mm Hg: indicates patient **is not** fluid responsive.
- Measure RAP at nadir of "a" wave.

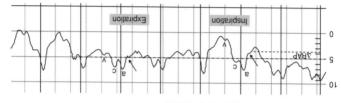

FIGURE 34   Example of evaluation of ΔRAP during spontaneous ventilation. Read the CVP (or RAP) at the base of the "a" wave or the base of the "c" wave. The ΔRAP is approximately 1.5 mm Hg, indicating that this patient may respond to a fluid bolus. The end-expiratory CVP is 5 mm Hg.

■ Cardiac Trauma

Blunt Cardiac Injury

History: Suspect blunt cardiac injury (BCI) with major blunt trauma to the thorax (bent steering wheel, crush injuries of the chest), deceleration injuries (can occur with deceleration from < 20 mph), or blast injury. Injuries may include myocardial contusion, myocardial rupture (usually fatal), acute aortic disruption (75-90% mortality), pericardial injury, hemopericardium, pericardial tamponade, valvular damage (mitral and aortic at higher risk), and disruption of major coronary vessels.

The following signs and symptoms suggest cardiac injury (or require further evaluation):

- Most common: nonspecific chest pain unrelieved by analgesia
- Thoracic trauma (bruising to chest wall or sternal, clavicular, or rib fractures)
- New murmur
- Pericardial friction rub
- Signs and symptoms of heart failure in absence of preexisting cardiac disease (the right ventricle is particularly susceptible due to its position behind the sternum)

Normal ECG in the absence of hemodynamic instability and chest pain rules out BCI. Changes in the ECG will be seen in 40-80% of cases:

- Nonspecific ST changes (rule out hypoxemia, hypotension, acidemia, electrolyte abnormalities)
- Arrhythmias: any ECG abnormality requires 24 hours of monitoring
  - Premature atrial complexes (PACs), premature ventricular complexes (PVCs), and atrial fibrillation are the most common arrhythmias associated with cardiac injury.
  - Heart block may include right bundle branch block, first-degree AV block, or third-degree block.
  - The presence of significant arrhythmias or heart block suggests cardiac injury.

Current guidelines from ATLS/EAST suggest that cardiac enzymes have no role in diagnosis of BCI. Echocardiography may show wall motion abnormalities (although TEE is not available in AOR and FAST may be difficult to use with concurrent thoracic injury).

Patient management includes the following measures:

- Supportive care (antiarrhythmics, inotropes): similar to management of cardiac disease

- Telemetry monitoring for 24-48 hours for patients with moderate chest injury and suspicion of cardiac trauma
- Pain management: treat concurrent injuries (thoracic epidural, opioids)
- Cardiac arrest: See Figure 35 JTTS Clinical Practice Guidelines for EMT thoracotomy

Cardiac Tamponade

Cardiac tamponade is defined as an acute or chronic accumulation of fluid in the pericardial space with compression of cardiac chambers, ultimately leading to obstructive shock. It is diagnosed with the following techniques:

- FAST exam (can detect 100 mL fluid) or CT scan
- CXR: widened mediastinum (requires 200 mL fluid in pericardium)
- Pericardiocentesis (diagnostic and temporarily therapeutic)

Signs and symptoms are as follows:

- ECG: sinus tachycardia and low-voltage, electrical alternans
- Elevated jugular venous pressure, manifested as distended neck veins (may be absent with hemorrhage/hypovolemia)
- Pulsus paradoxus (> 10 mm Hg decrease in SBP during spontaneous inspiration)
  - May be absent with hemorrhage/hypovolemia
  - Use manual blood pressure cuff; deflate more slowly than usual.
  - During deflation, the first Korotkoff sound is heard only during expiration; with further deflation, Korotkoff sounds are heard throughout respiratory cycle.
  - The difference between the SBP (first Korotkoff sound) heard initially and when Korotkoff sounds are heard throughout entire respiratory cycle is used to diagnose pulsus paradoxus.
- Pulseless electrical activity (PEA): consider tamponade in the differential diagnosis

Patient management includes the following measures:

- High-flow O_2 (maintain SpO_2 > 92%)
- Hemodynamically stable patient: avoid hypovolemia
- Hemodynamically unstable patient:
  - Temporizing measure: fluid resuscitation in hypovolemic patient
  - Emergent pericardiocentesis (temporary stabilization) performed by MD; followed by definitive surgical repair
- Emergent thoracotomy

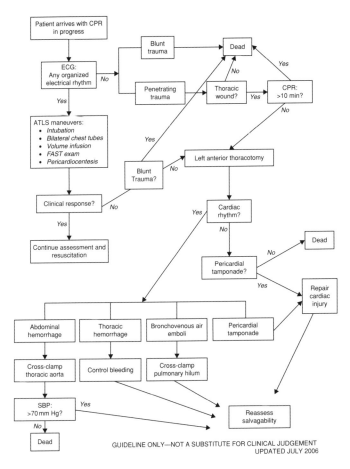

FIGURE 35 JTTS Clinical Practice Guidelines for EMT Thoracotomy.

References

American Heart Association. Part 10.7: Cardiac arrest Associated with trauma. *Circulation* 2005;112:IV146-IV149.

El-Chami F, Nicholson W, Helmy T. Blunt cardiac trauma. *J Emerg Med* 2007 (in press).

Emergency War Surgery Handbook (Chapter 16, p. 16.3), October 2006.

JTTS Clinical Practice Guidelines for EMT Thoracotomy, July 2006.

National Association of Emergency Medical Technicians. *Prehospital Trauma Life Support: Military Version* (6th ed., pp. 283-286). St. Louis: Mosby, 2007.

■ Abdominal/Gastrointestinal

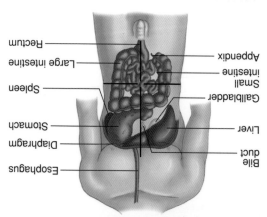

Esophagus
Bile duct
Diaphragm
Stomach
Liver
Spleen
Small intestine
Large intestine
Appendix
Rectum
Gallbladder

FIGURE 36   Solid abdominal organs.

Assessment

History:

Determine the cause of injury or presentation; time of last oral intake; pain, nausea, vomiting, or diarrhea; use of seatbelt/restraining harness, if a fall occurred (height of fall); urge to urinate/defecate; and last menstrual period/possibility of pregnancy.

Inspect for signs of blunt or penetrating injury, internal bleeding, bruises, scars, rashes, and trauma:

- Penetrating injury
  - Identify fragment, gunshot, or stab wounds.
  - If a penetrating foreign object (e.g., knife, pipe): stabilize in place; *do not remove.*
  - External wound appearance does not determine extent of internal injury.
- Evisceration of bowel: cover with a sterile moist (normal saline) dressing; *do not force* bowel back into abdominal cavity

Auscultate for the presence or absence of bowel sounds (if the environment allows).

Palpate the four quadrants counterclockwise, starting in RUO and ending in LUO (spleen may be injured):

- If the patient is complaining of pain, palpate that quadrant last.
- Note tenderness, involuntary muscle guarding, rebound tenderness, and rigidity.

- Gently squeeze inward on the pelvis, noting any pain or tenderness; *do not rock the pelvis.*

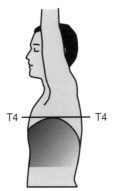

FIGURE 37 Level of injury to abdominal structures. Penetrating thoracic injuries below the T4 level or nipple line, to include the axillary line (level of the diaphragm), have a high probability of injuring abdominal structures.
Source: U.S. Department of Defense. *Emergency War Surgery Handbook.* The Borden Institute, Washington, D.C. (2006).

Note any concurrent injuries, such as rib fractures (especially if liver/splenic injury), thoracic trauma (particularly if esophageal/gastric injuries), and bladder injury (pelvic trauma).
In case of blunt trauma, the initial examination of the abdomen may be unremarkable. Ongoing assessment may reveal increasing signs of tenderness, rebound pain, guarding, and loss of bowel sounds.

Initial Nursing Management: Abdominal Trauma
- ABCs
- Tubes: decompress the stomach and bladder using nasogastric (use with caution in case of facial trauma) and urethral tubes, respectively
- Stabilize (temporarily) pelvic fractures.

Initial Diagnostic Exams
Perform the following assessments per MD order:
- Labs: CBC, chemistry panel, amylase, lipase, type and cross, PT/PTT/INR, UA
- Radiographs: flat and upright abdomen
- Rectal exam; occult blood testing
- Focused Assessment with Sonography for Trauma (FAST)–performed by MD

Postoperative Care: Abdominal Surgery

Manage dressings:
- Cover incision with sterile dressing for 24–48 hours after surgery.
- Wounds heal best in moist environment, so it may be appropriate to use a semi-occlusive dressing that is impermeable to bacteria but allows passage of moisture vapor.

Monitor for postoperative bleeding:
- Bleeding along incision that saturates the dressing; apply gentle pressure, reinforce dressing, and notify surgeon immediately
- Signs and symptoms requiring further exploration: tachycardia, hypotension, abdominal pain or distention (rule out other causes of hypotension, such as epidural analgesia or anesthesia)

A post-splenectomy patient will require the following immunizations: pneumococcal, *Haemophilus influenzae*, and meningococcal. Perform drain management. Dislodgement of a surgical drain is an emergency; notify the surgeon immediately.

TABLE 2-28   Common Postoperative Drains

Penrose
• Drainage of fluid, pus, blood, or necrotic debris
• Secured with a safety pin to prevent migration
• Cover with dry gauze (change when saturated) or an ostomy bag
• Remove dressing with caution as the Penrose drain may not be sutured in place

Negative-Pressure Drains (Jackson-Pratt/Hemovac)
• When fully charged, apply approximately 75 mm Hg of suction pressure
• Ensure tubing is without kinks
• Initial drainage is sanguineous or serosanguineous, but should become more serous
• Empty reservoir and recharge prn when half-full
○ Jackson-Pratt should remain concave or somewhat flat; it should not be fully inflated
• During drain removal, make sure the device is open (no negative pressure)
• Tubing may be gently milked to unclog it
• Attachment of drainage device to wall suction: set suction pressure to IAW MD order (generally low-pressure suction is 20–80 mm Hg)

T-Tube (Gravity Drain of Bile)
• Place patient in semi-Fowler's position and maintain drainage bag below insertion site
• Expect 300–500 mL of thick, blood-tinged, bright yellow to dark green bile drainage during the first 24 hours after surgery
• Drainage will decrease to < 200 mL/day by post-op day 4
• Report drainage greater than 500 mL/day
• Protect skin; bile drainage will irritate skin

Salem Sump
• Nasogastric decompression is appropriate on a selective basis for any patient in whom severe nausea, vomiting, or gastric distention develops; in patients with intestinal obstruction; or in patients with severe prolonged ileus
• Apply low continuous suction (20–80 mm Hg); if Levin tube use low intermittent suction
• Sump Port (only on Salem sump tube)
○ Keep sump port patent; prevents excessive suction pressure that could damage the stomach mucosa
○ Keep sump port above patient's midline/stomach
○ If irrigation is needed, follow fluid with 15–20 mL air bolus to reestablish a buffer of air between the gastric contents and the reflux valve
○ Never clamp sump tube to prevent reflux

(Continued)

TABLE 2-28 Common Postoperative Drains *(Continued)*

Medication Administration
- Make sure medication can be crushed (never crush enteric medications)
- Disconnect suction and aspirate contents; if < 100 mL, reinstill
- Flush tube with 30–50 mL water
- Dilute medication in water or apple juice and administer
- Flush tube
- Wait 30 minutes before reattaching tube to suction
- In patients who have undergone gastric surgery, if the nasogastric tube becomes dislodged, do not reinsert it. Instead, notify the surgeon immediately.

Damage-Control Surgery

Damage-control surgery entails rapid initial control of hemorrhage and contamination, temporary closure, resuscitation to normal physiology in the ICU, and subsequent re-exploration and definitive repair. Recovery will take place in the ICU, where the patient's hemodynamic status will be stabilized, coagulopathy reversed, and the patient rewarmed.

Injuries that typically require damage control techniques include upper abdominal injuries that are not isolated spleen injuries (e.g., duodenal injuries, large liver injuries, pancreas injuries), major penetrating pelvic trauma of more than one system, and any retroperitoneal vascular injury.

Acute Management of Casualty with Open Abdomen (Laparostomy)

The abdomen may be left open in the following circumstances:
- After damage-control surgery. The abdomen is packed and the patient is brought to the ICU for stabilization and then returned to the OR in less than 48 hours for definitive procedures.
- If there is excessive edema from blunt or penetrating trauma and fluid resuscitation
- In case of secondary peritonitis
- In case of postoperative wound dehiscence

The goal is to avoid increase intra-abdominal pressure and allow for surgical re-exploration if necessary. Note that a patient with an open abdomen can still develop intra-abdominal hypertension (IAH) and abdominal compartment syndrome (ACS).

Closure:
- For temporary closure, the abdomen is covered with a 3-L sterile plastic bag (Bogota bag) or large plastic abdominal dressing.
- Vacuum-assisted closure may be used (See the "See the "Soft-Tissue Trauma" section.)

Nursing care issues are as follows:
- Initial care: stabilize hemodynamic status, resolve acidosis, coagulopathy, and hypothermia
- Risk for IAH/ACS due to further bowel and retroperitoneal edema from volume resuscitation; patient may also have surgical packing left in place

- Fluid imbalance: 2-3 L fluid loss per day into dressing; include this fluid loss when assessing the patient's overall fluid balance
- Infection: severity of injury and inability to close abdomen increase the patient's risk for ventilator-associated pneumonia, bloodstream infections/central line infections, and surgical site infection
- Acute respiratory failure: initial management focuses on using lung-protective ventilation strategy (see the "Pulmonary/Thoracic" section); following extubation, the patient will have decreased effectiveness of breathing and coughing if the abdominal wall remains open
- Nutrition: enteral feeding is generally initiated after coverage or closure of the abdomen and the patient is resuscitated

References

Damage Control Surgery: DMRTI Emergency War Surgery Course.

Emergency War Surgery: Third United States Revision (Chapter 11), 2004. http://www.brookside-press.org/Products/Emergency_War_Surgery/Chp11CriticalCare.pdf

Emergency War Surgery: Third United States Revision (Chapter 12), 2004. http://www.brookside-press.org/Products/Emergency_War_Surgery/Chp12DamageControl.pdf

Sagraves SG, et al. Damage control surgery: The intensivist's role. J Intensive Care Med 2006;21:5-16.

Vertrees A, et al. Early definitive closure using serial abdominal closure technique on injured OEF/OIF casualties. http://www.facs.org/education/gs2005/gs63vertrees.pdf

Intra-abdominal Hypertension and Compartment Syndrome

Definitions

- Abdominal perfusion pressure (APP) = Mean arterial pressure (MAP) - Intra-abdominal pressure (IAP)
- Intra-abdominal pressure: in critically ill patient, 5-7 mm Hg
- Intra-abdominal hypertension (IAH): sustained or repeated IAP ≥ 12 mm Hg
- Abdominal compartment syndrome (ACS): sustained IAP ≥ 20 mm Hg (with or without APP < 60 mm Hg) that is associated with new organ dysfunction/failure

TABLE 2-29 Risk Factors for Intra-abdominal Hypertension/Abdominal Compartment Syndrome	
Diminished abdominal wall compliance	Capillary leak/fluid resuscitation
Acute respiratory failure, especially with elevated intrathoracic pressure	Acidosis (pH < 7.2)
Abdominal surgery with primary fascial or tight closure	Hypotension
Major trauma/burns	Hypothermia (core temperature < 33°C)
Prone positioning, HOB > 30°	Polytransfusion (> 10 units blood/24 h)
High BMI, central obesity	Coagulopathy (platelets < 55,000/mm³; PT > 15 sec, or INR < 1.5)
Increased intra-abdominal contents	Massive fluid resuscitation (> 5 L/24 h)
Gastroparesis, ileus, colonic pseudo-obstruction	Pancreatitis
Increased abdominal contents	Oliguria
Hemo/pneumoperitoneum	Sepsis
Ascites/liver dysfunction	Major trauma/burns
	Damage-control laparotomy

Monitoring for IAH/ACS proceeds as follows:

Collect the necessary equipment and supplies:

- Urinary catheter (two or three port)
- Pressure monitoring system (0.9% sterile saline; pressure tubing/transducer; pressure bag, if continuous monitoring is planned); prepare pressure line in same manner as for other pressure monitoring (See the "Hemodynamic Monitoring" section.)
- 18-gauge angiocatheter or three-way stopcock
- Chlorhexidine swab (cleanse sampling port)
- Clean gloves

Set up the system as demonstrated in Figure 38.

Position the patient supine (0° HOB).

Reference the transducer to the iliac crest (mid-axillary line). (Previous recommendation was to the symphysis pubis.)

Drain the bladder and clamp the drainage tube.

Instill 25–50 mL sterile saline (volume > 50 mL overdistends the bladder).

Measure IAP at end-expiration.

Remove the angiocatheter (or leave in place for frequent monitoring per local policy).

Unclamp the tubing.

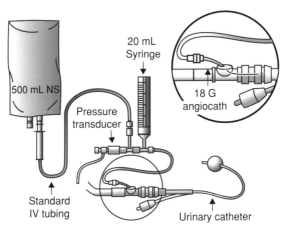

FIGURE 38 Setup for IAP monitoring.

References

Cheatham ML, Malbrain M, Kirkpatrick A, et al. International Conference of Experts on Intra-abdominal Hypertension and Abdominal Compartment Syndrome. II. Recommendations. *Intensive Care Med* 2007;33:951-962.

Gallagher JJ. Ask the experts: Describe the procedure for monitoring intra-abdominal pressure via an indwelling urinary catheter. *Crit Care Nurse* 2007;27(5):64-70.

Malbrain M, Cheatham ML, Kirkpatrick A, et al. Results from the International Conference of Experts on Intra-abdominal Hypertension and Abdominal Compartment Syndrome. I. Definitions. *Intensive Care Med* 2006;32:1722-1732.

World Society of the Abdominal Compartment Syndrome. http://www.wsacs.org

Diarrhea

Incidence: In a sample of deployed troops, 45% reported a decrease in job performance due to diarrhea for a median of 3 days, 62% sought medical care for diarrhea, and 33% required IV fluid rehydration (Sanders et al., 2005).

Assessment of a patient with diarrhea should include the following, obtain a history of illness, to include the characteristics of the diarrhea, nausea, vomiting, and where eating and obtaining water took place (on-base versus off-base).

Characteristics of diarrhea may aid in diagnosis of its cause. Traveler's diarrhea is mostly caused by *Escherichia coli* and presents as watery diarrhea without vomiting or fever. *Shigella* and *Campylobacter* typically cause bloody diarrhea and fever. Norovirus (Norwalk-like virus) typically causes vomiting. Monitor for multiple cases, and consult with the public health officer as appropriate.

Care consists of the following measures:

- Antidiarrheal: loperamide (Imodium)
- Antibiotic: medication selection based on etiology; refer to local policy
- Pepto-Bismol
- Rehydration (oral or IV)

References

Putnam SD, Sanders JW, Frenck RW. Self-reported description of diarrhea among military population in Operations Iraqi Freedom and Enduring Freedom. *J Travel Med* 2006;13(2):92-99.

Sanders JW, Putnam SD, Riddle MS, et al. Military importance of diarrhea: Lessons from the Middle East. *Curr Opin Gastroenterol* 2005;21(1):9-14.

Nutrition in Critically Ill/Injured Patients

Source: Adapted from Landstuhl Regional Medical Center Nutritional Support of the ICU Patient, July 27 2007. Note that this source is not a replacement for clinical judgment.

Indications for total peripheral nutrition are as follows:

- Unable to meet 60% of caloric needs enterally by day 7 from time of injury
- Any contraindications for enteral nutrition and a patient without nutritional support for 7 days
- Massive small bowel resection refractory to enteral feeds
- High-output fistula after failure of elemental diet

Ensure that the patient has a clean, dedicated central intravenous line for administration.

TABLE 2-30 Enteral Nutrition

Indications
· Any trauma patient who is anticipated to remain unable to take full oral intake on his or her own for more than 5 days from the time of injury · Any patient who has oral intake that is inadequate to meet current nutritional needs

Contraindications	
· High risk for non-occlusive bowel necrosis (active shock or ongoing resuscitation, persistent MAP < 60 mm Hg) · Generalized peritonitis · Intestinal obstruction · Surgical discontinuity of bowel · Paralytic ileus · Intractable refractory vomiting/diarrhea	· Mesenteric ischemia · Major GI bleed · Continuous neuromuscular blockade · Temperature < 96°F · Increasing requirement for vasoactive support to maintain MAP > 60 mm Hg · Bladder pressure trending higher and > 20 mm Hg

Source: Landstuhl Regional Medical Center.

General care for patient receiving enteral nutrition:
- Maintain HOB > 30° at all times or in reverse Trendelenburg position if spine not cleared.
- Obtain portable abdominal radiograph within 12 hours of CCATT or AE movement to confirm that feeding tube location is within jejunum.
- Enteral nutrition administered into the jejunum (past the ligament of Treitz) does not need to be stopped prior to going to the OR, diagnostic tests, CCATT/AE transport, lying flat.
- Keep OG on intermittent low suction while initiating/advancing tube feeds via feeding tube.

Table 2-31 Managing Intolerance of Enteral Feedings

Indicator	Severity	Definition	Treatment
Vomiting	(Occurrence)	Any	· If no OG, then place OG and start intermittent low wall suction · Check existing OG function/placement · IF OG placement is correct, decrease TF infusion rate by 50% and call MD
Abdominal distention and/or cramping or tenderness (if detectable)	Mild	History and/or physical exam	· Maintain TF infusion rate
	Moderate	History and/or physical exam	· Maintain TF infusion; do not advance · Order AP supine KUB X-ray · Assess for small bowel obstruction If moderate distention for ≥ 24 h, switch to elemental formula
	Severe	History and/or physical exam	· Stop TF infusion · Monitor fluid status · Consider CBC, lactate, ABG, Chem7, CT scan abdomen · Check bladder pressure

(Continued)

TABLE 2-31 Managing Intolerance of Enteral Feedings (Continued)

Diarrhea	Mild	1-2×/24 h or 200-400 mL/24 h	• Increase Tf infusion rate per protocol
	Moderate	3-4×/24 h or 400-600 mL/24 h	• Maintain Tf infusion rate; do not advance • Check for C. difficile in 3 sequential stools
	Severe	>4×/24 h or >600 mL/24 h	• Decrease Tf infusion rate by 50% • Review MAR; note antibiotic, bowel regimen, prokinetics, elixirs • Send stool for C. difficile toxin assay in 3 sequential stools • If C. difficile is positive, then treat with Flagyl and hold antidiarrheals for 48 h • If C. difficile is negative, give 2 mg loperamide after each loose stool • Order AP supine KUB x-ray to evaluate location of feeding tube • Consider switching to elemental formula • Monitor fluid and electrolyte status
High NG output	(measured)	> 1200 mL/12 h	• Stop Tf • Order AP supine KUB to evaluate location of OG and feeding tube • If OG is past the pylorus, pull back into stomach and resume tube feeds at previous rate • If NJ is in the stomach, consult GI to replace • If both tubes are in the correct positions, decrease tube feed rate by 50%; assess patient entirely • Check OG aspirate for glucose by lab ○ If glucose > 110, hold Tf, reassess in 12 hours ○ If OG aspirate is glucose negative, resume Tf at 50% of previous rate
Medication considerations	Inotropic agents (e.g., dobutamine, milrinone)		• Advance feeding per protocol
	Paralytics and vasoactive agents • Any paralytic continuous infusion • Vasopressin > 0.04 unit/min • Dopamine > 10 mcg/kg/min • Norepinephrine > 5 mcg/min • Phenylephrine > 50 mcg/min • Any epinephrine		• Elemental formula at 20 mL/h; do not advance • Continue Glutasolve; hold Prostat • Consider concurrent TPN starting ICU day 7

Source: Landstuhl Regional Medical Center (2 July 2007).

Reference
Jacobs DG, Jacobs DO, Kudsk KA, et al. Practice management guidelines for nutritional support of the trauma patient. Eastern Association for the Surgery of Trauma, 2003.
http://www.east.org/tpg.asp

Enteral Feeding During Aeromedical Evacuation

Refer to HQ AMC Surgeon General Policy Letter, December 21, 2005, for more information.

- Jejunal feeding tubes will be used for patients requiring enteral feeding during transport.
- KUB confirmation of placement beyond the ligament of Treitz either the day before or day of transport is required (Figure 39).
- Continuous low-flow feeding may be provided by an approved IV pump.
- Patients will have an NG or OG tube for stomach decompression; do not clamp this tube.
- Patients should be accompanied by CCATT or Burn Team. If a routine AE patient has need for enteral feedings during transport, a CCATT member on the aircraft can provide supervision.
- Enplane the patient's head forward to alleviate risk of aspiration.
- Use a backrest on the litter if safe for the patient (thoracic/lumbar spine clearance is required for trauma patients). If the patient's condition prevents use of a backrest, hold feedings 30-60 minutes prior to takeoff and landing.
- If the feeding tube or administration set becomes occluded during transport, discontinue feeding until the patient arrives at the destination facility.
- Flush the feeding tube with 20 mL saline q 8 h to prevent occlusion.
- Provide oral care q 12 h; moisturize the oral mucosa and lips q 2 h.

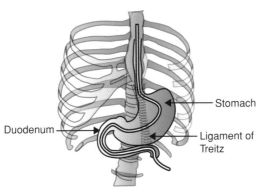

FIGURE 39   KUB demonstrating correct placement of enteral feeding tube beyond the ligament of Treitz (junction of duodenum and jejunum).

Gastric Tube Placement for Feeding

A radiograph (chest, KUB) is the only method that accurately assesses correct tube placement when instillation of any substance (e.g., char-coal, mucomyst, enteral nutrition) is planned. Mark the tube at the patient's nares to allow for rapid assessment of tube position.

The following methods are not recommended for verification of tube placement:

- The "whoosh" test (instillation of air down the tube with auscultation over epigastrum)
- Testing pH of aspirate using blue litmus paper
- Monitoring for bubbling of air at the end of the tube
- Characteristics of feeding aspirate (respiratory/gastric secretions may look similar)

Continuous monitoring:

- Evaluate the most recent (< 24 h) CXR or KUB.
- Determine if the mark on the tube at the exit site indicates that the tube has not moved.
- For intermittent feeding via NG tube, wait at least 4 h after last feeding. Insufflate 30 mL air and attempt to aspirate fluid. Indicators of correct gastric tube placement include pH < 5 and a gastric color (grassy green, clear and colorless, or cloudy white with feeding residual)
- For continuous feedings, verify the tube marking; pH is not useful in this circumstance. If pH < 5, it suggests the intestinal tube may have migrated to the stomach. A sudden increase in feeding residual may indicate tube migration to stomach.

References

American Association of Critical Care Nurses. Practice Alert: Verification of feeding tube placement.

Metheny NA. Preventing respiratory complications of tube feedings: Evidence-based practice. *Am J Crit Care* 2006;15(4):360–365.

Metheny NA, Schnelker R, McGinnis J, et al. Indicators of tubesite during feedings. *J Neuroscience Nurs* 2005;37(6):320–325.

Ostomy Care

- Assess the stoma q 4 h and at every patient care hand-off; it should normally be reddish-pink.
- Evaluate the surrounding skin for redness, induration, hardness, warmth, purulence, and pain.
- Ensure that a wafer ring is present: approximately ⅛ inch around stoma to prevent stoma constriction and fecal leakage.
- Using standard precautions change the bag when it is full and at least daily.
- Document I&O as well as liquid drainage postoperatively.

En route/in-flight considerations for ostomy are as follows:
- Ensure that the patient has extra bags, wafers, and stoma adhesive—at least a 24-h supply.
- Advise the patient to expect an increase in flatus and stool during ascent and in flight.
- Vent the collection bag (poke two holes above the wafer ring) to avoid excess gas from dislodging the bag.

In-flight Considerations for Patients with Gastrointestinal Injury/Disease
- Barometric pressure changes: Gas expansion may cause abdominal discomfort, decreased lung expansion and volume, ↑nausea and vomiting. These effects may require NG/OG tube decompression preflight or in-flight. Elevate HOB to 30° to prevent aspiration. Monitor for increased abdominal pressure.
- Vibration/thermal changes: May exacerbate the patient's underlying condition or diagnosis and increase the patient's sensitivity to motion sickness.
- G forces: May ↑ risk of aspiration. Place an OG/NG tube; elevate HOB to 30°. The physician may order a head-forward position for the patient (toward the cockpit in a fixed-wing aircraft).

■ Genitourinary/Renal
Renal/Genitourinary Problems
Renal colic was the most common urologic indication for aeromedical evacuation from CSH during first 6 months of Operation Iraqi Freedom (Baker et al., 2007).
The incidence of STDs in patients seeking outpatient gynecologic care at one deployed medical clinic was 2.5% (Wright et al., 2006).

Renal Colic
Renal colic (urinary stones) has the following presentation:
- Pain (upper ureteral or renal pelvic obstruction—unilateral flank pain or tenderness; lower ureteral obstruction pain radiating to ipsilateral testicle or labia)
- Hematuria (gross or microscopic); note that 10-30% of patients present without hematuria
- Other signs/symptoms: nausea/vomiting, dysuria, urgency

Care proceeds as follows:
- Hydration
- Normal saline or Ringer's lactate; the goal is urine specific gravity < 1.010 and daily urine output > 2 L
- Analgesia: a combined approach may be superior to use of a single agent alone
  ○ Ketorolac: 15-60 mg IV

○ Morphine: average dose 5–10 mg IV; may cause nausea/vomiting
- Antiemetics

Monitoring/diagnostics for renal colic include the following measures:
- UOP/urinalysis; note that a work-up of incidental asymptomatic microscopic hematuria is usually not warranted
- Strain urine: analysis of the stone may allow for tailored therapy
- Radiographic imaging: kidney–ureter–bladder (KUB) radiograph, ultrasonography or computed tomography (CT), intravenous pyelography

Urinary Retention
Urinary retention has the following presentation:
- Lower abdominal pain, hesitancy, urgency, frequency with small voids, lower abdominal pain
- Ask about history of prostatism, prostate surgery
- Can occur postoperatively after administration of general or regional anesthesia
- Urge to void with palpation of suprapubic region
- Bladder stone is a *rare* cause of urinary retention in the United States, but is much more common in less developed countries, espe-cially when protozoans are found in the water supply.

Diagnosis and treatment considerations are as follows:
- Urge to void with palpation of suprapubic region
- Ultrasound will show a very distended bladder.
- Urinary catheter is diagnostic and therapeutic.
- Leave the catheter in until the patient is evaluated by a urologist, unless postoperative (leave in 24 h)

Urinary Tract Infection
UTI has the following presentation:
- Frequency, urgency, dysuria, back/flank pain, possible cloudy malodorous or dark urine, suprapubic discomfort, pyuria
- Rule out sexually transmitted disease as cause.
Care proceeds as follows:
- Antibiotics
  ○ Trimethoprim 100 mg q 12 h × 3 days (not in formulary)
  ○ Trimethoprim-sulfamethoxazole 160/800 mg q 12 h × 3 days (not in formulary)
  ○ Levofloxacin 250 mg q 24 h × 3 days
- Pain relief: phenazopyridine 200 mg PO TID

TABLE 2-32	Management of Sexually Transmitted Diseases
Disease	Treatment
Herpes simplex 2 (genital herpes)	Acyclovir (assess patient for immunocompetence): • IV: initial episode, severe: 5 mg/kg q 8 h for 5-7 days • PO: initial episode: 200 mg q 4 h while awake (5 times/day) × 10 days • PO: recurrence: 200 mg q 4 h while awake (5 times/day) × 5 days
Condyloma acuminate (genital warts)	Chemical or physical destruction, immunologic therapy, or surgical excision
Chlamydia trachomatis	Azithromycin 1 gm PO as a single dose or Doxycycline 100 mg oral BID × 7 days (Note: doxycycline not recommended in pregnancy or if significant sun exposure is expected)

Renal Trauma

TABLE 2-33	Causes/Presentation of Renal Trauma
Renal trauma accounts for approximately 2% of all battle injuries.	
Bladder injury	Suspect in penetrating lower abdominal wounds, pelvic fractures with gross hematuria, or inability to void following abdominal or pelvic trauma
Urethral injury	• Suspected or known pelvic fracture, scrotal hematoma, blood at the meatus, rectal bleeding or a floating/high-riding prostate, inability to void • Catheterization is contraindicated until urethral integrity is confirmed via retrograde urethrogram (RUG)
Testicular pain	• Possible torsion, epididymitis, orchitis, STDs, hernia, mass, or trauma • Torsion: sudden onset of pain, pain-induced nausea/vomiting, swelling, abnormal lie of testicle; symptoms increase with elevation, activity • Epididymitis: gradual onset of worsening pain, ± fever, ± dysuria, ± trauma • Testicular tumor (usually M > 30 years old): is usually a painless mass, found incidentally; may first be noticed on self-exam after trauma

Care of renal trauma includes the following elements:

ABCs: conduct a primary/secondary assessment.

Inspect abdomen/flank: look for symmetry and ecchymosis over posterior ribs 11 and 12.

Palpate the abdomen, flank, lower rib cage, and lower vertebrae:

- Pain, masses (tamponade or perirenal hematoma), crepitus, bony deformation
- Gross hematuria is usual diagnostic clue

During trauma evaluation, place a urethral (Foley) catheter unless contraindicated.

- Contraindications include blood at the meatus, perianal or scrotal hematoma, or other signs of pelvic instability.
- If the patient has a urethral injury, a surgeon/urologist should place the urethral catheter as appropriate.

Retrograde urethrogram (RUG) should be performed first if there is blood at the meatus, a high-riding prostate, or other evidence of urethral injury.

- Obtain a kidney-ureter-bladder (KUB) plain film first; then place a 14-16 Fr urethral catheter (primed with contrast to rid air) in the urethra past the balloon. Add 1-2 cc saline to fill the balloon snugly in the fossa navicularis. A pelvic film in a semi-lateral position is obtained after injecting approximately 30 cc of straight contrast (con-ray) under steady, gentle pressure. A study is considered normal only if contrast enters the bladder without extravasation.
- In a patient with suspected pelvic or spine injury, study in the supine position with a supine anterior-posterior (AP) or cross-table RUG.

Other diagnostics include ultrasound (not good for grading) and CT scan.

Use the following system for renal injury grading:
- Grade 1: subcapsular hematoma
- Grade 2: small parenchymal laceration
- Grade 3: deeper parenchymal laceration without entry into collecting system
- Grade 4: laceration into collecting system with extravasation; vascular injury with contained hemorrhage
- Grade 5: shattered kidney or renal pedicle avulsion

Obtain the following lab tests:
- CBC
- Chem 10
- PT
- PTT/UA
- Type and screen or type and cross-match for 4 units of blood.

Treatment considerations:
Hemodynamically stable patients may be managed without surgery. The goal is hemorrhage control, collecting system continuity, and restoration of renal blood flow.
Patients with isolated, blunt minor renal trauma (Grade I-III) may be discharged with instructions to hydrate and follow-up urologic evaluation (refer to doctor's orders). Severe renal trauma requires definitive management.

Ileal Conduit
There is no need to vent an ileal conduit collection bag for flight.

Suprapubic Catheter
Manage a suprapubic catheter as follows:
- Assess the insertion site for signs of infection, bleeding, and leakage of urine.
- Change the dressing q 24 h or prn.
- If a suprapubic tube comes out and has been present for fewer than 10 days, do not attempt to reinsert it. Call a surgeon.

References

Baker K, et al. Demographics, stone characteristics, and treatment of renal calculi at 47th Combat Support Hospital during the first six months of Operation Iraqi Freedom. *Mil Med* 2007;172(5):498-503.

Emergency War Surgery (Chapter 18), 2004. http://www.brooksidepress.org/Products/Emergency_War_Surgery/index.htm

Hudak SJ, et al. Battlefield urogenital injuries: Changing patterns during the last century. *Urology* 2005;65(6):1041-1046.

JTTS Clinical Practice Guidelines for Urologic Trauma, July 2006.

Rozanski TA, Edmondson JM. Treatment of urinary calculi in the combat zone. *Mil Med* 2005;170(6):460-461.

Wright J, et al. Sexually transmitted diseases In Operation Iraqi Freedom/Operation Enduring Freedom. *Mil Med* 2006;171(10):1024-1026.

Rhabdomyolysis

Causes of rhabdomyolysis include the following:

- Multiple trauma/compression
- Crush injuries (increased risk with prolonged entrapment)
- Severe penetrating injuries (rare)
- Vascular or orthopedic surgery (if injury involves ischemia or massive tissue injury)
- Large or deep burns
- Immobilization
- Extreme exertion
- Hyperthermia/heat stroke
- High voltage electrical injury
- Snake bite
- Drugs: alcohol, methyl alcohol ethylene glycol, aspirin cocaine, heroin, amphetamines, MDMA (ecstasy)

Signs and symptoms are as follows:

- Classic triad: muscle pain, weakness, dark urine
- Creatine kinase (CK) levels: most sensitive indicator of myocyte injury
  - Normal: 45-260 U/L; CK generally increases to > 5× normal to 10,000 U/L
  - CK rises within 12 h, peaks in 1-3 days, and then declines in 3-5 days.
  - Peak CK may be predictive of acute renal failure (> 5000 U/L is r/t renal failure).
- Myoglobin: appears in urine (myoglobinuria–reddish/brown urine) when plasma level > 1.5 mg/dL
- Positive urine dipstick for blood with no red blood cells on micro exam is diagnostic.

Rhabdomyolysis is associated with the following complications:

- 10-50% of patients will develop acute renal failure.
- Hyperkalemia, hypocalcemia, hypercalcemia: avoid calcium administration during ARF

- Elevated liver function tests (LFTs)
- Cardiac arrhythmias, cardiac arrest
- Disseminated intravascular coagulation (DIC)

To prevent and treat acute renal failure, use these measures:
Early fasciotomies for crush, ischemia, or injured muscle can minimize or prevent rhabdomyolysis.
Early volume resuscitation consists of normal saline 1-2 L/h until blood pressure is stabilized and UOP is established or signs of fluid overload develop.

- Goal UOP: 2 mL/kg/h (200-300 mL/h) until myoglobinuria resolves and serum CK > 5000 U/L
- Start volume resuscitation as early as possible—before crushed body part is relieved.
- Place urinary catheter after evaluation for pelvic trauma/urethral damage.

Mannitol may be as effective as aggressive fluid resuscitation (based on small retrospective studies and animal data).

- 1 gm/kg IV over 30 min or 25 gm IV followed by 5 gm/h IV
- Total dose: 120 gm/day

The effectiveness of sodium bicarbonate urine alkalinization is based on small retrospective studies and animal data.

- Use caution: This treatment may increase the patient's risk of hypocalcemia.
- Add one ampule sodium bicarbonate (NaHCO$_3$) to 1 L normal saline (NS) or 2-3 ampules in 1 L D$_5$W at 100 mL/h; maintain urine pH > 6.5 and serum pH at 7.40-7.45.
- In patients with CK > 5000 IU/L, bicarbonate/mannitol (BIC/MAN) did not prevent renal failure, dialysis, or mortality (Brown et al., 2004)
- Alkaline diuresis may be protective in cases of rhabdomyolysis from prolonged entrapment

Furosemide may be given if UOP is not adequate despite adequate volume resuscitation. This drug has equivocal effectiveness and may acidify urine.
Dialysis is a possible treatment but is not available in AOR.

- Hyperkalemia: for rapid/temporary decrease in potassium treat with IV insulin/IV glucose: bolus 10 units regular IV plus 50 mL D$_{50}$, followed by glucose infusion (to prevent hypoglycemia).

References

Bagley WH, et al. Rhabdomyolysis. *Intern Emerg Med* 2007;2(3):210-218.
Brown CV, et al. Preventing renal failure in patients with rhabdomyolysis: Do bicarbonate and mannitol make a difference? *J Trauma* 2004;56(6):1191-1196.

■ Heat-Related Injuries

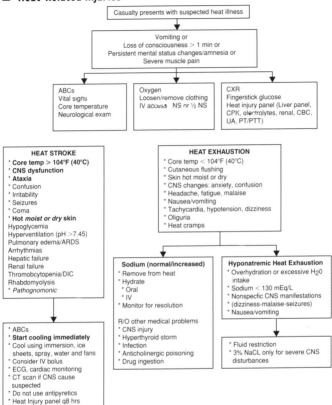

FIGURE 40 Management of suspected heat casualties.
Source: Data from U.S. Army Research Institute of Environmental Medicine. Heat Stress Control and Heat Casualty Management (TB MED 507/AFPAM 48-152). USARIEM, Natick, M.A. (2003).

Mild Heat Illness

Treat mild heat illness as follows:

Place the patient at rest in a cool environment.

Use the patient's core temperature as a guide.

Ensure adequate hydration:
- Oral rehydration: if casualty is alert and not at risk for vomiting, give 1 tsp salt/quart H_2O or sports drink.
- IV: 250–500 mL NS bolus until symptoms resolve; generally require 1–2 L. After 2 L, the type of IV fluid should be guided by lab analysis of sodium/potassium/bicarbonate.

Follow-up lab values include electrolytes with creatinine and a liver function panel with CK.

The patient should rest overnight in cool environment and avoid maximal exercise for several days.

Hyponatremic Exertional Heat Exhaustion

This type of heat-related illness is due to excessive hypotonic fluid intake (water) or excessive sodium loss. Treat the patient with fluid resuscitation.

- Normal saline or 3% saline and free water restriction
  - Rate of correction 1–2 mEq/L/h (do not exceed 2.5 mEq/L/h; do not increase sodium > 8–12 mEq/L over 24 h)
  - Estimated sodium deficit = total body water × (desired sodium – actual sodium)
  - Total body water ≈ lean body weight × 0.5 (women) or 0.6 (men)

Example: 90-kg male with sodium = 118 mEq/L; desired 130 mEq/L

Sodium deficit = 90 × 0.6 (130 – 118) = 648 mEq

3% saline = 0.5 mEq Na⁺/mL

The patient requires 1296 mL 3% saline over 24–36 h.

Heat Stroke

Pathognomonic findings include hyperpyrexia (core temperature > 40°C) and CNS dysfunction; younger casualties may have hot moist or dry skin. Use the patient's core temperature; continuous temperature monitoring method is preferred.

Monitor the patient's glucose as it may vary depending on the cause of the heat stroke: hypoglycemia (exertional heat stroke) and hyperglycemia (classic heat stroke).

KCl replacement should be with NS or ½ NS with ECG monitoring. Cooling methods should be performed as quickly as possible. There is no evidence to suggest that any one method is superior to the others, but avoid methods leading to peripheral vasoconstriction.

- Evaporative heat loss: spray lukewarm water (15–40°C) on naked casualty (or wrap in gauze) and fan with room temperature or 45°C air

- Immersion: leads to more rapid heat loss than evaporation; may be used for patients < 35-45 years; may be poorly tolerated in elderly patients
  - Field-expedient solution: dig a pit and line it with plastic (cool earth will cool water)
  - Place the casualty on stretcher and lower the buttocks and lower back into iced water and continuously massage extremities
  - Approximate cooling time 10-60 min
  - Can be performed with casualty in clothes; allows for culturally appropriate care
- Ice packs to groin/axilla/neck: effective but not well tolerated In awake casualty
- Wrap extremities in wet single layer of sheet or cotton underwear and fan the air at room temperature or apply cooling blanket

There is no consistent evidence regarding when to stop cooling. TB MED 507/AFPAM 48-152 recommends stopping when the patient's core temperature reaches 101°F (38.3°C).

In case of shivering, give lorazepam (Ativan) 1-2 mg IV or diazepam (Valium) 5 mg IV.

Antipyretics are ineffective in case of heat stroke and may exacerbate renal/hepatic dysfunction.

In heat stroke, the hemodynamic profile is generally consistent with distributive shock.

- Evaluate for comorbidities.
- No specific resuscitation regimen; consider using guidelines for septic shock hemodynamic support

The vasopressor of choice is dopamine. Avoid an alpha-adrenergic agonist (e.g., norepinephrine).

Rhabdomyolysis may be severe with exertional heat stroke. (See the "Soft-Tissue Trauma" section for its management.)

References

Bouchama A, et al. Cooling and hemodynamic management in heatstroke: Practical recommendations. *Crit Care* 2007;11:R54-R64.

Gardner JW, Kark JA. Clinical diagnosis, management and surveillance of exertional heat illness. *Med Aspects Harsh Environ* 2001;1:231-279.

Glazer JI. Management of heatstroke and heat exhaustion. *Am Family Phys* 2005;71(11):2133-2140.

Surgeon General of the United States. NOTAM: Change to heat stroke symptoms in the airman's manual, May 1, 2007.

Technical Bulletin: Heat Control and Heat Casualty Management. TB MED 507/AFPAM 48-152(1).

Heat Index

Dry Bulb Temperature

°F	80	82	84	86	88	90	92	94	96	98	100	102	104	106	108	110
°C	26.7	27.8	28.9	30	31.1	32.2	33.3	34.4	35.6	36.7	37.8	38.9	40	41.1	42.2	43.3

Relative Humidity (%)

RH	80	82	84	86	88	90	92	94	96	98	100	102	104	106	108	110
40	80	81	83	85	88	91	94	97	101	105	109	114	119	124	130	136
45	80	82	84	87	89	93	96	100	104	109	114	119	124	130	137	
50	81	83	85	88	91	95	99	103	108	113	118	124	131	137		
55	81	84	86	89	93	97	101	106	112	117	124	130	137			
60	82	84	88	91	95	100	105	110	116	123	129	137				
65	82	85	89	93	98	103	108	114	121	128	136					
70	83	86	90	95	100	105	112	119	126	134						
75	84	88	92	97	103	109	116	124	132							
80	84	89	94	100	106	113	121	129								
85	85	90	96	102	110	117	126	135								
90	86	91	98	105	113	122	131									
95	86	93	100	108	117	127										
100	87	95	103	112	121	132										

Likelihood of heat disorders with prolonged exposure or strenuous activity:

Caution   Extreme caution   Danger   Extreme danger

FIGURE 41 Heat index chart, NOAA National Weather Service.
Source: Courtesy of the National Weather Service/NOAA.

Windchill Chart

$$\text{Wind Chill (°F)} = 35.74 + 0.6215T - 35.75(V^{0.16}) + 0.4275T(V^{0.16})$$

Where, T= Air Temperature (°F)   V= Wind Speed (mph)   *Effective 11/01/01*

Frostbite Times: 30 minutes   10 minutes   5 minutes

Temperature (°F)

Wind (mph)	Calm 40	35	30	25	20	15	10	5	0	-5	-10	-15	-20	-25	-30	-35	-40	-45
5	36	31	25	19	13	7	1	-5	-11	-16	-22	-28	-34	-40	-46	-52	-57	-63
10	34	27	21	15	9	3	-4	-10	-16	-22	-28	-35	-41	-47	-53	-59	-66	-72
15	32	25	19	13	6	0	-7	-13	-19	-26	-32	-39	-45	-51	-58	-64	-71	-77
20	30	24	17	11	4	-2	-9	-15	-22	-29	-35	-42	-48	-55	-61	-68	-74	-81
25	29	23	16	9	3	-4	-11	-17	-24	-31	-37	-44	-51	-58	-64	-71	-78	-84
30	28	22	15	8	1	-5	-12	-19	-26	-33	-39	-46	-53	-60	-67	-73	-80	-87
35	28	21	14	7	0	-7	-14	-21	-27	-34	-41	-48	-55	-62	-69	-76	-82	-89
40	27	20	13	6	-1	-8	-15	-22	-29	-36	-43	-50	-57	-64	-71	-78	-84	-91
45	26	19	12	5	-2	-9	-16	-23	-30	-37	-44	-51	-58	-65	-72	-79	-86	-93
50	26	19	12	4	-3	-10	-17	-24	-31	-38	-45	-52	-60	-67	-74	-81	-88	-95
55	25	18	11	4	-3	-11	-18	-25	-32	-39	-46	-54	-61	-68	-75	-82	-89	-97
60	25	17	10	3	-4	-11	-19	-26	-33	-40	-48	-55	-62	-69	-76	-84	-91	-98

FIGURE 42 Wind chill chart, NOAA National Weather Service.
Source: Courtesy of the National Weather Service/NOAA.

Temperature Conversion

Celsius (C) = 5/9 (F − 32)
Fahrenheit (F) = (9/5 C) + 32

F	32	40	50	60	70	80	82	84	86	88	90
C	0	4.4	10	15.6	21.1	26.7	27.7	28.9	30	31.1	32.2

F	92	94	96	98	100	102	104	106	108	110
C	33.3	34.4	35.6	36.7	37.8	38.9	40	41.1	42.2	43.3

■ Hypothermia Treatment

For further guidance on hypothermia prevention and treatment, see
JTTS Clinical Practice Guidelines for Hypothermia Prevention, Monitoring and Management, October 2006.

Hypothermia Prevention

*The following measures must be immediately implemented across
the theater of operations until further notice (implementation date:
October 2006):*

- Temperature dots must be placed on all immediate/urgent litter
  casualties (forehead) at Level II and during CASEVAC to Level III.
- Keep EMT/OR temperature at > 85–90°F during casualty resuscitation.
- Use warmed IV fluids, warm blankets and, where available, forced-air
  warming devices (Bair Hugger) prn.
- Mandatory documentation of patient temperature on arrival and
  discharge from all Level II and III facilities. If the patient's non-core temperature (oral, axilla, tympanic) is high or low, use the core temperature
  (rectal, esophageal).
- Use of hypothermia prevention/management kits (HPMK) is mandatory for all rotary-wing evacuation/ground evacuation for urgent
  litter or intubated or immediate triage category casualties (Level I-II
  and Level II-III).

Use the following equipment for hypothermia prevention in any patient
who has suffered hypotension (SBP < 90 mm Hg), is intubated, has
received > 1000 mL of fluid, or has received a blood transfusion. Use in
a layered fashion across the evacuation chain.

TABLE 2-34 Hypothermia Prevention Equipment

	Description/Comments
Blizzard rescue blanket	Baffled reflective blanket—shake out fully to create pockets of air inside the blanket. Reduces severity of hypothermia, but should be used in combination with active warming methods.
TechTrade "Ready-Heat" blanket	Self-contained blanket—activated with exposure to air. Heats to 40°C in ~30 min, lasts ~8 h. Use in combination with passive warming methods. Approved for use in AE. Must place clothing or layer of sheet between Ready-Heat and patient's skin.
Thermo-Lite Hypothermia Prevention System cap	Use in combination with blizzard rescue blanket and TechTrade Ready-Heat blanket.
Space blanket (heavy duty)	Single-layer reflective blanket. Use in combination with active warming methods; is not effective alone.
Wool blanket (green)	Use in combination with active warming methods; is not effective alone. Warm blankets increase patient comfort but do not prevent hypothermia or rewarm patients.
Hypothermia Prevention and Management Kit	Includes a blizzard rescue blanket, TechTrade Ready-Heat blanket, and Thermo-Lite Hypothermia Prevention System cap.
Thermal Angel	Portable fluid warmer. Battery lasts through 2 units of 4°C blood. Use for bolus fluid administration only; is not effective for slow rates (e.g., 100 mL/h). Combine with passive warming methods.
Belmont FMS 2000	Requires electricity. Effective in preventing hypothermia. Use in fixed medical facility.
Bair Hugger	Requires electricity. Effective in preventing hypothermia. Use in fixed medical facility. Not approved for use in AE.
Temp Dots	Use in field for initial temperature monitoring.

Passive warming methods alone (e.g., wool blankets, space blankets) are not effective in preventing hypothermia. A combination approach using a passive warming method plus an active warming method (e.g., Ready Heat, Thermal Angel, Chillbuster, Belmont FMS) is effective in preventing hypothermia. These devices should be either disposable or PMI, exchanged upon transport.

FIGURE 43 Example of combined hypothermia prevention intervention including the blizzard rescue blanket, Ready-Heat blanket, and Thermo-Lite Hypothermia Prevention System cap. With the Ready-Heat blanket, a sheet or clothing must be placed between the device and the patient's skin. Place the Ready-Heat blanket on the patient's back/chest and wrap the patient in Blizzard Blanket.
Source: Courtesy of North American Rescue, Inc.

TABLE 2-35 Levels of Hypothermia Prevention				
Levels of Hypothermia Prevention	Level 1	Level IIa	Level IIb/III	Any Evacuation Platform
Hypothermia Prevention and Management Kit	X	X		X
Blizzard Rescue Blanket	X	X	X	X
TechTrade Ready-Heat blanket	X	X	X	X
Thermo-Lite Hypothermia Prevention System cap	X	X	X	X
Thermal Angel		X	X	X
Bair Hugger		X	X	
Temp Dots			X	
Belmont FMS 2000			X	
Foley Temp Sensing Kit			X	X

Notes:
1. Use Hypothermia Prevention and Management Kit or combination (blizzard blanket + Ready-Heat blanket + Thermo-Lite Hypothermia Prevention System cap).
2. Level IIa: Use Thermal Angel and Bair Hugger.
3. Level IIb/IIIa: Keep EMT/OR temperature at 78–90°F; use warmed IV fluids and blankets; use Bair Hugger + Thermal Angel or Belmont FMS.
4. Any evacuation platform: Use Thermal Angel + blizzard blanket.

Care under fire:
- Get the patient to cover.
- Stop any life-threatening external bleeding.

Tactical field care proceeds as follows:

- All attention should be directed toward preventing heat loss.
- Stop the patient's bleeding and resuscitate appropriately. If available, use warm fluids.
- Place Thermo-Lite HyPothermia Prevention System cap on the patient's head.
- Place the patient on the Blizzard Rescue Blanket.
- Remove any wet clothing and replace it with dry clothes, if possible.
- Place the Ready-Heat blanket on the torso and back of the patient, *with a layer of clothing or a sheet between the patient's skin and the blanket.*
- Wrap the Blizzard Rescue Blanket around the patient.
- If you do not have a survival blanket of any kind, then find dry blankets, poncho liners, space blankets, sleeping bags, body bag, or anything that will retain heat and keep the casualty dry.
- Place a temperature dot on the forehead of the patient for continuous monitoring.

CASEVAC considerations:

- During CASEVAC, the patient should remain wrapped in the Ready-Heat blanket, Blizzard Rescue Blanket, and hypothermia cap.
- If these items are not available, check with the air crew to see if they have them or any other similar items that can be used to prevent heat loss.
- Wrap the casualty in dry blankets and try to keep wind from open doors from blowing over or under the casualty.
- Use a Thermal Angel or other portable fluid warmer on all IV sites.

Here are some field-expedient "tricks of the trade":

- Warm IV fluids using two MRE heaters (sandwich an IV bag between heaters and insert back into MRE packet).
- Use a "hot pocket": Wrap the patient in a wool blanket and/or space blanket and place in a body bag, leaving the patient's face exposed.

■ Infection Control/Infectious Diseases

TABLE 2-36 Infection Control Precautions

Precautions	Gloves	Mask/Eye Shield	Gown	Comment
Standard	Touching blood, body fluids (B/BF), contaminated items, mucous membranes, or nonintact skin	During care activities likely to generate splashes or sprays of B/BF, secretions, especially during suctioning, intubation	When contact with B/BF, secretions, or excretions is anticipated	Wash hands between each patient whether or not gloves have been worn. Wear gloves when preparing/handling unwrapped food items.
Contact	When providing direct care in the immediate environment	Whenever procedures are performed that may cause splashes of B/BF	When providing direct care in the immediate environment	Private room or cohort with limited providers. Austere environment: Hang sheets around the bed in an open ward and enforce precautions when entering/exiting the "room." Examples: hemorrhagic fever (e.g., Ebola, Lassa, and Marburg), risk for colonization or infection with MDRO, *C. difficile*, acute diarrhea in incontinent patient, RSV, croup or bronchiolitis in young infants, skin infection (e.g., impetigo, major abscess, cellulitis, or decubiti), staphylococcal furonculosis, pediculosis, scabies or cutaneous infections with *C. diphtheriae*, Herpes simplex virus, zoster.
Droplet	When entering the room or if the patient is not in a room when in the immediate environment	Within 3 feet. Patient wears a surgical mask during transport. Request patient to cough/sneeze in a tissue.		Should be in a private room or cohort with limited providers. Austere environment: Hang sheets around the bed in an open ward and enforce precautions when entering/exiting the "room." Examples: meningitis, (suspected) invasive infection with *Haemophilus influenzae* type B or Neisseria meningitides, diphtheria, *M. pneumoniae*, pertussis, influenza, adenovirus, mumps, parvovirus B19, rubella, streptococcal pharyngitis, pneumonia, scarlet fever in young children.

(Continued)

TABLE 2-36   Infection Control Precautions (Continued)

Airborne	When in the immediate environment or times when in the immediate environment. Patient wears N95 during transport.	Fit-tested N95 mask or higher at all times when in the immediate environment. Patient wears N95 during transport.	Examples: pulmonary or laryngeal (suspected) tuberculosis, measles, varicella; disseminated zoster.

Austere Settings (Consult with Public Health)

Tent with patients with the same airborne-transmitted diseases should be placed downwind of the main care facility. Avoid grouping respiratory patients with infections due to different etiologies.

- Enteric outbreaks: Cohort patients with the same known/suspected diagnosis who are in the same stage of the disease.
- AE considerations:
  1. Infectious patients on a ventilator have a HEPA filter connected to the suction and ventilator expiratory ports. Secure ventilation tubing connections and use in-line suctioning.
  2. Austere ground settings (Ambus, tent): Patient with potential for airborne transmission wears an N95 mask and is placed in a low-traffic area, lowest litter position, near the air flow exit, and away from other patients/personnel. When in confined areas and/or in areas with poor air circulation, the patient and healthcare worker wear N95 masks. Refer to AFI 41-307, Aeromedical Evacuation Patient Guidelines and Standards of Care.

Sources: J. D. Siegel, et al. 2007 Guideline for Isolation precautions: Preventing transmission of infectious agents in healthcare settings, June 2007, http://www.cdc.gov/hicpac/pdf/isolation/Isolation2007.pdf; Diagnosis and treatment of diseases of tactical importance to central command. USACHPPM Technical Guide 273. October 2005, http://www.cdc.gov/flu; CDC medical care of ill disaster evacuees, http://www.bt.cdc.gov/disasters/medcare.asp.

Clean Hands Save Lives

Hand hygiene is the most important method for preventing the spread of infection:

- Hand washing: Wash hands with bacterial/nonbacterial soap and *clean* running water for at least 15 seconds if hands are visibly soiled or contaminated with blood or body fluids. Not effective against C. *difficile* spores.
- Alcohol-based solution: Use if hands are not visibly dirty.

When possible, dedicate patient-care equipment to a single patient or a cohort of patients who are infected or colonized with a multidrug-resistant organism (MDRO). If use of common equipment is unavoidable, then adequately clean and disinfect items before use for another patient with approved hospital germicide (refer to local policy).

Follow these recommendations if bedpans must be shared:

- Use of bedpans for several patients is accomplished by lining bedpans with a plastic bag and taping the bag securely to prevent slippage and spillage.

- Dispose of waste via a toilet, then carefully remove bag, keeping the soiled portion of the bag to the inside, roll/gather the bag closed and dispose of it as hazardous waste.

Do not share linen among patients.

Wound Management/Dressing Changes

Cohorting: Separate long-term (> 72 hours) and short term (< 72-hour stay) patients when possible to reduce the risk of cross-contamination with resistant hospital-associated organisms. Patients with known or suspected MDRO infections (*C. difficile*, MRSA), should be separated from the noninfected patients.

Skin care: All ICU patients should undergo a daily SAGE "bath" unless the patient refuses or has a sensitivity. On arrival bathe the patient to remove visible dirt using soap/water with 30 mL Hibiclens diluted in the basin. Avoid facial wounds and 2nd/3rd degree burns. Wait 6 hours after initial bath and bathe patient with Antiseptic Body Cleaning Washcloths once a day (see JTTS CPG for specific steps).

Source: Petersen K, et al. Trauma-related infections in battlefield casualties from Iraq. *Ann Surg* 2007;245(5):803-811.

Antibiotics used for prophylaxis or to treat wound infection should be directed by local policy (See JTTS CPG: Guidelines to Prevent Infection). The goal is to effectively prevent/treat infection but to avoid inappropriate use of antibiotics to decrease the risk of developing resistant organisms.

Acinetobacter baumannii

A. baumannii is a gram-negative bacterium that is found in water and soil. It spreads via exposure to the environment, person-to-person contact (inadequate hand washing and colonized skin), or contact with contaminated surfaces. Suspect this infection in all combat wounds until proven otherwise.

A. baumannii may be an MDRO; use cultures to guide therapy. *The key is prevention.*

Antibiotic use should be directed by local policy. Consult with an infectious disease MD as necessary.

Implement Contact Precautions.

For extended care, cohort patients if single rooms are not available.

If *A. baumannii* is sensitive to antibiotics, contact isolation may not be necessary. Consult with an Infection Control Nurse or Infectious Disease Physician.

References

Acinetobacter baumannii infections among patients at military medical facilities treating injured U.S. service members, 2002-2004. *MMWR* 2004;53:1063-1066.

Scott P, et al. An outbreak of multi-drug resistant *Acinetobacter baumannii-calcoaceticus* complex infection in the US military healthcare system associated with military operations in Iraq. *Clin Infect Dis* 2007;44(12):1577-1584.

Cholera

Contact a public health officer immediately if cholera is suspected.

Ingestion of *Vibrio cholerae* may occur via contaminated water and food or through direct oral-fecal contamination in areas with inadequate clean (potable) water. This pathogen is a potential biological warfare threat.

Onset of the disease occurs 2 h to 5 days after contamination.

Signs and symptoms are as follows:

- Mild or profuse amounts of "rice-water" diarrhea with or without vomiting, abdominal pain
- Severe cases: fluid loss > 5–10 L/day, severe dehydration, ↑ HR, ↓BP, lethargy

Prevention consists of providing potable water and ensuring adequate toilet/sanitation facilities. Mass chemoprophylaxis is not effective in preventing infection.

Treatment includes the following measures:

Isolate/cohort patients.

Use Standard and Contact Precautions–stool and emesis are highly infectious.

The majority of patients can be treated with oral rehydration salts (ORS) according to the World Health Organization:

- Recipe: NaCl, 2.6 gm; trisodium citrate dehydrate, 2.9 gm; KCl, 1.5 gm; anhydrous glucose, 13.5 gm. Dilute in 1 L potable water (http://www. who.int/medicines/publications/pharmacopoeia/OralRehySalts.pdf).
- If ORS packets are not available, add ½ small spoon salt + 4 big spoons sugar to 1 L potable water.
- Excellent resource to guide ORS volume requirements: http://www. who.int/child-adolescent-health/publications/CHILD_HEALTH/ WHO_FCH_CAH_06.1.htm.

Ringer's lactate is the preferred IV fluid; give as 100 mL/kg in 3-h period.

Give antibiotics in severe cases to diminish the duration of diarrhea, decrease the volume of rehydration fluids needed, and shorten the duration of Vibrio excretion. Consult with infectious disease specialist for specific recommendations.

References

http://www.cdc.gov/travel/yellowBookCh4-cholera.aspx

http://www.who.int/topics/cholera/publications/en/first_steps.pdf

Leishmaniasis

Leishmaniasis is a parasitic disease spread by the bite of infected sand flies (¼ the size of typical mosquitoes). It is endemic to the Middle East and Central/South America.

Sand fly season in Iraq is April to November; the peak is September to October. Flies are most active from dusk to dawn.

Prevention is key:

- Stay in air conditioning or well-screened structures.
- Wear long sleeves/pants and socks.
- Use insect repellents and treat clothing with permethrin insecticides per IAW command directives.
- Avoid dogs and rodents.
- Sleep in treated bed netting if sleeping outside.

The infection may spread via contaminated needles and blood transfusions.

Three types of infection are distinguished:

Cutaneous

- Most common; either painful or painless
- Lesions start as papules that often enlarge/rise, then ulcerate in the center—"volcano" like
- Lesions may be surrounded by concentric silvery scales or pink plaques, may have enlarged lymph nodes near lesions.

Visceral:

- Accounts for 90% of cases in Iran, India, Bangladesh, Nepal, Sudan, and Brazil
- Signs and symptoms: fever, weight loss, hepato/splenomegaly, swollen glands, anemia, leukopenia, thrombocytopenia, and elevated liver function tests
- Onset: weeks to months

Mucocutaneous:

- Found in Central/South America (Bolivia, Brazil, Peru)
- Occurs if a cutaneous lesion on the face spreads to involve the nose or mouth
- May occur months to years after the original skin lesion

References

Confer with Infectious Disease consultants at WRAMC: http://www.pdhealth.mil/leish.asp
http://www.cdc.gov/ncidod/dpd/parasites/leishmania/factsht_leishmania.htm

Malaria

Malaria is a mosquito-transmitted parasitic disease that is endemic throughout the tropics and in some temperate regions (Figure 44). Worldwide 300-500 million cases of malaria occur annually, causing as

many as 2 million deaths. In U.S. military personnel, a small number of
cases have been reported in Afghanistan, Korea, and Guam.
Four species cause malaria: *Plasmodium falciparum*, *P. malariae*,
P. ovale, and *P. vivax*. The incubation period is 7-30 days following
infective bite (depending on the species).
Humans are the primary reservoir for malaria, but there is no
human-to-human transmission of the disease.
Malaria has the following clinical presentation (maintain a high index of
suspicion in endemic regions):

- Fever, chills, profuse sweats, headaches, nausea/vomiting, body
  aches, general malaise, splenomegaly
- Additional findings in *P. falciparum*: mild jaundice, hepatomegaly,
  tachypnea
  - Sequelae with severe malaria caused by *P. falciparum*: cerebral
    malaria (mental status changes, decreased level of consciousness,
    seizures, coma); pulmonary edema, coagulopathy, severe anemia,
    hemoglobinuria, shock

Diagnosis requires confirmation with blood smear.
Presumptive treatment without a confirmed diagnosis is not generally
recommended. Treatment depends on the infecting species, the clinical
status of the patient, and knowledge of the geographic area where the
infection was acquired. Consult with an infectious Disease specialist
and refer to the CDC guidelines (http://www.cdc.gov/malaria/diagno-
sis_treatment/tx_clinicians.htm).

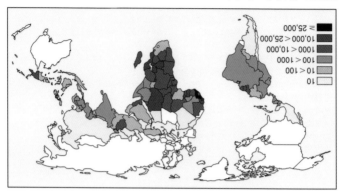

FIGURE 44 Distribution of malaria.
Source: Data from the WHO/Malaria Department.

References
Centers for Disease Control and Prevention, Malaria, http://www.cdc.gov/malaria/

Diagnosis and Treatment of Diseases of Tactical Importance to Central Command. USACHPPM Technical Guide 273. October 2005 (http://chppm-www.apgea.army.mil/)

USACHPPM. Deployment Medication Information Sheets. http://chppm-www.apgea.army.mil/dmis/ (Note: This site offers excellent teaching tools for prevention.)

USACHPPM. Just the Facts: Malaria. http://usachppm.apgea.army.mil/documents/fact/18-040-0107_malaria.pdf

Mycobacterium Tuberculosis (TB)

The initial infection may be asymptomatic. Later signs and symptoms of TB include the following:

- Fever (may be intermittent)
- Night sweats
- Anorexia and weight loss
- Fatigue
- Cough—productive or nonproductive for more than 3 weeks
- Hemoptysis
- Chest pain (pleuritic)
- Dyspnea

Diagnosis is made with the following techniques:

- Skin testing: positive PPD. As many as 25% of individuals with pulmonary disease will have a negative PPD. PPD may be negative in early-stage disease.
- Chest radiograph: depends on the character and extent of the disease.
- Invasive procedure: bronchoscopy or gastric aspirate if no sputum can be produced.

Treatment:

For U.S. military personnel, treatment is generally not started in the theater unless the patient presents with indications of disseminated disease or they are otherwise unstable. Consult with an infectious disease specialist for management of patients in the theater.

Take the following precautions when TB is suspected or confirmed:

- Persons with suspected or confirmed infection should wear a surgical mask when contact with other personnel is likely.
- Personnel in contact with individuals with suspected or confirmed infection should wear N95 masks. When masks are not available, consider conducting evaluations outdoors, where UV light will kill the infectious organism.
- Avoid use of unpasteurized dairy products.

References
Centers for Disease Control and Prevention, Division of Tuberculosis Elimination. http://www.cdc.gov/tb/

Diagnosis and Treatment of Diseases of Tactical Importance to Central Command. USACHPPM Technical Guide 273, October 2005. http://chppm-www.apgea.army.mil/

Guidelines for preventing the transmission of Mycobacterium tuberculosis in health care settings–2005. *MMWR* 2005;54(RR17):1-141. http://www.cdc.gov/mmwr/preview/mmwrhtml/rr5417a1.htm?s_cid=rr5417a1.htm?s_cid=rr5417a1.e

Norwalk Virus

During September 2-12, 2005, approximately 6500 of the estimated 24,000 evacuees from Hurricane Katrina who were sheltered at the Houston Astrodome visited the Reliant Park medical clinic; 1169 (18%) persons reported symptoms of acute gastroenteritis. An outbreak of norovirus gastroenteritis might have affected approximately 1000 evacuees and relief workers in three facilities at Reliant Park and other Houston evacuation facilities.

The Norwalk virus is the most common cause of acute outbreaks of gastroenteritis in the United States. In 2002-2003, it also caused out-breaks in military personnel in Afghanistan.

Indications of an outbreak include the following signs and symptoms:

- Acute onset of vomiting and/or nonbloody diarrhea lasting 12-60 h, with an incubation period of 24-48 h
- Acute outbreak of gastroenteritis in crowded setting; rapid transmission

Treatment consists of the following measures:

- Rapid rehydration (oral or intravenous depending on the severity of dehydration)
- Antibiotic therapy; there are resistant strains, so therapy is guided by cultures

It is important to prevent secondary transmission of the Norwalk virus by taking the following steps:

- Contact isolation
- Proper hand washing
- Cleaning/disinfecting soiled surfaces (consult with Public Health/infection control specialists)

References

Norovirus in Health Care Facilities: Fact sheet. http://www.cdc.gov/ncidod/dhqp/id_norovirusFS.html

Norovirus outbreak among evacuees from Hurricane Katrina–Houston, Texas, September 2005. http://www.cdc.gov/mmwr/preview/mmwrhtml/mm5403a3.htm

Outbreak of acute gastroenteritis associated with Norwalk-like viruses among British military personnel–Afghanistan, May 2002. *MMWR* 2002;51(22):477-479.

Thornton SA et al. Gastroenteritis in US Marines during Operation Iraqi Freedom. *Clin Infect Dis* 2005;40:519-525.

Q Fever

Q fever is caused by rickettsia (*Coxiella burnetii*). The pathogen may be obtained by inhalation of contaminated aerosols or handling of infected material–organisms are found in the urine, feces, milk, and birth products of infected cattle, goats, and sheep. On rare occasions, infection develops after ingestion of contaminated milk. Person-to-person transmission has rarely occurred, though the pathogen may be transmitted via breast milk. Person-to-person transmission should be considered a possibility for medical personnel performing obstetrical procedures on infected pregnant women. Q fever is a potential biological warfare agent.

Signs and symptoms:
- Sudden onset of high fever (104–105ºF), fatigue, severe headache, chills and/or sweats, myalgia, nausea, vomiting, diarrhea, and abdominal and pleuritic chest pain
- Hepatomegaly, splenomegaly

In the event of suspected or confirmed Q fever, implement Isolation Precautions; Standard Precautions may be used during health care.

Treatment includes the following measures:
- Doxycycline: the treatment of choice (consult with an Infectious Disease specialist)
- Antibiotic therapy most effective if initiated within first 3 days of illness

References

Centers for Disease Control and Prevention. Bioterrorism: Q fever. http://www.bt.cdc.gov/agent/qfever/

Centers for Disease Control and Prevention. Q fever. http://www.cdc.gov/ncidod/dvrd/qfever/index.htm (for naturally occurring Q fever)

Diagnosis and Treatment of Diseases of Tactical Importance to Central Command. USACHPPM Technical Guide 273, October 2005. http://chppm-www.apgea.army.mil/

Heyman DL. *Control of Communicable Diseases Manual*, 18th ed. APHA, 2004.

■ Mental Health

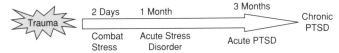

FIGURE 45   Stages of traumatic stress.

Combat/Ongoing Military Operation Stress (COSR)

Symptoms of COSR may occur after any life trauma event *and* may result from accumulating stress:
- Exhaustion/burnout
- Hyperarousal and anxiety
- Somatic complaints (GI, GU, CV, respiratory)
- Behavior changes
- Emotional dysregulation
- Anger/irritability
- Depression, guilt, or hopelessness

- Conversion disorder symptoms
- Amnestic and/or dissociative symptoms
- Brief, manageable "psychotic symptoms" (e.g., hallucinations, sleep deprivation, mild "paranoia")

In such a case, secure all weapons, ammunition, and explosives to eliminate opportunities for violence.

Assessment of COSR considers the following factors:
- Risk of harm to self or others; personal safety
- TBI/exposure to explosion/blast
- Primary/secondary assessment
- Hypoxia or infection
- Neurotoxicant exposure
- Use of over-the-counter and prescription drugs
- Substance/alcohol abuse (toxicology screen)
- History: stressors, function and/or impairment on operation or mission

Questions to Consider

"In your life, have you ever had any experience that was so frightening, horrible, or upsetting that, in the past month, you . . ."
- Had nightmares about it or thought about it when you did not want to?
- Tried hard not to think about it or went out of your way to avoid situations that reminded you of it?
- Were constantly on guard, watchful, or easily startled?
- Felt numb or detached from others, activities, or your surroundings?

A positive response is a "yes" answer to any three of the above items. Contact local mental health or chaplain services or advanced practice provider for assistance.

Acute interventions for COSR include the following measures:
- Treat the person according to his or her prior role and not as a "patient."
- Provide a reunion or contact with the primary group.
- Provide a respite from intense stress. The patient should avoid further traumatic events until he or she is recovered for full duty.
- Provide thermal comfort, oral hydration and food, hygiene, sleep (rest and restoration), and social/spiritual support.
- Consider medication, but avoid benzodiazepines.
- Provide voluntary group debriefings for members of preexisting and continuous groups. Avoid individual debriefings.
- Assign appropriate limited-duty tasks and recreational activities that will restore the patient's focus and confidence and reinforce teamwork.
- *Always include commanders in planning the best care approach during all aspects of care, especially for transfer to definitive care.*

Suspected Substance Abuse
- Hyperarousal
- Agitation
- Anxiety
- Nausea and vomiting
- Increased heart rate and temperature
- Weakness
- Diaphoresis
- Dilated/reactive pupils
- Major: "shakes," seizures, and hallucinations; symptoms of organ damage: brain syndrome, cirrhosis, esophageal varices

Detoxification follows IAW Theater Policy. Symptoms of withdrawal typically last 5-7 days. Evacuation usually occurs after the 3- to 5-day detoxification period.

Assess the patient for risk of suicide, self-harm, or violence:
- Personal safety a concern due to impaired cognition
- Alone and able to care for himself or herself
- Medications or weapons/ammunition available that could result in dangerous behavior
- Hopelessness; substance abuse disorder
- Failure at important personal endeavors
- Disruption of important personal relationships
- Expressed thoughts of potential harm to self or others; expressed great hostility toward political or prominent figures
- Current suicidal/homicidal ideas/plans
- History of suicidal behavior, violence, or impulsivity
- Presence of active mental illness (depression or psychosis): hears voices or sees visions that are telling person to harm self or others

The presence of definite intent (suicidal/homicidal ideation, intent, and/ or plan) to harm self or others requires voluntary/involuntary emergency inpatient psychiatric treatment.

Anger
Military veterans and individuals who encountered a major stressful event often experience anger afterward. Symptoms include a racing heart, thoughts of revenge, and feelings of betrayal; these symptoms may be experienced prior to an angry outburst.

Recognize as early as possible the person's point in the anger cycle and take active steps to avoid escalation to aggression (e.g., by taking a timeout, using relaxation strategies). Refer the patient to a local mental health professional as needed.

Verbal De-escalation

- Speak in a calm, matter-of-fact voice.
- Acknowledge the patient's struggles:
  - "What you are experiencing is more common than you think. Would you like to talk about it?"
  - "The deployments have been stressful for a lot of people."
  - "How has this experience been for you?"
  - "What can I do to make this easier for you?"
- Remind the patient that he or she is in a safe place and the patient's care and well-being are top priorities.
- Re-explain operational constraints, timelines, medical procedures, and the need for medication.
- Ask (or remind) the patient where he or she is right now. Reorient the patient as needed.
- If the patient is experiencing flashbacks, remind him or her where the patient is at a specific time in a specific place (grounding).
- Offer fluids and comfort items.
- Ask if prn medication would be helpful.
- Implement a verbal contract with the patient, with an explanation of consequences for not changing behavior.

Patient's Verbal Contract for Safety

- Patient agrees to notify medical team/attendant/escort of active suicidal/homicidal thoughts and/or need for medication.
- Patient accepts limits (i.e., stays within patient care area, escort for meals, toileting).
- Patient understands consequences for not changing behavior: medical team taking control, medication, and/or physical restraint if considered a threat to self or others.

Transferring to Definitive Care

- Reassess the patient, provide appropriate care (treat hypoxia; give medication; have one-on-one, verbal contract), and report/document interventions throughout the continuum.
- Safeguard the patient's personal dignity; show respect for his or her cultural, psychological, and spiritual values; and ensure the personal safety and the safety of others.
- Maintain strict confidentiality and release medical records and information only on a need-to-know basis. This is particularly important for individuals with legal, financial, or domestic difficulties.
- **Work with commanders** for the best care/approach.

Documentation

- Assessment, including results of a brief neurological exam, pulse oximetry, and behavior
- Justification for medication and/or restraint application
- Date/time of notification of the physician
- For women of childbearing age, last menstrual period
- Date/time of administration medication and/or application of restraints and outcome

TABLE 2-37 Side Effects of Antipsychotic Drugs

Drug/Dose Range	EPS	Anticho-linergic	Orthos-tatic/Hypostatic	Sedation	Comments
Conventional Antipsychotics					
Chlorpromazine PO: 10-25 mg q 4-6 h IM: 25-50 mg q 3 h	++	+++	+++	+++	Also for hiccups
Loxapine PO: 10-25 mg × 2 or 4 daily	++	+++	+	+	
Haloperidol PO: 0.5-5 mg × 2-3 daily; maximum dose = 100 mg/day IM: 2-5 mg q 1-8 h	+++	+	+	+	
Second-Generation Antipsychotics					
Clozapine Start: 12.5 mg × 1 or 2 daily; up to 150-600 mg/day	0/+	+++	+++	+++	Monitor for agranu-locytosis; seizure risk
Risperidone PO: 1 mg × 2 daily; increased slowly up to 8 mg daily	+	+	++	+	
Olanzapine PO: 5-25 mg daily IM: 2.5-10 mg; maximum dose = 10 mg q 2-4 h × 3)	+	+/++	+	+++	Upper-level dosages may be ap-propriate; monitor for hypoten-sion
Quetiapine PO: 25-100 mg × 2-3 times daily; increased slowly up to 800 mg	0/+	+	++	++	Observe for cataracts
Ziprasidone Start: PO: 20 mg × 2 daily; increased slowly up to 160 mg daily	+	+	+	+	Mild QT prolonga-tion; give with food

0 = none
+ = mild
+ = moderate
+++ = severe

Source: Adapted from Veterans Administration/U.S. Department of Defense, Clinical Practice Guideline Management of Psychoses Pocket Guide. http://www.oqp.med.va.gov/cpg/PSY/G/PsychPoc.pdf

Extrapyramidal Symptoms (EPS)

High-potency conventional neuroleptics (haloperidol, chlorpromazine) may cause EPS within hours or a few days after starting medication.

Symptoms are as follows:

- Tightness/stiffness of the muscles, particularly the jaw, neck, back, and arm muscles
- Opisthotonus (tetanic spasm in which the spine and extremities are bent with convexity forward; body rests on head/heels), oculogyric crisis (extreme, sustained upward deviation of the eyes), laryngeal dystonia, and Parkinson-type symptoms
- Arrhythmias, hypotension, respiratory suppression, and oversedation

In case of EPS, hold the patient's medication, provide supportive care, notify the physician, and document your actions. If previously untreated EPS symptoms are present on a preflight basis, the patient is not considered to be stable.

Neuroleptic Malignant Syndrome (NMS)

NMS is a rare, life-threatening emergency. Body temperature ≥102°F along with mental status change, rigidity, tachycardia, and labile BP while on antipsychotic medications (particularly haloperidol). If these symptoms appear, hold medication and treat supportively. Document and notify a physician. If NMS occurs preflight, the patient is not stable.

Patients Requiring Restraints

Restraints may be necessary for emergent and dangerous behavior—that is, when a patient poses an immediate danger to self and others, or the patient is too agitated/violent to be given sedatives.

- Perform a brief neurological exam and rule out hypoxia.
- Always use the least restrictive means for controlling behavior: verbal de-escalation, medication, education/counseling, and family/unit involvement. Note that any history of physical or sexual abuse may affect reactions to physical contact and place the individual at greater psychological risk.
- Restraints will not be applied as punishment or for medical team/crew convenience.
- A physician's written order is required for the initial application and continuation of restraints. PRN orders are prohibited.
  - Within 24 h and based on age, restraints are limited:
    - 4 h for adults
    - 2 h for children and adolescents age 9-17
    - 1 for patients younger than age 9

A physician will perform a face-to-face reassessment of the patient to determine whether restraints are to be continued.

Ongoing Assessment When Leather Restraints are On

Perform the following monitoring when leather restraints are used:
- Perform neurovascular assessment q 15 min.
- Maintain line-of-sight observation.
- Assess toileting and nutritional needs and offer fluids q 2 h.
- Change position, and remove one extremity restraint at a time to check skin integrity; perform skin care to the area and range of motion (ROM) exercises q 2 h.
- Monitor I&O if in four-point restraints for more than 24 h.

Other Types of Restraints for Managing Patients at Risk for Dislodging Vital Therapeutic Devices

Warning: These types of restraints are not routinely used in-flight because they are secured to the litter. Be readily available to untie or cut the restraint.

Mitten/Glove
- Wash and dry the patient's hands; roll up a washcloth or gauze pad and place in palm; close the patient's hand over the pad and restrict arm movement as required. Remove every two hours to reassess and allow for range of motion (ROM) exercise.
- Perform circulation and neurological assessments of all extremities with devices q 60 min (minimal requirement).
- Maintain line-of-sight observation (minimal requirement).

Vest and Soft Restraints
- Perform circulation and neurological assessments of all extremities with devices, and safety checks q 60 min.
- Maintain line-of-sight observation.

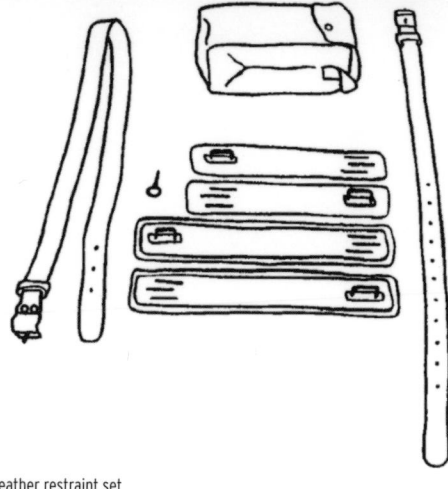

FIGURE 46A   Leather restraint set.

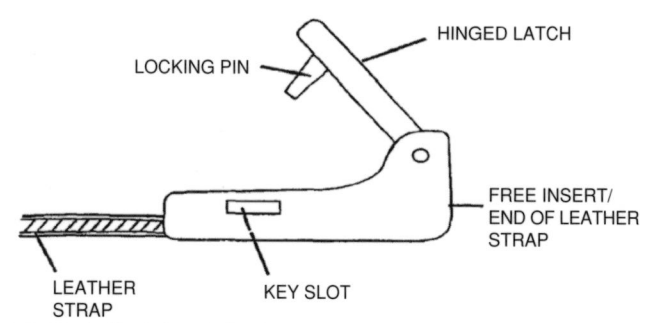

FIGURE 46B   Locking device on leather straps.

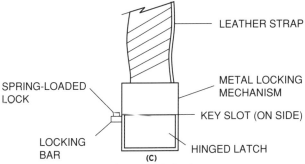

FIGURE 46C Leather restraint set, locking device on leather straps.
Source (for parts A-C): U.S. Air Force. Aeromedical Evacuation Equipment Standards (AFI-309). October 15, 2001.

Preparing for Application of Leather Restraints

- Inspect the short and long straps, and all cuffs, for cuts, tears, and excessive wear.
- Confirm that compatible restraint keys are available, the locking devices function, and caregivers know their location.
- Assemble a team of at least three individuals current in leather restraint application; one is the team leader.

Application of Leather Restraints

Four individuals are needed to apply leather restraints in emergency situations.

1. Place cuffs around the wrists and ankles, with the padded side toward the patient.
   - Attach smaller cuffs to wrists; metal loop faces palmar aspect of the wrist.
   - Attach larger cuffs above ankles; metal loop faces medial aspect of the lower leg.
   - Remove bulky material and footwear above the ankle (boots).
2. Push a metal loop through one of the three slots. The cuff should be snug but not constricting.
3. Place the long strap:
   - Hold the metal buckle and thread the other end through the metal loop of one of the wrist cuffs. Keep the locking device on lateral side of patient—it protects the medical staff.
   - Bring the strap across the abdomen, insert the end through the metal loop on the other cuff, and continue around the back. *Warning:* Do not secure the restraint straps to or around the litter.
   - Thread the strap through the buckle and adjust it to allow enough movement that the patient can touch nose.

- Depress the small round metal post on the side of the locking hinge until it is flush with the square metal bar and push the metal bar in. This locks the locking mechanism.

4. Place the short strap:
   - Thread the strap through the ankle loops, leaving a length of approximately 12 inches for walking.
   - Lock the device.

5. Pad all restraint cuffs when feasible.

6. Assess extremity neurovascular status, and then repeat the assessment q 15 min.

Source: Joint Commission, Behavioral Health Care Restraint and Seclusion, April 2005. http://www.jointcommission.org/AccreditationPrograms/Hospitals/Standards/FAQs/Provision+of+Care/Restraint+and+Seclusion/Restraint_Seclusion.htm

En Route/AE Patient Preparation

- Litter (1A/1B) patients: PJs/robe and appropriate footwear—no boots.
- May carry eyeglasses, toothbrush, and a small amount of money (not to exceed $25.00), wedding band, rings, wristwatch, ID card, and wallet.
- Uniforms should be packed in checked baggage.
- Inpatient psychiatric patients will not carry own medications or self-medicate.
- Use AF Form 3899, PMR for restraint orders/observation, and medication administration.
- Search all baggage and person for sharps, matches, lighters and cigarettes, and medication. Ask the patient. Items not allowed will be inventoried and accounted for.
- Some patients who may not need restraints in an MTF may present a clear risk to flight safety and require restraints.
- Use AF IMTS 3899F Physician Orders for Behavior Management and Restraints for 1A patients.
- For patients in leather restraints, use AF IMT 3899G, Patient Movement Observation Flow Sheet.

Stresses of Flight

The decrease partial pressure of O_2 and low humidity onboard aircraft exacerbate the effects of medication.

- Sedation: ↓ level of consciousness and respiratory rate/volume; encourage deep-breathing, monitor respiratory rate, monitor UOP, and give O_2 if pulse oximetry < 91%
- Give PO fluids and offer toileting q 2 h.
- If overly sedated, hold medication, document, and notify physician.

Noise, fatigue, prolonged confinement in the aircraft, and vibration may increase irritability, confusion, and the occurrence of agitation and hallucinations.

Healthcare Worker/Provider Care

It is important to cultivate a professional culture in which people take regular breaks, get reasonable sleep and food, and have regular contact with their own colleagues, friends, and family to support their continued work with casualties and their families.

Work schedules may be 12-hour shifts, six days per week. When there's a lull, being "on call" may be appropriate.

Find relaxing activities away from people you work and live with. E-mail, call, or write family and friends; encourage "care packages" from home. Such contact reduces feelings of isolation.

Symptoms of burnout include feeling strained by having to work with people, increasing difficulty sustaining concentration and attention levels throughout prolonged periods of work, decreasing memory for work-related details, and reacting to challenges with increasing cognitive rigidity rather than with cognitive flexibility.

■ Neurological

Spinal Immobilization/Application of Spinal Board

- Approach the patient in his or her direct view and instruct the patient not to move.
- A rescuer (team leader) stabilizes the patient's head (front or behind).
- Add padding behind the head to maintain proper alignment prn: Maintain the opening of the external auditory canal in-line with the point of the shoulder, and keep the face mid-line to prevent hyperextension/hyperflexion.
- Assess motor and sensory functioning.
- Assign at least three assistants to perform the following tasks:
  - Remove neck chains/dogtags.
  - Apply and secure the appropriate-size rigid cervical collar.
  - Place the patient's arms at his or her sides and straighten the legs; immobilize/splint prn.
  - Logroll the patient using three rescuers: Maintain the head/chin in mid-line position, and turn the body as a "unit."
  - Inspect the back/posterior legs.
  - Position the backboard behind and close to the patient.
  - Logroll and reposition the patient onto the center of the backboard as a "unit."
  - Place the backboard straps to encircle the patient's (1) shoulders, (2) hips, and (3) legs, proximal to knees.
  - Place lateral head support devices.
  - Place tape across the patient's forehead to secure the head. Do *not* place tape across the chin.

- Continue to maintain manual stabilization of the head/neck until the patient is fully secured to the board.
- After the patient is fully secured to board, reassess motor and sensory functioning.
- Release manual stabilization measures.

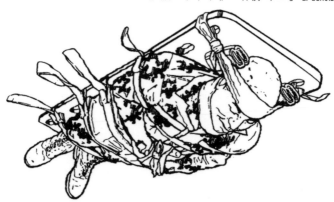

FIGURE 47 Example of field expedient spine immobilization.

Cervical-Collar Application

This description is meant as an example only. The actual procedure may vary depending on the brand of c-collar. Follow the manufacturer's guidelines.

- One rescuer manually stabilizes the head and neck in a neutral position throughout the process.
- A second rescuer sizes the collar:
  - Using the rescuer's hand/fingers, measure the distance horizontally just below the patient's chin to the shoulder.
  - Compare the finger distance with the collar "sizing reference" to the bottom of collar panel, not including the foam.
  - Adjust the collar size by unlocking tabs; move the collar up or down to achieve the desired size. Relock the tabs.
  - Pre-form the collar (roll, squeeze).
- Slide the rear panel behind the patient's neck (supine) or apply collar around the neck (upright). Place the chin support well under the chin. Maintain a neutral position of the patient's chin and neck. Adjust the c-collar's size, as needed.
- Hold the front panel in place and secure it until the c-collar is snug, but not tight or constricting. Fasten the strap.
- Reassess the patient's neurological status.

TABLE 2-38 Vacuum Spine Board	
Indications	Thoracolumbar Fracture that is Potentially Unstable
Transport considerations	• Patient in VSB must be transported by CCATT • Theater spine surgeon/CCATT must agree on suitability of VSB deflation and log rolling to reduce stress on pressure points
Pressure ulcer prevention	• Log rolling in a VSB without deflation does not decrease skin pressure • Padding/pressure reduction should be considered under occiput/heels • Maximum transport time without deflation: 10 h • If transport time > 10 h, CCATT should oven valve, release straps, log roll patient (maintain proper alignment) and provide adequate time for relief of pressure points as part of their normal turning schedule

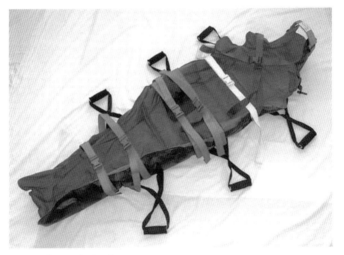

FIGURE 48   Vacuum spine board.

Neurological Assessment

- ABCs
- History of event/mechanism of injury
- Signs and symptoms (history): loss of consciousness, amnesia, neck or head pain, numbness

- Level of consciousness (AVPU):

  Alert

  Verbal (responds to verbal stimuli)

  Pain (does not respond to verbal stimuli/responds to painful stimuli)

  Unresponsive (does not respond to painful stimuli)

- Pupil reactivity to light: note pupil size, reactivity (brisk, sluggish, or nonreactive), and accommodation to light

Pupil Scale in Millimeters

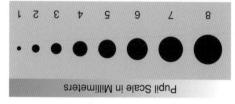

8   7   6   5   4   3   2   1

FIGURE 49   Pupil scale (millimeters).

TABLE 2-39   **Glasgow Coma Scale**

Each score is given for the patient's *best* response. The range of possible scores is 3–15.

Adult		Child	
Eye Opening (Note if eyes are swollen/injured.)			
Opens spontaneously	4	Opens spontaneously	4
Opens to verbal stimulation	3	Opens to verbal stimulation	3
Opens to pain	2	Opens to pain	2
None	1	None	1
Verbal Response (Note if an ETT or tracheostomy is present.)			
Oriented	5	Appropriate words/coos	5
Confused	4	Inconsolable cry to pain	4
Inappropriate words	3	Persistent cry to pain	3
Incomprehensible	2	Moans to pain	2
None	1	None	1
Motor Response			
Obeys command	6	Spontaneous movement	6
Localizes pain	5	Localizes pain	5
Withdraws to pain	4	Withdraws to pain	4
Flexion to pain	3	Flexion to pain	3
Extension to pain	2	Extension to pain	2
None	1	None	1
Total		**Total**	
15: Normal			
≤ 14: Abnormal; rule out TBI and/or other			
≤ 8: Airway compromised–protect airway			
3: Severe brain injury			

If the patient is chemically sedated, paralyzed, or intubated, he or she is scored as 3T.

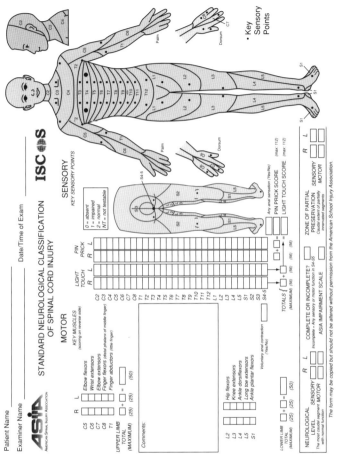

FIGURE 50   Spinal cord assessment.
Source: Reproduced from American Spinal Injury Association: International Neurological Classification of Spinal Cord Injury, revised 2002, Chicago, IL.

Spinal Cord Injury

This discussion is based on the standards developed by the American Spinal Injury Association.

To conduct a sensory examination, assess dermatomes for light touch, pinprick and external anal sphincter sensation (prn).

Light Touch

Use a cotton swab or cotton strand on a cotton applicator swab.

- 0 = Absent
- 1 = Impaired (any sensation that differs from sensation on a normal area)
- 2 = Normal
- NT = Not tested

Pinprick

Lightly touch the sharp end of a safety pin to the patient's face (normal) and dermatomes.

- 0 = Absent (includes sensation of being touched but not sharpness or inability to differentiate dull from sharp)
- 1 = Abnormal (sensation is somewhat sharp, but not as sharp as the normal area or sharper than the normal area)
- 2 = Normal (sensation in area tested is the same as the normal area)
- NT = Not tested

Anal Sphincter

- Test for light touch and pinprick.
- Using a gloved finger, apply pressure (any pressure sensation indicates an incomplete injury).

To conduct a motor examination, test 10 myotomes and assign one of the following grades. Assign a score of 0–4 only if the muscle is neurologically weak, not in case of weakness due to disuse.

- 0 = Total paralysis (no visible or palpable contraction)
- 1 = Palpable or visible muscle contraction
- 2 = Active movement, full ROM with gravity eliminated
- 3 = Active movement, full ROM against gravity
- 4 = Active movement, full ROM against full resistance
- 5 = Normal active movement, full ROM against full resistance

TABLE 2-40	Motor Examination	
Vertebral Level	Dermatome Level	Associated Function
C4	–	Spontaneous ventilation
C5	Clavicles/upper arm (lateral)	Shoulder abduction/shoulder shrug/elbow flexors
C6	Thumb/forearm	Supination/wrist extension
C5–C7	Lateral upper limbs/middle finger	C7: wrist flexion, elbow extensors
C8	Ring and little finger	Finger flexors (distal phalanx of middle finger)
T1	–	T1: finger abductors (little finger)
T2	Axilla/upper arm/medial	–
T4	Nipple line	–
T7	Xiphoid/epigastrum	–
T10	Umbilicus level	–
		T1–T12: accessory respiratory and abdominal muscles

(Continued)

TABLE 2-40	Motor Examination (*Continued*)	
T12	Inguinal/groin area	–
L1-L4	Anterior/inner lower limbs	L2: hip flexors L3: knee extension L4: ankle dorsiflexion
L4-L5, S1	Lower leg/foot	L5: long toe extensors S1: ankle plantar flexors
S3-S5	Perineum	

3 Question DVBIC TBI Screening Tool
Instruction Sheet

Purpose and Use of the DVBIC 3 Question TBI Screen

The purpose of this screen is to identify service members who may need further evaluation for mild traumatic brain injury (MTBI).

Tool Development

The 3 Question DVBIC TBI Screening Tool, also called the Brief Traumatic Brain Injury Screen (BTBIS), was validated in a small, initial study conducted with active duty service members who served in Iraq/Afghanistan between January 2004 and January 2005.

Schwab, K.A. Baker, G., livins, B., Sluss Tiller, M., Lux, W., & Warden. D.(2006), The Brief Traumatic Brain injury Screen (BTBIS): Investigating the validity of a self-repost instrument for detecting traumatic brain injury (TBI) in troops returning from deployment in Afghanistan and Iraq. *Neurology*: 66(5)(Supp. 2), A235.

Who to Screen

Screen should be used with service members who were injured during combat oprations, training missions or other activities.

Screening Instructions

Question 1: A checked [√] response to any item A through F verifies injury.

Question 2: A checked [√] response to A-E meets criteria for a positive (+) screen. Further interview is indicated. A positive response to F or G does not indicate a positive screen, but should be further evaluated in a clinical interview.

Question 3: Endorsement of any item A-H current symptoms which may be related to an MTBI if the screening and interview process determines a MTBI occurred.

Significance of Positive Screen

A service member who endorses an injury [Question 1], as well as an alteration of consciousness [Question 2 A-E], should be further evaluated via clinical interview because he/she is more highly suspect for having sustained an MTBI or concussion. The MTBI screen alone does not provide diagnosis of MTBI. A clinical interview is required.

For more information contact:
Telephone: 1-800-870-9244   Email: info@DVBIC.org   Web: www.DVBIC.org

FIGURE 51 DVBIC TBI screening tool.
Source: Defense and Veterans Brain Injury Center, 3 Questions DVBIC TBI Screening Tool [www. dvbic.org].

3 Question DVBIC TBI Screening Tool

1. Did you have any injury(ies) during your deployment from any of the following?
(check all that apply):

A. Fragment
B. Bullet
C. Vehicular (any type of vehicle, including airplane)
D. Fall
E. Blast (Improvised Explosive Device, RPG, Land mine, Grenade, etc.)
F. Other specify: _____

2. Did any injury you received while you were deployed result in any of the following?
(check all that apply):

A. Being dazed, confused or "seeing stars"
B. Not remembering the injury
C. Losing consciousness (knocked out) for less than a minute
D. Losing consciousness for 1–20 minutes
E. Losing consciousness for longer than 20 minutes
F. Having any symptoms of concussion afterward
(such as headache, dizziness, irritability, etc.)
G. Head Injury
H. None of the above

> NOTE: Endorsement
> of A–E meets criteria for
> positive TBI Screen

> NOTE: Confirm F and G
> through clinical interview

3. Are you currently experiencing any of the following problems that you think might be related to
a possible head injury or concussion?
(check all that apply):

A. Headaches
B. Dizziness
C. Memory problems
D. Balance problems
E. Ringing in the ears
F. Irritability
G. Sleep problems
H. Other specify: _____

Military Acute Concussion Evaluation (MACE)

Defense and Veterans Brain Injury Center

Patient Name: _____

SS#: _____-_____-_____ Unit: _____

Date of Injury: ____/____/_____ Time of injury: _____

Examiner: _____

Date of Evaluation: ____/____/____ Time of Evaluation: _____

History: (I – VIII)

I.   Description of Incident
     Ask:
     a) What happened?
     b) Tell me what you remember.
     c) Were you dazed, confused, "saw stars"? ☐ Yes ☐ No
     d) Did you hit your head? ☐ Yes ☐ No

II. Cause of Injury (Circle all that apply):
     1) Explosion/Blast   4) Fragment
     2) Blunt object   5) Fall
     3) Motor Vehicle Crash   6) Gunshot wound
     7) Other _____

III. Was a helmet worn? ☐ Yes ☐ No   Type _____

IV. Amnesia Before: Are there any events just BEFORE the
     Injury that are not remembered? (Assess for continuous
     memory prior to injury)
     ☐ Yes ☐ No If yes, how long _____

V.   Amnesia After: Are there any events just AFTER the
     Injury that are not remembered? (Assess time untill
     continuous memory after the injury)
     ☐ Yes ☐ No If yes, how long _____

VI. Does the Individual report loss of consciousness or
     "blacking out"? ☐ Yes ☐ No If yes, how long _____

VII. Did anyone observe a period of loss of consciousness or
     unresponsiveness? ☐ Yes ☐ No If yes, how long _____

VIII. Symptoms (Circle all that apply):
     1) Headache   2) Dizziness
     3) Memory Problems   4) Balance problems
     5) Nausea/Vomiting   6) Difficulty Concentrating
     7) Irritability   8) Visual Disturbances
     9) Ringing in the ears   10) Other _____

07/2007   DVBIC.org   800–870–9244
This form may be copied for clinical use.

**Military Acute Concussion
Evaluation (MACE)**

Defense and Veterans Brain Injury Center

Examination: (IX – XIII)

Evaluate each domain. Total possible score is 30.

IX. Orientation: (1 point each)

Month	0	1
Date	0	1
Day of week	0	1
Year	0	1
Time	0	1

Orientation: Total Score _____/5

X. Immediate Memory:
Read all 5 words and ask the patient to recall them in any order. Repeat two more times for a total of three trials. (1 point for each correct, total over 3 trials)

List	Trial 1	Trial 2	Trial 3
Elbow	0 1	0 1	0 1
Apple	0 1	0 1	0 1
Carpet	0 1	0 1	0 1
Saddle	0 1	0 1	0 1
Bubble	0 1	0 1	0 1
Trial Score			

Immediate Memory: Total Score _____/15

XI. Neurology Screening
As the clinical condition permits, check
Eyes: pupillary response and tracking
Verbal: speech fluency and word finding
Motor: pronator drift, gait/coordination
Record any abnormalities. **No points are given for this.**

XII. Concentration

Reverse Digits: (go to next string length if correct on first trial. Stop if incorrect on both trials) 1 pt. for each string length.

4–9–3	6–2–9	0	1
3–8–1–4	3–2–7–9	0	1
6–2–9–7–1	1–5–2–8–5	0	1
7–1–8–4–6–2	5–3–9–1–4–8	0	1

Months in reverse order: (1 pt. for entire sequence correct)
Dec-Nov-Oct-Sep-Aug-Jul-Jun-May-Apr-Mar-Feb-Jan
0   1
Concentration Total Score _____ /5

XIII. Delayed Recall (1 pt. each)

Ask the patient to recall the 5 words from the earlier memory test. (Do Not reread the word list.)

Elbow	0	1
Apple	0	1
Carpet	0	1
Saddle	0	1
Bubble	0	1

Delayed Recall Total Score _____ /5
TOTAL SCORE _____ /30

Notes: _____

_____

Diagnosis: (circle one or write in diagnoses)

No concussion
850.0 Concussion without Loss of Consciousness (LOC)
850.1 Concussion with Loss of Consciousness (LOC)

Other diagnoses _____

_____

Defense & Veterans Brain Injury Center
1–800–870–9244 or DSN: 662–6345

07/2007   DVBIC.org   800–870–9244
This form may be copied for clinical use.

119   Trauma/Medical   »   Neurological

Military Acute Concussion Evaluation (MACE)

Defense and Veterans Brain Injury Center

Instruction Sheet

Purpose and Use of the MACE

A concussion is a mild traumatic brain injury (TBI). The purpose of the MACE is to evaluate a person in whom a concussion is suspected. The MACE is used to confirm the diagnosis and assess the current clinical status.

Tool Development

The MACE has been extensively reviewed by leading civilian and military experts in the field of concussion assessment and management. While the MACE is not yet a validated tool, the examination section is derived from Standardized Assessment of Concussion (SAC) (McCrea, M., Kelly, J. & Randolph, C. (2000) the Standardized Assessment of Concussion (SAC): Manual for Administration Scoring, and Interpretation (2nd ed) Waukesa, WI: Authors.) which is a validated, widely used tool in sports medicine. Abnormalities on the SAC correlate with formal comprehensive neuropsychological testing during the first 48 hours following concussion.

Who to Evaluate

Anyone who was dazed, confused, "saw stars" or lost consciousness, even momentarily, as a result of an explosion/blast, fall, motor vehicle crash, or other event involving abrupt head movement, a direct blow to the head, or other head injury is an appropriate person for evaluation using the MACE.

Evaluation of Concussion

History: (I–VIII)

I. Ask for a description of the incident that resulted in the injury: how the injury occurred, type of force. Ask questions A–D.

II. Indicate the cause of injury.

III. Assess for helmet use. Military: Kevlar or ACH (Advanced Combat Helmet). Sports helmet, motorcycle helmet etc.

IV–V. Determine whether and length of time prior to injury and after the injury. Approximate the amount of time in seconds, minutes or hours, whichever time increment is most appropriate. For example, if the assessment of the patient yields a possible time of 20 minutes, then 20 minutes should be documented in the "how long?" section.

VI–VII. Determine whether and length of time of self reported loss of consciousness (LOC) or witnessed/observed LOC. Again, approximate the amount of time in seconds, minutes or hours, whichever time increment is most appropriate.

VIII. Ask the person to report their experience of each specific symptom since injury.

07/2007   DVBIC.org   800-870-9244

Military Acute Concussion Evaluation (MACE)

Defense and Veterans Brain Injury Center

Examination: (IX-XIII)

Standardized Assessment of Concussion (SAC)
Total possible score = 30
Orientation = 5
Immediate memory = 15
Concentration = 5
Memory Recal = 5

IX. Orientation: Assess patient's awareness of the accurate time
Ask: WHAT MONTH IS THIS?
WHAT IS THE DATE OR DAY OF THE MONTH?
WHAT DAY OF THE WEEK IS IT?
WHAT YEAR IS IT?
WHAT TIME DO YOU THINK IT IS?
One point for each correct response for a total 5 possible points. It
should be noted that a correct response on time of day must be
within 1 hour of the actual time.

X. Immediate memory is assessed using a brief repeated list learn-
ing test. Read the patient the list of 5 words once and then ask
them to repeat it back to you, as many as they can recall in any
order. Repeat this procedure 2 more times for a total of 3 trials,
even if the patient scores perfectly on the first trial.
Trial 1: I'M GOING TO TEST YOUR MEMORY. I WILL READ
YOU A LIST OF WORDS AND WHEN I AM DONE, REPEAT
BACK AS MANY WORDS AS YOU CAN REMEMBER, IN ANY
ORDER.
Trial 2 & 3: I AM GOING TO REPEAT THAT LIST AGAIN. AGAIN,
REPEAT BACK AS MANY AS YOU CAN REMEMBER IN ANY
ORDER. EVEN IF YOU SAID THEM BEFORE.
One point is given for each correct answer for a total of 15 possible
points.

XI. Neurological screening
Eyes: check pupil size and reactivity.
Verbal: notice speech fluency and word finding
Motor: pronator drift—ask patient to lift arms with palms up, ask
patient to then close their eyes, assess for either arm to "drift"
down. Assess gait and coordination if possible. Document any
abnormalities.
No points are given for this section.

07/2007   DVBIC.org   800–870–9244
This form may be copied for clinical use.

Military Acute Concussion Evaluation (MACE)

 Defense and Veterans Brain Injury Center

XII. Concentration: Inform the patient:
I'M GOING TO READ YOU A STRING OF NUMBERS AND
WHEN I AM FINISHED, REPEAT THEM BACK TO ME BACK-
WARDS. THAT IS, IN REVERSE ORDER OF HOW I READ
THEM TO YOU. FOR EXAMPLE, IF I SAY 7–1–9, YOU WOULD
SAY 9–1–7.

If the patient is correct on the first trial of each string length,
proceed to the next string length. If incorrect, administer the 2nd
trial of the same string length. Proceed to the next string length if
correct on the second trial. Discontinue after failure on both trials
of the same string length. Total of 4 different string lengths: 1
point for each string length for a total of 4 points.

NOW TELL ME THE MONTHS IN REVERSE ORDER, THAT IS,
START WITH DECEMBER AND END IN JANUARY.
3 points if able to recite ALL months in reverse order.
0 points if not able to recite ALL of them in reverse order.
Total possible score for concentration portion: 5.

XIII. Delayed Recall
Assess the patient's ability to retain previously learned information
by asking he/she to recall as many words as possible from the
initial word list, without having the word list read again for this trial.
DO YOU REMEMBER THAT LIST OF WORDS I READ A FEW
MINUTES EARLIER? I WANT YOU TO TELL ME AS MANY
WORDS FROM THE LIST AS YOU CAN REMEMBER IN ANY
ORDER.
One point for each word remembered for a total of 5 possible
points.
Total score = Add up from the 4 assessment domains: Immediate
memory, orientation, concentration and memory recall.

Significance of Scoring

In studies of non-concussed patients, the mean total score was 28.
Therefore, a score less than 30 does not imply that a concussion
has occurred. Definitive normative data for a "cut-off" score are
not available. However, scores below 25 may represent clinically
relevant neurocognitive impairment and require further evaluation
for the possibility of a more serious brain injury. The scoring system
also takes on particular clinical significance during serial assessment
where it can be used to document either a decline or an improvement
in cognitive functioning.

Diagnosis

Circle the ICD-9 code that corresponds to the evaluation. If loss
of consciousness was present, then circle 850.2. If no LOC, then
document 850.0. If another diagnosis is made, write it in.

MACE Form B

Due to test-retest issues (e.g., service members memorizing words and numbers), validated, alternative versions B or C should be used.

Immediate Memory

Read all 5 words and ask the patient to recall them in any order. Repeat two more times for a total of three trials. (1 point for each correct, total over 3 trials.)

List	Trial 1	Trial 2	Trial 3
Candle	0 1	0 1	0 1
Paper	0 1	0 1	0 1
Sugar	0 1	0 1	0 1
Sandwich	0 1	0 1	0 1
Wagon	0 1	0 1	0 1
Total			

Concentration

Reverse Digits: (go to next string length if correct on first trial. Stop if incorrect on both trials.) 1 pt. for each string length.

5–2–6	4–1–5	0	1
1–7–9–5	4–9–6–8	0	1
4–8–5–2–7	6–1–8–4–3	0	1
8–3–1–9–6–4	7–2–4–8–5–6	0	1

Delayed Recall (1 pt each)

Ask the patient to recall the 5 words from the earlier memory test (DO NOT reread the word list.)

Candle	0 1
Paper	0 1
Sugar	0 1
Sandwich	0 1
Wagon	0 1

07/2007   DVBIC.org   800–870–9244
This form may be copied for clinical use.

Military Acute Concussion Evaluation (MACE)

Defense and Veterans Brain Injury Center

MACE Form C

Due to test-retest issues (e.g., service members memorizing words and numbers), validated, alternative versions B or C should be used.

Immediate Memory

Read all 5 words and ask the patient to recall them in any order. Repeat two more times for a total of three trials. (1 point for each correct, total over 3 trials.)

List	Trial 1	Trial 2	Trial 3
Baby	0 1	0 1	0 1
Monkey	0 1	0 1	0 1
Perfume	0 1	0 1	0 1
Sunset	0 1	0 1	0 1
Iron	0 1	0 1	0 1
Total			

Concentration

Reverse Digits: (go to next string length if correct on first trial. Stop if incorrect on both trials.) 1 pt. for each string length.

1–4–2	6–5–8	0	1
6–8–3–1	3–4–8–1	0	1
4–9–1–5–3	6–8–2–5–1	0	1
3–7–6–5–1–9	9–2–6–5–1–4	0	1

Delayed Recall (1 pt each)

Ask the patient to recall the 5 words from the earlier memory test (DO NOT reread the word list.)

Baby	0	1
Monkey	0	1
Perfume	0	1
Sunset	0	1
Iron	0	1

TABLE 2-41	Types of Brain Injuries
Primary/ secondary injury	Primary: Brain injury due to trauma, mass, hemorrhage, ischemia, infection, chemical Secondary: Progressive brain insult due to cerebral edema, hypotension, hypoxemia, intracranial hypertension, increased intracranial pressure (ICP) • Abnormal cerebral perfusion pressure • Correctable with selective interventions • Hypotension and hypoxia are the most common causes
Traumatic brain injury (TBI)	• Sudden acceleration/deceleration, penetrating/nonpenetrating forces, explosion/blast wave • Direct impact or motor vehicle/aircraft crash • May be missed, especially in the presence of other more obvious injuries: heat or toxic injury, hypovolemic shock/dehydration, eye and spinal injury, and acute stress reactions (See MACE instrument.) Due to numerous deployments and the nature of enemy tactics, troops are at risk for sustaining more than one mild TBI (mTBI) or concussion in a short time frame. Individuals who experience three of the above events during a single deployment should remain in light-duty status, be redeployed, or be evacuated.
Closed head Injury	• Concussion: transient alterations of consciousness • Cerebral contusion: focal brain injury that may be associated with cerebral tissue injury and hemorrhage
Skull fractures	• Basilar: Battle's sign (oval-shaped bruise over the mastoid) or raccoon eyes (ecchymotic areas around the eyes) • Depressed: associated with lacerations of the dura • Penetrating: due to blast injuries, gunshot wounds, and impaled objects (rocks, metal, bone) • Complications: intracranial infection, hematoma, meningeal and brain tissue damage, pneumocephalus, hemorrhage, diffuse brain injury, infection, blood behind tympanic membrane, bleeding from ears and nose, and CSF rhinorrhea and CSF from ears
Hemorrhage	• Subdural hematoma: contusion or laceration of the brain with bleeding from the bridging veins; may be associated with skull fractures • Classifications: acute (within 24 hours), subacute (2-10 days), and chronic (after 2 weeks) • Epidural hematoma: associated with blunt injuries with or without skull fractures; arterial bleeding; may be acute or delayed. Classic symptoms are a transient LOC, return to normal neurological status, and then onset of headache and decreasing LOC, with dilated ipsilateral pupil.

JTTS In-Theater Management of Mild Traumatic Brain Injury has been superseded by DTM 09-033–"Policy Guidance for Management of Concussion/Mild Traumatic Brain Injury in Deployed Setting." Military providers should refer to this official use only document for revised guidance.

Anyone involved in an explosion/blast, fall, blow to the head and/or motor vehicle crash who was dazed, confused, "saw stars" or lost consciousness (even momentarily) should be considered to have suffered a concussion.

NOTE Certain signs or symptoms will warrant a prompt medical evaluation*, potentially including neuro imaging (see Red Flags # below)

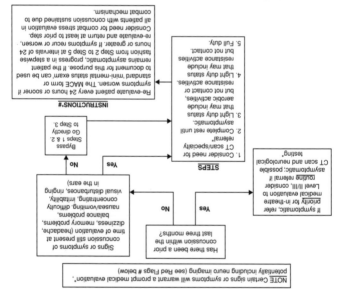

Red Flags#: Serious signs to watch for over first two days after injury:

*Neuro imaging, specialty referral and neuro testing at discretion of healthcare provider based on H&P/expertise

Refer for medical evaluation† immediately for any of the following:

Double vision	Seizures
Breathing difficulties	Slurred speech
Headache that worsens	Unsteady on feet
Can't recognize people or places/Disorientation	Repeated vomiting
Can't be awakened easily	Weakness or numbness in arms/legs
Behaves unusually or seems confused and irritable	Progressively declining neurological examination

#NOTE: any patient with concussion who is either admitted to the hospital for >24 hours or develops a Red Flag sign/symptom should remain at Step 4 and NOT be returned to full duty status or resume any "off-FOB" activity until 4 weeks from the time symptoms resolve. Casualties suffering 3 such events during a single deployment should remain in "no off-FOB activity" status, be re-deployed or evacuated.

GUIDELINE ONLY—NOT A SUBSTITUTE FOR CLINICAL JUDGEMENT AND SUBJECT TO OVERRIDING OPERATIONAL CONSIDERATIONS. Updated: August 2006

FIGURE 52 JTTS Clinical Practice Guidelines for In-Theater Management of Mild Traumatic Brain Injury (Concussion). – Superseded by DTM 09-033.

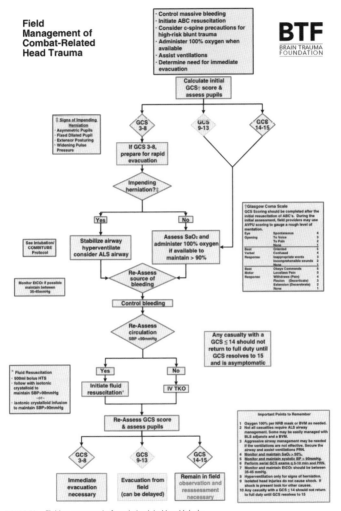

FIGURE 53 Field management of combat-related head injuries.
Source: Courtesy of the Brain Trauma Foundation [www.braintrauma.org].

TABLE 2-42. JTTS Clinical Practice Guideline for Severe Head Trauma (30 Jun 2010)

Monitoring and Lab Evaluation	General Indications
Intracranial pressure (ICP)	Glasgow Coma Score of 3-8 with an abnormal CT scan (hematomas, contusions, edema, or compressed basal cisterns) or 2 or more of the following adverse features are present in a patient with severe head injury and a normal head CT scan: (Age > 40 yr, unilateral or bilateral motor posturing, SBP < 90 mm Hg).
Arterial line	Any head trauma that requires tracheal intubation and/or for other medical indications.
Central venous pressure	When ICP or CPP management requires anything beyond simple measures and/or for other medical indications. Trendelenburg position will raise ICP. Line site of choice is SCV.
Exhaled CO$_2$	Desirable when active measures are required to control ICP. Correlate to PaCO$_2$ initially/periodically.
Neuroimaging	Noncontrast head CT upon admission then within 24 h after admission (or earlier to document stability of the bleed). Additional scans obtained as indicated (e.g., clinical deterioration).
Labs	ABG, CBC, Chem 10, TEG, PT, PTT, and INR *at least* q 8 h during the acute phases.

General Management Principles	
Philosophy	• Maintain continuous communication between the care teams. • Maintain the patient in a "hyperosmolar-but-euvolemic" state with adequate oxygen carrying capacity and a constant substrate delivery via adequate cerebral perfusion pressure (CPP) of > 60 mm Hg. • Aggressively avoid hypotension, hypoxemia, fever (> 99°F), hyponatremia and other CNS insults. • The longer the ICP is elevated (> 20), and the MAP and CPP are low (< 60), the worse the outcome! • Brain injury is heterogeneous amongst patients and the process is dynamic: Treatment and management goals must be tailored accordingly.
Resuscitation fluid	Normal or 3% saline.
Maintenance fluid	D$_5$ NS (Dextrose in maintenance fluids mandatory if insulin is utilized)
Sedation	Propofol first choice up to 72 hours. Other short-acting agents (fentanyl, Versed) upon discretion of SICU or neurosurgical staff. Typical ICU propofol sedation dose range: 20-75 mcg/kg/min.
Ulcer prophylaxis	All patients.
DVT prophylaxis	Recognize high DVT risk in traumatic brain injury patients. Intracranial neurosurgical procedures: Sequential Compression Device (SCD) with or without Graduated Compression Stocking (GCS): high risk neurosurgery patients: SCD and/or GCS. OK to use Lovenox following stable CT scan in consultation with neurosurgeon.
Seizure prophylaxis	Prophylactic anti-epileptic treatment is optional and is maintained for 7 days if no seizure activity is documented. Treat acute seizure with lorazepam 1-2 mg IV or midazolam 5-10 mg IV followed by loading dose of phenytoin 20 mg/kg infused at < 50 mg/min for fosphenytoin 20 PE (phenytoin equivalent)/kg infused at < 150 PE/min. The daily dose thereafter is 300 mg phenytoin or 300 PE fosphenytoin q HS or may be divided TID.
Antibiotics	If using antibiotic impregnated ventriculostomy, then no IV prophylactic antibiotics is required. Otherwise, Ancef 1 gm IV TID while ventriculostomy in place only (neurosurgeons' discretion). For all penetrating head trauma, use Ancef 1 gm IV TID.
Nursing	Hourly neurologic assessments. Document ICP/CPP and ventriculostomy output. Notify physician of all pertinent changes.
Steroids	Steroids are not recommended for head or spine trauma and should not be used.
Nutrition	Enteral feeding should be begun as soon as it is safe to do so. Avoid agitation/ICP during nasal or oral tube placement. Full enteral nutritional goal ≤ 7 days.

(Continued)

TABLE 2-42   JTTS Clinical Practice Guidelines for Severe Head Trauma (*continued*)

* General management goals: Goals may be individualized/altered according to specific patient requirements			
Neurologic	ICP	< 20 mm Hg	
	CPP	> 60 mm Hg	
Hemodynamic	Mean BP	Maintain to avoid ↓BP	• Hypotension (SBP < 90 mm Hg worsens mortality)
	CVP	> 5 mm Hg	• Provide a rapid physiologic resuscitation
Pulmonary	SpO₂	> 93%	Avoid routine hyperventilation
	PaCO₂	35–40 mm Hg in first 24 hours; 30–35 in first 7 days	
Hematologic	INR	≤ 1.3	Fresh frozen plasma
	Platelets	≥ 100,000 mm³	Platelets
	Hemoglobin	≥ 10 g/dL	Packed red blood cells
	TEG	Normalized values	As indicated by results
Metabolic	Glucose	> 80 < 150 mg/dL	Have low threshold for insulin drip
Renal	Serum osmolarity	> 280 & < 320 mOsm	See sodium disorders
	Serum sodium	> 138 & < 165 meq/L	

Intracranial Pressure Management (For individual patient management, consult neurosurgeon)

General Measures	Head in midline position, avoidance of tight cervical collars and tight circumferential ETT ties; elevate the head of the bed to 30 degrees. (Consider reverse Trendelenburg if suspected spine injury)
Sedation	Propofol first choice up to 72 hours. Other short-acting agents (fentanyl, Versed) upon discretion of SICU or neurosurgical staff. Typical ICU propofol sedation dose range: 20–75 mcg/kg/min. Prefer intermittent narcotics over continuous infusion.
Temperature	Aggressive temperature management. Consider cooling measures (Tylenol, cooling blanket) even for *modest* temperature elevations (> 98.6° F).
Intracranial Dynamics	• Treat sustained ICP elevations > 20 mm Hg • Always consider an expanding mass lesion with ICP elevations refractory to therapy.

Treatment Paradigm for the Traumatic Brain Injury Patient

Titrate to Effect Goal of ICP < 20 mm Hg	Ensure sedation and adequate analgesia	• Titrate lowest possible dose to achieve desired RASS score and/or BIS 60–80. • Avoid routine over sedation.
	InInitiate CSF drainage via ventriculostomy	Consider ventriculostomy drainage to control ICP to < 20 mm Hg
	Initiate osmotic therapy. Hold if [Na⁺] is > 159 and/or the SOsm is > 329	Hypertonic saline (3%): bolus therapy is 100–250 mL over 10 min and/or infusion rates range between 25–100 mL/h. As optional or adjunctive therapy consider mannitol: 0.25–1 gm/kg over < 20 minutes then 0.25 gm/kg q 6 h
	Initiate paralysis	Vecuronium: 10 mg IV push or 0.1 mg/kg. Cisatracurium (if available): Loading dose 0.2 mg/kg. Maintenance infusion rates: 1–3 mcg/kg/min
	Titrate ETCO₂	PaCO₂ ≥ 35 mm Hg

(Continued)

TABLE 2-42 JTTS Clinical Practice Guidelines for Severe Head Trauma (continued)

Cerebral Perfusion Pressure Management (CPP = MAP – ICP)

CPP Goal > 60 mm Hg	Ensure euvolemia	Utilize endpoints of resuscitation (exam, VS, arterial line, CVP, PA catheter)
	Control the ICP	• First line: 3% saline • Second line mannitol **Do not use mannitol in hypovolemic patients**
	Consider vasoactive drugs	Consider patient physiology. Vasopressin is the agent of choice, followed by phenylephrine or norepinephrine

Acute Clinical Deterioration (e.g., acute mental status change, blown pupil, or other obvious signs of cerebral herniation, new focal neurological symptoms, progressive and refractory ICP elevation)

Verify oxygenation and ventilation	
Hyperventilate (PaCO$_2$ 30-35 mm Hg to temporize only)	Uncal Herniation Syndrome • Unilaterally dilating pupil–progressing to fixed and dilated • Progressive impairment of consciousness–comatose • Contralateral Babinski's sign–contralateral weakness–bilateral decerebrate rigidity
Call neurosurgery	
Redose osmotic agent	
Arrange for emergent CT scan	

Glasgow Coma Scale	Eye Opening	Best Verbal Effort	Best Motor Effort
1	None	None	Flaccid
2	To pain	Nonspecific sounds	Decerebrates to pain
3	To verbal stimuli	Inappropriate words	Decorticates to pain
4	Spontaneous	Confused	Withdraws to pain
5		Oriented	Localizes to pain
6			Follows commands

Common Sodium Disorders Seen in Head Trauma (Discuss therapy with staff prior to initiation)

Disorder	Na$^+$	Diagnostic Clues	Treatment
SIADH	↑	Low serum Osm, usually euvolemic, ↓ Uosm	Free water restriction, hypertonic saline if severe
Cerebral salt wasting	↑	SOsm may be normal, ↓ UOP, signs of volume depletion and hemoconcentration, very high U$_{Na}$	• Volume replacement with NS or hypertonic saline • Oral sodium • Beware of rapid Na$^+$ correction
Mannitol use	↓	Polyuria, ↓ Na$^+$ and ↓Osm	Hold mannitol if SOsm > 329 mOsm; Na$^+$ > 159
Diabetes insipidus	↓	Polyuria (> 250 mL/h), ↓ Na$^+$ and SOsm > 250, U$_{spgr}$ < 1.005	DDAVP 2-4 mcg SQ/IV BID as permitted by neurosurgeon

Hypertonic (3% saline) may be delivered via peripheral IV or intraosseous access. Use for patients with moderate head injury who deteriorate and those with severe head injury
- Give 250 mL 3% saline bolus IV (children 5 mL/kg) over 10-15 minutes
- Follow bolus with infusion of 3% NaCl at 50mL/h
- If awaiting transport: check serum Na$^+$ levels every hour:
  - If Na$^+$ < 150 mEq/L, re-bolus 150 mL over 1 h then resume previous rate
  - If Na$^+$ 150-154, increase NaCl infusion 10 mL/h
  - If Na$^+$ 155-160, continue infusion at current rate
  - If Na$^+$ >160, hold infusion, recheck in 1 hour

Microsensor ICP Monitoring
Based on USAF Competency Checklist:
- Measures pressure only; no CSF drainage capability

- Placed either in the subdural space, intraventricularly, or into the brain tissue
- ICP catheters from one manufacturer are compatible only with ICP monitors from the same manufacturer
- The zero reference number is established during ICP catheter insertion and should be written on the cable connection end of the catheter; it is specific to the individual patient catheter (See the manufacturer's guidelines for the procedure to use while zeroing the monitor.)

CSF Drainage with Codman External Ventricular Drainage Device (Ventriculostomy): Codman System II and Codman EDS 3

The on/off stopcock orientation for the Codman System II and the Codman EDS 3 external drainage devices (ventriculostomies) are *opposite* of each other.

- Wash hands and use sterile technique as appropriate.
- Position the patient per doctor's orders—maintain a midline head position.
- Secure the ventriculostomy to the IV pole. If one is available, attach the leveler to the system.
- Replace all vented caps with nonvented caps.
- If the system is not primed:
  - Clamp the tubing below the collection chamber.
  - Using sterile technique and PRESERVATIVE FREE NORMAL SALINE, completely prime the tubing from the proximal end to the collection chamber. Ensure there are no air bubbles in the system.
  - Clamp the tubing between the patient and the patient's catheter.
  - Connect the ventriculostomy to the patient's catheter.
- Level the "0" (mm Hg or cm H_2O per MD orders) on the ventriculostomy system to the appropriate patient landmark (external auditory canal or as prescribed).
- Unclamp the tubing between the patient and the collection chamber.
- Confirm that all stopcocks and clamps are in the correct position for drainage.

Ventriculostomy ICP Setup/Monitoring

Source: Adapted from AF Nurse Corps competency checklist for ICP monitoring, March 2007.

ICP monitoring is to be performed only by registered nurses who have completed competency evaluation. Always follow the manufacturer's operational guidelines, especially as they relate to stopcock orientation.

- Position the patient per MD orders—maintain a midline head position.
- Secure the ventriculostomy to the IV pole.

Warning: The CSF drainage device may become inoperable and will not drain if it is inverted and the air filter becomes wet/clogged. In such a case, replace the drainage device if necessary.

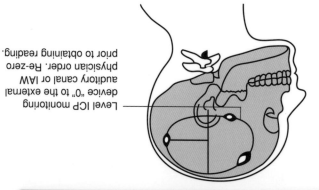

Level ICP monitoring device "0" to the external auditory canal or IAW physician order. Re-zero prior to obtaining reading.

FIGURE 54 Example of reference point for ICP monitor; reference to the external auditory meatus. Regardless of the reference level, the external transducer must be secured at a stationary point and maintained at that point for the duration of monitoring.

- Level the "0" on the ventriculostomy to the external auditory meatus.
- Adjust the height of the collection chamber to the prescribed height on scale (mm Hg or cm H_2O as prescribed).
- Using sterile technique, disconnect the transducer from an invasive pressure tubing set.
- Completely flush the transducer and collection system with *sterile preservative-free normal saline*. Ensure NO air bubbles are present.
- Attach the transducer to the port at the "0" level on the ventriculostomy system.
- Cap the distal end of the transducer and all access ports with sterile *nonvented caps*.
- Clamp the tubing above the port located at the "0" level on the ventriculostomy.
- Attach the transducer cable to monitor and "zero" it. Follow the manufacturer's instructions.
- *Warning:* Do not attach an ICP transducer to an IV pressure bag or flush fluid into the patient. *Be aware that injecting even 1 mL of fluid can lead to significant patient complications and mortality.*
- Unclamp the tubing above the port located at the "0" level on the ventriculostomy.
- Set the stopcock to "Monitor."
- Set the ICP monitor scale and alarm limits.
- CSF will drain when the stopcock is set to open to "Drain." For example, CSF will drain when the height is set at 15 mm Hg and ICP exceeds 15 mm Hg or the device is below the prescribed height.

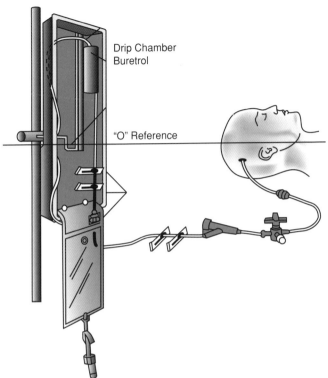

FIGURE 55 Intracerebral ventricular catheter connected to a collection chamber/system and secured (top and bottom) to an IV pole. This system uses transducer and invasive pressure monitor to measure ICP. *Source:* U.S. Department of Defense. *Emergency War Surgery Handbook.* The Borden Institute, Washington, D.C. (2006).

Continuous ICP Monitoring with Intermittent CSF Drainage

- Identify the amount (mL) of CSF to be drained over prescribed time per IAW MD's orders.
- Open the ventriculostomy to DRAIN: Set the stopcock OFF to the TRANSDUCER and ON to DRAIN.
- Observe the patency of the system and drainage characteristics.
- Close the system to drain and set it ON to MONITOR when pre-scribed parameters are met.
- Continue monitoring.

- Document ICP; CPP; MAP; CSF drainage amount, quantity, and color; and the patient's neurological status.

Continuous CSF Drainage with Intermittent ICP Monitoring
- Identify the amount of CSF drainage/monitoring parameters per IAW MD's orders.
- Close the ventriculostomy to drain: Set the stopcock off to the patient and on to the monitor.
- Return to drain: Set the stopcock off to monitor and on to drain.
- Document ICP; CPP; MAP; CSF drainage amount, quantity, and color; and the patient's neurological status.
- Double-check the stopcock orientation with another provider.

Complications of ICP Monitoring
Be alert for any of the following complications:
- Intracranial infection: Use strict sterile technique, and avoid breaching the system.
- Intracerebral hemorrhage: Observe changes in characteristics and volume of CSF drainage.
- Hematoma.
- Injury to brain parenchyma (tissue).
- Air in ventricle or subarachnoid space: Eliminate all air bubbles in tubing. Use *nonvented* caps.
- CSF leak.
- Over-drainage of CSF leading to ventricular collapse and herniation: Closely monitor the prescribed level and amount of drainage.
- Occlusion of catheter (blood, brain tissue):
  ○ Assess system patency by lowering the device below the reference level and observing 2-3 drops of CSF entering the collection chamber.
  ○ If it is clogged, the ventriculostomy may be flushed with sterile, preservative-free, physiologic saline.
  ○ Using strict sterile technique, flush away from the patient only. *Do not flush into the patient.*
- Dislodged catheter: Do not reinsert the catheter.
- Inadvertent fluid instillation. *Do not use an IV pressure bag and do not flush the line into the patient.*

Patient Movement/Aeromedical Evacuation Considerations
- The physician may elect to place the patient in a head-forward or head-aft position on the aircraft. Note that some rotary-wing aircraft fly in a "nose down" attitude; in such a case, position the patient in a head-aft/feet-forward position.

- Consider turning the ICP drainage system off to drain during take-off and landing and significant patient movement. No drainage should occur while moving the patient to the aircraft. Do not turn drainage off for more than *15 minutes*.
- Use AE-approved ICP monitoring equipment.
- Ensure cable and transducer compatibility prior to patient care hand-offs.
- Maintain any occlusive dressing. Do not remove the dressing, and reinforce it as needed.

Adult Stroke

Assessment of stroke involves assessing the ABCs and use of the Cincinnati Prehospital Stroke Scale:

Facial droop: Have the patient smile or show the teeth.
- Normal: Both sides of the face move equally.
- Abnormal: One side of the face does not move at all.

Arm drift: Have the patient close his or her eyes and hold the arms out for 10 seconds.
- Normal: Both arms move equally or not at all.
- Abnormal: One arm drifts compared to the other.

Abnormal speech: Have the patient say, "You can't teach an old dog new tricks."
- Normal: Patient uses correct words with no slurring.
- Slurred or inappropriate words or is unable to speak

Any one of these three signs is abnormal; the probability of stroke in such a case is 72%.

Source: Kothari RU, et al. Cincinnati Prehospital Stroke Scale: Reproducibility and validity. *Ann Emerg Med* 1999;33(4):374. Reproduced with permission.

Hospital assessment of an adult stroke patient includes the following steps:
- Determine when patient was last normal.
- Obtain SaO_2, vital signs, IV, labs (ABG, CBC, PT/PTT, INR, glucose, electrolytes, BUN/creatinine, blood alcohol), complete neurological exam, ECG, emergent noncontrast CT if available (for differential diagnosis of hemorrhagic versus nonhemorrhagic stroke).

Treatment of stroke involves the following measures:
- Oxygen goal: maintain $SaO_2 > 92\%$
- If patient is not a candidate for fibrinolysis (or not available), give aspirin 325 mg PO/PR.
- Treat hyperglycemia (glucose >140 mg/dL) or hypoglycemia.
- Treat fever (> 37.5°C/99.5°F); goal is to maintain normothermia.
- Investigate source of fever; give acetaminophen (1 gm 4 ×/day).

TABLE 2-43 Guidelines for Blood Pressure Control in Acute Ischemic Stroke

Blood Pressure	Treatment
SBP > 220 mm Hg or DBP > 120 mm Hg	• Do not treat blood pressure acutely with ischemic stroke unless there is other end-organ involvement (e.g., active MI, pulmonary edema, hypertensive encephalopathy, acute heart failure, aortic dissection) • Treat other symptoms of stroke (e.g., headache, pain, agitation, nausea/vomiting) • Treat other acute complications (e.g., hypoxia, ICP, seizures, hypoglycemia)
SBP > 220 mm Hg or DBP 121–140 mm Hg Goal: 10–15% ↑ BP	• Labetalol: 10–20 mg IV over 1–2 min; may repeat or double q 10–20 min; maximum dose = 300 mg • Nicardipine: infusion 5 mg/h, titrate up to desired effect by increasing 2.5 mg/h every 5 min to maximum of 15 mg/h
DBP > 140 mm Hg Goal: 10–15% ↑ BP	• Nitroprusside: 0.5 mcg/kg/min IV infusion

Source: Reproduced from 2005 American Heart Association Guidelines for Cardiopulmonary Resuscitation and Emergency Cardiovascular Care, *Circulation* 112 (2005): iv-117. Used with permission of Lippincott Williams & Wilkins. [http://lww.com]

TABLE 2-44 Guidelines for Blood Pressure Control in Acute Intracerebral Hemorrhage

Intracerebral hemorrhage	• SBP > 170 mm Hg: labetalol, nitroprusside, nicardipine (goal SBP: 140–160 mm Hg) • BP can generally be lowered by 15%
Subarachnoid hemorrhage	• If patient is alert, consider lowering blood pressure to reduce risk of rebleeding • Optimal therapy for subarachnoid hemorrhage is not yet clear • If level of consciousness is impaired, do not decrease blood pressure unless guided by ICP measurement
	Maintain CPP > 60–70 mm Hg.

Source: Broderick, J., et al., "Guidelines for the management of spontaneous intracerebral hemorrhage in adults (2007 update)." *Stroke* 38 (2007): 2001-2023.

Seizures/Status Epilepticus

Status epilepticus is characterized by ongoing seizures that persist after first- and second-line drug therapy. To manage this condition, take the follow measures:

Manage the patient's ABCs.

Assess the patient: neurological exam, SaO$_2$, labs (electrolytes, glucose, toxicology, CBC, LFTs, Ca^{++}, Mg), continuous ECG, two IV sites.

Medications:

• First line drug: lorazepam, 0.02–0.03 mg/kg IV (2 mg/min); wait 1 min, then repeat (maximum dose = 0.1 mg/kg) Alternatives: diazepam, 0.1 mg/kg IV, or midazolam, 0.05 mg/kg IV

• First line drug: Phenytoin, 20 mg/kg at 25–50 mg/min (monitor ECG/BP) and start infusion 20 mg/kg at 25–50 mg/min (incompatible with benzodiazepines)

Correct metabolic abnormalities.

If seizures are refractory to first-line drugs:

• Phenytoin, 10 mg/kg IV, and lorazepam, 0.05 mg/kg IV

• If hemodynamically stable: phenobarbital 20 mg/kg at 100 mg/min. If seizures continue, infuse a 10 mg/kg dose of phenobarbital. Additional doses of phenobarbital may be administered until the seizure stops. Closely monitor the patient's EEG (if available) and hemodynamic status. Maintenance infusion 1-4 mg/min × 24 h. Consult with a neurologist.

- If hemodynamically unstable: midazolam 0.2 mg/kg IV, followed by infusion 0.5 mg/kg/h
- If seizures persist for 45-60 min: add propofol 1-2 mg/kg/h, titrate to stop seizures

References

2005 American Heart Association guidelines for cardiopulmonary resuscitation and emergency cardiovascular care: Part 9: Adult stroke. *Circulation* 2005;112(24):IV-111-IV-120.

Adams HP, et al. Guidelines for the early management of adults with ischemic stroke: A guideline from the American Heart Association/American Stroke Association Stroke Council. *Stroke* 2007;38(5):1655-1711.

American Association of Neuroscience Nurses. Guide to the care of the patient with intracranial pressure monitoring (2005).

Defense and Veterans Brain Injury Center (DVBIC), Working Group on Acute Management of Mild Traumatic Brain Injury in Military Operational Settings. Clinical practice guidelines and recommendations (December 22, 2006). http://www.pdhealth.mil/downloads/clinical_practice_guideline_recommendations.pdf

Deployment Health Clinical Center. Traumatic brain injury. http://www.pdhealth.mil/TBI.asp

Guidelines for the acute medical management of severe traumatic brain injury in infants, children and adolescents. *Crit Care Med* 2003;4(3). (Note: This patient group is not covered in this book.)

Guidelines for field management of combat related head trauma. http://www.braintrauma.org/site/DocServer/btf_field_management_guidelines.pdf?docID=121

Guidelines for the management of severe traumatic brain injury (3rd ed). *J Neurotrauma* 2007;24(suppl 1):S1-S106.

JTTS Clinical Practice Guideline: In-theater Management of Mild Traumatic Brain Injury (concussion). http://www-nehc.med.navy.mil/Postdep/docs/Web_TBI%20clinical%20practice%20guideline%20and%20MACE1.pdf

JTTS Clinical Practice Guidelines for Adult Severe Head Trauma.

Military Acute Concussion Evaluation. http://www.dvbic.org/pdfs/DVBIC_instruction_brochure.pdf

War Surgery (Chapter 15), 2005.

■ Obstetrics

History

To find the patient's expected date of delivery (EDD), use Naegle's rule: Add 7 days and subtract 3 months from the woman's last menstrual period (LMP). Alternatively use the Rule of Nines: Add 9 to the month and day of LMP to find the due date. Primiparous women (primips—first pregnancy beyond 20 weeks gestation) compared to multiparous women (multips—more than one pregnancy beyond 20 weeks' gestation) are more likely to deliver late than early.

The following terms are used to describe phases of pregnancy:

- *Term* pregnancy: 37-42 weeks' gestation
- *Near term*: 35-36 6/7 weeks' gestation (need close attention to oxygenation, glucose levels, and temperature control of newborn)
- *Preterm*: 20 to 34 6/7 weeks' gestation

- **Viability:** generally beyond 23 weeks' gestation (more medically aggressive attempts to maintain pregnancy)

Ultrasonography is the method most commonly used to determine gestational age.

When taking the history, include pregnancy information:

- **Gravida:** number of pregnancies
- **Para:** number of gestations beyond 20 weeks
- **Abortion:** number of gestations terminated before 20 weeks gestation either spontaneously (SABs or miscarriages) or intentionally/therapeutically (TABs)
- **Current OB/medical history:** sexually transmitted diseases, preterm labor, preeclampsia (increased BP and proteinuria in pregnancy), HELLP syndrome), eclampsia (seizures with increased BP and proteinuria in pregnancy), diabetes, previa, abruption, premature rupture of membranes, multiple gestation
- **Other medical conditions,** especially cardiac disease, thyroid disease, seizures, blood dyscrasias, chronic hypertension, and neurologic and oncologic conditions
- **Previous OB history:** previous complications (same as current OB history plus preterm birth, postpartum hemorrhage, infection), and vaginal or cesarean section
- **Other significant medical/social history:** age, headache, allergies, smoking, alcohol and drug abuse, psychosocial problems

Assessment

Primary assessment (ABCD) followed by secondary assessment of the mother takes priority.

Fetal heart rate (FHR) may be heard by Doppler or ultrasound on an external fetal heart monitor. It may be documented by 11–12 weeks, but is more likely to be heard after 20 weeks. Fetal heart rate by stethoscope is generally not reliable. If you are unsure whether you are hearing fetal heart rate, place the pulse oximeter on the mother at the same time as you listen to the FHR to verify it.

- **Normal range:** 120–160 beats/minute

Documentation of fetal movement can be accomplished starting at the 20th week of gestation.

- Maternal perception of fetal movement is typically between 16 and 18 weeks for multiparous women and 18–20 weeks for primiparous women.
- There is considerable variation in fetal movement, with less occurring earlier in pregnancy, and smaller movements toward the end of a term pregnancy, when the fetus has less room.

To assess contractions:
- Note the onset, duration, frequency, and intensity of any contractions.
  - Intensity can be determined by lightly palpating the fundus of the uterus during a contraction.
  - Intensity is described as mild, moderate, or strong.
- Note the presence of back, pelvic, and/or rectal pain.
- Contractions are timed from the beginning of one to the beginning of the next.

Vaginal examination:
- Determine whether the membranes are intact. If they are not, note the time of rupture and the amount, color, and odor of vaginal discharge.
- Avoid vaginal exams unless they are clearly needed. They are uncomfortable for the woman and, if they do not change management, probably are not needed.
- If membranes are ruptured, a vaginal exam should not be performed unless it is clearly necessary, to avoid increasing the risk of chorioamnionitis.

Assess the patient for active bleeding and estimate the amount of blood loss:
- Can use pad count—number of soaked maternity pads in 2 hours
- Weigh a dry pad and then weigh a soaked pad, and subtract the dry pad weight to find the number of cc difference.

Urinalysis:
- Pregnant women normally spill protein and glucose in small amounts.
- If preeclampsia is suspected, then a 24-h urinalysis for quantitative protein is desirable.
- Evidence suggests that the ubiquitous urine dipstick is not useful.

To check the fundal height, follow these steps:
- The woman lies supine.
- Identify the symphysis pubis.
- Place the end of the tape measure against the symphysis pubis.
- Stretch the tape over the abdomen.
- Gently apply pressure and palpate for the top of the fundus.
- Estimate fundal height,
- Evaluate using a fundal growth chart.

General Interventions

Maintain adequate oxygen transport across the placenta to the fetus.
- Administer O_2 at a rate of 10-15 L/min per mask. Maintain $SpO_2 > 92\%$.

- Keep the mother off her back and in the left lateral recumbent (LLR) position if possible. Either lateral position is acceptable, though the best blood flow occurs in the LLR position.
- If the mother must be on her back, use pillow to promote uterine displacement and relieve pressure on the superior vena cava, which can lead to hypotension and decreased oxygen flow to the fetus.

General Considerations for Aeromedical Evacuation

Patients who are beyond the 34th week of pregnancy are not routinely accepted for military AE but will be moved if determined necessary by a physician.

- An incubator will be carried and ready to use on board the military aircraft.
- The commercial flight guidelines are up to 32 weeks' gestation for international flights and up to 36 weeks' gestation for domestic flights.

Patients in preterm labor or with preterm premature ruptured membranes may be airlifted after labor is controlled on a case-by-case basis. Generally, the fetus should not be compromised by stressors of flight unless the mother is compromised.

Stresses of Flight

Consult the theater flight surgeon regarding the decision to transport. The following factors are considered as part of this decision:

- Decreased partial pressure of oxygen: May cause an increase in cardiac workload. Lower concentration of O_2 to the placenta may result in fetal hypoxia. Administer O_2 (10-15 L/min per mask) if the fetus potentially could be compromised during flight.
- Barometric pressure changes: Gas expansion may cause pain and uterine irritability and decrease capacity for lung expansion. Insert an NG tube if there is a high risk for aspiration.
- Noise/vibration: May increase the risk of seizure in preeclamptic patients, and may cause uterine irritability and excessive stimulation and movement of the fetus.
- Decreased humidity: Dehydration may induce or complicate preterm contractions or preterm labor (the patient may have contractions without any cervical change). Consider having a saline lock or IV infusion of Lactated Ringer's solution during the flight.
- Fatigue: Excess weight, physiological changes, overall effects of the previously mentioned stresses, and the length of time in the AE system may fatigue the patient. Maintain adequate hydration/nutrition during the flight.
- G-forces: May push the fetus onto the maternal vena cava or the placenta. To prevent this problem, keep the mother in a left or right lateral position during flight.

The literature strongly suggests that air transport is frequently extremely valuable in obstetric emergencies, although some "emergencies"—for example, hypoxic fetuses, severe preeclamptics, or severe bleeding due to previa or abruption—may not be good candidates for transport. In contrast, patients with early preterm labor, stable preeclampsia, previas, or abruptions may be able to be transported. AE has no impact in advanced uncomplicated pregnancy. Consult with the Theater Flight Surgeon.

References

Connor SB, Lyons TJ. U.S Air Force aeromedical evacuation of obstetrical patients in Europe. *Aviat Space Med* 1995;66(11):1090-1093.

Newlands JC, Barclay JR. Air transport of passengers of advanced gestational age. *Aviat Space Med* 2000;71(8):839-842.

Gestational Diabetes

With gestational diabetes, you are unlikely to see signs of hyperglycemia in the mother, but you may see signs of hypoglycemia.

Care proceeds as follows:

- Goal: blood glucose 80 to 120 mg/dL
- Terbutaline: relatively contraindicated for patients with IDDM or gestational diabetes because of its transient hyperglycemic effects
- Continuous insulin infusion: discontinue at delivery
- Maternal blood glucose: check q 2 h; if glucose is 80-99 mg/dL, keep on D_5LR at 125 ml/h; if glucose is 100-120 mg/dL, keep on LR at 125 ml/h
- If maternal blood glucose > 120 mg/dL, may start sliding-scale insulin infusion
- If maternal blood glucose < 80 mg/dL (hypoglycemia), consult with maternal fetal expert

Severe Preeclampsia

Clinical presentation consists of new-onset proteinuric hypertension and at least one of the following signs and symptoms:

- CNS dysfunction
- Liver capsule distention (RUQ pain, N/V)
- Hepatocellular injury
- SBP > 160 mm Hg or DBP > 110 mm Hg
- Thrombocytopenia (< 100,000)
- Proteinuria (> 5 gm/24 h)
- Oliguria (< 500 mL/24 h)
- Fetal growth restriction
- Pulmonary edema/cyanosis
- Cerebral vascular accident due to severe preeclampsia clotting disorders secondary to hepatocellular injury

Care proceeds as follows:

- O_2 (10-15 L/min): to maintain SpO_2 > 92%

- Hourly checks: vital signs, I&O, neurological status, deep tendon reflexes (DTRs), pulmonary status
- Continuous fetal monitor (if available): FHR in range 120-160 without late decelerations, severe variable decelerations, or prolonged decelerations
- Seizure precautions
- Magnesium sulfate infusion:
  ○ Usually 4-6 gm bolus; then 2 gm/h
  ○ Monitor for magnesium toxicity and administer maintenance infusion only if patellar reflex present, RR > 12 bpm, and UOP > 30 mL/h
  ○ Calcium gluconate (1 gm IV over 5-10 min) should be administered only to counteract life-threatening symptoms of magnesium toxicity (e.g., cardiorespiratory compromise)
- Hypertension: labetolol, hydralazine, nifedipine
- Cardiac monitor (prn)

HELLP Syndrome
This syndrome occurs primarily in the third trimester:
- **H**emolysis, decreased hematocrit
- **E**levated SGOT/SGPT
- **L**ow platelets ($< 100,000/\mu L$)
- **P**lus hyperreflexia

Care proceeds as follows:
- Primary interventions are aimed at stabilizing the mother, assessing the fetal status, and determining if prompt delivery is needed.
- Consult with a maternal-fetal expert to guide therapy.

Preparation for transfer:
- An inpatient record and/or narrative summary is essential.
- Send IV calcium gluconate 10% solution if the patient is receiving magnesium infusion therapy.

Trauma in Pregnancy
Blunt trauma puts the patient at increased risk for traumatic placental abruption or fetal-maternal hemorrhage. Penetrating trauma puts the patient at risk for maternal shock, uteroplacental injury, or fetal injury. *Treatment priorities are the same as with a nonpregnant woman:*
- ABCs.
- Reposition the uterus in left or right lateral position.
- Laparotomy is not an indication for cesarean section.
- Placental abruption usually occurs early after injury. Monitor the FHR (if applicable) beginning as soon as the mother is stabilized and then q 6 h.
- Draw a Kleihauer-Betke blood test (if available) to see if there is fetus blood in the maternal system due to trauma.
- If CPR is needed, position the mother with a wedge to lift the uterus off the great vessels.

■ Ocular

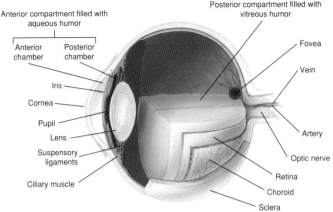

Anterior compartment filled with aqueous humor

Posterior compartment filled with vitreous humor

Anterior chamber
Posterior chamber

Iris
Cornea
Pupil
Lens
Suspensory ligaments
Ciliary muscle

Fovea
Vein
Artery
Optic nerve
Retina
Choroid
Sclera

FIGURE 56 Structure of the eye.

Assessment

For a conscious patient:

- Can the patient see? Check each eye—for example, by having the patient read a book page or newspaper.
- Eye pain or foreign-body sensation—further inspection is needed.
- PERRL: pupils equal, round, reactive to light.
- Can the patient blink/close the eye normally?
- Assess for afferent pupillary defect (Marcus-Gunn defect).

TABLE 2-45 Assessment for Afferent Pupillary Defect	
1. Conduct the assessment in a dark environment to cause dilation of the eyes.	**FIGURE 57** Pupils assessment
2. Shine a light into the unaffected eye—assess pupil constriction in both eyes.	
3. Swing the light quickly to the opposite eye: • Normal response: pupil size will not change • Abnormal response: bilateral pupil dilation (optic nerve damage)	
4. Swing the light back to the other eye—will cause bilateral pupil constriction.	

For an unconscious patient:

- PERRL
- Corneal abrasion, burn or foreign body (evert lids)
- Check that the eyelid shuts

- Assess for afferent pupillary defect (substitute for visual acuity assessment)

Visual acuity and afferent pupillary defect are the two most important measurements for predicting vision outcome in case of ocular trauma.

20/100 He told us that the
ship was never seen
again by human eyes.

20/80 Looking outside and
seeing snow made us
happy to be at home.

20/60 The speedy race car
zoomed by the crowd
for an easy victory.

20/50 The ocean waves are
high and have white
caps across the top.

20/40 My best friend goes
to second grade and
sits near my sister.

20/30 The lemonade tastes
good after the long
bike ride from town.

20/25 Collecting a set of
trading cards was a
contest in my class.

20/20 Permitting and hiking
are activities that
are offered at camp.

20/15 The ducks is softly
gliding in the water
along on the wide river.

FIGURE 58 Snellen chart.
Source: Dr. Charles Wormington. Used with permission of Tom Cockley, Gulden Ophthalmics.

General Rules for Treatment of Ocular Injury

- Remove a non-impaled foreign body from the conjunctiva or cornea using irrigation.
- *Do not* remove an impaled foreign body.
- Treat any patient with a history of a possible intraocular foreign body as a possible penetrating eye injury (evacuate the patient for an ophthalmology consult).
- Do not give out topical anesthetics (tetracaine/proparcaine) for self-medication.
- At forward medical facilities, apply a Fox shield or Styrofoam cup. Ensure that the protective cover rests on the cheekbone, not on the eye. Do not put a patch under the shield.
- *Evacuate urgently (4–6 h) for open globe repair.*
- Assess visual acuity and get a history of the injury.

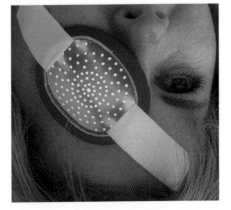

FIGURE 59   Fox shield. Do not apply an eye patch; avoid all pressure on the eye (a patch could worsen the injury).

Source: Courtesy of Eye Shield Technology, Inc. (800-800-1722)

Uveitis

Uveitis is an intraocular inflammation that may be caused by a viral or bacterial pathogen or an inflammatory process (e.g., sarcoid). The signs and symptoms depend on the affected location in the eye:

- Anterior (iris, ciliary body): redness at junction of cornea and sclera, pain
- Posterior (choroids): painless; floaters

Treatment depends on the cause; consult with an ophthalmology specialist. Note that topical steroids should be prescribed only by an ophthalmologist.

Corneal Abrasions

Suspect a corneal abrasion with a history of blunt or sharp trauma. Rule out open globe injury (no pressure on the eye), and observe for the following signs:

- Eye pain
- Photophobia
- Tearing

Treatment includes an antibiotic ointment:

- Polysporin (polymyxin B/bacitracin): 1-2 gtt/q 4-6 h; ointment ½ inch q 4 h
- Erythromycin ophthalmic ointment: ½-inch ribbon in conjunctival sac 2-6×/day
- Bacitracin: ½-inch ribbon in conjunctival sac q 6 h

Avoid patching, as it does not improve the healing rate or increase patient comfort.

Pain management:

- Ocular anesthetic: use for initial assessment only
- Ophthalmic diclofenac: 0.1% drops qid; wait at least 5 min before using other types of eye drops
- Cycloplegic agents (not for chronic use): 1% tropicamide (Mydriacyl) 1-2 drops, may repeat in 5 min; or 1% cyclopentolate (Cyclogyl) 1 drop, may repeat in 5-10 min
- Severe photophobia: 0.25% scopolamine 1 drop bid; will cause blurred vision and pupil dilation for 5-6 days

Ruptured or Lacerated Eyeball/Open Globe Injury

This type of injury involves a full-thickness injury of the cornea, the sclera, or both.

Signs are as follows:

- Prolapse of intraocular tissues through the wound
- Hemorrhagic swelling of the conjunctiva
- Hyphema (blood in the anterior chamber): indicates severe blunt or penetrating trauma
- Pupillary distortion: may indicate open globe injury
- Loss of vision

Care proceeds as follows:

- *Avoid pressure on the eye*—no dressing on the eye.
- Place Fox shield or cup over the eye.
- No ointment on open globe
- Give ciprofloxacin 500 mg IV/PO bid or levofloxacin 500 mg IV/PO daily.
- Give tetanus toxoid: if indicated.
- Prevent nausea and vomiting.
- Ensure urgent evacuation (< 48 h) for an ophthalmology consult.

Orbital Floor (Blowout) Fracture

History generally includes blunt trauma. Rule out an accompanying spinal cord or head injury.

Signs will include the following:

- Enophthalmos: recession of the eyeball within the orbit
- Diplopia: double vision
- Decreased ocular motility
- Hypoesthesia (diminished sensitivity) of trigeminal nerve (lower eyelid, zygoma, upper lip)
- Subconjunctival hemorrhage/hyphema
- Oculocardiac reflex: bradycardia and syncope (vagus mediated) caused by entrapment of extraocular muscles into the fracture site with globe restriction. Attempts to move the globe may initiate this reflex.

Care proceeds as follows:

- Pseudoephedrine 60 mg PO q 6 h
- Broad-spectrum antibiotic
- Ice pack
- Avoid blowing nose
- Ophthalmology consult

Eyelid Lacerations

Only repair eyelid lacerations that do not involve the eyelid margin and are without fat prolapsing through the wound. In all other cases, evacuate the patient for an ophthalmology consult. Do not discard eyelid tissue that is amputated or partially amputated. Wrap it in moist gauze and send it with the patient.

Thermal Burns to the Eyes

- Perform a fluorescein exam (early, before swelling occurs) for all patients with burns above the clavicles.
- If a corneal abrasion is present, apply ophthalmic antibiotic ointments.
- *No steroids*

Chemical Injuries

- Apply copious irrigation: 30–60 min with normal saline/lactated Ringer's solution; nonsterile water only if no other fluid available. Make sure to irrigate under the eyelids.
- Do not attempt to neutralize the chemical.
- Perform a fluorescein test:
  ○ No epithelial injury: treat with liquid tears
  ○ Epithelial injury: use ophthalmic ointment 4x/day

Considerations for Aeromedical Evacuation

Consult with the Flight Surgeon before the flight to determine if altitude restrictions will be required.

Give in-flight O_2 for transport at altitudes above 4000 ft mean sea level for patients with retinal/choroids injury.

TABLE 2-46   Flight Considerations

Blood Pressure	Physiological Response	Management
Decreased partial pressure of O_2	• May ↑ intraocular pressure and vasodilatation from hypoxia • Aggravates retinal hemorrhage, detached retina, and glaucoma	• May require O_2 4 L/min via nasal cannula • Restrict altitude as a last resort
Barometric pressure changes (expanding air at altitude)	• ↓ blood flow and/or extrusion of eye contents • Closed penetrating eye injury may have trapped air in globe; normally reabsorbed in 3 days • Postoperative eye surgery patients may have trapped air in the globe; certain gases used in surgery may persist 3-9 weeks • Sinus/tooth pain	• Give decongestants preflight, except for tooth pain • Move jaw and/or swallowing to clear ears • Valsalva and politzer bag to clear ears • Contraindicated for eye injuries/surgery, glaucoma, retinal detachment, nasal/facial fractures • ↓ mean cabin altitude as last a resort (< 2000 ft)
Decreased humidity	Excessive drying of the eyes leads to corneal irritation and abrasions of the sclera, especially in comatose patients or patients whose eyes do not completely close	• Artificial tears, if not contraindicated • Tape eyelids closed (only if no eye injury—no pressure on the eye)
Vibration/thermal/turbulence	• Causes motion sickness, vomiting, and ↑intraocular pressure and pain	• Antiemetics • Cool cabin

References

Kim WI. Recommendations for initial care of ocular and adnexal injuries at 1st and 2nd Echelons.

Ocular injuries. In *Emergency War Surgery* (3rd U.S. Revision, pp. 14.1-14.13), 2004.

Thach A (Ed.). *Textbooks of Military Medicine: Ophthalmic Care of Combat Casualty*. Washington, DC: Borden Institute, Walter Reed Army Medical Center, 2003.

■ Orthopedic-Musculoskeletal

See the "Soft-Tissue Trauma" section.

• Approximately 70% of war wounds involve the musculoskeletal system (Covey, 2006).
• Among the 39 survivors of the attack on the *USS Cole*, there were 81 total injuries, of which 40% were musculoskeletal (Lambert et al., 2003).
• In a study of critically injured patients transported by USAF CCATT in support of OEF/OIF in casualties with a single body area injured, 35% had extremity trauma (orthopedic and soft-tissue trauma) and 76% of polytrauma victims had injuries to the extremities.
• Splinting and external fixation are the most common methods of stabilization used in the AOR.

Initial Assessment/Management

• Maintain the patient's ABCs.
• Perform an initial assessment: complete primary assessment (ABCDE) and secondary assessment.

- The only immediately life-threatening musculoskeletal injury is associated hemorrhage.
- Stabilize obvious/suspected fractures. This step is imperative to prevent further soft-tissue and neurovascular trauma and to decrease hemorrhage and pain.

Orthopedic-Specific Assessment

- Check the extremities for deformities, hematomas, open wounds, ecchymotic areas, and tender/painful areas. Any obvious fractures should be immobilized immediately.
- Maintain spinal precautions as appropriate.
- Check for the presence of edema—ensure that all constricting garments or jewelry are removed.

Neurovascular Evaluation

The CMS evaluation should compare findings in the extremities:

- Circulation:
  ○ Pulses proximal and distal to injury: strong and palpable, weak, only obtainable by Doppler, absent
  ○ Capillary refill: normal < 2 sec or sluggish
  ○ Color: pink and warm, pale, dusky and cool to touch
- Motor: move all motor units distal to the injury (wiggle fingers and toes)
- Sensation: ability to feel touch (intact, diminished, absent); see the "Neurological" section for more specific evaluation

Constantly monitor the patient for the presence of compartment syndrome (the six P's). Note that approximately 24% of casualties with musculoskeletal injuries have concomitant vascular injuries, which may diminish pain sensation (Covey, 2006).

TABLE 2-47 Signs of Vascular Compromise on Physical Examination

Hard Signs	Soft Signs
• Active hemorrhage	• History of hemorrhage
• Expanding/pulsatile hematoma	• Stable hematoma
• Pulselessness	• Diminished pulse
• Palpable thrill	• Neurologic deficit
• Bruit	• Unexplained hypotension
	• Distal ischemia

Reference

Stockinger ST. Assessing for vascular injury in penetrating extremity trauma. *Emerg Med* 2004;36(2):44B-44H.

Doppler Pulse Assessment

- Use ultrasound gel or surgilube; place over the approximate location of the arterial pulse point.
- To obtain the best signal, place the Doppler probe at a 60-90 °angle to the artery.

- Slowly move the Doppler probe across (perpendicular to the expected path of the artery) to identify the center of the artery.
- Avoid rapid motion, as it distorts the Doppler signal.
- If most distal pulses are normal (e.g., radial DP), it is not necessary to assess more proximal pulses in that extremity.

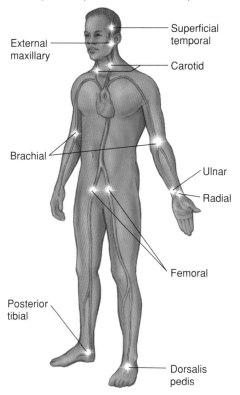

External maxillary

Superficial temporal

Carotid

Brachial

Ulnar

Radial

Femoral

Posterior tibial

Dorsalis pedis

FIGURE 60 Pulse points.

Ankle-Brachial Index
An ankle-brachial index (ABI) measures ankle systolic pressure and brachial systolic pressure.
- ABI > 0.90: acceptable
- ABI < 0.90: requires further evaluation

Evaluation of the ABI is unnecessary if the patient has obvious vascular compromise.

To perform this measurement:

- Place the patient in supine position.
- Measure the systolic brachial pressure in both arms using Doppler technology; use the higher of the two measurements. Note that SBP is detected as the first sounds with cuff deflation.
- Place the blood pressure cuff on the patient's leg just above the malleoli. Measure the dorsalis pedis and posterior tibial arterial systolic pressures. Select the higher of these two values as the ankle pressure measurement to be used as the ankle systolic pressure in the ABI calculation.
- For trauma assessment, use the following formula to calculate this index: Systolic BP in injured extremity ÷ Systolic BP in uninvolved arm.

Management of Sprains and Strains

Immediate treatment follows the RICE protocol:

- **Rest:** limit weight bearing (crutches) until the patient able to walk with a normal gait
- **Ice:** 15-20 min in 2-3 h for first 48 h or until swelling is improved
- **Compression:** apply an elastic bandage in the distal to proximal direction
- **Elevation:** keep the injured extremity above the level of the heart

Splinting

Splints should be used to manage fractures without significant associated wounds/soft-tissue damage; for low-energy, stable fractures; and for wounds that are not amenable to external fixation. They should also be used to stabilize a fracture until a patient can be transported to a higher level of care.

During initial splinting, do not attempt to manipulate the extremity. A splint is designed to minimize the motion of the extremity, so it may require modifying the splint to fit the fracture.

If the extremity has no pulse, manipulation is appropriate to attempt to return blood flow. Reducing the fracture also reduces pain and bleeding and may make transport easier for the patient. Absence of a pulse is a medical emergency with a fracture; the reduction procedure should be performed only by a trained provider.

When splinting, follow these guidelines:

- Long bone fractures: immobilize joints above or below the injury
- Joint injuries: the splint should extend beyond the long bone above and below the joint

Always assess the pulse distal to the fracture both before and after splinting. If the pulse is worse or absent after splint placement or fracture reduction, the splint must be removed and the fracture reduced.

Cast Care

Aeromedical evacuation considerations for a patient with a cast are described in Air Force Instruction 41-307. Also consider the following points:

- Ideally, plaster/fiberglass casts should be at least 48 hours old to allow for possible soft-tissue expansion after an acute injury.
- Plaster casts should be bivalved if swelling is expected or if the cast restricts emergency egress (i.e., Spica). If bivalving jeopardizes alignment of the fracture, then the physician must be informed that there may not be cast cutters available in-flight. Also write the order "Do Not Bivalve" on the appropriate patient treatment form.
- If the cast covers a surgical wound site, "window" the cast to allow for tissue expansion and examination, especially over the location of pulses to be checked.
- Assess the cast for proper drying, cracks, rough edges, drainage and bleeding (outline, date and time, and site), foul odor, and pressure points.
- Perform circulation and neurological checks prior to flight. If they are abnormal, contact the MTF to bivalve the cast or loosen the bivalved cast.
- Any drainage or malodor must be investigated, up to and including cast removal by physician if available.

FIGURE 61   Bivalve cast on both sides to allow for potential soft-tissue expansion.

Fractures

Triage

During triage, fractures of the hands/feet have a lower triage priority (although high morbidity). Long bone fractures have a higher triage priority for the following reasons:

- Higher risk for hemorrhage, compartment syndrome, infection, and amputation

- Rule out concurrent injuries: pelvic fracture, cervical or thoracolumbar spine injuries, visceral injuries, hemo/pneumothorax, head injuries

Be aware that high-velocity gunshot wounds can cause devastating soft-tissue and orthopedic trauma that may not be readily apparent from the external injury.

General Principles for Care of Fractures

Minimize movement, as this reduces the risk of bleeding and further neurovascular trauma and pain. In case of an open fracture, do not attempt to reposition the protruding bone ends.

Treatment goals are as follows:

- Decrease/stop hemorrhage. (See the "Shock Management/Hemorrhage Control" section.)
- Prevent infection. (See the "Soft-Tissue Trauma" section.)
- Decrease risk of venous thromboembolism. (See the "Venous Thromboembolism Prophylaxis" section.)
- Decrease risk of pulmonary complications (e.g., fat embolism) by reducing fracture.

Clinical diagnosis is usually made on the basis of the patient's signs and symptoms:

- ○ Usually manifest 24–72 h after the initial injury
- ○ Classic presentation: hypoxemia, neurologic abnormalities, petechial rash

Treatment focuses on prevention of complications by early immobilization of the fracture. Care is supportive in nature.

Use of Antibiotics in Fractures: General Principles

- Prophylactic antibiotics should be used only for 24 h. Continued antibiotic use should be guided by clinical conditions and culture results. Refer to your local policy for guidelines for appropriate antibiotic use.
- For scheduled procedures, administer an antibiotic 60 minutes before wound incision.

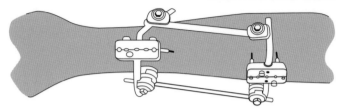

FIGURE 62 Example of external fixator.

External Fixator Management

There is no standardized evidence-based definition of pin site infection.

- During the first 72 h, copious serous drainage and erythema around insertion sites may be present.
- Persistent erythema after 72 h with increasing exudates, visible drainage of pus, and loosening of the pins suggests colonization or infection.

Pin Care: There is no evidence-based consensus on the appropriate regimen for pin care. Decisions on the appropriate solution depend on wound characteristics. Refer to your local policy.

TABLE 2-48 Example of Pin Care Policy	
Supplies	**Key Points**
• Sterile cotton-tip applicators • Hydrogen peroxide • Sterile saline • Sterile specimen cup for saline peroxide mixture • Clean gloves	• Keep the skin around the sites clean and dry. • Chlorhexidine 2 mg/mL solution may be the most effective cleansing solution for pin site care. Limited results from randomized controlled trials are available from which to draw a definitive conclusion about the preferred treatment.
Procedure	**Key Points**
• Wash hands. • Trim hair from the pin site if necessary. • Don clean gloves. • Using aseptic technique, clean each pin site with a separate sterile cotton-tip applicator dipped in a mixture of ½ saline and ½ peroxide. • Perform pin site care once daily with mechanically stable bone-pin interfaces. • The removal of crusting is based on the caregiver's discretion. • Leave open to air. • Inspect pin sites for inflammation, drainage, pain, swelling, tenderness, and odor. Routine topical antibiotic treatment is *not* recommended unless ordered by the healthcare provider.	• Avoid manipulation of pins. • Pin site care should be increased if mechanical looseness or early signs of infection are present. • No direct research exists with regard to removing crusting. Crusts are a normal protective mechanism and their removal can disturb healthy tissue. However, removing crusts allows exudates to escape. • Notify physician of suspected infection, pain, or clicking noises. Topical antibiotics are known to disturb the normal flora of the skin.

Source: From James A. Haley, Veterans' Hospital, Tampa, FL: June, 2007.

References

Holmes SB, Brown SJ. Skeletal pin care: National association of orthopaedic nurses guidelines for orthopaedic nursing. *Orthopaedic Nursing* 2005;24(2):99-107. http://www.orthonurse.org/portals/0/images/pdf/pincare2005.pdf

Temple J, Santy J. Pin site care for preventing infections associated with external bone fixators and pins (review). *Cochrane Database Systematic Review*, 2004.

Walker JA. Evidence for skeletal pin site care. *Nursing Standards* 2007;21(45):70-76.

Pelvic Fracture

Refer to JTTS Clinical Practice Guidelines for Pelvic Fracture Care, October 2006.

Pelvic fractures indicate injury from massive force. Assessment includes the following considerations:

- Assess/monitor for concurrent hemorrhage and organ damage. In particular, assess for hemodynamic stability, as an unstable fracture can lead to massive blood loss.
- Pelvic rocking should *not* be performed, as it could worsen the fracture. Instead, gently compress the pelvis during the initial assessment.
- Assess for concurrent genitourinary injury, especially urethral transection (male/female patients–blood at meatus; male patients–high prostate).
- Assess for distal neurological injuries.

Care is based on fracture stability and hemodynamic stability. Note that there is a high risk for blood loss, particularly with vertical shear fracture and anteroposterior compression fracture. Decreased bleeding may occur with external fracture stabilization.

Crush Injuries

Crush Syndrome

The consequences of crushed limbs, that sustain prolonged ischemia, muscle necrosis, and release of cellular components into the circulation when the trapped limb is freed and reperfused (Newton, 2007). It has a relatively low incidence in battlefield trauma, but increased incidence is associated with disasters (particularly earthquakes) and acts of terrorism causing building collapse. Crush syndrome may also occur with motor vehicle crashes.

Risk for crush syndrome is increased if the victim has a history of being trapped for a prolonged period of time. The severity of injury is directly related to degree of compression and duration. Hypovolemic shock is the most common cause of death in the first 48 hours after such an injury.

Initial assessment includes the following considerations:

- Maintain the patient's ABCs.
- Conduct primary and secondary surveys.
- Extremities may initially appear normal, but with reestablishment of perfusion and volume resuscitation the crushed area may begin to develop compartment syndrome.

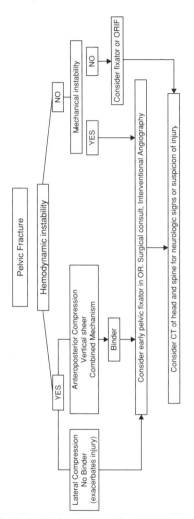

FIGURE 63 JTTS Clinical Practice Guidelines: Recommendations for Pelvic Fracture Care (October 2006)
There has been limited use of pelvic binders in the AOR.
Source: Department of Defense, Deployment Health Clinical Center, Joint Theater Trauma System (JTTS) *Clinical Practice Guidelines for In-Theatre Management of Mild Traumatic Brain Injury (Concussion),* August 2006. [www.pdhealth.mil/TBI.asp]

Additional monitoring:

- Monitor for renal failure/rhabdomyolysis. (See the "Genitourinary/Renal" section.)
- Monitor for compartment syndrome (discussed next).
- Excessive pain out of proportion to injuries may indicate development of compartment syndrome in the trunk or buttocks.

Treatment/Prevention:

- Initiate fluid resuscitation while victim is trapped. Administer at least 1 L IV fluids before extrication to decrease the risk of hypovolemia.
- Do not use potassium/lactate-based solutions. (Refer to the "Renal" section for specific guidelines.)

Compartment Syndrome

Acute compartment syndrome may occur with high-energy and crush injuries and long-bone fractures, prolonged immobilization (e.g., individual who collapses), snake bite, burns, and extravasation of vasoactive medications. It may also be caused or exacerbated by a tight dressing, splint, or cast.

Compartment syndrome can lead to tissue necrosis and permanent nerve damage. Rapid recognition and treatment are needed to prevent irreversible damage.

Signs and symptoms of compartment syndrome include the "6 P's":

- **Pain** out of proportion (or unrelieved by appropriate analgesia)/pain with passive stretch (e.g., dorsiflexion of the foot and toes will cause pain in the posterior calf compartment). Pain is often the earliest symptom and is generally considered the only reliable sign.
- **Paresthesia:** later symptom—described as a burning or prickly sensation
- **Pallor:** late sign
- **Paralysis:** late sign
- **Pulselessness.** Pulses may persist indefinitely as compartment pressure is generally less than SBP.
- **Poikilothermia:** temperature the same as the environment.

Other monitoring methods:

- Pulse oximetry monitoring is not a reliable method for diagnosis of compartment syndrome.
- Compartment pressure measurement may or may not be done.

Care:

- Bivalve cast and/or removal of dressing
- Place the extremity at the level of the heart; *do not* elevate above heart

- Fasciotomy: performed by MD as soon as feasible, with removal of dead muscle
- Post-fasciotomy wound care: wound left open; cover with moist sterile dressing

References

Bongiovanni MS, Bradley SL, Kelley DM. Orthopedic trauma: Critical care nursing issues. *Crit Care Nurs Q* 2005;28(1):60-74.

Bridges EJ, Evers K. *Report: Wartime critical care air transport (2001-2006).* TriService Nursing Research Program.

Camuso MR. Far-forward fracture stabilization: External fixation versus splinting. *J Am Acad Orthop Surg* 2006;14:S118-S123.

Covey DC. Combat orthopaedics: A view from the trenches. *J Am Acad Orthop Surg* 2006;14:S10-S17. (Excellent review of Level II care)

Ingari JV, Powell E. Civilian and detainee orthopaedic surgical care at an Air Force Theater Hospital. *Techn Hand Upper Extremity Surg* 2007;11(2):130-134.

Lambert EW, Simpson RB, Marzouk A, et al. Orthopaedic injuries among survivors of USS Cole attack. *J Orthop Trauma,* 2003, 17(6), 436-441

Lin DL, Kirk KL, Murphy KP, et al. Evaluation of orthopedic injuries in Operation Enduring Freedom. *J Orthop Trauma* 2004;18(5):300-305.

Mazurek MT, Ficke JR. The scope of wounds encountered in casualties from the Global War on Terror: From the battlefield to the tertiary treatment facility. *J Am Acad Orthop Surg* 2006;14:S18-S23. (Excellent review of injury types; useful for developing training scenarios)

Newton EJ, Love J. Acute complications of extremity trauma. *Emerg med clin North Am* 2007;25(3):751-761.

■ Pediatrics

TABLE 2-49 Quick Reference: Basic Pediatric Dosing and Equipment Guide

Broselow Color Zone	Gray			Pink	Red	Purple	Yellow	White	Blue	Orange	Green		
Approximate weight	3	4	5	6	8	10	13	16	20	26	32	40	45
Approximate age	Newborn	Newborn	2 mo	4 mo	8 mo	1 yr	2 yr	4 yr	5-6 yr	7-8 yr	9-10 yr	12 yr	13 yr
Heart rate	100-160	100-160	100-160	100-160	100-160	90-150	90-150	80-140	70-120	70-120	70-120	60-100	60-100
Respiratory Rate	30-60	30-60	30-60	30-60	30-60	24-40	24-40	22-34	18-30	18-30	18-30	12-24	12-20
Minimum systolic blood pressure	40	40	50	60	60	70	70	80	80	80	90	90	90
Endotracheal tube (use cuffed if > 5.5 years)	3.0	3.0	3.5	3.5	3.5	4.0	4.5	5.0	5.5	6.0	6.5	6.5	7.0
Nasogastric tube/ Foley catheter	5 Fr	5 Fr	5 Fr	5-8 Fr	8 Fr	8-10 Fr	10 Fr	10 Fr	12 Fr	14 Fr	14 Fr	14 Fr	16 Fr
Chest tube	10-12 Fr	10-12 Fr	10-12 Fr	10-12 Fr	10-12 Fr	16-20 Fr	20-24 Fr	20-24 Fr	24-32 Fr	28-32 Fr	32-36 Fr	36 Fr	36 Fr
Fluid bolus (mL)	60	80	100	120	160	200	260	320	400	520	640	800	900
Maintenance fluids (mL/h)	12	16	20	28	35	40	45	55	65	70	75	100	115
PRBC (mL) [unit = 350 mL]	30-45*	40-60*	50-75*	60-90*	80-120	100-150	130-195	160-240	200-300	260-390	320-480	400-600	450-675
FFP (mL)	30-45	40-60	50-75	60-90	80-120	100-150	130-195	160-240	200-300	260-390	320-480	400-600	450-675
Platelets (mL)	15-30	20-40	25-50	30-60	40-80	50-100	65-130	80-160	100-200	130-260	160-320	200-400	225-450
Cryoprecipitate (units)	1	1	1	1	1	1-2	1-2	2	2-3	3	4	4-6	4-6

(Continued)

TABLE 2-49 Quick Reference: Basic Pediatric Dosing and Equipment Guide (Continued)

Broselow Color Zone	Gray	Pink	Red	Purple	Yellow	White	Blue	Orange	Green		
Acetaminophen PO (mg)	40	80	80-120	120	160	160-240	240	320	320-400	650	650
Fentanyl IV (mcg)	6-9	12-18	16-24	20-30	26-39	16-32	20-40	26-52	32-64	20-40	22-45
Flumazenil IV (mg)	0.03	0.06	0.08	0.1	0.13	0.16	0.2	0.2	0.2	0.2	0.2
Glucose IV (mL of $D_{25}W$)	6 (D10)	6-12	8-16	10-20	13-26	16-32	20-40	26-52	32-64	40-80	45-90
Lorezapam IV (mg)	0.15-0.3	0.3-0.6	0.4-0.8	0.5-1	0.65-1.3	0.8-1.6	1-2	1.3-2.6	1.6-3.2	2-4	2-4
Mannitol IV (gm)	3	6	8	10	13	16	20	26	32	40	45
Metoclopramide IV (mg)	0.3	0.6	0.8	1	1.3	1.6	2	2	2	2	2
Midazolam IV (mg)	0.15-0.3	0.3-0.6	0.4-0.8	0.5-1	0.65-1.3	0.8-1.6	0.5-1	0.65-1.3	0.8-1.6	0.5-2	0.5-2
Morphine IV (mg)	0.15	0.3	0.4-0.8	0.5-1	0.65-1.3	0.8-1.6	1-2	1.3-2.6	1.6-3.2	2-4	2.2-4.5
Naloxone IV (mg)	0.3	0.6	0.8	1	1.3	1.6	2	2.6	3.2	4	4.5
Oxycodone PO (mg)	0.15 -0.45	0.3-0.9	0.4-1.2	0.5-1.5	0.65-1.9	0.8-2.4	1-3	1.3 - 3.9	1.6 - 4.8	2-6	3-8
Pancuronium IV (mg)	0.3	0.6	0.8	1	1.3	1.6	2	2.6	3.2	4	4.5
Phenobarbital: IV load (mg)	60	120	160	200	260	320	400	520	640	800	900
Phenytoin: IV load (mg)	45	90	120	150	195	240	300	390	480	600	675
Vecuronium IV (mg)	0.3	0.6	0.8	1	1.3	1.6	2	2.6	3.2	4	4.5

*Call blood bank.
Source: Harborview Medical Center, Seattle, Washington.

TABLE 2-50 Vital Signs for Pediatric Patients

Age	Heart Rate	Respiratory Rate	Blood Pressure	Urinary Output
Infant	120-180	30-60	>1 year average SBP: (Age in years × 2) + 90 mm Hg. Lower limit: (Age in years × 2) + 70 mm Hg (< lower limit indicates hypotension)	2 mL/kg/h
Toddler	90-160	20-40		> 2 yr: 1 mL/kg/h
Preschool	80-110	20-30		
School age	75-110	18-30		
Adolescent	60-90	12-16		

Heart Rate
• Count apical pulse for a full minute.
• Bradycardia is life-threatening in pediatric patients and is associated with hypoxemia; CPR is indicated if the child is bradycardic with poor perfusion or is pulseless.

Respiratory Rate
• Count for a full minute.
• A respiratory rate greater than 60/min is abnormal for any child.

Assessment of Dehydration
• Palpate the depressed anterior fontanel (infants).
• Poor skin turgor is a late sign, occurring after 10-15% fluid loss.
• A good check is moisture in mouth; the buccal area should be smooth and moist.
• Once babies have tears (usually develop about 1-3 months of age), no tears is an important marker of fluid loss.
• In any baby who previously had tears with crying, no tears means immediate attention to fluid status is needed.

Skin Color
• Cyanosis is a late sign of hypoxia.

Mental Status/Level of Activity
• Check the child's mental status/level of activity: Active and alert? Hearty cry? Lethargic or unresponsive?

TABLE 2-51 Indications of Volume Deficit in Infants

	Mild	Moderate	Severe
Body weight	< 5% loss	5-10%	10-15%+
Fluid volume loss	< 50 mL/kg	50-90 mL/kg	> 100 mL/kg
Skin color	Pink and warm/pale	Pale/gray, cool	Mottled, cyanosis, cold
Skin turgor	Normal	Poor	Very poor
Capillary refill	2-3 sec	> 3 sec	> 3-4 sec
Urine output	< 2 mL/kg	Oliguria (< 1 mL/kg)	Marked oliguria and azotemia
Mucous membranes	Dry	Very dry	Parched
Blood pressure	Normal	Normal/decreased	Decreased
Heart rate	Normal/increased	Increased	Rapid/thread
Tears	Normal	No tears	No tears

In case of volume deficit, isotonic crystalloid is the solution of choice, to be given at 10 mL/kg prn. Avoid too-rapid infusion, as it increases the risk for intraventricular hemorrhage.

Neonatal

Immediate care of the newborn includes the following steps:

- Clear the airway through suctioning (either with a bulb syringe or with 5-60 mm Hg suctioning). Suction the mouth first, then the nose. Newborns are obligatory nose breathers.
- Visualization of the vocal chords and possible tracheal suctioning is reserved for meconium if the baby is not vigorous.
- Dry the newborn.
  - A baby that is already crying needs no additional stimulation; avoid overstimulation. *Warning:* If meconium staining is present, avoid stimulation until the airway is clear.
- Assess vital signs.
- Ensure the umbilical cord remains clamped to avoid bleeding.
- Ensure that the baby is kept warm.
  - In a radiant warmer, the infant should be naked.
  - Wrap the infant in clothes/hat/blanket if the newborn is placed in an incubator; avoid overheating.
  - In an emergency situation, place the infant in skin-to-skin contact with the mother (or other person's chest), and then apply a wrap over the infant, keeping the face exposed.
- *Critical:* Prevent hypothermia from heat loss caused by radiation (between the body and surrounding objects), convection (air flow over the body), evaporation (wet infant), and conduction (between the body and contact with objects).
- Per AHA neonatal resuscitation guidelines, avoid use of 100% oxygen for resuscitation of term and preterm infants. Use positive-pressure ventilation with self-inflating bag in the absence of an O_2 source. Monitor oxygen therapy with oximetry or blood gas. (In the field, 100% oxygen may be the only option.)
- The current practice recommendation is to use information from the Neonatal Resuscitation Program for initial assessment and to guide therapy (rather than APGAR scores).

Neonatal Resuscitation

Source: Adapted from the neonatal resuscitation algorithm that appears in the following article: AHA guidelines for cardiopulmonary resuscitation and emergency cardiovascular care, *Circulation* 2005;112(24): IV189. Refer to the complete AHA guidelines for more information.

Upon the child's birth, evaluate the following issues:

Term gestation, amniotic fluid clear, breathing or crying, good muscle tone?

- Yes: routine care (provide warmth, clear airway prn, dry, assess color)
- No: Provide warmth, position/clear airway (? ETT), dry, stimulate, reposition

Evaluate respirations, heart rate, and color.

- Breathing, HR > 100, and pink: observe
- Breathing, HR > 100, and cyanotic: give supplemental O_2
  - If persistent cyanosis: provide positive-pressure ventilation
  - Effective ventilation, HR > 100, and pink: give post-resuscitation care
  - HR < 60: see below
- Apneic or HR < 100: provide positive-pressure ventilation
  - HR < 60: provide positive-pressure ventilation/chest compressions
    - HR remains < 60: administer epinephrine (0.01-0.03 mg/kg/dose) and/or volume (10 mL/kg isotonic crystalloid)
    - HR < 60: continue positive-pressure ventilation; Effective ventilation, HR > 100, and pink: give post-resuscitation care

Respiratory Distress
Respiratory distress is defined as RR > 60/min (see age-specific parameters), grunting/forced expiration, head bobbing, and tachycardia. It may be accompanied by the following signs and symptoms:

- Use of accessory muscles: sternal retractions, chest muscles visibly pulling, prolonged expiratory time
- Nasal flaring: infants are obligated nose breathers for the first 4 months of life; keep the nares clear of secretions
- Cardiovascular symptoms: poor peripheral perfusion (capillary refill > 2 sec, cool/mottling) and tachycardia
- Neurological symptoms: decreased muscle tone, altered mental status.
- Pallor preceding cyanosis: assess capillary refill (Note that newborns normally have acrocyanosis.)

Respiratory Failure
Respiratory failure is defined as RR < 10/min and/or irregular respirations. It is accompanied by the following signs and symptoms:

- Cardiovascular: slower than normal or absent heart rate, weak or absent peripheral pulses, hypotension
- Neurological: unresponsiveness, limp muscle tone
- All symptomatic, high-risk, or unstable pediatric patients should be placed on high-flow oxygen, have IV/IO access, and be placed on a cardiac monitor and pulse oximetry.

Glucose Management (High-Risk or Symptomatic Neonate)

Source: Adapted from Merenstein GB, Gardner SL. *Handbook of Neonatal Intensive Care* (p. 382). St. Louis: Mosby, 2006. Used with permission.

Signs of hypoglycemia include jitteriness, tremors, poor tone, change in level of consciousness, apnea, bradycardia, cyanosis, tachypnea, poor sucking or feeding, hypothermia, and seizures.

Treatment includes the following measures:

- Serum glucose < 25-30* mg/dL or < 40-50 mg/dL and symptomatic:* IV bolus 2 mL/kg $D_{10}W$; infuse $D_{10}W$ at 4-8 mg/kg/min; recheck glucose in 30 min
  - Recheck glucose < 40-45 mg/dL:* repeat $D_{10}W$ bolus; increase infusion rate 10-15%; recheck serum glucose in 30 min
  - Recheck glucose > 40-45 mg/dL: continue glucose infusion; recheck serum glucose q 1-2 h
- Glucose < 40-50 mg/dL:* symptomatic; begin feeding formula or breast milk (not sugar water); recheck serum glucose within 30 min
  - Recheck glucose < 40-45 mg/dL or not tolerating feed: give treatment for symptomatic neonate
  - Recheck glucose > 40-45 mg/dL: continue feeding q 3 h; recheck serum glucose q 1-2 h
- Glucose > 40-45 mg/dL: begin feeding; follow clinically; if symptomatic, consider IV glucose therapy

*These levels are arbitrary and should not be considered "normal" or "hypoglycemic."

TABLE 2-52 Medications	
Cardiac Emergency Medications	
Amiodarone	Pulseless VT/VF: 5 mg/kg IV Perfusing rhythm: 5 mg/kg over 20-60 min Infusion: start at 5 mcg/kg/min; may increase to maximum dose of 10 mcg/kg/min or 20 mg/kg/24 h
Atropine	0.01-0.02 mg/kg IV/ET Minimum dose = 0.1 mg/dose Maximum cumulative dose = 1 mg
Calcium chloride 10%	20 mg/kg/dose every 10 min
Epinephrine IV/IO	IV/IO: 0.01 mg/kg IV, 1:10,000 concentration ETT: 0.1 mg/kg IV, 1:1,000 concentration
Lidocaine	1 mg/kg IV over 2-4 min
Sodium bicarbonate	1-2 mEq/kg IV
Seizures	
Phenobarbital	Status epilepticus: 15-20 mg/kg IV, not to exceed 1 mg/kg/min; may give additional 5 mg/kg q 15-30 min up to a maximum dose of 30 mg/kg
Phenytoin	Status epilepticus: 15-20 mg/kg IV, not to exceed 1 mg/kg/min; may give additional dose if seizure persists, 5 mg/kg over 12 hours for goal serum of 10 mg/L
Glucose	If hypoglycemic, 2-4 mL/kg bolus of $D_{25}W$, then infusion at 8 mg/kg/min

(Continued)

TABLE 2-52 Medications (Continued)

Cardiac Emergency Medications

Analgesia

Acetaminophen	10-15 mg/kg PO or PR q 4-6 h; do not exceed 5 doses/day
Fentanyl	Intermittent: 1 mcg/kg IV q 30-60 min Infusion: 1-5 mcg/kg/h
Ibuprofen	15-10 mg/kg PO q 6-8 h; maximum dose = 40 mg/kg/24 h
Ketorolac (Toradol)	0.5 mg/kg IV/IM q 6 h
Morphine	Intermittent (floor): 0.05-0.1 mg/kg IV, IM q 4-6 h Intermittent (ICU): 0.1 mg/kg IV or IM q 1-2 h Infusion: 10-40 mcg/kg/h
Oxycodone	0.05-0.15 mg/kg PO q 4-6 h
Oxycodone + acetaminophen (Percocet)	Dose based on oxycodone and acetaminophen (see each drug for dosing) Most common strength: oxycodone HCl 5 mg + acetaminophen 325 mg

Sedation

Naloxone (Narcan)	0.01 mg/kg IV or ET; 0.001 mg/kg IV or ET (maximum dose = 2 mg)
Diazepam (Valium)	Seizures: 0.2-0.5 mg/kg IV (up to 6-10 mg) PO: 0.25-0.3 mg/kg
Diphenhydramine (Benadryl)	1.25 mg/kg IV, IM, or PO q 6 h
Lorazepam (Ativan)	Seizures: 0.05-0.1 mg/kg IV (up to 4-6 mg) Intermittent (floor): 0.025 mg/kg IV, IM, or PO prn q 4-6 h Intermittent (ICU): 0.05 mg/kg IV, IM, or PO q 2-4 h
Midazolam PO/IV	PO: 0.5-0.8 mg/kg IV sedation: 0.1 mg/kg up to 0.25 mg/kg Infusion: 1-2 mcg/kg/min
Flumazenil (Mazicon)	0.01 mg/kg up to 0.2 mg IV over 15 sec; repeat (maximum dose = 1 mg)

Other

Mannitol	0.25-1.0 g/kg IV; repeat q 4 h prn
Metoclopramide (Reglan)	0.1 mg/kg IV or PO q 6 h
Ondansetron	0.1 mg/kg IV or PO q 8 h

TABLE 2-53 Infusions

Drug	Dose	Drug	Dose
Dopamine	2-20 mcg/kg/min	Nitroglycerin	0.25-5 mcg/kg/min
Dobutamine	2-20 mcg/kg/min	Nitroprusside	0.25-8 mcg/kg/min
Epinephrine	0.1-1 mcg/kg/min	Norepinephrine	0.05-1 mcg/kg/min
Heparin	20-30 unit/h	Phenylephrine	0.05-1 mcg/kg/min
Insulin	0.05-0.1 unit/kg/h	Vecuronium	Loading dose: 0.1 mg/kg IV Infusion: 0.05-0.1 mg/kg/h (must be intubated)
Lidocaine	20-50 mcg/kg/min		

IV Voluton with microdrip tubing and infusion pumps will be used for all neonatal/pediatric patients. During resuscitation, give small IV boluses (20 mL/kg) and reassess.

Cardioversion	0.5 J/kg; if ineffective, increase to 1 J/kg and repeat
Defibrillation	2 J/kg; if ineffective, increase to 4 J/kg and repeat

General Pediatric Considerations
- Primary assessment (ABCD) followed by secondary assessment takes priority.
- The presence of a parent or other family member may decrease the child's anxiety and agitation.
- Hypoxia and respiratory dysfunction are the most common cause of cardiac arrest.
- Start CPR if the child is bradycardic with poor perfusion or pulseless.
- A child's trachea is narrow, the tongue is large, and the intercostal muscles are weak. For all these reasons, proper positioning is essential. Use the head-tilt/chin-lift technique to open the airway.
- For spinal immobilization, use the jaw-thrust maneuver. *Warning:* Hyperextension or flexion of the neck will cause airway compression.
- A rolled towel placed under the shoulders of the infant or child aids in maximizing airway size and reducing resistance. For neutral alignment of the c-spine, align the external auditory meatus with the shoulders.
- Calculate the endotracheal tube (ETT) based on the child's size in pediatric patients 1-10 years of age (or refer to length-based resuscitation tapes for children up to 35 kg).
  - Uncuffed ETT size (mm) = (age in years ÷ 4) + 4
  - Cuffed ETT size (mm) = (age in years ÷ 4) + 3
  - Standby: one size larger and one size smaller (0.5 mm) ETT or tracheotomy tubes
- Rule out hypoxia, hypovolemia (dehydration, hemorrhage), hypothermia, hypoglycemia, congenital heart disease, accidental ingestion, and acid–base imbalance.
- Refer to the AHA pediatric advance life support guidelines for specific resuscitation protocols.

Stresses of Flight
The following characteristics must be considered before evacuating a pediatric patient by air:
- Decreased partial pressure of oxygen: Infants and younger children are more reactive to hypoxia, and will become hypoxic earlier than adults, especially cardiac patients.
- Barometric pressure changes: Encourage the use of a pacifier/bottle on descent to help the infant/child clear the ears. Gastric compression may restrict diaphragmatic movement, especially if the child is supine; elevate the head and consider decompression with an oral or nasogastric tube.

- **Decreased humidity:** Infants and children are more susceptible to dehydration. If not NPO or receiving IV/IO or tube feedings, give fluids at least every 2 h. Decrease insensible loss by covering the patient.
- **Thermal:** Thermal changes have the greatest impact on infants and young children, because they have a very sensitive thermoregulation system. The primary intervention to prevent heat loss is to cover the patient (including head), while leaving the face visible.
- **Vibration:** Ensure infants are padded when in car seats (consider wrapping around car seat). Avoid padding between the baby and the seat, as it can create an unsafe head position.
- **Noise:** Infants/children are sensitive to excessive noise. Earplugs should be cut in half (vertically) to fit their smaller ear canals.

Patient Movement/Transfer

If operationally feasible, place infants and children through 8 years old or 57 inches tall in a car seat. Avoid padding between the baby and the seat; it can create an unsafe head position.

Ensure adequate age-appropriate food and care items, including baby bottles, formula, medication, and diapers for duration of travel.

References

American Heart Association. Part 13: Neonatal resuscitation guidelines. *Circulation* 2005; 112(24):IV188-IV195.

Hockenberry MJ, et al. Wongs *Nursing Care of Infants and Children*, 8th ed., 2006.

Johns Hopkins. *The Harriet Lane Handbook: A Manual for Pediatric House Officers*, 17th ed., 2005.

McGuigan R, Spinella PC, Beekley A, et al. Pediatric trauma: Experience in a combat support hospital in Iraq. *J Ped Surg* 2007;42:207-42210.

■ Pulmonary/Thoracic

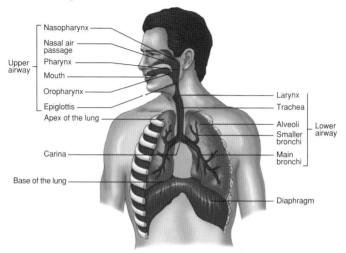

FIGURE 64 Anatomical upper and lower airway.

Pulmonary Assessment

Inspect the chest for symmetry of movement and use of abdominal/accessory muscles.

Inspect and palpate to detect injuries, using the DCAP-BTLS protocol:

- **D**eformity
- **C**ontusions
- **A**brasions
- **P**unctures
- **B**urns
- **T**enderness
- **L**acerations
- **S**welling

Note any tracheal deviation and/or jugular vein distention (JVD).

Palpate the chest wall for crepitus and deformities of the clavicles, ribs, and sternum; flail chest; tender areas; and subcutaneous air.

Auscultate breath sounds. Be systematic, and auscultate both lung fields for comparison.

In austere environments, assessment may be limited to inspection and palpation.

Open Airway
Jaw Thrust/Chin Lift
Suction
Insert Oral/Nasopharyngeal Airway

Assist Breathing
Pocket Mask
100% O2 BVM

Indications for Endotracheal Intubation and Mechanical Ventilation:

- Inability to ventilate/oxygenate
- Obstruction
- Inability to maintain airway

Prepare for ETT Intubation

- IV Patent
- Suction, BVM, laryngoscope, ETT with stylet, CO_2 detector

Sedative/Hypnotic (Anesthesia administer)

- Etomidate (*Decreases adrenal function*)
  - 0.3 – 0.4 mg/kg IV (stable)
  - 0.1 – 0.2 mg/kg IV (unstable)
- Propofol - Inducton: 40 mg q 10 sec

Paralytic

- Succinylcholine 1.5 mg/kg IV *or*
- Rocuroniun 1.2 mg/kg IV (Causes prolonged paralysis)

Suction Ranges all Ages
80–120 mm Hg

NOTE: In flight: Suction flow rates decrease with increasing altitude, ne-cessitating increased suction pressure. *Caution. Closed-system suction pressure* > 125 *mm Hg may cause ventilator failure* (*Eagle* 754) *requiring re-start.*

Difficult Airway/Alternate Airways—Assist provider

- Re-position, suction available; BVM 100% O_2
- Alternate Airways:
  - Nasal ETT
  - ETT placement with lighted stylet or Bullard laryngealscope
  - "Fastrach" laryngeal mask airway (LMA): pediatric-adult
  - Esophageal-Tracheal Combitube (ETC)/double lumen—adult only
  - Surgical Cricothyrotomy/Tracheostomy

FIGURE 65 Ineffective airway/breathing.

References

- JTTS Clinical Practice Guidelines for Trauma Airway Management, July 2006,
- Emergency War Surgery, Ch 11, Critical Care,
- AFI 41–307, Aeromedical Evacuation Patient Considerations and Standards of Care, Ch 4, Airway and Respiratory Management
- Schmelz j, et al. Preventing suctioning induced hypoxemia at altitude. Am J Crit Care, 2000, 9, 218.
- Bridges E, Schmelz J et al. Endotracheal suctioning at altitude. Implications for practice. Am J Crit Care, 2000, 9, 218.

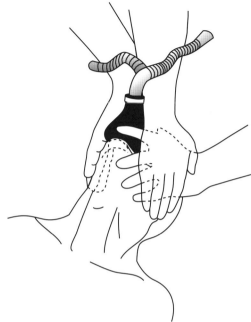

FIGURE 66   Correct hand placement for two person bag-valve-mask ventilation.
Source: U.S. Department of Defense. *Emergency War Surgery Handbook.* The Borden Institute, Washington, D.C. (2006).

Confirm ETT/Alternate Airway Placement

Ventilate every five sec with BVM at 100% O_2; perform CPR if indicated.

- Inflate tube cuff.
- Place CO_2 indicator between the tube and BVM; "go for the gold".
- Note rise/fall of chest.
- Auscultate epigastrum, lung bases, apices.
  - Gastric gurgling: esophageal intubation
  - Absent breath sounds on left lung fields: ETT down right main stem deflate cuff and withdraw ETT a few centimeters; reassess lung sounds
  - Absent breath sounds/difficult ventilation with ETT in correct position: possible tension pneumothorax
- Note tube condensation/fog and the level of the teeth in relation to the tube.

- Apply pulse oximeter.
- Obtain CXR and ABGs.
- Check cuff air leak/manometer to minimize tissue trauma.
  ○ Fill cuff with air while listening over the larynx area for leak.
  ○ Manometer cuff pressure: 20-30 cm H_2O

ETT/Trachea Troubleshooting

Assess the patient for excessive coughing, skin color, rise/fall of chest, breath sounds, tracheal deviation, JVD, neck/chest crepitus, anxiety, and SpO_2. Note the ventilator alarm indicators, cuff pressure, tube kinking, or the presence of water in the tubing.

When in doubt, immediately disconnect from ventilator and assist with BVM 100% O_2; use PEEP-capable BVM prn.

Possible causes of ETT problems (DOPE):
- **D**islodged: right main stem bronchus or tube out
- **O**bstructed: secretions (suction); biting on tube (sedate)
- **P**neumothorax: needle decompression/chest tube
- **E**quipment: failure, leaks, water, kinks, disconnected

There is no evidence to support instillation of saline down the ETT, and this practice may cause worsening of the patient's pulmonary status. If secretions are problematic, evaluate the patient's hydration status (free water) and ensure in-line humidification.

Source: Adapted from JTTS Clinical Practice Guidelines for Trauma Airway Management, July 2006, and AFI 41-307, Aeromedical Evacuation Patient Considerations and Standards of Care (Chapter 4).

Tension Pneumothorax

A tension pneumothorax occurs when trapped air in the pleural space compresses the lungs, heart, and great vessels. *It is a life-threatening condition!* Pneumothorax is the cause of 33% of preventable combat deaths.

Signs and symptoms are as follows:
- Cardinal signs: decreased breath sounds, hyperresonance in the affected hemithorax, hypotension
- Late signs: distended neck veins, tracheal shift to opposite side, cyanosis, feeling of "impending doom"

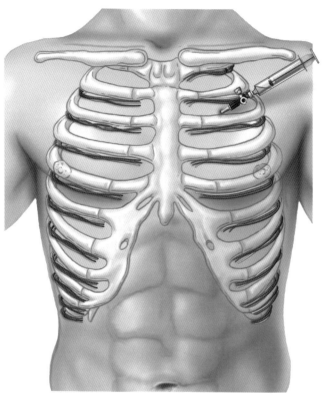

FIGURE 67A   Example of correct location for insertion of needle for emergency decompression.

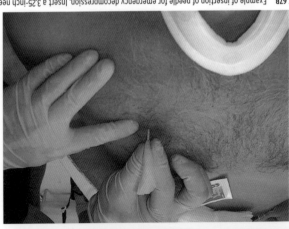

FIGURE 67B Example of insertion of needle for emergency decompression. Insert a 3.25-inch needle into the second intercostal space at the midclavicular line.

Needle Decompression

Needle decompression is a life-saving procedure in case of tension pneumothorax:

- Locate the second intercostal space at the midclavicular line.
- Cleanse the area with betadine or alcohol prep pads.
- Insert a 10- to 14-gauge, **3.25-inch** IV catheter over the needle (a shorter needle may not reach the pleural space) into the chest cavity over the superior edge of the third rib at a 90° angle.
- Listen for a gush of air, and reevaluate the patient for improvement of symptoms.
- Tape the catheter in place with a cap or three-way stopcock to prevent reentry of air into the chest.
- If necessary, place an Asherman chest seal or the finger of procedure glove over the secured catheter.
- Dress any open chest wound (prn).
- Prepare for insertion of a chest tube.

TABLE 2-54	Causes of Chest Injuries		
Penetrating Injuries	**Blunt Trauma**	**Injuries**
Gunshot wound	Motor vehicle crash	Tension pneumothorax
Stab wound	Motor vehicle versus	Sucking chest wound
Shrapnel wound	pedestrian	Hemothorax
	Fall	Flail chest/rib fractures
	Crush injury	Cardiac injury/tamponade
	Blast injury	Injury to aorta and great vessels
		Injury diaphragm, liver, and spleen

Open Pneumothorax (Sucking Chest Wound)

Signs and symptoms are as follows:

- Penetrating chest wound/impaled object in chest
- "Sucking" or "hissing" sound with inhaling
- Difficulty breathing
- Froth or bubbles around injury
- Coughing up blood or blood-tinged sputum
- Pain in chest or shoulder

Management of an open pneumothorax proceeds as follows:

- Expose the chest; check for exit wounds.
- Secure impaled objects in place.
- Seal the wounds with airtight material, covering the larger wound first.
- Cover the wounds completely and tape down three sides to provide a flutter-type valve for air escape; may use Asherman chest seal

Treat *all* penetrating chest wounds in this manner. Continually reassess the patient for tension pneumothorax and shock. If respiratory distress worsens, remove the wound dressing to allow trapped air to escape.

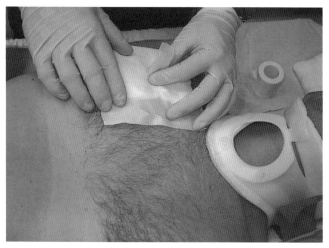

FIGURE 68 Asherman chest seal: commercial transparent occlusive dressing with inherent flutter valve. Placed over open chest wound or needle/catheter used for chest decompression. Wipe area dry prior to application.

Hemothorax

A hemothorax arises when there is blood in the pleural space due to bleeding from the chest wall, lungs, intercostal spaces, or pulmonary and/or great vessels.

Signs and symptoms, which are usually seen with open chest wound/ pneumothorax or flail chest, as follows:

- Chest pain and tightness
- Shortness of breath
- Signs of shock (early and late)
- Cyanosis (late)
- Dullness to percussion
- Coughing up frothy red blood

Treatment:

- Cover and dress open chest wounds.
- Treat tension pneumothorax: decompress if suspected.
  ○ Prepare for chest tube and possible autotransfusion.
  ○ Treat shock from massive hemorrhage (1000–1500 mL from chest); administer lactated Ringer's solution and blood products.
- Patient requires immediate evacuation to surgical assets.

Source: Adapted from National Association of Emergency Medical Technicians, *Prehospital Trauma Life Support (PHTLS), Military Version* (Chapter 10).

Flail Chest

Flail chest occurs when two or more adjacent ribs are fractured in more than one place or a fractured sternum leads to loss of chest wall stability.

Signs and symptoms are as follows:

- Severe pain at site
- Rapid shallow breathing with splinting
- Paradoxical chest movement (may be difficult to detect initially): flail segment moves in during inspiration and out during expiration
- Pulmonary contusion, possible pneumothorax, and/or lacerated lung leading to hypoxia
- Other organs may be injured (e.g., heart, liver, great vessels)

Treatment may require intubation and mechanical ventilation. Sandbags or other stabilization of flail segment is contraindicated.

Source: National Association of Emergency Medical Technicians, *Prehospital Trauma Life Support (PHTLS), Military Version* (Chapter 10).

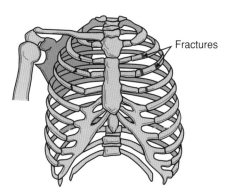

FIGURE 69 Flail chest.

Assisting with Chest Tube Insertion
Supplies
  Sterile scalpel
  Curved clamp
  Local anesthetic
  Povidone-iodine
  Chest drainage system
  Chest tube
  Petroleum gauze or dry sterile dressing
  Suture set
  Suture
  Sterile 4 × 4s
  Tape
  1% or 2% lidocaine
Select the appropriate chest tube size:
  • Adult, pneumothorax, stable condition: 16-22 Fr chest tube
  • Adult, large pneumothorax, unstable condition: 24-28 Fr chest tube
  • Children, young adults: 16-24 Fr chest tube (See the "Pediatrics" section for weight-based recommendations)
  • Infants, young children: 10-12 Fr chest tube
Administer pain medication as needed, based on the patient's clinical condition:
  • Morphine: 2-10 mg IVP over 5 min
  • Fentanyl: up to 50 mcg, slow IVP

Place the patient in a semi-recumbent position with the ipsilateral arm maximally abducted or put behind head.
Use full Barrier Precautions during the insertion procedure.
After the insertion is complete:
- Connect the chest tube to the drainage system; maintain the sterility of the system.
- Keep the collection system *upright*, secure, and below the level of the chest.
- Connect suction to the system, usually at 20 cm H_2O.
- If suction is not ordered, follow the manufacturer's directions for venting.
- Apply a chest tube dressing (note and dress flank wounds as needed):
  ○ Petroleum gauze or dry sterile dressing around insertion site, covered with sterile pre-split dressing or folded V-shaped sterile gauze; tape securely in place; or
  ○ Large transparent adhesive dressing (12 inches by 12 inches, or larger) over site
- Tape all connections lengthwise, rather than wrapping around the tube and connections.
- *Evidence-based recommendation:* Keep the chest tube drainage tube flat at the patient level; do not allow it to drape (i.e., form a dependent loop). If draping occurs, drain the tubing every 15 minutes to maintain adequate drainage (Schmelz, 1998).
- Prevent kinking, and minimize the length of dependent tubing to prevent draping/looping.
- *Do not* clamp the tube when moving the patient.
- Note the drainage, and mark its level (with the date and Zulu time).
- If the initial insertion yields $\geq$ 1000-1500 mL indicates hemorrhage; notify the MD immediately.
- If the blood drains at a rate of 200 mL/h for 2 consecutive hours, notify the MD.
- Obtain a CXR when feasible.

Sources: Adapted from Atrium University, Managing Chest Drainage Continuing Education Program (May 2006), Chest tubes, p. 11; Steps for chest insertion and drain setup, pp. 21-22.

"Wet Seal" Chest Drainage Systems

For all chest drainage systems, follow the manufacturer's guidelines for setup, suction, and operation.

A "wet seal" or "water seal" system (e.g., Pleur-evac) typically includes three chambers: water seal, suction control (in cm H_2O) (controls negative pressure), and drainage. There is no integral one-way valve. A Heimlich valve is required for patients who will be evacuated by air.

The basic setup for a wet-seal system includes the following steps:
- Fill the water seal chamber to the specified level to provide the water seal.
- Leave the vent tube (short tube) open to the air for straight drainage.
- Fill the suction control chamber to the level ordered by the physician.
- Connect the suction tube (short tube) to the suction source, and increase suction until the water in the suction control chamber gently bubbles.
- When the system is functioning properly, water rises and falls in the water seal chamber.
- Monitor suction control and water seal level; add water as needed.

"Dry Seal" Chest Drainage Systems

A "dry seal" system (e.g., Atrium ExpressT Dry Seal Chest Drain 4050–Autotransfusion System) typically includes two chambers: air leak indicator and drainage. Mechanically regulated suction is possible with the integral mechanical one-way valve. A Heimlich valve is not required for patients who will be evacuated by air.

The basic setup for a dry-seal system includes the following steps:
- Connect the chest tube to the drainage system patient tubing.
- Secure the drainage system below the patient's chest.
- Attach suction to the drainage system port.
- Turn on suction to –80 mm Hg.
- The regulator is preset to –20 mm Hg; adjust it according to the physician's order.
- Note the "bellows" indicator (▲ mark or beyond); increase suction, as needed.
- When feasible, fill the air leak monitor with sterile water or saline up to the line marker (the port is in back of system); if bubbles flow right to left, it indicates an air leak.
- The system has a built-in Heimlich valve, so do not add an external Heimlich valve to it.

Assessment/Care of Patients with Chest Tube (q 2 hours)

If not contraindicated, elevate HOB $\geq 30°$.

Assess pain status.

Auscultate breath sounds; check vital signs, SpO_2.

Inspect/palpate insertion site dressing, security of all connections, tubing for drainage, clots, kinks; ensure all proximal holes of the chest tube are not exposed.

Note drainage/mark level (date/time); add to 24 h output documentation.

Check tube patency with the suction off:
- Water seal fluctuation during respiration:
  - Present: expected in unexpanded lung
  - Absent: lung expanded or system occlude; check for kinks, clots
- Bubbling in the air leak/water seal chamber:
  - Present: air leak. This is normal in an unexpanded lung, but abnormal if the lung was expanded; check for system leak.
  - Absent: no air leak. The lung is expanded or the system occluded; check the system.

Encourage coughing and deep breathing every 2 h. Ensure adequate pain management and splint chest.

TABLE 2-55	Ventilator Settings
Pressure cycled	Delivers a predetermined amount of pressure during inspiration (Example: pressure-controlled inverse ratio ventilation)
Flow cycled	Inspiration terminated when a specific flow rate is achieved (Example: pressure support ventilation)
Volume cycled	Delivers a predetermined volume of air during inspiration (Example: controlled, ACV, SIMV)
Control mode	• Preset tidal volume and rate delivered regardless of patient's respiratory effort • Patient cannot initiate breaths or change the ventilatory pattern • Used when respiratory drive is absent or excessive
Assist-control (ACV)	• Delivers a minimum ventilatory rate, preset inspiratory time, and preset tidal volume; assists patient-initiated breaths • Controlled ventilations delivered when effort falls below minimum settings
Synchronized intermittent mandatory ventilation (SIMV)	• Permits spontaneous breathing while periodically delivering ventilator-generated breaths
Fraction inspired oxygen (FIO2)	• 0.21 (room air) to 1.0 (100% O_2) • Critical patients are usually started at an FIO_2 of 1.0 and weaned to 0.40 • May require adjustment at altitude
Ventilation rate	• Initial rate: 10-14 breaths/min • Titrate to normalize $PaCO_2$
Tidal volume (Vt) based on ARDSNet protocol	Calculate Vt using predicted body weight (PBW) • PBW Males = 50 + 2.3 [height (in inches) − 60] • PBW Females = 45.5 + 2.3 [height (in inches) − 60] Vt = 6-8 mL/kg PBW (Example: 72-inch male: 50 + 2.3[72 − 60] = 77.6; Vt = 466-621 mL)
Inspiration/expiration ratio (I:E)	Usually 1:3
Positive end-expiratory pressure (PEEP)	Delivered during inhalation and exhalation to prevent alveolar collapse (usually 5 cm H_2O) Increased PEEP may be required in acute respiratory distress syndrome (ARDS), but generally not higher than 15 cm H_2O Avoid high pressure with pulmonary blast injury Settings remain constant at altitude
Continuous positive airway pressure (CPAP)	Positive airway pressure in the spontaneously breathing patient improves oxygenation in the same manner as PEEP

Initial settings for a 6-foot male: FIO = 1.0, mode SIMV/ACV, rate 12, Vt 500 mL, PEEP 5 cm H_2O

Source: U.S. Army Institute of Surgical Research. *Emergency War Surgery Handbook* (Chapter 11). October, 2006. Additional data from ARDSNet protocol.

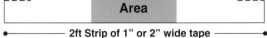

**Lay Piece of Tape Over 1ft section
to create nonstick area for back of neck**

Cut 3" Flaps

Nonstick
Area

2ft Strip of 1" or 2" wide tape

FIGURE 70   Securing an endotracheal tube. Commercial ETT holders may not be available, and they may not adequately secure the tube for CCATT transport.

To secure the endotracheal tube, follow these steps:
- Clean the skin with mild soap and water.
- Use alcohol wipes to remove oil from skin; allow skin to dry.
- Apply skin adhesive (i.e., benzoin tincture) only to area of taping to enhance adherence.
- Cut a 1-inch- or 2-inch-wide silk/twill tape, 2 feet long.
- Place a second piece of tape, 1 foot long, on top of the first piece to create a nonstick area.
- On each end of the sticky side, make an approximately 3-inch cut to create a "V."
- Place double-sided tape behind the midcervical area, just below the earlobe.
- Attach the proximal end of the tape right above the upper lip.
- Wrap the remaining tape edge around the ETT.
- Repeat these steps to secure the tape on the opposite side.
- Attach the ETT to the ventilator circuit/tubing.
- Change the tape and tube position q 24 h.

Note that tape will not adhere to burned tissue. In such cases, use umbilical tape and secure the ETT with non-slip knots.

Care of Ventilated Patients
Ventilated patients require a dedicated BVM with 100% O_2, PEEP, and suction apparatus and supplies. Check the following at every patient care hand-off and every 2 h:
- Assess ETT placement, lung sounds, vital signs
- Change position, but maintain HOB at 30° if possible
- Provide oral care

Assess the following at every patient care hand-off and hourly; also check them on a pre-flight, on ascent/descent, and during cruising when the patient is being evacuated by air:
- Ventilator settings (Vt, rate, FiO_2, alarms on, humidifier fluid level)
- In-line Mini-Ox
- Cuff pressure

Continuous care measures for ventilated patients include the following:

- Cardiac monitoring
- Pulse oximetry *(Patients with vasoconstriction may have a delay in a change in peripheral SpO_2 by as much as 60–90 sec; monitor for changes in heart rate as another indicator of hypoxemia.)*
- NG suction (per MD order)
- Therapeutic soft restraints (per MD order)
- Temperature q 4 h

For airborne infection control precautions, a HEPA filter is placed in-line, after the exhalation port or per IAW manufacturer's guidelines. A second filter is placed on intake valve; consult with Respiratory Therapy specialists. If expired body fluids block the filter, replace the filter and continue patient ventilation.

Source: Adapted from AFI 41-307, *Aeromedical Evacuation Patient Considerations and Standards of Care* (Chapters 4 and 12).

Preventing Ventilator-Acquired Pneumonia

Elevate the HOB 30–45° (unless contraindicated). During flight, use backrest for the patient.

- Mechanical ventilation
- High risk of aspiration
  - TBI/decreased LOC
- All enteral feeding tubes
  - Gastric distention
  - Trauma to face or neck

Routine changing of ventilator circuits is not recommended.
To care for the patient, provide the following measures:

- Brush/clean the patient's teeth, gums, and tongue with normal saline or distilled water and a soft toothbrush or gauze q 12 h.
- Moisturize the oral mucosa and lips q 2 h with normal saline or distilled water; petroleum jelly may be applied to the lips.
- Use oral chlorhexidine gluconate (0.12%) rinse q 12 h per physician's order. (The evidence supporting this practice came from studies in cardiac surgery patients with controlled intubation.)

TABLE 2-56 Conditions Requiring Supplemental Oxygen

Major trauma/burns	Hemothorax/pneumothorax	Primary blast lung injury
Shock (any cause)	Pulmonary embolism	Atelectasis
Ischemic chest pain	COPD (use with caution)	Carbon monoxide poisoning
Neurological trauma	Cerebrovascular accident	Status asthmaticus

In-Flight Oxygen Requirements

- All conditions requiring O_2 on the ground will require O_2 during ground/rotor-wing transport and in-flight.

- Cabin altitude restrictions are coordinated with the validating Flight Surgeon and the sending physician. (Note that cabin altitude restrictions increase fuel consumption and decrease aircraft range.)

TABLE 2-57   In-Flight Oxygen Requirements

Condition	In-Flight O_2 Requirements (Maintain $SpO_2 > 91\%$)
Chronic low Hgb: • 8.5-10 gm/dL • 7.0-8.5 gm/dL • < 7.0 gm/dL	O_2 available Start at 2 L/min AE validating Flight Surgeon concurrence
Post-op low Hgb (acute): • 9.0-10 gm/dL • 8.0-9.0 gm/dL • < 8.0 gm/dL	• O_2 available • Start at 2 L/min • AE validating Flight Surgeon concurrence; Hgb < 8 requires transfusion prior to flight
Penetrating eye injuries	4 L/min via nasal cannula or mask; altitude restriction if known air in globe
Decompression Sickness: • Skin: "creeps" • Joints: "bends" • Respiratory: "chokes" • CNS: "staggers"	100% via tight-fitting mask or aviator's mask Maximum cabin altitude: destination field level

Source: U.S. Air Force. Aeromedical Evacuation Patient Considerations and Standards of Care (AFI 41-307). U.S. Air Force, Washington, D.C. (2003).

TABLE 2-58   Oxygen Delivery Methods

Method	L/min	$O_2\%$
Nasal cannula: dependent on minute ventilations	2	23-28
	3	28-30
	4	32-36
	5	40
	6	Maximum 44
Simple mask: start > 5 L/min to clear CO_2 from mask	5	40
	6	44-50
	8	55-60
Partial rebreathing mask	6	55-60
	8	60-80
	10	80-90
	12	90
	15	90
Non-rebreathing mask: used during resuscitation	6	55-60
	8	60-80
	10	80-90
	12	90
	15	> 90

Source: U.S. Air Force. Nursing Considerations: Aeromedical Evacuation Crew (AEC) Checklist (AFI 11-2AE-3V3, CL-21). U.S. Air Force, Washington, D.C. (2005): p. 14.

Calculation of O_2 Requirements

O_2 flow (L/min) = Duration of (total pressure − residual pressure) × cylinder constant

Residual pressure = 200 psi

Cylinder constants: D = 0.16, E = 0.28, H = 3.14, G = 2.41, K = 3.14, M = 1.56

Example: Determine the life of an M cylinder that has a pressure of 2000 psi and a flow rate of 10 L/min.

$$\frac{(2000 - 200) \times 1.56}{10} = \frac{2808}{10} = 281 \text{ min (4 h, 41 min)}$$

For liquid oxygen (LOX) calculations:

1. Add the O_2 flow of each patient (including ventilator use) to get a total O_2 flow (L/min).
2. Add estimated flight times to the estimated ground times for a total mission time (hours).
3. Multiply the total mission time (hours) by 60 to get a total mission time (minutes).
4. Multiply the total mission time (minutes) by the total O_2 flow (L/min) to get the mission's total gaseous O_2 requirement (liters–gaseous)
5. Since 1 L of LOX equals 804 gaseous L of O_2, divide the total gaseous O_2 requirement (liters–gaseous) by 804 to get the mission's total LOX requirement (liters–LOX)

Example: A mission has 5 patients on supplemental oxygen at 5 L/min and 2 patients on ventilators. For the patients on ventilators, one requires requiring a flow of 8 L/min and the other requires a flow of 12 L/min.

- Total O_2 flow = (5 + 5 + 5 + 5 + 5 + 8 + 12) = 45 L/min
- Estimated flight time = 8 h + 3 h ground time (660 min)
- Total gaseous O_2 requirement = 660 min × 45 L/min = 29,700 L

$$\text{Total LOX requirement} = \frac{29{,}700 \text{ L gaseous oxygen}}{804 \text{ L LOX/L gaseous oxygen}} = 37 \text{ L of LOX}$$

A ventilator must be placed on a separate PT LOX to allow for a 60 L/min flow rate. Consult with Respiratory Therapy specialists.

Source: AFI 11-2AE-3V3, CL-2 1 (June 2005), *Nursing Considerations: Aeromedical Evacuation Crew (AEC) checklist*, pp. 6-7.

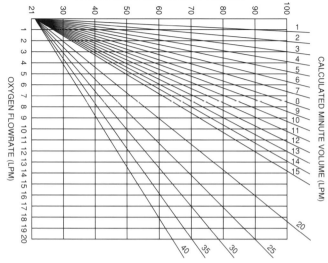

FIGURE 71 Oxygen flow chart.
Source: U.S. Air Force. Aeromedical Evacuation Patient Considerations and Standards of Care (AFI 41-307). U.S. Air Force, Washington, D.C. (2003).

Using the Oxygen Flow Chart

Before starting, calculate the minute volume using the following formula:

$$\text{Tidal volume} \times \text{Rate} \times 0.001 = \text{Minute volume}$$

Example

Tidal Volume		Rate			Minute Volume
500	×	16	× 0.001		= 8 L/min
900	×	8	× 0.001		= 7.2 L/min

1. Find the nearest calculated minute volume line (to the nearest whole number) at the top of the chart. With a ruler and pen, trace over the diagonal line (minute volume line).
2. Find the prescribed O_2 concentration ordered on the left of the graph. With a ruler and pen, draw a line across the chart at the level of the O_2 concentration.
3. At the point where the minute volume line and the oxygen line drawn intersect, draw a vertical line down to the bottom of the chart.

4. Follow the vertical line down to the bottom of the graph and read the number to the nearest ½ L/min.
5. Set the number found in step 4 on the O_2 flow meter. Be sure to read the center of the flow meter ball.
6. Measure the O_2 concentration with an O_2 analyzer.
7. After 2 minutes, adjust the flow meter slightly to achieve the ordered O_2 concentration.

Source: USAF School of Aerospace Medicine Critical Care Air Transport Team "Blue Book."

Using the Conversion Chart for In-flight Oxygen Administration

TABLE 2-59	Conversion for In-flight Oxygen Administration																
10,000	30	36	44	51	58	65	73	80	87	94	100						
9,000	29	35	42	49	56	63	70	77	84	91	98	100					
8,000	28	34	40	46	54	61	67	74	81	87	93	100					
7,000	27	32	39	45	52	58	65	71	78	84	91	97	100				
6,000	26	31	37	44	50	56	62	69	75	81	87	94	100				
5,000	25	30	36	42	48	54	60	66	72	78	84	90	96	100			
4,000	24	29	35	41	46	52	57	64	70	75	81	87	93	97	100		
3,000	23	28	33	39	45	50	56	61	67	73	78	84	89	95	100		
2,000	23	27	32	38	43	48	54	59	64	70	75	81	86	91	97	100	
1,000	22	26	31	38	41	47	52	57	62	67	72	78	83	88	93	98	100
FiO_2	21	25	30	35	40	45	50	55	60	65	70	75	80	85	90	95	100

CABIN ALTITUDE
Desired Sea Level Equivalent (SLE) Oxygen Percentage

☐ Even though the delivered O_2 may be at 100%, the partial pressure of oxygen necessary to deliver 100% SLE cannot be obtained (ex: 100% O_2 @ 8,000 feet only provides 75% O_2 SLE).
☐ Desired % O_2 SLE cannot be obtained at these altitudes.

Source: U.S. Air Force. Aeromedical Evacuation Patient Considerations and Standards of Care (AFI 41-307). U.S. Air Force, Washington, D.C. (2003).

Example: A patient receiving FiO_2 of 30% while on the ground and who will be flying at a cabin altitude of 8,000 feet will need to have the FiO_2 increased to 40% to deliver the same partial pressure of O_2 as the patient was receiving on the ground.

Example: Physician orders FiO_2 30% via nasal cannula. On the ground, run O_2 at 3 L/min. Inflight, maximum cabin is 6000 feet; give 37% O_2 to maintain FiO_2 30% by adjusting flowmeter to 4-5 L/min.

Autotransfusion

Autotransfusion involves the collection of uncontaminated blood from the chest for IV infusion. When performing this procedure, always follow the manufacturer's guidelines for infusion/anticoagulation.

Basic instructions for use of a "chest in-line blood collection bag" are to use aseptic technique and BBF precautions when administering blood products. A citrate anticoagulant may be added to the collection bag to minimize clotting as prescribed by a physician or IAW local policy.

Example: ACD-A solution dose:
- 140–250 mL blood: instill 20–35 mL ACD-A
- 250 mL blood: instill 14 mL ACD-A for each 100 mL blood

Example: CPD solution dose: 14 mL CPD for each 100 mL blood

Warning: Rapid infusion of blood with citrate anticoagulation may produce citrate toxicity (hypocalcemia/hyperphosphatemia: circumoral paresthesia, abdominal cramps, arrhythmias, and myocardial depression).

Follow this procedure for autotransfusion:
- Close all clamps, and remove the tube caps on the blood collection bag.
- Clamp the patient chest drainage tubing when you are ready to attach the collection bag.
- Disconnect the patient tubing and connect it to the collection bag; cap the system connection.
- Open all the clamps on the collection bag.
- Open the clamp on the patient tube; continue chest drainage. Be sure to prevent kinks, looping, and accidental clamping of patient drainage tube.
- Document the output.
- Prime the microemboli blood filter (40 micron) and nonvented blood administration set with saline; minimize air bubbles.
- When bag is full, don personal protection equipment (PPE).
- Securely close the bag and the patient clamps.
- Disconnect the collection bag.
- Immediately reconnect the patient to the chest drainage system and open the patient clamp.
- Close the blood collection bag system.
- Invert the bag; using aseptic technique, spike the bag with the filter/blood administration setup.
- Hang the bag on an IV pole. If the pressure infuser is *not* used, open the vent on top of the bag.
- When using a pressure infuser, keep the blood bag vent closed and the pressure < 150 mm Hg.
- Open the IV tubing clamp to finish priming.
- Connect the blood tubing to the patient and monitor the transfusion. Blood should be started within 6 hours of starting collection. Store blood according to IAW local policy.
- Leave approximately 50 mL of blood in the bag to prevent air emboli.
- Use a new microemboli filter with every new blood collection bag.

Source: Adapted from Atrium, Personal guide to managing chest drainage autotransfusion: In-line ATS Bag (2550), p. 20; Anticoagulants, pp. 24–27; Autotransfusion precautions, pp. 37–38.

Heimlich Valves

A Heimlich valve is a sterile one-way "flutter valve" that is attached to
a chest tube. It is used to prevent the flow of air or fluid back into the
chest cavity during chest transport.

FIGURE 72   Heimlich valve.
Source: Courtesy and © Becton, Dickinson and Company.

Note: If a one-way valve is built into the chest drainage unit (e.g., a
dry-seal system), a Heimlich valve is contraindicated. All chest tubes
attached to an AE-approved wet-seal chest drainage system (e.g., Pleur-
evac) or straight drainage (i.e., drainage bag) require a Heimlich valve.

Source: Air Mobility Command Aeromedical Evacuation Equipment Standards (Chapter 5).

Patient Movement/Aeromedical Evacuation

Chest tubes may be left in position during patient movement and
evacuation. Use AE-approved dry-seal drainage systems in such
a case.

Two large clamps for each chest tube are mandatory. If the chest
tube is clamped, it increases the patient's risk for tension pneumothorax.
Release clamps as soon as possible.
Do not allow the chest drainage system to be positioned above
the level of the chest. Do not clamp the chest tube while moving the
patient.
Maintain and document I & O on each trip segment and as required.

Post-Chest Tube Removal Requirements

- Aeromedical evacuation must wait for a minimum of 24 hours post
  removal.
- Expiratory and lordotic chest X-rays should be taken at least
  24 hours post chest tube removal, with their interpretation being
  documented in the patient's medical records. This step may not be
  feasible in contingency operations.
- Apply an occlusive dressing to the chest tube site once the tube is
  removed.

TABLE 2-60   Hospital-Based Management of Acute Exacerbations of Asthma

Refer to complete guidelines for specific information on management of asthma. This table is not intended as a replacement for MD orders or clinical judgment.

Signs/Symptoms	Management

Mild
 	
• Dyspnea only with activity (walking)
• Talks in sentences
• ↑ RR
• Moderate end-expiratory wheezes
• Peak expiratory flow (PEF) > 70% predicted or personal best
• SaO_2 > 95%
• HR < 100
	• Supplemental O_2 to achieve SaO_2 > 90%
	• Albuterol (short-acting beta, agonist [SABA]) :
	  ○ Metered-dose inhaler (MDI) using a spacer
	  ○ Nebulizer (if patient unable to use MDI or MDI is ineffective):
	    ⊙ Pediatric: 0.1-0.5 mg/kg q 20 min × 3 doses (maximum dose, 15 mg/h), then 0.15-0.30 mg/kg (up to 10 mg) q 1-4 h prn or 0.5 mg/kg by continuous nebulizer or MDI 4-8 puffs q 20 min × 3 doses, then q 1-4 h prn
	    ⊙ Adult: 2.5-5 mg q 20 min × 3, then 2.5-10 mg q 1-4 h prn or 10-15 mg/h continuously or MDI 4-8 puffs q 20 min up to 4 h, then q 1-4 h prn
	    ⊙ Dilute to 3 mL and administer at gas flow of 6-8 L/min

Moderate
 	
• Dyspnea at rest limits activity
• Infant: softer, shorter cry or difficulty feeding
• Talks in phrases
• PEF 40-69% predicted or personal best
• ↑ RR, HR 100-120/min
• ↑ accessory muscles; substernal retractions
• Loud wheezes during expiration
• SaO_2 90-95%
• ± Pulsus paradoxus (10-25 mm Hg)
	• PO corticosteroids if no immediate response to SABA or recent course of oral corticosteroids (prednisone, methlyprednisolone):
	  ○ Pediatric: 1 mg/kg in 2 divided doses (maximum dose, 60 mg/day)
	  ○ Adult: 40-80 mg/day in 1-2 divided doses
	Moderate Exacerbation
	• Inhaled SABA q 60 min; continue treatment for 1-3 h (consider admission)
	• Oral corticosteroids

Severe
 	
• Dyspnea at rest—interferes with conversation
• Infant: stops feeding
• PEF < 40% predicted or personal best
• RR > 30/min; HR > 120/min
• ↑ Accessory muscle use
• Substernal retractions
• Loud inspiratory/expiratory wheezes
• SaO_2 < 90%; PaO_2 < 60 mm Hg
• PCO_2 > 42 mm Hg; possible respiratory failure
• Pulsus paradoxus
	• Supplemental oxygen to maintain SaO_2 > 90%
	• Use higher dose of SABA plus ipratropium bromide repeatedly (3 dose in first hour) or continuously
	• Ipratropium (not first-line therapy)
	  ○ Pediatric: nebulizer solution 0.25-0.5 mg q 20 min × 3, then prn or MDI 4-8 puffs q 20 min × 3, then prn
	  ○ Adult: nebulizer solution 0.5 mg q 20 min × 3, then prn or MDI 8 puffs q 20 min prn up to 3 h
	• Ipratropium (Atrovent) + albuterol (ED patients only—severe exacerbations only; not for hospital management)
	  ○ Pediatric: nebulized 1.5 mL q 20 min × 3, then prn or MDI 4-8 puffs q 20 min prn up to 3 h (each puff = 18 mcg ipratropium + 90 mcg albuterol)
	  ○ Adult: nebulized 3 mL (0.5 mg ipratropium + 2.5 mg albuterol) q 20 min × 3, then prn or MDI 8 puffs q 20 min prn up to 3 h
	• Corticosteroids (give immediately)

Life-Threatening: Respiratory Arrest, Imminent • Drowsy, confused • PEF < 25% (may not be needed with very severe attack) • Bradycardia • Paradoxical chest/abdominal movement • No wheezes • No pulsus paradoxus; indicates respiratory muscle fatigue	• Supplemental oxygen (100%), intubation/mechanical ventilation (do not delay intubation if respiratory failure is impending) • Permissive hypercapnia: recommended ventilator strategy; minimize high airway pressure and avoid air trapping • Nebulized albuterol + ipratropium • IV corticosteroids (methylprednisolone); see above dosing

(Continued)

TABLE 2-60   Hospital-Based Management of Acute Exacerbations of Asthma *(Continued)*

Refer to complete guidelines for specific information on management of asthma. This table is not intended as a replacement for MD orders or clinical judgment.

Evaluation of Effectiveness of Therapy

Patient's subjective response

Symptom resolution (use of accessory muscles, inspiratory/expiratory wheezing, pulsus paradoxus, cyanosis, respiratory rate)

- PEF: goal is sustained increase in PEF > 70% of predicted or personal best
- SpO_2; goal at ABG: goal is correction of significant hypoxemia (SpO_2 < 90%)

Reference: National Asthma Education and Prevention Program: Expert panel report III. *Guidelines for the diagnosis and management of asthma*. Bethesda, MD: National Heart, Lung, and Blood Institute, 2007. (NIH publication no 08-4051). Full text is available online at www.nhlbi.nih.gov/guidelines/asthma/asthdln.htm (accessed October 23, 2007).

Source: Adapted from NHLBI guidelines for the diagnosis and management of asthma. Section 5: Managing exacerbations of asthma, August 28, 2007.

■ Shock Management/Hemorrhage Control

In diagnosing shock, it is important to rule out hemorrhagic shock, tamponade, and tension pneumothorax.

Signs and symptoms of shock are as follows:

- Tachycardia; weak pulse, narrowing pulse pressure
- ↓ BP/ MAP (late signs)
- ↑ RR
- Pale/dusky, cool, moist skin
- ↑ Mental status
- Distant heart sounds
- Jugular venous distention
- ↑ UOP

Apply direct pressure.

- Bandaging is not direct pressure.
- Reinforce the first dressing to prevent dislodgement of a clot.

Initial Treatment

- Tourniquet
- Give high-flow O_2; maintain SaO_2 > 92%.
- Use two large-bore IVs or intraosseous delivery to administer Ringer's lactate (warmed).
- Prevent hypothermia.
- Rule out TBI and tension pneumothorax.

Controlled resuscitation:

- SBP ~ 80-90 mm Hg; MAP ~ 60 mm Hg

Blood for typing, CBC, coagulation, chemistry, ABG

Splint/align fractures

Rule out internal bleeding (chest, abdomen, or orthopedic)

Assist with performance of a diagnostic peritoneal lavage (DPL) or focused abdominal sonography for trauma (FAST); obtain a CT scan. Determine whether the patient might have another type of shock.

TABLE 2-61	Initial Fluid Resuscitation
Controlled Resuscitation	
Use before definitive surgical control to maintain perfusion; target MAP ≈ 60 mm Hg	
Fluid Resuscitation	
· Ringer's lactate 1 L, given at 250 mL/h · 6% Hetastarch (Hextend): maximum 1 L, given at 600-800 mL/h · 3% Hypertonic saline: maximum 500 mL, given at 250-700 mL/h	
Evaluate Response to Fluids	
· Responder: BP increases and is maintained; monitor—may require surgery · Transient responder: BP increases and then decreases; requires blood transfusion—emergent · Nonresponder: no increase in BP/continued bleeding; urgent surgery/blood transfusion/futility	
Resuscitation Goals	
· SBP > 100 mm Hg; MAP > 70 mm Hg · SaO₂ > 92% · Normothermia · Urine output	· Correct acidosis · Base deficit < 2 · Lactate < 2.5 mmol/L · Clinical coagulopathy resolved

Hemorrhage control is vital and takes priority over fluid resuscitation, especially in austere environments.

Source: U.S. Army Institute of Surgical Research. *Emergency War Surgery Handbook*, October, 2006.

Hemorrhage Control

Hemorrhage from extremity wounds accounts for 24% of preventable combat deaths.

Take these steps to control hemorrhage:

- Apply direct pressure to the wound.
- Apply a pressure dressing.
- If bleeding continues, consider a tourniquet.

Tourniquet

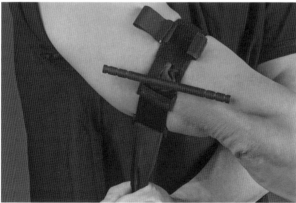

FIGURE 73A   Combat Application Tourniquet® (C-A-T®; Phil Durango, LLC; NSN 6515-01-521-7976).
Source: Courtesy of North American Rescue, Inc.

FIGURE 73B   Special Operations Forces Tactical Tourniquet (SOFTT®; NSN 6515-08-137-5357); Tactical
Medical Solutions, LLC).
Source: Courtesy of Tactical Medical Solutions, Inc.

FIGURE 73C   Emergency Medical Tourniquet (EMT Delfi Medical Innovations).
Source: Courtesy of Delfi Medical Innovations, Inc.

A tourniquet may be appropriate under tactical conditions where it is difficult to maintain pressure or monitor a wound. Apply a tourniquet if other methods to control bleeding fail. Use a tourniquet early, rather than allowing for blood loss.

The tourniquet should not be removed until advanced hemostatic or surgical control is available.

Be aware that it may not compress vessels under long bones.

Tourniquets on the arm should be placed on the upper arm.

If a tourniquet for an injury on the lower leg does not stop bleeding, it should be moved to the upper thigh, where vessels are more easily compressed.

Ischemia damage is rare if the tourniquet is applied for less than 1 hour.

To apply a tourniquet, follow these general directions:
- Place the tourniquet around the extremity, a minimum of 2 inches above the wound or amputation.
- The tourniquet should be a minimum of 2 inches wide.
- Once the tourniquet is applied and secured in place, twist the windlass device (stick) or inflate the cuff until it stops the bleeding.
- Secure the device.
- Mark the casualty with a "T" on his or her forehead.

References

Butler, F, Holcomb JB, Giebner SD, et al. Tactical combat casualty care 2007: Evolving concepts and battlefield experience. *Mil Med* 2007;172(11 suppl):1-19.

Emergency War Surgery Handbook. The Borden Institute, Washington, DC.

Navein J, Coupland R, Dunn R. The tourniquet controversy. *J Trauma* 2003;54(5):S219-S220.

Prehospital Trauma Life Support, Military Version. St. Louis: Mosby, 2006.

Smhelz J, Johnson A, Norton J, et al. Effect of chest drainage tube position on volume and pressure. *Am J Crit Care* 1999;8:319-323.

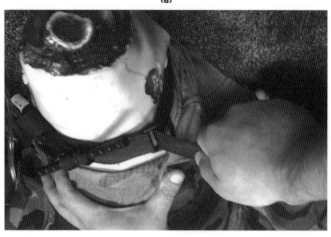

(A)

(B)

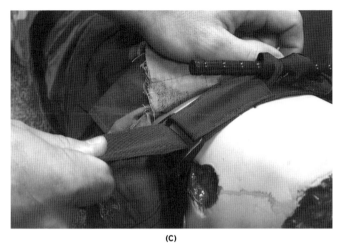

(C)

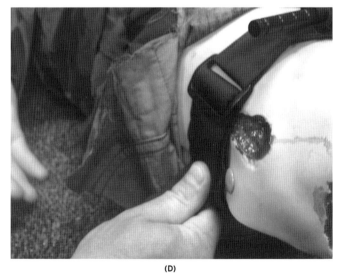

(D)

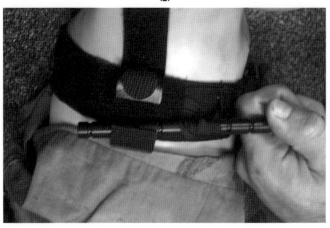

(E)

(F)

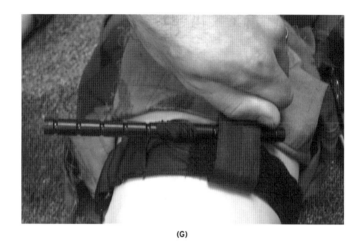

(G)

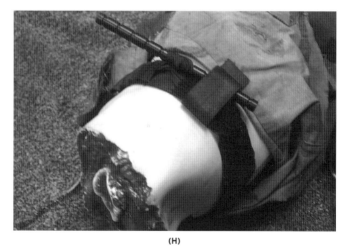

(H)

FIGURE 74   Application of C.A.T.

Hemostatic Dressings

Stop the Bleeding

First, evaluate the wound. Apply direct pressure and bandage the wound. If bleeding does not stop, apply tourniquet if appropriate.

If bleeding does not stop (or a tourniquet is not appropriate), use QuikClot® Combat Gauge™.

Consider these points:

- *Do not* apply near the patient's eyes.
- Use should be delayed until after a trial of a conventional dressing.
- Do not use on minor wounds.
- Use of these measures in case of internal wounds is not yet recommended.
- The provider must apply pressure to the bleeding site after application of these measures (usually 2–8 min).

QuikClot® Combat Gauze™

QuikClot® Combat Gauze™ is applied as follows:

- Blot away excess blood, water, or dirt from the wound with a sterile gauze pad or the cleanest, driest product available (can be placed in blood).
- Tear open the QuikClot pack.
- Place over or pack the dressing on the wound (may require more than one QuikClot® dressing).
- Apply direct firm pressure to the wound using a sterile gauze bandage or the cleanest product available. Apply pressure for 3 minutes (minimum) or until bleeding stops. Do not remove QuikClot®. (Continued pressure may be required.)
- Apply an absorbent dressing and a pressure bandage. If no pressure bandage is available, continue to apply manual pressure.
- Send the QuikClot® packaging with the wound dressing to notify medical team of use.
- Note: Research is currently ongoing to evaluate the use of QuikClot® for penetrating trauma; however, there are no current recommendations for this use.

FIGURE 75 QuikClot® Combat Gauze™.
Source: Courtesy of Z-Medica Corporation.

Reference

Arnaud F, et al. Comparative efficacy of granular and bagged formulas of the hemostatic agent QuikClot. *J Trauma* 2007;63(4):775-782.

Cardiogenic Shock

Cardiogenic shock may result from pump failure due to heart failure, myocardial infarction (MI), arrhythmias, valvular pathology, or sepsis. Severe left ventricular dysfunction is the cause of 80% of shock associated with MI.

Signs and symptoms of cardiogenic shock are as follows:

SBP < 90 mm Hg or acute decrease in SBP > 30 mm Hg

Hypoperfusion:
• UOP < 20 mL/h
• Decreased CNS function
• Peripheral vasoconstriction (cool, moist skin of trunk and extremities)
• CI < 2.2 L/min/m²

Congestion
• Pulmonary congestion (crackles)
• PAOP > 18 mm Hg

Supportive care:

Treat the cause, and stabilize the patient's hemodynamic status:
• Oxygen (4-8 L/min): maintain SpO_2 > 92%.
• Ventilatory support as needed.
• Furosemide: 10-20 mg IV over 1-2 min; infusion 0.05 mg/kg/h. A vascular effect may be observed within 5 min; the diuretic effect is delayed.
• Nitroglycerin: start at 5-10 mcg/min and titrate 10 mcg/min q 3-5 min. Use in patients with acute pulmonary edema with adequate BP; use in combination with dobutamine. Avoid in patients with inferior MI with suspected RV involvement.

Do not use if SBP < 90 mm Hg or 30 mm Hg below baseline, or if patient has extreme bradycardia (HR < 50 bpm) or tachycardia (>100 bpm).

- Fluids: may be necessary with right ventricular MI and inferior MI.
- Vasopressors: use with caution to maintain MAP > 65 mm Hg; avoid excessive vasoconstriction, as it may further decrease CI.
  - Dopamine: 3-10 mcg/kg/min (use for inotropic and vasopressor effect)
  - Norepinephrine: 0.02-0.04 mcg/kg/min (use for profound hypotension)
  - Dobutamine: 2-20 mcg/kg/min (use for ↓CI and ↑PAOP; avoid with hypotension)
- Morphine: 2-4 mg IV; repeat q 5-15 min. Use for acute pulmonary edema. Note: it may cause hypotension.
- Arrhythmia control
- Revascularization for acute MI: fibrinolytic therapy (See the "Cardiac" section for dosing.)

Obstructive Shock
Mechanical obstruction of blood flow through great veins, aorta, heart, and pulmonary vasculature.

Cardiac Tamponade
Cardiac tamponade occurs when blood, fluid, or a mass is present in the pericardium as a result of blunt or penetrating trauma.
Signs and symptoms are as follows:
- Tachypnea, tachycardia, hypotension, or shock
- Pulsus paradoxus (SBP > 10 mm Hg during spontaneous inspiration); not reliably elicited if ventilated
- Chest radiograph (CXR–rarely used acutely in trauma): enlarged cardiac silhouette and absence of pulmonary congestion
- FAST exam: primary method for diagnosis
- ECG: low-voltage complexes; may progress to PEA
- Jugular venous distention may be absent if the patient is hypovolemic

Pericardiocentesis performed by an MD.

Tension Pneumothorax
Tension pneumothorax occurs when air enters the pleural space of the injured lung on inspiration and does not escape during expiration. The increased intrathoracic pressure collapses the injured lung, leading to a mediastinal shift in which the great vessels, heart, and uninjured lung are pushed to the opposite side.

Signs:

- **Severe respiratory distress**
- Decreased or absent breath sounds (on the affected side)
- Hypotension
- Distended neck veins
- Deviated trachea to the opposite side (late sign)
- Cyanosis (late sign)

If the patient is being ventilated, he or she will exhibit increased peak inspiratory pressure, decreased tidal volume. *Remove the patient from the ventilator* and use a bag-valve-mask to ventilate.

Treatment consists of needle decompression, followed by placement of a chest tube. Use a 3.25-inch needle to ensure entry into pleural space; a shorter needle will not reach in large individuals.

Pulmonary Embolism

Selected risk factors for pulmonary embolism include age > 40 years, trauma, immobilization, major surgery, MI, and central venous catheterization.

The most common signs and symptoms include these:

- Dyspnea
- Tachypnea
- Pleuritic chest pain
- Crackles
- Cough
- Leg swelling
- Tachycardia
- Leg pain

Diagnosis relies on the following measures:

- CXR/ECG is not specific; may show RV strain
- ABG: shows hypoxemia with increased A-a gradient
- Echocardiography: less sensitive and specific than CT angiography scan
- Vascular duplex scan of legs and upper body if central venous catheter has been placed: to evaluate for venous thromboembolism (VTE)

Use the following treatments:

Full systemic anticoagulation is contraindicated in trauma, postoperative, and head injury patients.

- Enoxaparin (low-molecular-weight heparin [LMWH])
  - 1 mg/kg SQ q 12 h or 1.5 mg/kg daily
  - Severe renal failure: 1 mg/kg daily

- Unfractionated heparin (UFH): IV
  - Bolus 100 units/kg, then 18-20 units/kg/h
  - Goal aPTT: 1.5-2.0 times control values (measure q 6 h)
- Inferior vena cava filter (preventive): if contraindications to UFH/ LMWH or recurrent VTE; placed at LRMC or Echelon (Role) 5 MTF
- Supportive care (massive PE)
  - Cautious fluid administration: augment right ventricular function
  - O_2, intubation, mechanical ventilation
  - Dobutamine may increase RV function but worsen hypotension
- Sequential compression devices (SCDs)

Distributive Shock
Distributive shock consists of hypotension and relative hypovolemia due to decreased vascular tone and blood maldistribution.

Neurogenic Shock
Neurogenic shock involves disruption of sympathetic innervations; it is usually seen with spinal cord injury above T6.
Signs and symptoms are as follows:
- Hypotension, bradycardia (or absence of compensatory HR), decreased vascular resistance
- Bounding peripheral pulses (absent if hypotensive)
- Skin warm and dry
- Flaccid paralysis: loss of sensation, autonomic function, and reflexes below the level of injury

Treatment:
In case of trauma, assume the cause of hypotension is blood loss until proven otherwise.
First-line therapy is IV fluids.
Give vasopressors, titrate to maintain the patient's MAP/SBP:
- Phenylephrine: start infusion at 100-180 mcg/min until BP is stable; maintenance: 40-60 mcg/min
- Norepinephrine: start infusion at 0.5 mcg/min (range 2-12 mcg/min)

Anaphylactic Shock
Anaphylactic shock may occur within minutes after exposure to the allergen.
Patients will exhibit the following signs and symptoms:
- Skin: flushed, itching, hives; edema of face and tongue
- Respiratory: laryngeal edema, bronchospasm, cough, stridor, wheezing, chest pain or tightness
- Circulatory: hypotension, tachycardia, arrhythmia, palpitations, pallor, dizziness, and syncope
- Neurological: anxiety, fatigue, lethargy and coma; sudden loss of consciousness and seizures

Treatment proceeds as follows:

- Epinephrine 1:1000: 0.3 mL SQ q 15 min. Repeat × 3 prn for moderate bronchospasm, facial, and laryngeal edema.
- Diphenhydramine (Benadryl): 50 mg IV push × 1 if unresponsive to SQ epinephrine.
- Epinephrine 1:10,000: 0.5-1 mg IVP q 5-10 min if unresponsive to previously applied measures
- Early intubation

Sepsis/Septic Shock

Treat sepsis per the JTTS protocol. This condition involves a clinical source of infection or positive blood culture and at least 2 or more of the following findings:

- Core temperature > 38.3°C or < 36°C
- WBC > 12,000/μL or > 4000/μL or > 10% immature bands
- Positive blood culture (rule out contamination)
- HR > 90 bpm
- RR > 20 breaths/min (or PaCO$_2$ < 32 mm Hg)

Severe sepsis consists of sepsis plus at least one of the signs of organ hypoperfusion or organ dysfunction:

- Areas of mottled skin or capillary refilling > 3 sec
- Urine output < 0.5 mL/kg for at least 1 h
- Lactate > 2 mmol/L
- Abrupt change in mental status
- Platelet count < 100,000 cells/mL or disseminated intravascular coagulation (DIC)
- Acute lung injury (ALI) or acute respiratory distress syndrome (ARDS)
- Cardiac dysfunction

Septic shock consists of severe sepsis plus one of the following conditions:

- MAP < 60 mm Hg (< 80 mm Hg if previously hypertensive) after 20-30 mL/kg colloid or 40-60 mL/kg crystalloid
- Need for dopamine > 5 mcg/kg/min or norepinephrine > 0.25 mcg/ kg/min to maintain MAP > 60 mm Hg (> 80 mm Hg if previously hypertensive)

Initial management includes these measures:

Perform cultures before administering antibiotics.
Start broad-spectrum antibiotics within 1 h of recognition of severe sepsis or 3 h from ED: Time to administration of antibiotics is crucial.
Measure serum lactate.
If the patient is hypotensive and/or lactate > 4 mmol/L:

- Give crystalloids: 500-1000 mL over 30 min (initial volume 20 mL/kg)

- If after fluids MAP ≤ 65 mm Hg or lactate > 4 mmol/L, give the following agents:
  - Norepinephrine: 2-12 mcg/min
  - Dopamine: 2-20 mcg/kg/min
  - Vasopressin: 0.04 unit/min (if refractory to norepinephrine and dopamine)
- Give dobutamine (2-20 mcg/kg/min) if MAP, central venous pressure (CVP), and hemoglobin (Hgb) are within the target ranges but central venous O_2 saturation (ScvO2) < 70%.
- Transfuse: $ScvO_2$ < 70% and goal Hgb 7-9 gm/dL (10 gm/dL if cardiac disease, acute CVA).
- Return to OR for extensive irrigation/drainage and surgical debridement.

Resuscitation goals are as follows:
- MAP ≥ 65 mm Hg
- CVP 8-12 mm Hg (12-15 mm Hg if ventilated)
- Central venous O_2 saturation ($ScvO_2$) > 70% or mixed venous O_2 saturation ($ScvO_2$) > 65%
- Resolution of lactate: > 10% decrease from baseline in first 6 h of therapy associated with improved outcomes
- Base deficit (BD) may be used as a surrogate for lactate, although a patient may have increased lactate without an increase in BD

Maintenance therapy includes the following measures:
- Steroids: give if patient is refractory to vasopressors/fluids—hydrocortisone 200 mg/day (4 doses) × 7 days
- Blood glucose: maintain between 80 and 150 mg/dL; monitor for hypoglycemia
- Inspiratory plateau: maintain at < 30 cm H_2O for patients with ARDS
- Activated protein C is not currently available in AOR

■ Soft-Tissue Trauma

In Operation Iraqi Freedom/Operation Enduring Freedom, 53% of extremity wounds were penetrating soft-tissue trauma and 26% were fractures and 4% were amputations. The remaining injuries were contusions, abrasions, burns, vascular trauma, and dislocations. Among the fractures, 82% were open fractures (Owens, 2007), which is similar to the 83% open fracture rate in Operation Desert Storm.

Acute Management
- The first step for all soft-tissue trauma is direct pressure to stop bleeding. Do not remove the dressing; apply another dressing on top of it.

- If necessary, apply a tourniquet.
- Use hemostatic agents (Combat Gauze applied with at least 3 minutes of direct pressure) if direct pressure and tourniquet do not stop bleeding.
- If there is significant trauma lacking definitive hemorrhage control, use hypotensive resuscitation: SBP ≈ 85–90 mm Hg (Holcomb, 2003). Note that there is limited evidence to definitively indicate that a barely palpable radial pulse is equivalent to an SBP ≈ 90 mm Hg, although this is frequently cited as a recommendation.
  - The purposes of hypotensive resuscitation are to avoid disturbing clot formation and causing rebleeding, to prevent dilutional coagulopathy, and to avoid resuscitation-induced hypothermia.

All soft-tissue trauma wounds need debridement and/or exploration. Some small penetrating fragments can be managed without surgical exploration: In such a case, cleanse the wound with antiseptic and scrub brush. However, a patient may have suffered severe internal injury with only a small external wound; thus further evaluation of all injuries must be undertaken.

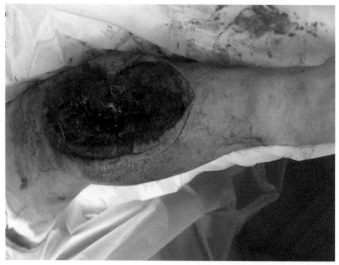

FIGURE 76   Soft-tissue trauma (fragment wound).
Source: Reproduced from the Defense Medical Readiness Training Institute (DMRTI), War Skills Surgery Course, Fort Sam Houston, TX.

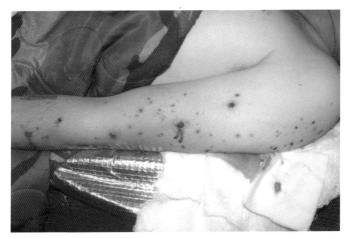

FIGURE 77 Multiple small explosive fragment wounds may be successfully treated with local wound care and prophylactic antibiotics.
Source: © 2006 American Academy of Orthopaedic Surgeons. Reprinted from the *Journal of the American Academy of Orthopaedic Surgeons*, Volume 14 (10), pp. S10-S17 with permission.

Wound Care

All war wounds are dirty, so wound irrigation is necessary to clean them.

- Perform *gentle* irrigation with a simple bulb syringe or gravity irrigation. Use of high-pressure pulse lavage is appropriate only in the OR and is a surgical decision.
- Use large-bore tubing (e.g., Baxter Y-Type TUR irrigation set; NSN 3218654401).
- The solution of choice is a warm, sterile, isotonic solution (alternatives: sterile water or potable water) with no additives.
- Volume for small wounds is 1-3 L; for moderate wounds is 4-8 L; and for large wounds or wounds with heavy contamination is > 9 L.

Source: JTTS Clinical Practice Guidelines for Irrigation of War Wounds.

Debridement and irrigation of major wounds will generally occur in the operating room.

Primary wound closure *should not* be performed in the field. Instead, wounds are generally left open for 4-5 days. If the wound is clean and granulating at that point, a decision will be made regarding closure. *Dressing considerations are as follows:*

- Do not plug the wound; allow for wound drainage.
- Initial field dressing: dry, nonocclusive
- Postoperative dressing: wet to moist

- Wet to dry dressing; used for wound debridement but may cause pain, bleeding, and damage of healthy tissue during removal Assess the wound for drainage and odor. A foul-smelling wound may require additional debridement.

Aeromedical evacuation considerations are as follows:
- Dressings are not changed during flight, but rather are reinforced.
- Consider the need to change the dressing before the flight and during any ground-based care.

With antibiotics, the goal is to effectively prevent/treat infection but avoid inappropriate use of antibiotics to decrease the patient's risk of developing antibiotic resistance. Because appropriate antibiotic selection may change over time, refer to your local policy and consult with an infectious disease MD as appropriate.

Confirm tetanus toxoid status in U.S./coalition forces. Assume that third-country nationals are not immunized (verify if possible); give them tetanus toxoid and consider tetanus immune globulin.

Amputation Care

Basic principles of care are described here:
- Maintain limb position in an anatomically neutral position. For example, with above-the-knee amputations, avoid excessive continual flexion at hip and abduction and minimize the natural tendency for lateral rotation of the residual limb. Avoid placement of pillows under the knee to prevent contractures.
- See the pain management section for recommendations for treatment of nociceptive versus neuropathic pain.
- Postoperative Management: soft dry dressing should be applied around the amputation site and extremity. Circumferential wraps with gauze rolls and ace wraps must be applied in a figure-eight fashion without excessive compression. Dressing should be tighter distally than proximally (i.e., graded compression) to prevent a tourniquet effect, promote venous drainage and minimize edema.

Below-the-knee, Below-the-Elbow, and Above-the-Elbow Dressings
Follow similar steps as for application of soft dressings (gauze) during initial wound management. *The key is to avoid creating a tourniquet effect with the dressing.*
1. Using a 4-inch-wide elastic bandage, go over the end of the limb, slightly stretching the bandage.
2. Relax the stretch and secure the bandage by going around the limb once.
3. Increase the stretch and go to one side of the center.
4. Decreasing the stretch, go around the back.
5. Go up the other side of the center as you increase the stretch again.

6. Repeat this figure-eight pattern until the end is securely bandaged, and then secure the bandage with Velcro or tape. Do not secure bandages with pins.
7. If the length below the knee/elbow is very short, you will need to make a similar figure-eight pattern above and below the joint and then secure the bandage.

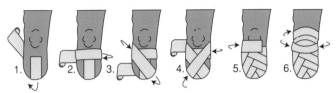

FIGURE 78 Dressing for below-the-knee, below-the-elbow, and above-the-elbow amputation.
Source: Courtesy of the Amputee Coalition of America [www.amputee-coalition.org].

Above-the-Knee Amputation Dressing

Use similar technique for gauze dressing during initial wound management.

1. Use two 6-inch-wide elastic bandages. If necessary, bandages can be sewn together.
2. Wrap around the waist twice.
3. Wrap around the end of the limb.
4. Wrap back around the waist.
5. Wrap around the end of the limb.
6. Wrap around the waist and secure. (This is the anchor for the next bandage.)
7. Take another 6-inch-wide elastic bandage and, similar to the technique used for below-the-knee amputations, go over the end of the limb, slightly stretching the bandage.
8. Relax the stretch and secure the bandage by going around the limb once, then increase the stretch and go to one side of the center.
9. Decreasing the stretch, go around back, and then go up the other side of the center as you increase the stretch again. Repeat this figure-eight pattern until the end is securely bandaged, making sure to bandage all of the way up into the groin area. Secure the bandage with Velcro or tape. Do not secure bandages with pins.

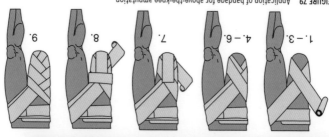

FIGURE 79 Application of bandage for above-the-knee amputation.
Source: Courtesy of the Amputee Coalition of America [www.amputee-coalition.org].

Negative Pressure Wound Therapy (NPWT)

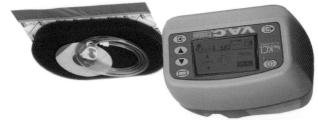

FIGURE 80 V.A.C.® Freedom. (Courtesy of KCI Licensing, Inc., 2007.) Do not substitute any parts/supplies when using this system.

The Vacuum-Assisted Closure (V.A.C.®) Freedom System (Kinetic Concepts, Inc., San Antonio, TX) is approved for use during aeromedical evacuation. Refer to the manufacturer's guidelines for further information (http://www.kcil.com/Clinical_Guidelines_VAC.pdf).

This kind of NPWT is used for acute and chronic wounds. It decreases edema, removes wound exudates, and promotes healing.

This therapy is contraindicated in the following types of wounds:

- Before complete wound debridement and hemostasis is achieved
- Malignancy in the wound
- Untreated osteomyelitis
- Non-enteric and unexplored fistulas
- Necrotic tissue with eschar present

See V.A.C.® Safety Information for further details: http://www.kcil.com/VAC_IFU.pdf. In general, take these precautions:

- *Do not* substitute any parts or supplies when using this system (e.g., do not use surgical drapes in place of the sponge or use an alternative suction source).

- *Do not* place foam dressings directly in contact with exposed blood vessels, anastomotic sites, organs, or nerves.
- *Protect vessels and organs.* All exposed or superficial vessels and organs in or around the wound must be completely covered and protected prior to the administration of V.A.C.® Therapy. Always ensure that V.A.C.® Foam Dressings do not come in direct contact with vessels or organs.
- *Closely monitor patients at increased risk for bleeding.* Patients at higher risk include those who have weakened or friable blood vessels or organs in or around the wound as a result of, but not limited to, the following conditions: suturing of the blood vessel (native anastamoses or grafts) or organ, infection, trauma, radiation, inadequate wound hemostasis, use of anticoagulants or platelet aggregation inhibitors, and inadequate tissue coverage over vascular structures.
- *Beware of infected blood vessels.* Use extreme caution when V.A.C.® Therapy is applied in close proximity to infected or potentially infected blood vessels.
- Remove the V.A.C.® Dressing if defibrillation is required in the area of dressing placement. Failure to remove the dressing may inhibit transmission of electrical energy and/or patient resuscitation.

TABLE 2-62 Nursing Care for Patient with V.A.C.®	
FIGURE 81 Foam Placement	
Always use V.A.C.® Dressings from sterile packages that have not been opened or damaged. • Cut the foam to fit the wound; avoid rough edges on the foam and do not trim it over the wound. • Multiple pieces of foam may be used, but ensure good piece-to-piece contact. • Gently place the foam into the wound. • Do not place any foam dressing into blind/unexplored tunnels. • Always count the total number of pieces of foam used in the wound and document that number on the drape and in the patient's chart. • Also document the dressing change date on the drape.	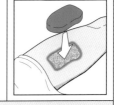
FIGURE 82 Wound Coverage	
Cover the wound and foam with an adhesive drape. • Several pieces may be required to cover the wound. • Allow for a 3- to 5-cm border around the wound/sponge. • Check for leaks, and use additional drape to seal any leaks found.	

(Continued)

TABLE 2-62   Nursing Care for Patient with V.A.C.® (Continued)

FIGURE 83   Pad Application
Source: Courtesy of KCI Licensing, Inc.

Pinch the drape and cut a 2-cm hole through it (not a slit, as a slit may self-seal during therapy). The hole should be large enough to allow for removal of fluid and/or exudate. It is not necessary to cut into the foam.

· Apply the pad, which has a central disk and a surrounding outer adhesive skirt.
· Remove both backing layers 1 and 2 to expose the adhesive.
· Place the pad opening in the central disk directly over the hole in the drape.
· Apply gentle pressure on the central disk and outer skirt to ensure complete adhesion of the pad.
· Pull back on the blue tab to remove the pad stabilization layer.

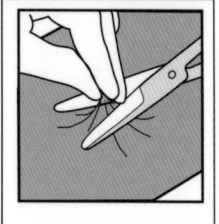

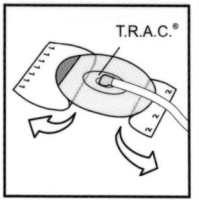

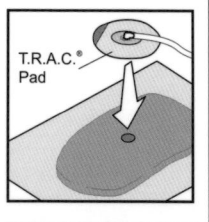

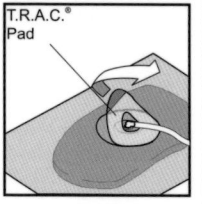

Negative-Pressure Settings

The initial pressure is generally set at -125 mm Hg continuous pressure. *Increase the pressure (in 25 mm Hg increments) for the following conditions:*

- Excessive drainage
- Large wound volume

Decrease the pressure (in 25 mm Hg increments) for the following conditions:
- Extremes of age
- Compromised nutrition
- Risk of excessive bleeding (e.g., patients on anticoagulation therapy)
- Circulatory compromise (e.g., peripheral vascular disease)
- Excessive granulation tissue growth
- Pain or discomfort not relieved by appropriate analgesia
- Periwound or wound bed ecchymosis

Foam Removal
V.A.C.® Foam Dressings are not bioabsorbable. Always count the total number of pieces of foam removed from the wound, and ensure that the same number of foam pieces is removed as was placed.

If the dressing adheres to the wound, consider introducing sterile water or normal saline into the dressing, waiting 15–30 min, and then gently removing the dressing from the wound.

Dressing Changes
In AOR, a dressing change may be carried out in the operating room.
- Change pads q 24–48 h if no infection (no less than 3×/week)
- Change pads q 12 h or prn if infected (no longer than q 48 h, depending on clinical/tactical conditions)
- Do not change pads during AE flight
- Keep V.A.C.® therapy on for at least 22 of 24 hours; if pump is off for > 2 h, remove pad and cover with standard dressing

Monitoring
Monitor patients for increased secretions, which may indicate possible hemorrhage. A sudden, rapid increase in bright red blood in the tubing and/or canister requires immediate treatment.

If significant bleeding develops, immediately discontinue the use of V.A.C.® Therapy, take measures to stop the bleeding, and do not remove the foam dressing until the treating physician or surgeon is consulted. Do not resume the use of V.A.C.® Therapy until adequate hemostasis has been achieved, and the patient is not at risk for continued bleeding.

Monitor patients for acute infection, indicated by fever, tenderness, redness, swelling, itching, rash, increased warmth in the wound area, purulent discharge, or a strong odor. In such a case, notify the MD for possible removal of the pad.

References
Emergency War Surgery, Third United States Revision (pp. 22.1–22.1414). Washington, DC, Borden Institute,. Walter Reed Army Medical Center, 2004.
Emergency War Surgery Course, 2007.

■ Venous Thromboembolism Prophylaxis

Venous Thromboembolism Prevention

Risk factors for venous thromboembolism (VTE) are as follows:

- Increasing age (> 40 years)
- Prolonged immobility, stroke, or paralysis
- Trauma (major or lower extremity)
- Major surgery (abdomen, pelvis, lower extremity)
- Smoking
- Recent myocardial infarction
- Central venous catheter use
- Acute medical illness
- Infection
- Previous VTE
- Cancer
- Obesity
- Varicose veins
- Cardiac or pulmonary failure
- Inflammatory bowel disease
- Nephrotic syndrome
- Pregnancy/postpartum
- Estrogen use
- Thrombophilia

Sources: Geerts, 2004; Nutescu, 2007.

Signs and Symptoms

Reliance on signs and symptoms of early VTE is unreliable, as the first indication of VTE may be a pulmonary embolism. Current guidelines recommend that decisions regarding thromboprophylaxis be based first on the patient's risk (see JTTS for risk-based prophylaxis).

Holcomb, JB. Fluid resuscitation in modern combat casualty care: Lessons learned from Somalia. J Trauma 2003;54:846-851.

JTTS Clinical Practice Guideline. Amputation. (Mar 2010).

Langworthy MJ, Smith JM, Gould M. Treatment of mangled lower extremity after a terrorist blast injury. Clin Orthop Related Res 2004;422:88-96.

Leininger BE, Rasmussen TE, Smith DL, et al. Experience with wound VAC and delayed primary closure of contaminated soft tissue injuries in Iraq. J Trauma 2006;61:1207-1211.

Owens BD, Kragh JF, Macaitis J, et al. Characterization of extremity wounds in Operation Iraqi Freedom and Operation Enduring Freedom. J Orthoped Trauma 2007;21:254-257.

TABLE 2-63   JTTS Clinical Practice Guidelines for the Prevention of Deep Vein Thrombosis (Nov 2008)

Note that this table is a guideline only; it is not a substitute for clinical judgment.

Trauma Surgery	
• Emergency trauma surgical procedures in patients with prohibitive risk of bleeding, or ongoing coagulopathy	• Sequential compression device (SCDs) until able to be anticoagulated • Start lovenox within 12 hours of cessation of coagulopathy (ideal)
• Emergency trauma surgical procedures in all patients except patients with prohibitive risk of bleeding (once coagulopathy not present)	• Lovenox 30 mg SQ BID • Strongly consider adding SCDs
• Isolated major orthopedic surgery of extremities, spine, and pelvis	• SCDs *and* • Lovenox 30 mg SQ BID • Continue treatment for 7-10 days • Consider eligibility for IVC filter

General Surgery	
• Low risk: minor procedures in patients < 40 years of age, no risk factors	• Early mobilization
• Moderate risk: minor procedures with additional risk factors for thrombosis; non-major surgery in patients 40-60 years old, with no additional risk factors; major surgery in patients with no additional risk factors	• Unfractionated heparin 5000 units BID *or* • Lovenox 40 mg SQ daily
• Moderate risk or higher with high risk of bleeding	• Graduated compression stockings (GCS) or SCDs
• Higher risk: non-major surgery in patients > 60 years of age or who have additional risk factors; major surgery in patients > 40 years or who have additional risk factors	• Unfractionated heparin 5000 units TID *or* • Lovenox 30 mg SQ BID
• High risk: patients with multiple risk factors	• Unfractionated heparin 5000 units TID *or* • Lovenox 30 mg BID *plus* GCS or SCDs

Vascular Surgery	
• Patients without additional thromboembolic risk factors	• No need for thromboprophylaxis
• Patients with additional thromboembolic risk factors	• Unfractionated heparin 5000 units BID *or* • Lovenox 40 mg SQ daily

Urologic Surgery	
• Low-risk urologic surgery	• Early ambulation
• Major, open urologic procedures	• Unfractionated heparin 5000 unit BID or TID
• Patients actively bleeding or at risk for bleeding	• GCS or SCDs
• Patients with multiple risk factors	• GCS or SCDs *and* • Unfractionated heparin 5000 units SQ BID or TID *or* • Lovenox 40 mg SQ daily

Neurosurgery	
• Intracranial neurosurgical procedures	• SCDs with/without GCS
• High-risk neurosurgery patients	• SCDs and/or GCS. OK to use lovenox following stable CT scan in consultation with neurosurgeon.

In hospitalized patients in the United States, medical patients account for 70-80% of fatal pulmonary embolisms and 50-70% of thromboembolic events.

References

Büller HR, et al. Antithrombotic therapy for venous thromboembolic disease: The Seventh ACCP Conference on Antithrombotic and Thrombolytic Therapy. *Chest* 2004;126(3 suppl):401S–428S.

Geerts WH, et al. Prevention of venous thromboembolism: The Seventh ACCP Conference on Antithrombotic and Thrombolytic Therapy. *Chest* 2004;126(3 suppl):338S–400S.

Nutescu EA. Assessing, preventing, and treating venous thromboembolism: Evidence-based approaches. *Am J Health-Syst Pharm* 2007;64(suppl 7):S5–S13.

Segal JB, et al. Management of venous thromboembolism: A systematic review for a practice guideline. *Ann Intern Med* 2007;146(3):211-222.

SECTION

Treatment

■ Blood/Blood Products

Follow all regulations for blood product storage and administration.
Administer compatible blood when clinically and operationally feasible.

- O-negative blood is the universal donor.
- Echelon (Role) 2 MTFs provide Rh-negative PRBCs to Rh-negative males and females.
- Echelon (Role) 3 and higher MTFs have the capability to group, type, and cross-match blood before transfusion of O-negative patients when operationally or clinically feasible.
- In case of a shortage of Rh-negative blood, priority is given to Rh-negative females.
- Do not withhold life-saving transfusions because of Rh incompatibility.

Recipient	Donor
O	O
A	A (O)
B	B (O)
AB	AB (A, B, O)
Rh+	Rh+ or Rh—
Rh—	Rh—

TABLE 3-1   Blood Products

Either hang blood products within 30 minutes or return them to the blood bank or an approved blood storage container.

Product	Notes
Whole blood	• ABO compatible required • Total volume ≈ 500 mL/unit • Infuse IV/IO < 4 h to minimize hemolysis and bacterial contamination • Administer via blood warmer (fresh whole blood is already warmed)
Packed red blood cells (PRBCs)	• ABO compatible preferred • Total volume ≈ 425 mL/unit • Administer via blood warmer • Infuse /IO < 4 h to minimize hemolysis and bacterial contamination
Fresh frozen plasma (FFP)	• ABO compatible preferred (A or AB) (A or AB until blood compatibility determined) • Total volume ≈ 250 mL/unit • Infuse IV/IO 15-30 min depending on the volume via blood tubing • Precise storage conditions must be adhered so as to prevent serious harm to patient; plasma not stored under precise conditions should be discarded immediately (See Joint Theater Blood Program guidance.) • Thawed plasma for emergency should be type A or AB; no more than 2 units of untyped plasma should be administered until ABO typing has been completed
Platelets	• May be transfused at room temperatures 68-75°F (20-24°C) • Total volume < 50 mL/unit • Complete within 20-60 min depending on total volume
Cryoprecipitate	• ABO compatible preferred • Once thawed, must be infused immediately; infuse over 3-15 min • 1 dose cryoprecipitate = 10 single units

Recombinant Factor VIIa (rFVIIa)

The use of rFVIIa should be reserved for patients likely to require massive transfusion (e.g., significant injury and 3 or 4 of the following risk factors and is at the discretion of the treating physician. It should be the judgment of the provider that the casualty has a life-threatening hemorrhage and coagulopathy.

Risk factors for massive transfusion upon hospital admission in seriously injured patients (at least 3 of 4):
1. Systolic blood pressure < 110 mm Hg
2. Heart rate > 105 bpm
3. Hematocrit < 32%
4. pH < 7.25

Note: Patients with 3 of the above 4 risk factors have approximately a 70% risk of massive transfusion; patients with all 4 of the above have an 85% risk.

5. Other risk factors for massive transfusion include: INR level > 1.4, NIR-derived $StO_2 < 75\%$.

rFVIIa Dosing is as follows
- Dose 90-120 mcg/kg IV/IO push
- If coagulopathic bleeding continues 20 minutes after infusion administer 2 additional units fresh whole blood or 4 U FFP and/or 6 pack platelets. Redose rFVIIa 90-120 mcg/kg IV push and repeat up to a maximum of 3 doses within 6 hours.

Guidelines for Storage and use:
- Refrigeration at 4°C (range 2-8°C).
- Reconstitution with sterile water for injection at room temperature.
- The reconstituted solution may be used up to 24 hours after reconstitution.
- **The FDA has approved a non-heat sensitive rFVIIa. This product will be distributed throughout the AOR to replace expended stocks.**

Relative contraindications: Known hypersensitivity to rFVIIa or any of its components. Known hypersensitivity to mouse, hamster, or bovine proteins.

Absolute Contraindication: Active cardiac disease.

Source: JTTS Clinical Practice Guideline. Damage Control Resuscitation at Level IIb/III Treatment Facilities, Feb 2011. Note that this guideline is not a substitute for clinical judgment.

Damage Control Resuscitation (Role IIb/III)

Emergency department resuscitation includes (PRBC, plasma, and platelets [1:1:1 ratio] and rFVIIa) and should be initiated for patients at risk for massive transfusion (see rFVIIa–above). (Note: all platelets at US Level III facilities are apheresis platelets. 1 apheresis unit/pack = 6 units random donor platelets). Transfusion of products and administration of rFVIIa should be based on clinician judgment and the response of the patient to resuscitative therapy. Crystalloid and nonsanguinous colloid therapy should be limited in the patient with significant ongoing bleeding.

OR Resuscitation

Goal: stop bleeding, normalize the casualty's temperature and prevent/reverse coagulopathy and shock. In addition to component therapy resuscitation the following are suggested:
- The operating room must be kept as warm as possible; ideally ≥ 108°F.
- Consider a dose of rFVIIa for ongoing coagulopathic bleeding.
- Administer THAM (tromethamine), a nonbicarbonate buffer to maintain pH > 7.2. The required dose (mL of 0.3 molar solution) is equal to body weight (kg) x base deficit (mEq/L) x 1.1.

- Administer Ca^{++} after every 4 units of PRBCS and/or to keep ionized Ca^{++} > 1.0 (via iSTAT). Prevent citrate-induced hypocalcemia—administer calcium via a separate line.
  - 10% calcium-gluconate (10-20 mL for every 2 units of blood; total 20-40 mL for every 4 units PRBCS)
  - 10% calcium chloride (if hepatic failure) 5-10 mL for every 500 mL of PRBCs; total 10-20 mL for every 4 units PRBCS
  - *Avoid rapid bolus*, as it may cause cardiovascular compromise; administer 0.5 mL or fraction over 1 min

ICU Resuscitation

For patients who continue to have massive bleeding in the ICU the 1:1:1 approach in addition to all other damage control procedures principles are still required. Additional doses of rFVIIa may be indicated if acid/base and hematologic parameters are sufficient for its effectiveness (pH > 7.1, platelets > 50,000 and fibrinogen > 100).

Massive Transfusion (MT) Protocol

A flexible protocol for use in the ED, OR, and ICU that consists of batches as defined below, which vary in composition, but are directed toward approximating a 1:1:1 ratio of PRBC, FFP, platelets, and cryoprecipitate (cryo).

- **Pack One:** 4u PRBC and 4u FFP, should consider 6 pack platelets, one 10-unit bag cryo and ±Factor VII at this time if patient received 4uPRBC/4uFFP emergency release blood (uncrossmatched PRBC 2 units O+ and 2 units O- and 4 units AB FFP).
- **Pack Two:** 4u PRBC and 4u FFP
- **Pack Three:** 4u PRBC, 4u FFP, 6 pack platelets, one 10-unit bag of cryo and ±Factor VII
- **Pack Four:** 4u PRBC and 4u FFP
- **Pack Five:** 4u PRBC, 4u FFP, 6 pack platelets, and one 10-unit bag of cryoprecipitate
  - A reassessment of the progress of the resuscitation, hemostasis, and the need to continue the MT Protocol should be conducted between the providers taking care of the patient at that time
- Packs **Six** and **Seven** are identical to packs **Four** and **Five**
- Packs **Eight** and **Nine** are identical to packs **Four** and **Five**
  - *Thawed plasma* for emergency should be type A or AB until able to obtain casualty's blood type
  - *Cryoprecipitate:* 10 units contains 2,500 mg fibrinogen (1 unit fresh whole blood ~1000 mg fibrinogen; 1 unit FFP ~400 mg fibrinogen; 1 unit platelets ~80 mg fibrinogen).
  - *Fresh whole blood* should be reserved for casualties who are anticipated to require massive transfusion (10 or more units PRBCS in 24 hours), for those with clinically significant shock or coagulopathy (e.g., bleeding with associated metabolic acidosis.

thrombocytopenia or INR > 1.5) when optimal component therapy is unavailable or stored component therapy is not adequately resuscitating a patient with immediately life-threatening injuries. *Donor FWB must be an ABO type-specific match to the casualty.* If not matched, a fatal hemolytic reaction may occur. **TYPE O whole blood is NOT universal.**

Source: JTTS Clinical Practice Guideline. Damage Control Resuscitation at Level IIb/III Treatment Facilities, Feb 2011. *JTTS Clinical Practice Guideline.* Fresh Whole Blood (FWB) Transfusions, Mar 2011. Note: These guideline are not a substitute for clinical judgment.

Tranexamic Acid (TXA)—antifibrinolytic. The early use of TXA (i.e., *as soon as possible after injury but ideally not later than 3 hours post injury*) should be strongly considered for any patient requiring blood products in the treatment of combat-related hemorrhage and is most strongly advocated in patients judged likely to require a massive transfusion. Initial use of TXA after 3 hours post injury may not have benefit and may worsen survival. *It is strongly recommended that TXA **not** be administered to patients when the time from injury is known to be or suspected to be greater than 3 hours.* TXA may be administered to patients requiring massive transfusion if they have an associated TBI.

Ampoule: 1,000 mg in 10 mL water (premixed)
Dose:
- 1 g TXA in 100 mL 0.9% NS over 10 min via separated IV line from any containing blood or blood products. Avoid Hextend as a carrier fluid.
- Infuse second 1 g dose IV over 8 h with 0.9% saline carrier
  Storage: 59–86° F/15–30°C (storage at temperatures greater than these may reduce or destroy TXA efficacy.

Source: JTTS Clinical Practice Guideline. Damage Control Resuscitation at Level IIb/III Treatment Facilities, Aug 2011. (see for additional TXA details).

If the patient has an adverse reaction to any blood products, do the following:
- Stop the infusion immediately if symptoms are present.
- Notify the physician.
- Disconnect and change the IV tubing or retrograde flush the IV tubing with normal saline (flush toward the IV bag).
- Keep the vein open with normal saline. You may need to start a large-bore IV in another extremity.
- Start high-flow O_2 via NRB mask to maintain SpO_2 > 91% as needed.
- Place the patient on a cardiac monitor.
- Obtain temperature, vital signs, and pulse oximetry q 15 min.
- Monitor UOP hourly.
- Draw 5-7 mL of blood from the extremity not receiving blood products and send it to the blood bank.
- Reverify the blood unit and document.

TABLE 3-2   Reaction to Blood Products

Reaction	Signs and Symptoms	Treatment
Febrile	↑ Temperature 2°F or more, chills, flushing, tachycardia, headache, anxiety	• Acetaminophen 650 mg PO • Monitor vital signs every 15 min and observe for symptoms. Note that aspirin may interfere with platelet function.
Allergic/anaphylactic	Hives, itching, chills, flushing, nausea, and vomiting; coughing and/or wheezing, laryngeal edema	• Diphenhydramine (Benadryl) 50 mg IVP • Epinephrine per MD order
Acute hemolytic reaction	Rapid onset of the above symptoms, dyspnea, hypotension, hemoglobinuria; ↑ CVP, distended neck veins, dyspnea, cough, and/or crackles/rales	• Infuse normal saline to maintain UOP 30-50 mL/h • Treat for shock • Diphenhydramine, epinephrine SQ or IV • May require diuretics

- Save the blood bag, tubing/filter, and IV solution; send them to the blood bank.
- Document the date/end time of the transfusion on SF 518, Section III, Post-Transfusion Data, Progress Note, AF IMT 3829/3899.

Autotransfusion

Follow these steps for an autotransfusion:
- Collect blood from sterile cavities (chest or abdomen without visceral injuries).
- Blood is drained into sterile containers (chest drainage systems) and then infused.
- Blood from contaminated abdominal wounds may be used at an increased risk of systemic infection.

Refer to the manufacturer's guidelines for setup of specific autotransfusion devices. For steps for blood product administration, refer to the Joint Theater regulations.

Source: Adapted from JTTS Clinical Practice Guidelines, November 2006.

■ Glycemic Control

Note that the accuracy of single-channel point-of-care glucose monitors is affected when hematocrit < 34%. Anemia results in 15-30% over-*estimation* of serum glucose by the glucometer. When the appropriate correction formula is unavailable, validate the glucometer with serum glucose values. Arterial or venous blood samples reflect true serum glucose values better than do capillary samples in critically ill patients. Contact the Institute for Surgical Research for additional recommendations.

TABLE 3-3   Insulin

Insulin	Onset (hours)	Peak (hours)	Duration (hours)	Compatibility with Other Types of Insulin	Appearance
Available in AOR					
Regular (Novolin R, Humulin R)	0.5-1	2-4	5-8	NPH, lente, ultralente	Clear
NPH (Novolin N, Humulin N)	1-1.5	4-12	16-24	Regular	Cloudy
Not Listed in AOR Formulary					
Lispro (Humalog)	0.3-0.5	0.5-2.5	3-6.5	Human NPH, human ultralente	Clear
Aspart (Novolog)	0.2-0.3	1-3	3-5	Human NPH	Clear
Lente (Novolin L, Humulin L)	1-2.5	7-15	16-24	Regular	Cloudy
Ultralente (Humulin U)	4-6	8-20	24-28	Regular	Cloudy
Insulin glargine (Lantus)	~2	No peak	20 to > 24	Do not mix with other insulin	Clear

References

Mann E, et al. Error rates resulting from anemia can be corrected in multiple commonly used point-of-care glucometers. *J Trauma* 2008:64(1):15-21

Pidcoke HF, et al. Occult hypoglycemia in a burn ICU unmasked with correction of hematocrit effect in point-of-care glucometers (abstract). *J Burn Care Research* 2007;28(2):S92.

In-flight Considerations for Glycemic Control

- IStat
- Glucometers approved for in-flight use: Precision (Abbott) and Ascensia (Bayer Healthcare).

Sliding Scale Insulin Protocol

Refer to MD orders as needed.

TABLE 3-4   Sliding Scale Insulin Protocol
Accucheck q 4h

Blood Sugar (mg/dL)	Action
50	Give 1 amp D_{50}, notify MD
50-70	Give 1/2 amp D_{50}, notify MD
71-120	Do nothing
121-150	Give 2 units regular insulin SQ
151-180	Give 4 units regular insulin SQ
181-210	Give 6 units regular insulin SQ
211-250	Give 8 units regular insulin SQ
251-300	Give 10 units regular insulin SQ
>300	Give 12 units and notify MD

■ Insulin Infusion Protocol

Refer to local policy or MD orders as needed. *The following protocol applies to ICU only.*

Goal: 100–150 mg/dL.

Monitoring: Insulin infusion dose must be recalculated q 1 h with the latest blood glucose value.

Admixture: Regular insulin 100 units in 100 mL NS, to equal a concentration of 1 unit/mL. With the initiation of the insulin drip 20 mL of insulin solution from the insulin bag will be flushed through the infusion line to "prime" the tubing.

Initiate insulin infusion: The initial BG value will be used to calculate the beginning drip rate of the infusion. **The following formula will be used: (BG − 60) × 0.03.**

With each subsequent hourly BG value, the following formulas will be utilized to obtain the infusion rate:

BG > 150, (BG − 60) × 0.04
BG 100–150, (BG − 60) × 0.03
BG < 100, (BG − 60) × 0.02

Example: BG = 210 mg/dL

Initial dose = (210 − 60) × 0.03 = 4.2 units/h

If patient has not achieved the target BG range of 100–150 mg/dL within 12 hours of continuous insulin infusion therapy, assure that the following has occurred:

• All solution that is D_5 based has been changed to NS, unless contraindicated by pharmacy.
• Insulin infusion therapy is being administered through a dedicated IV line.

If both previous steps have been taken then proceed to Insulin *Resistant Infusion Guidelines.*

Insulin Resistant Infusion Guidelines

With each subsequent hourly BG value the following formulas will be utilized to obtain the infusion rate:

TABLE 3-5	Insulin Infusion Rate Formulas	
BG > 150	BG 100–150	BG < 100
(BG − 60) × 0.05	(BG − 60) × 0.04	(BG − 60) × 0.02

If after an additional 12 hours and patient has not reached goal of 100–150 mg/dL, then physician may increase the above (1) and (2) multiplier values by increments of 0.01–0.02 till goal is achieved. At no time should the 0.02 multiplier value be increased.

Hypoglycemia Guidelines

When the BG is < 80, the following multiplier will be used to calculate the D_{50} dose:

(100 − BG) × 0.3 = mL of D_{50} IVP

BG will be checked every 15 minutes after infusion of D_{50} and the insulin drip will be adjusted according to the previous multiplier formulas.

Reasons to Call Physician
- BG is less than 80.
- If feedings, TPN, other diabetic meds, or steroids are started or stopped.

Based on Brook Army Medical Center Insulin Infusion Protocol (not a substitute for clinical judgment).

Diabetic Ketoacidosis

Refer to MD orders as necessary.

Precipitating factors for diabetic ketoacidosis may include newly diagnosed diabetes, inadequate insulin treatment or compliance, infection, concomitant cardiovascular disease, trauma, heat stroke, severe burns, renal failure, or drugs. Signs and symptoms may include polyuria, polydipsia, weakness, or altered mental status.

Lab values will include the following findings:
- Blood glucose: 500-800 mg/dL
- Metabolic acidosis
  - pH: 7.0-7.30 (depends on severity of disease process)
  - Serum bicarbonate: < 18 mEq/L
- Urine/serum ketones: positive
- Anion gap (serum sodium – serum chloride + bicarbonate): > 10
- Mental status: may range from alert to stupor/coma

Treatment includes the following measures:

Management of ABCs

Fluid replacement (average fluid loss 3-6 L); correct estimated deficit within 24 h
- 0.9% saline at 15-20 mL/kg/h (~1-1.5 L in first hour), depending on condition (more aggressive if patient is in shock) and comorbidities (e.g., cardiac)
- Evaluate serum sodium, hydration, and UOP to guide further fluid choice; should be ~2 L over next 4 h
  - Normal or hypernatremia: 0.45% saline at 4-14 mL/kg/h
  - Hyponatremia: 0.9% saline at 4-14 mL/kg/h
- Monitor vital signs, UOP, mental status q 1 h and prn
- Reevaluate lab values after 4 hours; use results to guide fluid choice as above (0.9% saline or 0.45% saline)

Potassium supplementation: depletion will be unmasked with resolution of acidosis, hypovolemia, and hyperglycemia
- Establish normal renal function
- Delay initiation of insulin therapy until K^+ > 3.3 mEq/L

- If patient is normokalemic or hypokalemic on presentation, begin K+ supplementation immediately; add 20–30 mEq/L to replacement fluid (ensure UOP > 50 mL/h).
- If patient is hyperkalemic on presentation, start supplementation when K+ < 5.3 mEq/L (assuming adequate UOP).
  Phosphate supplementation (administer potassium phosphate):- routine use not recommended
- Replace if serum phosphate < 1.0 mg/dL or signs of cardiac dysfunction or respiratory depression.
- Dose: 0.08 to 0.32 mM/kg diluted and administered over 6 h

Insulin
- Bolus: regular insulin 0.1 unit/kg/h; continuous infusion: 0.1 unit/kg/h (↓glucose 50–70 mg/dL/h)
- Monitor glucose q 1 h and prn; if glucose does not decrease 50–70 mg/dL after 1 h, repeat bolus and double infusion rate
- When serum glucose reaches 200 mg/dL,- switch IV solution to D₅NS or D₅ or D₅½NS; consider decreasing insulin infusion rate (0.05–0.1 unit/kg/h)
- Indications of resolution of DKA (begin tapering insulin and convert to SQ insulin):
  ○ Glucose < 200 mg/dL
  ○ Anion gap < 12 mEq/L
  ○ Serum bicarbonate > 18 mEq/L
  ○ Venous pH > 7.30

Reference
Kitabachi AE, et al. Hyperglycemic crises in adult patients with diabetes: A consensus statement from the American Diabetes Association. Diabetes Care 2006;29(12):2739-2748.

■ Intraosseous Access

Intraosseous Fluid Administration

Indications for intraosseous (IO) fluid administration are as follows:
- Reliable venous access cannot be achieved quickly; placement of the IO by a skilled provider takes 1–2 min.
- As the first attempt at vascular access in full cardiopulmonary arrest or severe shock if IV access cannot be obtained

Contraindications to intraosseous fluid administration are as follows:
- Extremity with fracture or vascular injury (trauma or cutdown)
- Areas of cellulitis or burn should generally not be penetrated.

Locations for insertion of IO access are as follows:
- Optimal (adult): sternum (do not use for children < 3 years)
- Optimal (child): proximal tibia
- Alternative locations: femur (midline 3 cm above the lateral condyle); distal tibia (1–2 cm proximal to the medial malleolus)

Start IV fluids as soon as possible:
- Crystalloids: LR, normal saline, hypertonic saline, dextrose (administration of a large volume of isotonic solution may not be possible)
- Colloids, blood, plasma
- Flow rate (*can achieve same rates as with peripheral IV*): 20-25 mL/min with a pressure bag (300 mm Hg) or a high-pressure IV pump.

When administering medications via the IO route, note the following points:
- Onset similar to that with IV infusion
- Use same dose as with IV route
- Flush with 3-10 mL NaCl after drug administration to flush out of bone marrow.

TABLE 3-6	**Medications That Can Be Administered by the Intraosseous Route**				
Anesthetics	Cardiac Drugs	Analgesics	Neuromuscular Blocking Agents	Antimicrobial Agents	Other
Bupivacaine	Adenosine	Fentanyl	Atracurium	Amikacin	Calcium chloride
Etomidate	Amiodarone	Morphine	Pancuronium	Ampicillin	Calcium gluconate
Ketamine	Atropine	Naloxone	Rocuronium	Cefotaxime	Dextrose
Lidocaine	Digoxin		Succinylcholine	Ceftriaxone	Diazepam
Propofol	Dobutamine		Vecuronium	Chloramphenicol	Furosemide
Sodium pentothal	Dopamine			Chortetracycline	Heparin
	Ephedrine			Clindamycin	Insulin
	Epinephrine			Gentamicin	Mannitol
	Isoproterenol			Penicillins	Methylprednisolone
	Lidocaine			Sufadiazine	Phenobarbital
	Norepinephrine			Tobramycin	Phenytoin
	Vasopressin			Vancomycin	Sodium bicarbonate

Source: M. Dubick and J. Holcomb, "A review of intraosseous vascular access: Current status and military application, Mil Med 165 (2000): 552–559; and, M. L. Buck, et al., "Intraosseous drug administration in children and adults during cardiopulmonary arrest," *Ann Pharmacotherapy* 41 (2007): 1679-1686.

Complications occur in 1-12% of patients:
- Extravasation (12%): associated with multiple insertion attempts or improper insertion; increases risk for compartment syndrome
- Osteomyelitis: remove IO needle as soon as possible; use should not exceed 24 h
- Fat emboli: clinical significance ranges from undiagnosed to lethal (rapid DIC and cardiovascular collapse)
- Sternal and tibial fractures
- **Confirm all needle lengths. Not all needles are designed for sternal use.**

FAST™ Adult and Adolescent Intraosseous System

Follow the manufacturer's guidelines.

Indications for use of this system are as follows:

- Inadequate peripheral IV access
- Failed IV or central line insertions
- Temporary, rapid administration of fluids, blood, and medications

Contraindications are as follows:

- Children <12 years of age
- Injury/fracture to upper chest or previous sternotomy

In preparation, use *aseptic technique* and prepare the site with local anesthetic if the patient is conscious.

Steps for Insertion:

1. Cleanse the site with a chlorhexidene-based preparation tincture of iodine or 70% alcohol.
2. Locate the sternal notch.
   - Place the index finger of the nondominant hand at the sternal notch and align the IO patch indentation.
   - Place the IO patch; align the IO introducer *perpendicular to the manubrium;* off perpendicular insertion may result in under penetration of the infusion tube and/or infiltration.
   - Verify that the target zone is over the manubrium (~1-1.5 cm below the sternal notch).
3. Maintaining perpendicular alignment, insert with increasing pressure (20-30 lb) until the device releases; release will be felt and the infusion tube will separate from the introducer.
4. Remove the introducer by pulling straight back and insert the needles into the Post-use Sharps Cap.
5. Connect the infusion tube to the right-angle female luer of the adapter tube on patch.
   - Check patency; bone marrow should aspirate freely.
   - If bone marrow does not aspirate freely, flush with 5 ml saline.
   - If IO does not flush easily, discontinue and use alternative site.
   - If IO flushes easily, continue with procedure.
   - Connect IV tubing to male luer of the tube on the patch and ensure adequate flow.
6. Place the dome.
   - Use an IV bag pressure device

If low or no flow:

- Check for kinked tubing.
- Check patency and for clogged tube:1 ml normal saline flush.
- Incorrect insertion angle: infiltration

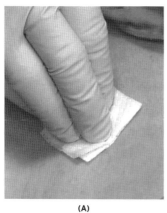

(A)

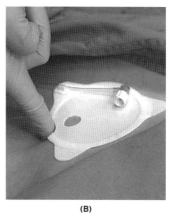

(B)

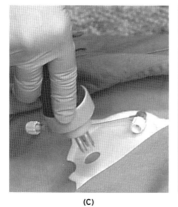

(C)

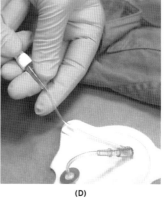

(D)

(E)

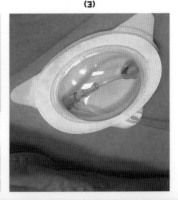

(F)

FIGURE 8A-G   Insertion of FAST 1O into sternum.
Source: Courtesy of Pyng Medical Corporation.

Remove FAST™ after 24 hours.

For the new version of the FAST™ with BLUE tipped luer:

- Stop IV flow and disconnect IV tubing.
- Remove the dome cover.
- Pull on the infusion tubing to remove it.
- Remove patch; apply dry sterile dressing.

For the original version of the FAST™ with remover tool attached to dome:

- Stop IV fluid flow and disconnect IV tubing.
- Remove the dome cover and open remover package.
- Hold insertion tube perpendicular to manubrium and maintain slight traction.
- Insert remover (threaded device); a gentle turn counterclockwise aids "seating."
- When remover is seated, turn remover clockwise until turning stops; engage remover into metal proximal end of infusion tube.
- Use only "T"-shaped knob on the remover; hold patch and pull remover perpendicular to manubrium [Do not pull on luer or tube. If the metal end breaks, it requires a small incision to remove. Report to FDA (http://www.pyng.com/contact-us/tell-us-your-story/)].
- Remove patch; apply dry sterile dressing.

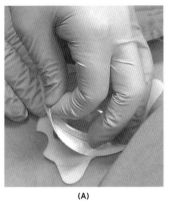
(A)

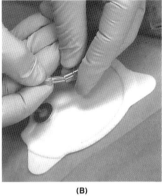
(B)

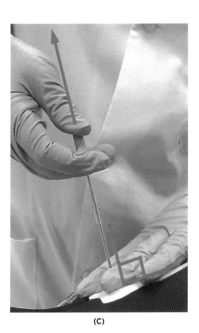
(C)

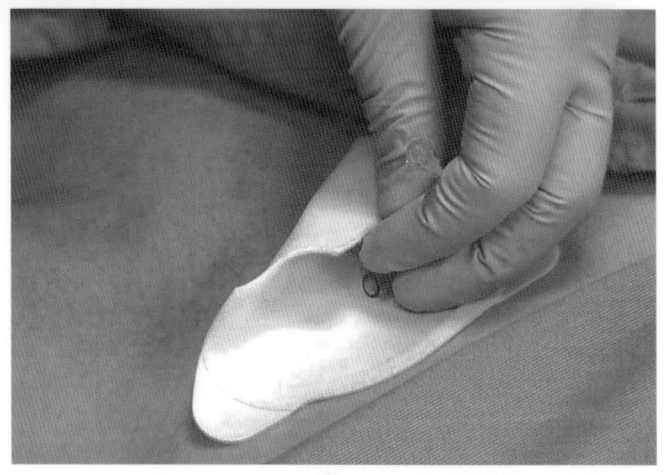

(D)

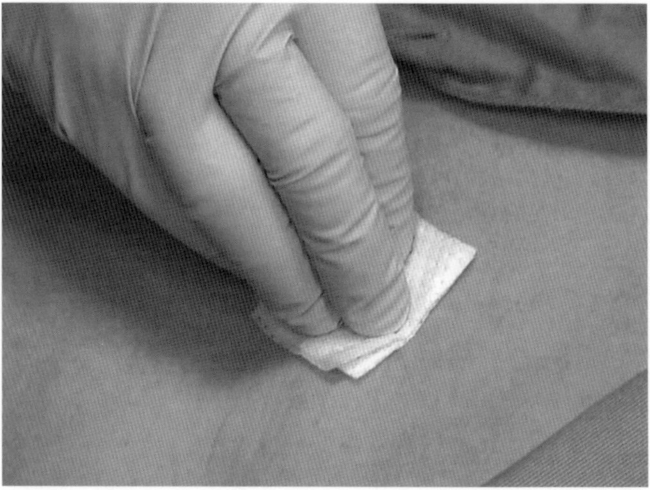

(E)

FIGURE 85A-E   Removal of FAST IO into sternum.
Source: Courtesy of Pyng Medical Corporation.

EZ-IO Catheter

For the EZ-IO AD, the patient's weight must be greater than 88 lb (40 kg). For the EZ-IO PD, the patient's weight must be in the range 6.6–86 lb (3–39 kg).

Follow these steps to insert the EZ-IO:

- Consider anesthetic for alert patients.
- Identify landmarks for insertion.
  - Usual site: anterior proximal tibia, 2 cm below tibial tuberosity, medial aspect of tibia (flat) to avoid growth plate
  - Alternative sites: proximal humerus, medial malleolus, distal anterior femur, anterior iliac crest
- Cleanse site with a chlorhexidine-based preparation, tincture of iodine, or 70% alcohol.
- Prepare the driver and needle set.
- Stabilize leg flex and support the patient's knee.
- Insert the EZ-IO needle set using aseptic technique: Insert the needle set perpendicular to the bone with constant gentle pressure and a screwing motion. The needle set will "give" or "pop" with decreased resistance when it is in the bone marrow space.
- Remove the driver from the needle set.
- Remove the stylet from the catheter.
- Confirm placement by aspirating marrow. If unable to aspirate, flush with 5–10 mL normal saline. Resistance should be minimal and without signs of infiltration.
- Attach EZ-Connect extension set. (Do *not* attach the syringe directly to the needle.)
- Flush IO with a 10 mL syringe bolus,
- Start the infusion under pressure. Use an IV pump or pressure infuser, or push fluid boluses.
- Secure the tubing and catheter.

Do not leave the EZ-IO catheter in for more than 24 h. Discontinue its use if infiltration occurs; apply direct pressure followed by a pressure dressing.

For additional educational materials, contact the manufacturer.

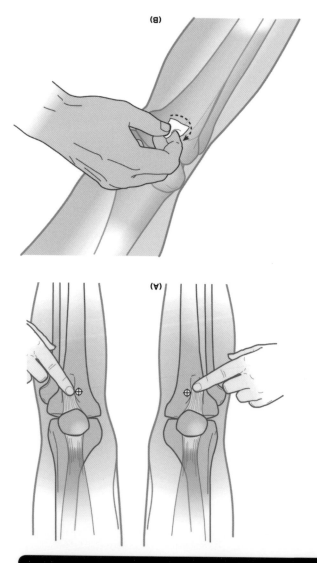

(A)

(B)

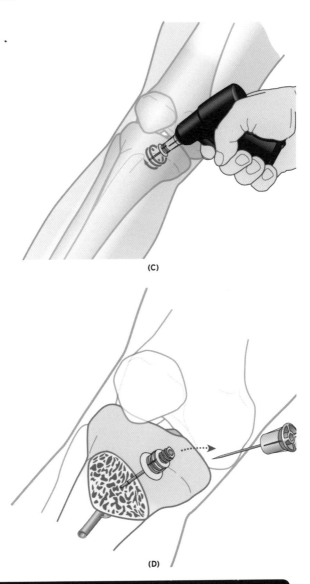

(C)

(D)

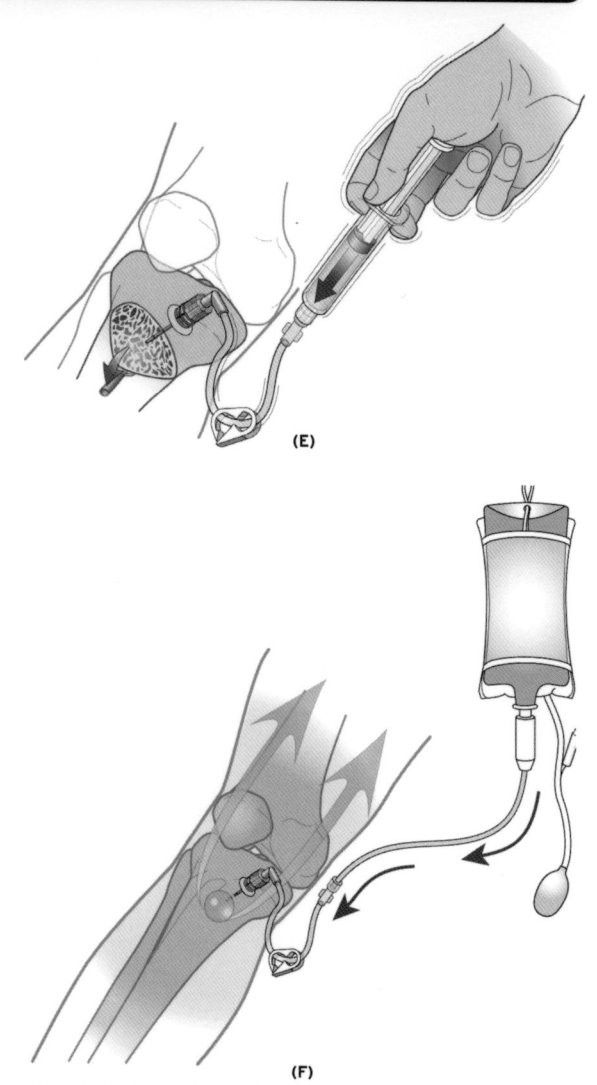

(E)

(F)

FIGURE 86A–F Use of EZ-IO for tibial insertion.
Source: Courtesy of VidaCare Corporation.

■ Labs

TABLE 3-7 Chemistry

Lab Value	Normal Range
Na⁺ (mEq/L)	135-145
K⁺ (mEq/L)	3.5-4.5
CL⁻ (mEq/L)	98-108
HCO_3^- (CO_2) (mEq/L)	22-32
Ca⁺⁺ (total) (mg/dL)	8.9-10.2
Ca⁺⁺ (ionized) (mmol/L)	1.18-1.38
Mg (mg/dL)	1.8-2.4
PO₄ (mg/dL)	2.5-4.5
Glucose (mg/dL)	60-125
BUN (mg/dL)	8-21
Creatinine (mg/dL)	0.3-1.2
Albumin (gm/dL)	3.5-5.2
Protein (gm/dL)	6.0-8.2
Total bilirubin (gm/dL)	0.2-1.3
Alkaline phosphatase (SGOT) (U/L)	15-40
Alanine aminotransferase (SGPT) U/L	Male: 10-64 Female: 6-40
Amylase (U/L)	27-144
Anion gap = $(Na^+) - (Cl^- + CO_2)$ (mEq/L)	12 ± 2
Lactate mmol/L	Arterial: 0.3-0.8 Venous: 0.5-2.1

Source: Available from IStat or Piccolo.

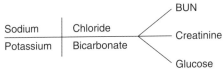

FIGURE 87 Chemical formula.

TABLE 3-8 Hematology

	Age	Range
Red blood cells (RBC)	Newborn 1 m 6 m-2 y 2 y-6 y 6 y-12 y 12 y-18 y >18 y	3.9-6.0 3.0-5.4 3.7-5.3 3.9-5.3 4.0-5.2 4.1-5.3 3.8-5.6
White blood cells (WBC) × 10⁹/L	Newborn 6 m-2 y 2 y-4 y 4 y-6 y 6 y-14 y >14 y	5.0-30.0 6.0-17.0 6.0-15.5 5.5-14.5 4.5-13.5 4.3-10.0

(Continued)

TABLE 3-8 Hematology *(Continued)*	Age	Range
Neutrophil count (1000/µL)	Newborn 1 m 6 m-1 y 1 y-4 y 4 y-10 y 10 y-12 y >12 y	6.0-26 1.5-8.5 1.5-5.0 1.5-5.0 1.5-7.5 1.8-7.0 1.8-7.0
Hemoglobin (Hgb) (gm/dL)	Newborn 1 m 6 m-2 y 2 y-6 y 6 y-12 y 12 y-18 y 18 y	14.5-22.5 10.0-18.0 10.5-13.5 11.5-13.5 11.5-15.5 12.0-15.5 11.5-18.0
Hematocrit (Hct) (%)	Newborn 1 m 6 m-2 y 2 y-6 y 6 y-12 y 12 y-18 y >18 y	45-64 31-55 33-39 34-40 35-45 36-49 36-50
Platelets (Plt) (1000/µL)	0-1 m 1 m-1 y 1 y-3 y 3 y-7 y 7 y-12 y >12 y	250-450 300-750 250-600 250-550 200-450 150-400
Prothrombin time (PT) (sec)		11-14
Partial thromboplastin time (PTT) (sec)		21-35
International normalized ratio (INR)		0.8-1.3
D-dimer (µg/mL)		<250
Activated coagulation time (ACT)		70-120 sec Therapeutic: 180-240 sec or 2 × normal range

FIGURE 88 Chemical formula.

TABLE 3-9 Urinalysis			
Lab Test	Normal Range	Prerenal	Intrarenal
pH	4.6-8.0		
Appearance	Clear		Muddy
Color	Amber		Brown granular epithelial casts

(Continued)

TABLE 3-9 Urinalysis (*Continued*)			
Lab Test	Normal Range	Prerenal	Intrarenal
Specific gravity	1.003-1.030	> 1.020	< 1.010
Osmolality	250-1000 mOsm/L	> 500 mOsm/L	< 350 mOsm/L
pH	5.0-8.0		
Albumin	Negative		
Ketones	Negative		
Bilirubin	Negative		
Occult blood	Negative		
Protein	Negative		
Na^+	10-40 mEq/L	< 10 mEq/L	10-40 mEq/L
K^+	< 8 mEq/L		
Cl^-	< 8 mEq/L		
BUN/plasma creatinine	10-15:1	> 20:1	
FeNa	–	<1%	>2%

Fractional excretion of sodium (FeNa): Use the following formula if the patient is oliguric:

$$FeNa = \frac{UNa \times PCr}{PNa \times UCr} \times 100$$

TABLE 3-10 Cerebrospinal Fluid Analysis	
Run CSF analysis within 60 minutes of obtaining a specimen	
Appearance	Crystal clear, colorless
Pressure (up to 250 mm H_2O with obesity)	60-200 mm H_2O
WBCs · ↑ PMNs with bacterial infection · ↑ Leukocytes with viral infection	0-5 cells
RBCs (confirm atraumatic lumbar puncture)	0-5 cells
Glucose (< 18 mg/dL with bacterial infection)	40-80 mg/dL
Protein (total) Increased with infection (bacterial > viral)	Lumbar: 15-45 mg/dL Cisternal: 15-25 mg/dL Ventricular: 5-15 mg/dL

TABLE 3-11 Blood Gas Values		
Lab	Arterial	Venous
PO_2 (mm Hg)	80-100	35-45
PCO_2 (mm Hg)	35-45	41-51
pH	7.35-7.45	7.31-7.41
HCO_3^- (mEq/L)	22-26	22-26
O_2 saturation (%)	98-99	60-80
Base excess	−2 to +2	0 to +4

When assessing blood gas values, consider the following questions:
  Is there acidemia or alkalemia?

  • pH: < 7.35 = acidemia
  • pH > 7.45 = alkalemia

Can the ∆pH be explained by ∆PCO₂?

- Acute ↑PCO₂ should cause ↓pH of 0.08 (respiratory acidosis)
- Acute ↓PCO₂ should cause ↑pH of 0.08 (respiratory alkalosis)
- Chronic

If ∆pH can be explained by ∆PCO₂, go to evaluation of oxygenation.

- $PaO_2 < 60$ mm Hg/$SaO_2 < 92\%$ = hypoxia

If ∆pH cannot be explained by ∆PCO₂, check serum bicarbonate.

- Normal HCO_3 = 22-24 mEq/L
- $HCO3 < 22$ mEq/L = metabolic acidosis
  - Calculate anion gap (normal = 12 ± 2)
  - AG > 17 = anion gap metabolic acidosis
- $HCO_3 > 24$ mEq/L = metabolic alkalosis

Rule of 80

- $pH + PaCO_2 < 70$: metabolic acidosis
- $pH + PaCO_2 > 90$: metabolic alkalosis
- $pH + PaCO_2 = 80$: pure respiratory acidosis

Alveolar-Arterial Gradient

$$PAO_2 = FiO_2 \cdot (PB - PH_2O) - (PaCO_2/R)$$

PaO_2: obtain from arterial blood gas

Example: Suppose a patient is on 40% O_2 at sea level (Pb = 760 mm Hg) and will be transported with ascent to a cabin altitude of 8000 feet (Pb = 565 mm Hg) onboard an aircraft with no change in ventilation (PaCO₂ = 40 mm Hg).

Sea-level $PAO_2 = 0.4 \cdot (760 - 47) - (40/0.8) = 235$ mm Hg).

Note that the alveolar-arterial gradient increases by 5-7 mm Hg for every 10% increase in FiO_2.

TABLE 3-12	Altitude-Barometric Pressure Chart		
Feet	Meters	Barometric Pressure (mm Hg)	Altitude of Selected Locations
0	0	760	Washington, D.C. (0-400 ft) London (50 ft) Incirlik (127 ft) Baghdad (183 ft)
500	152	746	Tikrit (380 ft) San Antonio (512 ft)
1000	305	733	Mosul (700 ft) Landstuhl (816 ft)
2000	610	707	Islamabad (2000 ft)
3000	914	681	
4000	1219	656	
5000	1524	633	Bagram (4900 ft) Denver (5280 ft)
6000	1829	609	Average cabin altitude AE

(Continued)

TABLE 3-12   Altitude–Barometric Pressure Chart (*Continued*)

Feet	Meters	Barometric Pressure (mm Hg)	Altitude of Selected Locations
7000	2134	587	"""
8000	2438	565	"""
9000	2743	543	
10,000	3048	523	Maximum cabin altitude AE
15,000	4572	429	

TABLE 3-13 Other Lab Values	
Human chorionic gonadotropin (hCG) (mIU/L)	Blood: • Negative: < 5 • Indeterminate: 6-24 (retest after 72-96 h) • Positive: > 25 Urine: • Positive: > 20
Dilantin	10-20 μg/mL
Heparin (based on APT)	Threshold: > 1.5 × control Range: 1.5-2.3 × control

Thromboelastogram

A thromboelastogram (TEG) is used as a global assessment of hemostatic function from initiation of coagulation through clot lysis. It is a more sensitive measure of coagulation and fibrinolysis than are other coagulation tests.

TABLE 3-14 Thromboelastogram Values			
Index	Normal	Comments	
R (reaction) time	4 min	Coagulation factor activation	↑R value: deficiency of coagulation factors • Treatment: FFP
K time	1-4 min	• Measure of the speed to reach a maximum amplitude of 20 mm • Measure of clotting factors, fibrinogen, platelet function	• K: treat by ↑fibrinogen (cryoprecipitates, FFP, whole blood) • ↓K: treat with anticoagulants
α angle	47-74	• Represents speed of clot strengthening • Measure of clotting factors, fibrinogen, platelet function	↓α angle results from hypofibrinogenemia and thrombocytopenia • Treatment: FFP, cryoprecipitates, rVIIa
MA (maximum amplitude)	55-73 mm	• Greatest vertical amplitude of the graphic tracing • Measure of clot strength relative to platelet number and function	↓MA – ↓clot strength • Treatment: Platelets
LY30	0-8%	• Rate of amplitude reduction 30 min after MA • Measure of clot stability	> 7.5% indicates hyperfibrinolysis that may be treated with antifibrinolytic agent (amino-caproic acid)

TEG-directed transfusion may be used upon admission for all patients who arrive in shock, arrive with a penetrating brain injury, require emergency release of blood, or have an anticipated need for massive transfusion. Repeat TEG after each phase of blood product resuscitation.

FIGURE 89 TEG-directed transfusion.

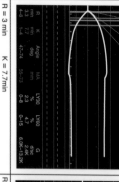

R min	K min	Angle deg	MA mm	LY30 %	LY60 %	G d/sc
3.3	7.7			2.3	4.7	2.4K
4-8	1-4	47-74	55-73	0-8	0-15	6.0K-13.2K

R = 3 min   K = 7.7min
α angle = —   MA = —
LY30: 2.3%

History: Gunshot Wound—injuries to rectum, small bowel, open femur fracture. Arrived in Class IV shock.

Interpretation: prolonged K time/no angle measured.
Recommended therapy: FFP or 4 units cryoprecipitate; whole blood and recombinant Factor VIIa if findings remain abnormal.

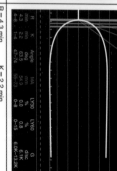

R min	K min	Angle deg	MA mm	LY30 %	LY60 %	G d/sc
4.3	2.2	63.5	54.9	0.0	0.8	6.1K
4-8	1-4	47-74	55-73	0-8	0-15	6.0K-13.2K

R = 4.3 min   K = 2.2 min
α angle = 63.5°   MA = 54.9 mm
LY30 = 0%

Intra-operatively after 11 units PRBC, 2 units platelets, 4 units cryoprecipitate, 6 units FFP, 3 units whole blood, and Factor VIIa.

Interpretation: decreased MA.
Recommended RX: whole blood (or platelets if available).

R min	K min	Angle deg	MA mm	LY30 %	LY60 %	G d/sc
5.8	2.3	58.5	57.1	0.0	0.0	6.1K
4-8	1-4	47-74	55-73	0-8	0-15	6.0K-13.2K

R = 5.8 min   K = 2.3 min
α angle = 57°   MA = 57.1
LY30 = 0%

Postoperatively after 19 units PRBC, 2 units platelets, 4 units cryoprecipitate, 6 units FFP, 6 units whole blood, and Factor VIIa.

Interpretation: normalization of profile.

R = reaction time.
K = period from 2 to 20 mm amplitude.
MA = maximum amplitude.
LY30 = lysis at 30 minutes.
FFP = fresh frozen plasma.
PRBC = packed red blood cells.

TABLE 3-15   TEG Interpretation and Treatment Decisions

Lab	Treatment Decision
Prolonged R time	Administer 4 U FFP
Prolonged K time or decreased α angle	• Administer 4 U FFP or 4 units cryoprecipitate if remain abnormal after FFP • Consider whole blood and Factor VIIa if values remain abnormal
Decreased maximum amplitude	Give platelets, if available, or transfuse 2-4 units of whole blood
Increased LY30	Amicar: 5 gm IV load over 1 h/1 gm/h infusion until normalization of LY30

■ Medications

Conversions

1 liter (L) = 1000 milliliters (mL)

1 gram (gm) = 1000 milligrams (mg)

1 mg = 1000 micrograms (mcg)

1 lb = 2.2 kg (lb/2.2 = kg)

TABLE 3-16   Example of IV Medication Calculations

Example: 100 mL over 1 h with 15 gtt/mL drip set

How many drops/min?	$\left[\left(\dfrac{\text{Volume to be given}}{\text{hours to given}} \right) \times \dfrac{\#gtt}{mL} \right] \div 60$
	$\dfrac{100}{1} \times 15 \div 60 = 25 \dfrac{gtt}{min}$

Example: 176-lb (176/2.2 = 80 kg) patient receiving dopamine 400 mg in 250 mL D_5W at 10 mL/h

How many mcg/kg/min?	$\left[\left(\dfrac{mg\ drug}{ml\ diluent} \right) \times 1000 \right] \div 60 \div kg \times \dfrac{ml}{hr}$
	$[(400 \div 250) \times 1000] \div 60 \div 80 \times 10 = 3.3 \text{ mcg/kg/min}$

Dosage increased to 8 mcg/kg/min

What is the rate (mL/h) required to achieve this dosage?	$\dfrac{(\text{Desired dose} \times 60 \times kg)}{\left(\text{drip concentration in } \frac{mcg}{mL} \right)}$
	$(8 \text{ mcg/kg/min} \times 60 \times 80)/(400/250 \times 1000) = \dfrac{38,400}{1600} = 24 \dfrac{ml}{hr}$

Example: 225-lb (225/2.2 = 102 kg) patient receiving norepinephrine (4 mg/250 mL) at 25 mL/h

How many mcg/min?	$\left[\left(\dfrac{mg\ drug}{ml\ diluent} \right) \times 1000 \right] \div 60 \times \text{infusion rate} \left(\dfrac{ml}{hr} \right)$
	$\left[\left(\dfrac{4}{250} \right) \times 1000 \right] \div 60 \times 25 = 6.6 \dfrac{mcg}{min}$

Decrease the dosage to 4 mcg/min

What is the rate (mL/h)?	(Desired dose $\times$ 60)/(drip concentration in mcg/mL)
	$(4 \text{ mcg/min} \times 60)/(4/250 \times 1000) = \dfrac{240}{16} = 15 \dfrac{ml}{hr}$

TABLE 3-17 Selected PO/IV Medications

Drug	Dosage/Notes
Acyclovir (Zovirax)	Herpes simplex: • IV: initial episode, severe: 5 mg/kg q 8 h for 5-7 days • PO: initial episode: 200 mg q 4 h while awake (5×/day) × 10 days • Recurrence: 200 mg q 4 h while awake (5×/day) × 5 days
Amikacin sulfate	15 mg/kg/24 h IV divided into 2 or 3 doses (5 mg/kg IV q 8 h or 7.5 mg/kg q 12 h); administer over 30-60 min
Ampicillin and subbactam (Unasyn)	1.5-3 gm IV q 6 h; do not exceed 4 gm subbactam/24 h. Reconstitute each 1.5 gm with at least 3.2 mL; dilute to final concentration of 3-45 mg/mL. Administer over 10-15 min.
Atropine sulfate ophthalmic solution	1-2 gtt up to 4 × per day; dilates pupils and causes cycloplegia
Azithromycin (Zithromax)	Community-acquired pneumonia: 500 mg IV daily × 7-10 days; administer over 1 h Chlamydia: 1 gm PO as a single dose
Bacitracin ophthalmic ointment	Thin bead into lower eyelid; after 1 min, wipe excess away with sterile pad
Bacitracin/polymixin B ointment (Polysporin)	1-2 gtt q 4-6 h; ointment: ⅓ inch q 4 h
Benoxinate HCl/ fluorescein 0.4-0.25% ophthalmic solution	1-2 gtt until effect; local anesthetic and diagnostic only–do not dispense
Cefazolin sodium (Ancef)	250 mg-1.5 gm IV q 6-8 h depending on source/severity of infection; dilute with 50-100 mL of D₅W or NS. Administer 1 gm over 3-5 min or longer depending on dilution. Use with caution if sensitive to penicillin.
Cefotixin sodium	1-2 gm IV q 4-8 h (depending on source/severity of infection), up to 12 gm/24 h. Reconstitute each 1 gm with 10 mL D₅W or NS and further dilute to 50-100 mL.
Ceftazidime (Fortaz)	250 mg-2 gm IV q 8-12 h (depending on source/severity of infection). Reconstitute with 5 mL and further dilute in 50-100 mL solution. Give as a single dose over 30 min.
Ciprofloxacin (Cipro)	400-500 mg IV q 12 h (depending on source/severity of infection). Administer over 60 min; note that rapid infusion increases risk for anaphylaxis. PO dose is also available.
Clindamycin	1.2-1.8 gm/24 h IV in 2-4 doses; dilute with 50 mL of D₅W or NS; administer over 10-60 min
Dexamethasone sodium phosphate (Decadron)	Anti-inflammatory: 0.5-24 mg daily, divided in 2-4 doses based on response Shock: 40 mg IV; repeat q 2-6 h prn Cerebral edema: 10 mg IV, then 4 mg IM/IV q 6 h × 2-4 days, then taper over 5-7 days Acute mountain sickness: 8 mg initially, followed by 4 mg after 6 and 12 h
Diazepam (Valium)	Anxiety: 2-10 mg BID-QID/IM or IV 2-10 mg q 3-4 h (depending on severity of symptoms) Seizures (recurrent) or status epilepticus: 50-10 mg IV q 10-15 min prn, up to max 30 mg; may repeat in 2-4 h if needed (See also the "Pain/Management" section.)
Doxycycline	Chlamydia: 100 mg PO q 12 h × 7 days Acinetobacter or O fever: 100 mg PO q 12 h on day 1, then 100 mg/day PO in 1-2 divided doses Severe infections: 100 mg PO q 12 h Also antibiotic of choice for post-exposure treatment of inhalational and cutaneous anthrax; consult infectious disease specialist.
Enoxaparin (Lovenox)	30-40 mg SQ daily (see discussion of VTE prevention)

(Continued)

TABLE 3-17   Selected PO/IV Medications (Continued)

Drug	Dosage/Notes
Erythromycin ophthalmic ointment	1/2-inch ribbon in conjunctival sac 2-6 × /day
Flumazenil (Romazicon)	Reversal agent for benzodiazepine overdose • IV push: 0.2 mg IV over 30 sec • If desired level of consciousness not obtained after an additional 30 sec: dose of 0.3 mg IV over 30 sec • Further doses of 0.5 mg IV over 30 sec may be given at 1-min intervals if needed to maximum total dose of 3 mg; most patients respond to 0.6-1 mg
Furosemide (Lasix)	Edema: initial dose, 20-40 mg IV over 1-2 min; may repeat same dose 2 h later or may be increased by 20 mg until desired response Acute pulmonary edema: 40 mg IV over 1-2 min; after 1 h, may increase to 80 mg IV over 1-2 min
Gentamycin sulfate	3-5 mg/kg/day IV in 3-4 equal doses (depending on source/severity of infection)
Haloperidol (Haldol)	Agitation/delirium: 2-5 mg IV (range: 0.5-10 mg) Acute psychosis: 2-50 mg IV (rate 5 mg/min) Antipsychotic: 0.5-5 mg PO BID-TID (maximum dose = 100 mg/day) Consult with mental health specialist. *Note that all IV doses are unlabeled.*
Hydrocortisone	Septic shock refractory to fluids and vasopressors: 200-300 mg/day IV for 7 days in 3-4 divided doses or by continuous infusion
Imipenem	Bacterial septicemia, mild: 250-500 mg IV q 6 h Moderate/severe severity: 500-1000 mg IV q 6-8 h (based on susceptibility)
Insulin	See the "Glycemic Control" section.
Labetolol	Give undiluted or mix 40 mL labetolol + 160 mL IV solution 20 mg (2 mg/min); repeat 40-80 mg at 10—min intervals until desired BP is achieved. Initial dose is followed by infusion of 2-8 mg/min. Maximum dose = 300 mg.
Levofloxacin	UTI: • Uncomplicated: 250 m IV/PO q 24 h × 1-3 days • Complicated: 750 mg IV/PO q 24 h × 3 days. Skin/subcutaneous infection: • Uncomplicated: 500 mg IV/PO q 24 h × 7-10 days • Complicated: 750 mg PO or IV q 24 h × 7-14 days • Traveler's diarrhea: 250 mg IV/PO q 24 h × 3 days
Loperamide (Imodium)	Diarrhea, acute: 4 mg PO followed by 2 mg after each loose stool, up to a maximum of 16 mg/day Traveler's diarrhea: 4 mg PO followed by 2 mg after each loose stool, up to a maximum of 8 mg/day
Lorazepam (Ativan)	Alcohol withdrawal syndrome: 2 mg PO q 6 h × 4 doses, then 1 mg q 6 h × 8 doses Anxiety: initial, 2-3 mg/day PO divided into 2-3 doses Sedation for a mechanically ventilated patient: • Continuous infusion: 0.01-0.1 mg/kg/h IV • Intermittent dose: 0.02-0.06 mg/kg IV q 2-6 h Note: Keep vials refrigerated and protected from light.
Mannitol	Increased ICP: 0.25-1 gm over 5-10 min; repeat 0.25-2 gm/kg q 4-6 h prn Acute renal failure: • Prophylaxis for oliguria: 50-100 gm IV as a 5-25% solution during surgery, immediately postoperatively or following trauma • Treatment of oliguria: 50-100 gm IV as a 15-25% solution (may require a test dose) Notes: Warm to dissolve crystals; infuse over 30-90 min.

(Continued)

TABLE 3-17   Selected PO/IV Medications (Continued)

Drug	Dosage/Notes
Phenobarbital	Status epilepticus: 10–20 mg/kg IV in single or divided dose over 10–15 min; give additional 5 mg/kg q 15–30 min. Maximum dose = 30 mg/kg; average dose range = 1–3 mg/kg/24 h.
Phenylephrine	Severe hypotension: 100–180 mcg/min infusion until BP is stabilized. Average dose range: 40–60 mcg/min. Admixture: 10 mg/100 mL NS or D₅W; may increase to 20–30 mg/500 mL.
Tetracycline	Skin infection: 1 gm/day PO in 2–4 doses; severe: 500 mg PO QID
Tetracaine hydrochloride ophthalmic solution 0.5%	Anesthesia for procedure on eyes: 1–2 gtt of 0.5% solution 5–10 min for 3–5 doses. Do not dispense to patient.
Ticarcillin disodium and clavulanate potassium (Timentin)	Infection of skin/subcutaneous tissue, lower respiratory tract infection, or septicemia: 3.1 gm (3 gm ticarcillin and 100 mg clavulanic acid) IV q 4–6 h (dose for patient weight > 60 kg)
Timolol maleate (Timoptic) 0.5% ophthalmic solution	One drop per eye BID
Tobramycin	Serious infection of skin/subcutaneous tissue, abdomen, lower respiratory tract, or urinary tract: 1 mg/kg IV every 8 h; maximum dose, 3 mg/kg/day. Life-threatening infection of skin/subcutaneous tissue, abdomen, lower respiratory tract, or urinary tract: 1.66 mg/kg IV every 8 h; maximum dose, 5 mg/kg/day; reduce dose to 3 mg/kg/day as soon as indicated
Tropicamide (Mydriacyl) ophthalmic solution	To induce mydriasis and cycloplegia: 1–2 gtt 15 minutes before procedure; may also acutely relieve pain. Do not dispense to patient.
Vancomycin	Staphylococcal infection, methicillin-resistant: 2 gm/day IV divided q 6–12 h administered over at least 60 min. Clostridium difficile infection: 500 mg–2 gm PO daily divided q 6–8 h × 7–10 days. Also consult with an infectious disease specialist.
Vasopressin	2 mL = 40 units. Mix 0.1–1 unit/mL; maximum concentration = 1 unit/mL. ACLS: 40 units IV/ETT. Pressure support: 0.04 unit/min. Infusion: 0.04 unit/min
Vecuronium	Patient must be intubated; 10 mL/100 mL D₅W (0.1 mg/mL); IV bolus 0.08–0.1 mg/kg. Wait 25–40 min, and then start 1 mcg/kg/min. Average dose range = 0.8–1.2 mcg/kg/min to maintain 90% of twitch response.
Warfarin sodium (Coumadin)	Venous thromboembolism prophylaxis/treatment: 2–5 mg PO daily; adjust dose based on INR; usual maintenance dose, 2–10 mg PO daily. Also see the discussion of VTE prophylaxis.

Note that this table is not a replacement for an MD order.
Source: B. L. Gahart and A. R. Nazareno. *2007 Intravenous Medications.* St. Louis: Mosby, 2007; Micromedex: Thompson Healthcare Series (accessed December, 2007).

■ Pain Management

Acute Pain/Sedation Management

As part of the rapid pain assessment, consider the following pain-related issues:

- Location of pain
- Quality of pain (use patient's own words to determine character and radiation of pain)

- Duration of pain (onset, pattern)
- Intensity of pain (use 0-10 scale, FACES, FLACC)
- Triggers of pain
- What relieves pain

Frequency of Assessment:
- If there is no pain, reassess in 4-8 hours.
- Check q 1-2 h in the first 24 h post-injury/postoperative.
- Check q 2-4 h around-the-clock while pain exists.
- Assess pain relief with interventions (30 min after parenteral administration; 60 min after PO administration; or more frequently depending on medication administered/severity of pain).

Faces

Point to each face using the words to describe the pain intensity. Ask the individual to choose the face that best describes his or her own pain.

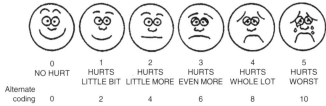

	0	1	2	3	4	5
	NO HURT	HURTS LITTLE BIT	HURTS LITTLE MORE	HURTS EVEN MORE	HURTS WHOLE LOT	HURTS WORST
Alternate coding	0	2	4	6	8	10

FIGURE 90 Wong-Baker FACES pain rating scale.
Source: From Hockenberry MJ, Wilson D, Wikelstein ML: Wong's Essentials of Pediatric Nursing, ed. 7, St. Louis, 2005, p. 1259. Used with permission. Copyright, Mosby.

TABLE 3-18 Faces, Legs, Activity, Cry, and Consolability (FLACC)			
Use the FLACC scale to assess and monitor pain in preverbal children.			
Category	Scoring		
	0	1	2
Face	No particular expression or smile	Occasional grimace or frown, withdrawn, disinterested	Frequent to constant quivering chin, clenched jaw
Legs	Normal position or relaxed	Uneasy, restless, tense	Kicking or legs drawn up
Activity	Lying quietly, normal position, moves easily	Squirming, shifting back and forth, tense	Arched, rigid, or jerking
Cry	No cry (awake or asleep)	Moans or whimpers, occasional complaint	Crying steadily, screams or sobs, frequent complaints
Consolability	Content, relaxed	Reassured by occasional touching, hugging or being talked to, distractible	Difficult to console or comfort

Source: Merkel S, et al. The FLACC: A behavioral scale for scoring postoperative pain in young children. *Pediatr Nurse* 1997;23(3):293-297. Printed with permission. ©, 2002, The Regents of the University of Michigan.

TABLE 3-19   Motor Activity Assessment Scale (MAAS) Sedation Scoring System (Goal: MAAS 2-3)

0	Unresponsive	Does not move with noxious stimuli (i.e., suctioning or 5 seconds of vigorous sterna or nail bed pressure)
1	Responsive only to noxious stimuli	Opens eyes, raises eyebrows, turns head towards stimulus or moves limbs with noxious stimuli
2	Responsive to touch or name	Opens eyes, raises eyebrows, turns head towards stimulus or moves limbs when name is spoken loudly
3	Calm and cooperative	No external stimulus required to elicit response, movements purposeful, follows commands
4	Restless and cooperative	No external stimulus required to elicit AND patient is picking at sheets or tubes OR uncovering self and follows commands
5	Agitated	No external stimuli required to elicit response AND attempting to sit up OR moves limbs out of bed AND does not consistently follow commands
6	Dangerously agitated, uncooperative	No external stimulus required to elicit response AND patient is pulling at tubes or catheters OR thrashing side to side OR striking others OR trying to climb out of bed AND does not calm down when asked

From Devlin JW et al. Motor Activity Assessment Scale: A valid and reliable sedation scale for use with mechanically ventilated patients in an adult surgical intensive care unit. *Crit Care Med*, 27(7), 1271-1275 (with permission).

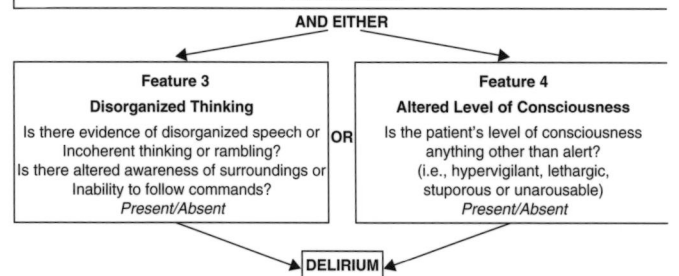

Confusion Assessment Method (CAM-ICU)

Delirium indicated if patient has Feature 1 and 2, plus either 3 or 4

Feature 1
Acute Onset of Changes or Fluctuations in the Course of Mental Status
Is there evidence of an acute change in mental status from baseline or fluctuating behavior over the past 24 hours
Present or Absent

AND

Feature 2
Inattention
Does the patient have difficulty focusing attention or following conversation or instructions?
Present or Absent

AND EITHER

Feature 3
Disorganized Thinking
Is there evidence of disorganized speech or Incoherent thinking or rambling?
Is there altered awareness of surroundings or Inability to follow commands?
Present/Absent

OR

Feature 4
Altered Level of Consciousness
Is the patient's level of consciousness anything other than alert?
(i.e., hypervigilant, lethargic, stuporous or unarousable)
Present/Absent

DELIRIUM

Pain Assessment in Cognitively Impaired Patients

There are no validated instruments for pain assessment in a cognitively impaired patient. Instead, use of simple pain scores (e.g., FACES) should be attempted for all responsive patients with multiple trauma.

If reliable reports of pain are not available, the use of behavioral manifestations, response to analgesia, knowledge of the various types of pain, and reports from family/unit members may be used to assess pain.

There is poor correlation between pain assessment and physiological indicators of pain, such as increased heart rate, blood pressure, respiratory rate; perspiration; or pallor (Puntillo et al., 1997).

Behavioral Manifestations of Pain

Procedural pain intensity and procedural distress are directly related to behavioral activity. Behaviors commonly observed during painful procedures include the following:

- Grimacing
- Body movements (clenched fists, rigid, wincing)
- Vocalization (moaning, verbal complaint)

Procedures Known to Produce Pain

The following procedures are usually associated with pain:

- Wound care (dressing change, packing wound, debridement, irrigation) causes acute pain (Stotts et al., 2004).
- Chest tube removal causes moderate to severe pain. Administration of 4 mg morphine IV (20 minutes before procedure) or 30 mg ketorolac IV (60 minutes before procedure) has been found to significantly decrease pain (Puntillo & Ley, 2004).
- Endotracheal suctioning causes a mean pain intensity score of 5/10 in surgical ICU patients and of 4.4/10 in burn/trauma patients (Arroyo-Novoa et al., 2007).

Medications Used to Relieve Acute Pain (See JTTS CPG Analgesia, Sedation, and Delirium)

General Principles of Acute Pain Management

- Intravenous medications most effective route for trauma patients—standard of care for acute/traumatic pain control.
  - Note: If a patient is in shock the administration of analgesics may not be appropriate due to hemodynamic side effects and need to perform lifesaving interventions.
- While opioids are the most commonly used analgesic, the most effective acute pain management plans utilize a multimodal approach that relies on a variety of pain medication classes in order to maximize effectiveness while reducing the side effects of any one drug.
- Fentanyl, morphine, naloxone can be administered through intraosseus needle.

- Consideration should be given for pre-procedure/pre-transport medication.
- The complexity/severity of combat injuries may preclude the use of narcotics as the sole mode of analgesia.
- The use of regional anesthesia (continuous peripheral nerve blocks) may be more effective than narcotics for certain localized injuries—orthopedic/soft tissue trauma.
- An example of a multimodal approach for perioperative pain management used at Walter Reed Army Medical Center may include peripheral nerve block, NSAIDS, narcotic analgesia, benzodiazepines, and gabapentin (Stojadinovic 2006).

TABLE 3-20   Suggested Dosages of Opioids in a 70-kg Opioid-Naïve Military Casualty

Opioid	IV/IM*	PCA†	Oral	Epidural‡
Morphine	5-15 mg q 3-4 h	1-2 mg q 6-12 min	10-30 mg q 2-3 h	1-4 mg
Hydromorphone	2-3 mg q 3-4 h	0.2-0.8 mg q 8-12 min	2-3 mg q 4-6 h	0.5-1 mg
Fentanyl	25-100 mcg q 10 min titrated to effect at bedside	Rare use	Sublingual used in field	50-100 mcg
Codeine	15-60 mg q 4 h IM only	N/A	30-60 mg q 4 h	N/A
Oxycodone§	N/A	N/A	10-20 mg q 4-6 h	N/A
Tramadol	50-100 mg q 4-6 h	N/A	50-150 mg q 4-6 h	N/A

*Generally, the IM administration of opioids should be avoided in favor of IV administration.

†Patient-controlled analgesia (PCA) is the preferred method for opioid pain control when equipment is available and the patient is able to operate the PCA device.

‡Epidural/intrathecal infusions or narcotics should be avoided in patients who may be transported to the next level of care within 24 hours.

§Combined with acetaminophen as Percocet.

Source: DVPMI Military Advanced Regional Anesthesia and Analgesia Handbook.

TABLE 3-21   Suggested Dosages of Nonsteroidal Anti-inflammatory Drugs (NSAIDs) for Acute Pain Management in Military Casualties

NSAID	IV/IM	PO	Comments
Acetaminophen*	NA	325-1000 mg q 4-6 h up to 3000 mg/day	Does not produce gastric irritation or alter platelet aggregation; weak anti-inflammatory; hepatotoxic in large doses
Ketorolac	30 mg, then 15-30 mg q 6 h	10 mg q 4-6 h	30 mg IV is equivalent to 10 mg morphine; moderate anti-inflammatory activity; may cause life-threatening bronchospasm in asthma patients

(Continued)

TABLE 3-21	Suggested Dosages of Nonsteroidal Anti-inflammatory Drugs (NSAIDs) for Acute Pain Management in Military Casualties *(Continued)*		
NSAID	IV/IM	PO	Comments
Ibuprofen	N/A	400-800 mg q 8 h	Low incidence of GI side effects
Naproxen	N/A	250-500 mg q 12 h	Longer half-life allows twice-daily dosing
Indomethacin	N/A	25-50 mg q 8 h	Potent anti-inflammatory

*Concurrent use of acetaminophen and morphine enhances the opioid effect.
Source: Courtesy of Chester Trip Buckenmaier, III, COL, US Army Medical Corps.

TABLE 3-22	Suggested Dosages of Anticonvulsants and Tricyclic Antidepressants for Acute Pain Management in Military Casualties	
Agent	Oral	Comments
Gabapentin (Neurontin)	100-300 mg q 8 h, gradually increased prn up to 3600 mg daily in 3 divided doses	Treat/prevent neuropathic pain
Amitriptyline	10-150 mg daily	Treat neuropathic pain
Nortriptyline	25 mg every night, up to a maximum of 150 mg daily	Treat neuropathic pain

Early use of tricyclic antidepressants may have some benefit in preventing acute progression to chronic pain.
Source: Courtesy of Chester Trip Buckenmaier, III, COL, US Army Medical Corps.

Post-Amputation Pain

Nociceptive pain is the result of direct injury to tissue (wounds, thermal, inflammatory).

- Regional nerve blocks are used frequently in acute pain management.
- Opioids are effective for nociceptive pain.
- NSAIDs (e.g., ketorolac, ibuprofen) and acetaminophen are useful adjuncts for nociceptive pain.

Neuropathic pain is pain due to a primary lesion or dysfunction in the nervous system. It occurs with amputation and spinal cord injury, and includes phantom limb pain (PLP). It may be described as sharp, shooting, stabbing, and knifelike and often has a sudden onset.

Military casualties who are 6 months or more post-amputation report using a number of nonmedical strategies that are effective in decreasing PLP, including tapping the limb, rubbing the limb, and exercise (Ketz, 2008).

Patients may also say that the phantom pain worsens when they void. This is normal and real and should not be discounted even if it is not experienced by everyone.

General pharmacological guidelines:

The literature does not provide adequate evidence for definitive recommendations about which medications to start with in case of PLP or medication dosage. Current practice for treating PLP in a young wounded military member is as follows (courtesy of Dr. Jennifer Meneterez), but is not a replacement for an MD order or clinical judgment:

Tricyclic antidepressants and anticonvulsants are often used for neuropathic pain:

- Neurontin: 300 mg tid (not 100 mg)
- Elavil: 25 mg 1-2 h before bedtime (rather than pamelor)

Opioids are only rarely useful in treating PLP.

- Opioids may be useful for short periods if nociceptive pain complicates the diagnosis.
- Try to avoid using methadone if possible, as it is difficult to wean off during the outpatient phase of care.

Flexeril 10 mg tid prn may be given if the PLP is associated with a twitching sensation, cramping, or a restless sensation in the residual limb (as an alternative to diazepam).

In case of *musculoskeletal pain*, anecdotal reports indicate that NSAIDs may be useful therapy (Garbez & Puntillo, 2005). Do not administer NSAIDs to patients with renal failure or aspirin sensitivity.

Epidural Anesthesia

For use as epidural anesthesia, an opioid (morphine) or low-dose anesthetic (e.g., ropivacaine) may be administered only by anesthesia provider or via continuous infusion.

For morphine, the following considerations apply:

- Onset, 30-90 min; peak effect, ~90 min
- Risk for respiratory depression: 2-12 h after bolus
- Dosing example: loading dose, 2-6 mg; PCEA, 0.2-0.5 mg; lockout, 10 min; basal: 0-0.8 mg/h.

With a low-dose anesthetic, the goal is to enhance analgesia without producing anesthesia. Potential side effects include sensory or motor deficit, mild orthostatic hypotension, urinary retention, and local or systemic toxicity (McCaffrey, 1999).

- Complete q 8 h sensory/motor assessment: assess for areas of numbness/tingling and ability to bend knees/lift buttocks off bed, as appropriate.
- If patient is ambulatory, assess for orthostasis before getting out of bed.
- Monitor for bladder distention and inability to urinate.
- Observe for signs of toxicity: circumoral tingling and numbness, ringing in ears, metallic taste, CNS abnormalities, cardiac arrhythmias. Toxicity is a medical emergency—stop the infusion and contact an MD immediately.

Aeromedical Evacuation (AE) Considerations for Patients with Epidural Infusion or Peripheral Nerve Block (PNB)

Refer to AMC Surgeon General's policy letter (12 May 2011) and note:

- Stable patients with epidural analgesia and peripheral nerve blocks may move through the AE system under the management of qualified personnel.

- Epidural or peripheral nerve block analgesic infusion must be in place and running without complication for a minimum of 4 hours prior to departing a sending facility.
- Any patient incurring a complication from epidural or PNB placement will wait a minimum of 24 hours before being manifested for aeromedical evacuation.
- Originating facility will send a minimum of 1000 mL of 20% IV intra-lipid solution physically with the patient.
- Before departing the originating facility, the analgesia level for the patient must be stable at T10 dermatome level or below (see page 113 for dermatome chart), with the patient exhibiting partial extremity motor control (T10 is approximately at the level of the umbilicus).
- Continuous epidural and PNB will contain only amides such as bupivicaine or ropivacaine.
- Narcotics, or any other medication, will not be added to the catheter infusions.
- If a patient with an epidural or PNB experiences breakthough pain greater than 3/10, manage with oral or IV narcotic by a single injection or PCA per written MD orders. Do not administer through the epidural line.
  - Before administration of supplemental narcotics, first check the integrity of the CPNB or epidural system: Tubing is connected without kinks and the pump is functioning.
- If patient with epidural develops worsening back pain at insertion site and/or deterioration of neurologic status (progressive leg weakness or bladder dysfunction) communicate with MD.
- All epidural analgesia or PNB infusions must be administered in an approved pain pump. Label the pump, tubing and infusion bag as "epidural infusion" or "peripheral nerve block infusion."
- Do not change the sterile dressing covering the insertion site in the aircraft. Reinforce the dressing as necessary.
- Epidural/PNB catheters will not be removed until evaluated by an anesthesia provider. Catheters will not be removed in flight.
- At each enroute location, an anesthesia provider or pain management team member will be contacted as needed for consultation on issues related to pain management. A change in the infusion rate/dosing can be performed only by an anesthesia provider (anesthesiologist or CRNA).

Patient-Controlled Analgesia (PCA)

The devices approved for PCA may vary. Refer to your local policy and the manufacturer's guidelines for information on programming and use of specific devices. Ensure that a device is approved for aeromedical evacuation before using it during an AE mission.

Notify Flight Surgeon for the following:

· Shortness of breath · Respiratory rate ≤ 10/min or 50% below baseline · Oxygen saturation < 93% on room air · Hypotension: postural BP drop > 15 mm Hg from baseline · High sensory block: Numbness above nipples · Motor blockade: inability to bend knees while lying on bed · Difficulty swallowing · Inadequate analgesia · Pain out of proportion to the clinical injury or out of character for the patient's history · Increasing sedation or presence of confusion · Pruritus or nausea/vomiting unrelieved after initial treatment · Leakage on catheter dressing · Catheter disconnection · Catheter dislodgement · Temperature > 101°F and/or presence of shaking chills	**Signs/Symptoms of Local Anesthetic Toxicity*** · Metallic taste · Lightheadedness or dizziness · Ringing in the ears · Excitation, restlessness · Feeling of impending doom · Loss of consciousness · Seizure · Cardiovascular instability *In event of any of these signs and symptoms, TURN OFF the pump, leave pump attached to catheter. Notify MD immediately and initiate resuscitation as needed.

TABLE 3-23   PCA Programming Parameters

The parameters are set by an MD and can be changed by MD order.

Parameter	Description	Example of PCA for Opioid-Naive Patient (Morphine)†
Drug concentration	Drug amount/mL	1 mg/mL
Loading dose	Administer to achieve desired level of pain control	2.5 mg IV repeat prn
PCA dose	Amount of drug the patient will receive with each bolus	0.6-2.0 mg
Bolus lockout time	The time period after the last bolus delivery during which another bolus is not allowed	5-10 min
Basal rate*	Continuous infusion rate (mL/h)	0-1.25 mg/h
Hour limit	Maximum dose potentially administered in 1 h	7.5-12.5 mg/h

*Use with caution in an opioid-naive patient (basal rate < half the projected hourly requirement).

Source: From M. McCaffrey M. Pasero, and C. Pain. *Clinical Manual*, Second edition. Mosby: St. Louis, IL (1999): p. 252. © Elsevier, 1999.

General considerations related to PCA follow:
- Morphine is the drug of choice for PCA in military AE systems (1 mg/mL).
- A continuous basal opioid infusion should be initiated only if the patient is monitored by a dedicated medical provider and continuous pulse oximetry is performed throughout all phases of transport.
- The patient may require an increased bolus dose during transport.
- Breakthrough pain may require a supplemental opioid bolus.
- Opioid PCA can be administered in conjunction with continuous peripheral nerve block.
- Monitor pain q 4 h or more frequently prn.
- The sending facility should send two additional AA batteries for the ambIT Pain Pump for patients in the AE system.

For more information, refer to the Army Regional Anesthesia and Pain Management Initiative (http://arapmi.org/).

Epidural or Continuous PNB – Local Anesthetic Toxicity

If any of the following signs/symptoms listed in the above table associate with Local Anesthetic Toxicity occur–TURN OFF the pump, leave pump attached to the catheter.

Treatment of Local Anesthesia Toxicity (LAST)
- *Get help.*
- *Initial focus.*
  - Airway management: ventilate with 100% oxygen.
  - Seizure suppression: benzodiazepines are preferred.
  - BLS/ACLS may require prolonged effort.
- Infuse 20% lipid emulsion (values in parenthesis are for a 70 kg patient).
  - Bolus 1.5 mL/kg (lean body mass) IV over 1 min (~100 mL).
  - Continuous infusion 0.25 mL/kg/min (~18 mL/min).

- ○ Repeat bolus once or twice for persistent cardiovascular collapse.
- ○ Double the infusion rate to 0.5 mL/kg/min if BP remains low.
- ○ Continue infusion for at least 10 minutes after attaining circulatory stability.
- ○ Recommend upper limit: approximately 10 mL/kg lipid emulsion over the first 30 min.
- Avoid vasopressin, calcium channel blockers, beta blockers or local anesthetics.
- Alert the nearest facility to have cardiopulmonary bypass available.
- Avoid propofol in patients having signs of cardiovascular instability.

References

Arroyo-Novoa CM, Figueroa-Ramos MI, Puntillo K, et al. Pain related to tracheal suctioning in awake acutely and critically ill adults: A descriptive study. *Intensive Crit Care Nurse* 2008 Feb; 24(1):20-7. Epub 2007 Aug 6.

Buckenmaier CC 3rd, Lee EH, Shields CH, et al. Regional anesthesia in austere environments. *Reg Anesth Pain Med* 2003;28:321-327.

Buckenmaier CC, McKnight GM, Winkley JV, et al. Continuous peripheral nerve block for battlefield anesthesia and evacuation. *Reg Anesth Pain Med* 2005;30:202-205.

Clark ME, Bair MJ, Buckenmaier CC, et al. Pain and combat injuries in soldiers returning from Operations Enduring Freedom and Iraqi Freedom: Implications for research and practice. *J Rehabil Res Dev* 2007;44(2):179-194.

Galluzi KE. Managing neuropathic pain. *JAOA* 2007;107(11 suppl 6):ES39-ES48.

Garbez R, Puntillo K. Acute musculoskeletal pain in the emergency department: A review of the literature and implications for advanced practice nurse. *AACN Clin Iss* 2005;16(3):310-319.

Ketz A. Pain management in the traumatic amputee. *Crit Care Clin North Am* 2008, 21(1), 51-57.

Li D, Puntillo K, Miaskowski C. A review of objective pain measures for use with critical care adult patients unable to self-report. *J Pain* 2008 Jan; 9(1): 2-10. Epub 2007 Nov 5.

Liu SS, Wu CL. The effect of analgesic technique on postoperative patient-reported outcomes including analgesia: A systematic review. *Pain Medicine* 2007;105(3):789-808.

McCaffrey M, Pasero C. *Pain Clinical Manual* (2nd ed), Mosby, 1999, p. 252.

Puntillo K, Ley SJ. Appropriately timed analgesics control pain due to chest tube removal. *Am J Crit Care* 2004;13(4):292-304.

Puntillo Ka, Miaskowski C, Kehrle K, et al. Relationship between behavioral and physiological indicators of pain, critical care patients' self-report of pain and opioid administration. *Crit Care Med* 1997;25(7):1159-1166.

Stojadinovic A, Auton A, Peoples GE, et al. Responding to challenges in modern combat casualty care: Innovative use of advanced regional anesthesia. *Pain Medicine* 2006;7(4):330-338.

Stotts N, Puntillo K, Bonham Morris, A, et al. Wound care pain in hospitalized adult patients. *Heart Lung* 2004;33:321-332.

Pediatric Pain Management

All children need the following measures prescribed:

- Background pain control: scheduled, not prn.
- Procedural pain control. If wound care or a procedure cannot be accomplished with the medications ordered or safely within the area where care is being provided, discuss with an MD the need for an anesthesia-assisted procedure or booking the procedure in the OR.

TABLE 3-24	Initial Dosage Guidelines, Pediatrics		
Initial Dosage for Opioid Analgesics			
Analgesic	**Route**	**Dose (Child < 50 kg)**	**Dose (Child > 50 kg)**
Morphine	IV	0.1 mg/kg q 2-4 h Infusion: 0.025 mg/kg/h Newborn: 0.004-0.01 mg/kg/h	5-8 mg q 2-4 h Infusion: 1.5 mg/h
Fentanyl	IV PO	0.5-1.0 mcg/kg q 1-2 h Infusion: 0.5-2.0 mcg/kg/h Oralet: 10-15 mcg/kg (maximum dose = 400 mcg)	25-50 mcg q 1-2 h Infusion: 25-100 mcg/h
Hydromorphone	IV	0.02 mg/kg q 2-4 h Infusion: 0.006 mg/kg/h	1 mg q 2-4 h Infusion: 0.3 mg/h
Oxycodone	PO	0.1-0.2 mg/kg q 3-4 h	5-10 mg q 3-4 h
Codeine	PO	0.5-1.0 mg/kg q 3-4 h	30-60 mg q 3-4 h
Hydrocodone + acetaminophen	PO	0.5-0.2 mg/kg q 4-6 h	5-10 mg q 4-6 h
Meperidine*	IV	0.1-1 mg/kg q 2-3 h	50-75 mg q 2-3 h
Dosage for Nonopioid Analgesics			
Analgesic	**Route**	**Dose (Child < 60 kg)**	**Dose (Child > 60 kg)**
Acetaminophen	PO PR	10-15 mg/kg q 4 h (maximum dose = 90 mg/kg) 20 mg/kg (loading dose, 35-40 mg/kg)	650-1000 mg q 4 h (maximum dose = 4000 mg daily) 1000 mg
Ibuprofen	PO	5-10 mg/kg q 6 h (maximum dose = 40 mg/kg/day)	400-600 mg q 6 h (maximum dose = 2400 mg/day)
Ketorolac (not for children < 2 years)	IV	0.25-0.5 mg/kg q 6 h (maximum dose = 2 mg/kg/day)	15-30 mg q 6 h (maximum dose = 120 mg/day)
Naproxen	PO	5-6 mg/kg q 12 h (maximum dose = 24 mg/kg/day)	250-375 mg q 12 h (maximum dose = 1000 mg/day)

*Meperidine should generally be avoided in pediatric patients if other opioids are available.

References

American Medical Association. Module 6: Pain management: Pediatric pain management. http://www.ama-cmeonline.com/pain_mgmt/module06/index.htm

Bauman BH, McManus JG. Pediatric pain management in the emergency department. *Emerg Med Clin North Am* 2005; 23(2):393-414.

Johns Hopkins. *The Harriet Lane Handbook: A Manual for Pediatric House Officers*, 17th ed. Elsevier, 2005.

Kotwal RS, O'Connor KC, Johnson TR, et al. A novel pain management strategy for combat casualty care. *Ann Emerg Med* 2004;44:121-127.

Sedation

TABLE 3-25 Ramsay Sedation Score

Clinical Status	Score
Patient anxious, agitated, or restless	1
Patient cooperative, oriented, and tranquil	2
Patient asleep, responds to commands only	3
Patient asleep, responds to gentle shaking, light glabellar tap, or loud auditory stimulus	4
Patient asleep, responds to noxious stimuli such as firm nailbed pressure	5
Patient asleep, has no response to firm nailbed pressure or other noxious stimuli	6

RSS Interpretation	
1	Inadequate sedation
2, 3, or 4	Acceptable sedation
5 or 6	Excessive sedation

TABLE 3-26 Sedation/Antipsychotic Therapy, Adult

Medication	Route	Intermittent Dose	Infusion Dose Range
Diazepam (Valium)	IV	0.03-0.1 mg/kg q 0.5-6 h	–
Lorazepam (Ativan)	IV	0.02-0.06 mg/kg q 2-6 h	0.01-0.1 mg/kg/h
Midazolam (Versed)	IV	0.02-0.08 mg/kg q 0.5-2 h	0.04-0.2 mg/kg/h
Propofol	IV	–	5-80 mcg/kg/min
Haloperidol (Haldol)*	IV	0.03-0.15 mg/kg q 0.5-6 h	0.04-0.15 mg/kg/h

Notes:
1. Propofol is preferred for rapid awakening (increased risk for increased triglycerides after 2 days infusion).
2. Midazolam and diazepam are useful for rapid sedation of acutely agitated patients.
3. Midazolam is appropriate for short-term use only.
4. Patients receiving haloperidol should have ECG monitoring for QTc.

TABLE 3-27 Sedation/Antipsychotic Therapy, Pediatric

Medication	Route	Intermittent Dose
Diazepam	PO	0.25-0.3 mg/kg
Lorazepam	PO, IV, IM	0.05 mg/kg
Midazolam	PO	0.5-0.8 mg/kg
	PR	0.5-1 mg/kg
	IM	0.15-0.2 mg/kg
	IV	0.1-0.25 mg/kg

Recommended Orders Set for Therapies for Analgesia, Sedation, and Delirium Management (Adult)

See JTTS Clinical Practice Guideline Management of Pain, Anxiety and Delirium of Injured Warfighters (Nov 2010) for additional recommendations.

Analgesia Goal is a pain level of 3 or less (or other specified level).

Intermittent Dosing

- Fentanyl 25-100 mcg IV q1 h prn for mild to moderate pain.
- If required more than q2 h, go to continuous IV.

Continuous Dosing (stop intermittent dosing if continuous infusion started).

- Fentanyl IV 25-250 mcg/h.
- Fentanyl IV bolus 25-100 mcg q10 min as needed for breakthrough pain.

Sedation Goal: MAAS score of 2-3.

Intermittent Dosing

- Lorazepam (Ativan) 1-4 mg IV q1 h prn for anxiety/agitation.
- If required more than q2 h, go to continuous IV.

Continuous infusion (stop intermittent dosing if continuous infusion started).

- Lorazepam IV infusion 1-5 mg/h.
- Lorazepam IV bolus 1-2 mg IV q20 min prn for breakthrough anxiety/agitation
- Midazolam (Versed) IV 1-6 mg/h (avoid with liver/renal dysfunction).
- Midazolam IV bolus 1-2 mg q2 min prn for breakthrough agitation/anxiety.

Dexmedetomidine Continuous Infusion

- *Indication*: Short term sedation in patients undergoing awake intubation or as a bridge to extubation in patients who are very agitated and do not tolerate spontaneous breathing trials. Avoid use > 24 hours if spontaneous respiration is desired.
- *Continuous Infusion*: 0.3-0.7 mcg/kg/h IV for 24 h (maximum dose 0.7 mcg/kg/h).
- Titrate in increments of 0.1 mcg/kg/h q10 minutes to achieve sedation score 2-3 and pain score < 4/10.
- Stop infusion for HR < 45 beats/min or if patient develops 2nd- or 3rd-degree AV block.
- For persistent hypotension unresponsive to fluid challenge, decrease dose by 50%.
- Discontinue if SBP and MAP do not return to established parameters within 10 minutes.

Delirium Assess for delirium using CAM Scale

Initiating therapy

- Haloperidol (Haldol) IV 2-10 mg IV ONE DOSE ONLY.
- Haloperidol IV prn 2-5 mg q15 min prn agitation. Recommend not to exceed 20 mg over 1 hour.

Maintenance Dosing

- Haloperidol 2-5 mg IV q1 h prn for delirium.
- Monitor QT$_c$ for patients receiving more than 10 mg haloperidol per day. Discontinue if QT$_c$ exceeds 500 msec or interval increases 60 msec from baseline.

Ketamine

Indication: An adjuvant to opioids when reduced narcotic use if desired.

IV or IM Loading Dose: 150-300 mcg/kg
Continuous infusion: 1-14 mcg/kg/min

- Admixture 250 mg ketamine in 250 mL NS.
- For patients < 60 years of age and greater than 70 kg, start infusion at 10 mg/h for acute and neuropathic pain. Patients outside these guidelines should receive ketamine 100 mcg/h.

Note: Recent evidence indicates no significant increase in CNS symptoms in patients receiving ketamine (PCA, IV, or epidural) compared to opioids alone.

■ Post-Anesthesia Care Unit (PACU) Recovery

Post-Anesthesia Assessment and Care

Source: Based on guidelines from the Department of Army's IBN Sina Hospital. Also refer to local policies and procedures.

The postoperative report to the PACU should include the following information:

- Patient's name, age, and surgical procedure
- Any complications that may have occurred in the operating room
- ASA grade (I-IV):
  - ASA 1: normal healthy patient
  - ASA 2: patient with mild systemic disease with no functional limitations
  - ASA 3: patient with moderate systemic disease with functional limitations
  - ASA 4: patient with severe systemic disease that is a constant threat to life
- Type of anesthesia:
  - If spinal or epidural anesthesia was used, the dermatome level and expected duration of the block should be reported (see the "Neurological" section for a dermatome chart).
  - If a nerve block was performed, the limb and expected duration of the block should be reported.
- Medications received in the OR:
  - Opioids
  - Sedatives
  - Reversal agents
  - Antiemetics
- Known allergies or medical history
- Fluids given in the OR:
  - Crystalloids
  - Colloids
  - Blood products
- Fluids lost in the OR
- Estimated blood loss
- Urine output
- NG output
- Ventriculostomy output
- Lines: all peripheral/central IV lines, arterial catheter, urinary catheter, other invasive devices (chest tubes, ventriculostomy, wound drains)

TABLE 3-28   Post-Anesthesia Recovery Score

Criterion	Description	Score
Motor	Able to move all extremities voluntarily or on command[*]	2
	Able to move 2 extremities on command	1
	Able to move 0 extremities voluntarily or on command	0
Respiratory	Spontaneous respirations; able to deep-breathe and cough freely[*]	2
	Dyspnea or limited breathing	1
	Apneic	0
SBP[†]	SBP ± 20% of pre-anesthetic level	2
	SBP ± 20–50% of pre-anesthetic level	1
	SBP ± 50% of pre-anesthetic level	0
Level of consciousness	Awake and alert, answers questions appropriately[*]	2
	Arousable on calling but falls back to sleep	1
	Unresponsive	0
SpO_2	$SpO_2 > 92\%$ on room air	2
	Supplemental O_2 required to maintain $SpO_2 > 90\%$	1
	$SpO_2 < 92\%$ with O_2 supplementation	0
Skin color	Normal skin color, acyanotic	2
	or	
	Skin is pale, blotchy, and/or dusky	1
	Cyanotic	0
	Total	

[*]Indicates score needed for discharge based on that criterion.
[†]The pre-anesthetic SBP may be hypotensive with massive trauma. When a pre-anesthetic SBP is presumed abnormal, compare it to predicted normal values for the specific patient (for age and/or condition).

Interpretation

Score	Interpretation
10	Optimal
8 or 9	Safe
≤7	Low or dangerous

Maximum points: 10. The higher the score, the better.
Source: This table was published in *J Perianesthesia Nursing,* 13(3), Aldrete JA. Modifications to the postanestesia score for use in ambulatory surgery, p 150, Copyright Elsevier (1998).

Typical Criteria for Discharge of Patient from a Level III PACU

This information is not a replacement for clinical judgment. Final approval for discharge must be given by the anesthesiologist or nurse anesthetist.

- PAR score > 8, with scores of 2 in motor activity, respiratory, and consciousness.
- Patient has stayed in PACU for at least 30 minutes after admission.
- Patient has stayed in PACU for at least 20 minutes from last IV narcotic administered.
- Patient's pain is at an acceptable level (4/10 or lower, or to a level the patient states is "tolerable").
- Patient's nausea/vomiting is controlled.
- Any extremity with a cast, splint, or brace is neurovascularly intact.
- Surgical dressings are intact, without excessive bleeding.
- All drainage has been recorded and is within normal limits.

- Appropriate ward or step-down orders are on the chart.
- IV access is patent and appropriately secured.
- If patient received reversal agents for neuromuscular blocking agents while in the PACU, patient has stayed in the PACU for at least 60 minutes.

Due to the rapid turnover in a combat environment, no patients will be discharged to home or return to duty from the PACU. All patients must transfer to the ward for full recovery prior to discharge out of the facility. *If regional anesthesia has been given, the following criteria must be met for discharge:*

- Patients receiving spinal or epidural anesthetic should be able to bend their legs and have recovered sensation to the L1 dermatome (hip/perineum).
- Patients receiving extremity blocks should have the blocked extremity adequately immobilized or protected if the block has not resolved.

Postoperative Pain Management

This information is not a replacement for an MD order or clinical judgment. Pain management is based on assessment of patient's pain and physiological stability.

Assess and record the patient's pain level every time vital signs are recorded and prn. Use pain scales (see the "Pain Management" section):

- 0-10 scale
- Visual analog scale
- FACES scale
- If culture or language makes assessment of pain difficult, consider evaluating the therapy based on "what is tolerable for patient."

TABLE 3-29 Adult Intravenous Analgesics (Routinely Ordered and Available in AOR)		
Analgesic	Intermittent Dose	Infusion Dose Range*
Morphine	0.01-0.15 mcg/kg IV q 1-2 h	0.07-0.5 mcg/kg/h
Fentanyl	0.35-1.5 mcg/kg q 0.5-1 h	0.7-10 mcg/kg/h
Meperidine (Demerol)	Not recommended	Not recommended
Hydromorphone (Dilaudid)	10-30 mcg/kg IV q 1-2 h	7-15 mcg/kg/h
Ketorolac	30 mg q 6 h If age > 65, weight < 50 kg, or patient has renal insufficiency, then 15 mg q 6 h	

*Patients requiring a continuous infusion for pain management may require transfer to the ICU.

Source: S. A. Nasraway Jr., et al., "Sedation, analgesia and neuromuscular blockade of the critically ill adult," *Crit Care Med* 30 (2002): 117-141.

Notes:
1. Dose and intervals between doses should be titrated according to the individual's response.
2. More frequent doses may be needed for acute pain management in mechanically ventilated patients.
3. Use caution when using multiple agents. Do not give agents so that they will peak at the same time, as this could increase adverse effects such as respiratory depression.

Pediatric Pain Management

Whatever is painful to an adult is painful to a child, unless proven otherwise.

TABLE 3-30	Pediatric Intravenous Analgesics	
Analgesic	Intermittent Dose (<50 kg)	Intermittent Dose (> 50 kg)
Morphine	0.1 mg/kg q 2-4 h	5-8 mg q 2-4 h
Fentanyl	0.5-1 mcg/kg q 1-2 h	25-50 mcg q 1-2 h
Hydromorphone	0.02 mg/kg q 2-4 h	1 mg q 2-4 h

Naloxone (Narcan) Administration

Source: Landstuhl Regional Medical Center (2 July 2007).

1. Patients who require naloxone (Narcan) usually meet all of the following criteria:
   • Unresponsive to physical stimulation
   • Shallow respirations or RR < 8 bpm
   • Pinpoint pupils
2. Stop the administration of the opioid and any other sedative drugs. If given IV, maintain IV access.
3. Summon help. Ask a coworker to prepare naloxone and bring it to you. Remain with the patient and continue to attempt to arouse him or her.
4. Mix 0.4 mg (1 ampule) of naloxone and 10 mL of normal saline in a syringe for IV administration.
   • Pediatrics: if patient is a child < 40 kg, dilute 0.1 mg (1/4 ampule) in 9 mL NS to make 0.01 mg/mL solution = 10 mcg/mL.
5. Administer the dilute naloxone IV very slowly (0.5 mL over 2 min) while you observe the patient's response (titrate to effect).
6. The patient should open his or her eyes and talk to you within 1-2 min. If not, continue IV naloxone at the same rate up to a total of 0.8 mg (20 mL dilute naloxone). If no response, begin looking for other causes of sedation and respiratory depression.
7. Discontinue naloxone administration as soon as the patient is responsive to physical stimulation and able to take deep breaths when told to do so. Keep the syringe nearby. Another dose of naloxone may be needed as early as 30 min after the first dose because the duration of naloxone is shorter than the duration of most opioids.
8. Assign a staff member to monitor the patient's sedation and respiratory status and to remind the patient to deep-breathe every 1-2 min until the patient becomes more alert.
9. Notify the MD.
10. Consider a nonopioid analgesic for pain relief if appropriate.

11. Resume opioid administration at half the original dose when the patient is easily aroused and respiratory rate > 9 breaths/min.

Giving too much Naloxone or giving it too fast can precipitate severe pain, which is extremely difficult to control and increases sympathetic activity, leading to hypertension, tachycardia, ventricular dysrhythmias, pulmonary edema, and cardiac arrest. In physically dependent patients, withdrawal syndrome can be precipitated; patients who have been receiving opioids for more than one week may be exquisitely sensitive to antagonists.

References

Johns Hopkins. The *Harriet Lane Handbook: A Manual for Pediatric House Officers*, 17th ed. Elsevier, 2005.

McCaffery M, Pasero C. *Pain: Clinical Management*. St. Louis: Mosby, 1999.

Practice guidelines for acute pain management in the perioperative period. *Anesthesiology* 2004;100:1573-1581.

Postoperative/Post-discharge Nausea and Vomiting (PONV)

The following factors may increase the risk of PONV:

- Female
- Nonsmoker
- History of PONV/motion sickness
- Intraoperative/postoperative opioids
- Duration of surgery > 60 min
- Emetogenic surgery: intra-abdominal surgery, strabismus surgery, ENT surgery, breast surgery

Postoperative patient management proceeds as follows (per MD order only):

Verify adequate hydration and blood pressure:

- ASPAN recommends supplemental IV fluids for ASA I-III patients who are at increased risk for PONV (Exact amount of supplemental fluid is not specified).

Supplemental oxygen may decrease PONV.

Give antiemetics as necessary:

- Ondansetron (Zofran)
  - Adult (> 40 kg): 4 mg IV undiluted over at least 30 sec (2-5 min preferred)
  - Pediatric (< 40 mg/kg): 0.1 mg/kg
- Metoclopramide (Reglan)
  - Adult: 10 mg IM/IV; administer over 1-2 min
  - Pediatric: rarely used; ondansetron is preferred in this population
    Age > 14 years: 10 mg IV over 1-2 min
    Age 6-14 years: 2.5-5 mg IV over 1-2 min
    Age < 6 years: 0.1 mg/kg over 1-2 min

- Promethazine (Phenergan)
  ○ Adult: 12–25 mg IV q 4–6 h prn; give each 25 mg over 1 min
  ○ Pediatric: 0.25–0.5 mg kg IV (IV only in children > 2 years)

References

ASPAN's evidence-based clinical practice guideline for the prevention and/or management of PONV/PDV. *J Perianesthesia Nursing* 2006;21(4):230-250.

Habib AS. Evidence-based management of postoperative nausea and vomiting: A review. *Can J Anesth* 2004;51(4):326-341.

PACU orders, IBN Sina Hospital.

Prevention of Perioperative Hypothermia

See the "Hypothermia Treatment" section.

- Preoperative warming may decrease the risk of perioperative hypothermia.
- Passive warming (insulating exposed body surfaces) can reduce heat loss by as much as 30%, with the most effect coming from a single layer.
- Active warming (forced-air warmer/circulating-water garments) are the only methods to effectively prevent perioperative hypothermia. Use active warming when patient's temperature is ≤96.0°F. Follow the manufacturer's instructions when using these devices.
- Warmed IV fluids may prevent fluid-induced hypothermia, but do not warm the patient.
- Warmed blankets may improve patient comfort, but do not prevent hypothermia or warm the patient.
- Forced Air Warming (follow manufacturer's instructions)
  Safety Alert
  ○ Do not "hose" (i.e., do not attach the hose to the blanket). This practice results in heated air blowing directly on the patient and has caused severe burns.
  ○ Use chemical warming blankets with caution. Place a wool blanket or sheet between the patient and the chemical blanket to prevent burns.

SECTION IV

Appendix

■ Abbreviations

A.b.	*Acinetobacter baumannii*
AE	Aeromedical evacuation
AELT	Aeromedical Evacuation Liaison Team
ASD	Acute stress disorder
AOR	Area of Responsibility
BBF	Blood and body fluid
BI	Battle injury
C2	Command and control
CASEVAC	Casualty evacuation
CASF	Contingency Air Staging Facility
CCATT	Critical Care Air Transport Team
CPG	Clinical practice guideline
CSH	Combat Support Hospital
DNBI	Disease and non-battle injury
FAST	Focused abdominal sonography for trauma
FFP	Fresh frozen plasma
FOB	Forward operating base
HN	Host nation
IED	Improvised explosive device
IO	Intraosseous
JFC	Joint Force Commander
JTTS	Joint Trauma Theater Surgeon
LZ	Landing zone
MH	Mental health
mcg	Microgram
mg	Milligram
mL	Milliliter
MOST	Mobile oxygen storage tank
MTF	Medical treatment center
NGO	Nongovernmental organization
NIPRNET	Non-secure Internet Protocol Router Network
ORM	Operational risk management

PAD	Patient administration director	**SMEED**	Special Medical Emergency Evacuation Device (for NATO litter)
PEP	Post-exposure plan		
PMI	Patient movement items (medical equipment)	**SOP**	Standing operating procedure
PMR	Patient movement record	**STD**	Sexually transmitted disease
PMRC	Patient movement requirements center (global, Joint, Theater)	**TACC**	Tanker Airlift Control Center (AF)
		T-AH	Hospital ship
POD	Port of debarkation (arrival)	**TBI**	Traumatic brain injury
		TMLMC	Theater Medical Logistic Management Center
POE	Port of embarkation (departure)	**TRAC2ES**	TRANSCOM Regulating and Command and Control Evacuation System
PROFIS	Professional Filler System		
PT LOX	Patient liquid oxygen (portable unit)	**UMT**	Unit ministry team
PTSD	Post-traumatic stress disorder	**VFS**	Validating flight surgeon
SI	Seriously wounded or ill	**VSI**	Very seriously ill or injured
SIPRNET	SECRET Internet Protocol Router Network	**Z, ZULU**	Military/international time reference at Greenwich, England; Greenwich Mean Time (GMT)
SITREP	Situation report		

Abbreviations That Should *Not* Be Used

IU International unit; write "International Unit"

MS, MSO₄, MgSO₄ Morphine sulfate or magnesium sulfate; write "morphine sulfate" or "magnesium sulfate"

QD (Q.D., qd, q.d.) Daily; write "daily"

QOD, Q.O.D., qod, q.o.d. Every other day; write "every other day"

U Unit; write "unit"

Trailing zero (X.0 mg) Write X mg

Lack of leading zero (.X mg) Write 0.X mg

■ Disaster-Specific Management
Disaster/Mass-Casualty Response

TABLE 4-1 Severity Predictor for Mass-Casualty Events		
Triage Category		
All casualties	One-third critical casualties: dead on scene or die at hospital, require emergency surgery or require hospitalization	• Black (dead/expectant) • Red (immediate) • Yellow (delayed-admitted)
	Two-thirds noncritical casualties: acute casualties treated and released from ED	• Yellow (delayed-released) • Green (minimal)
The following factors can change the pattern of casualties: use of manufactured weapons (i.e., military ordinance), explosion in a confined space, or collapse of buildings or other structures. If one of these factors is present, the pattern of casualties can change and the number of critical casualties may double.		

Mass Casualty Predictor
Source: Centers for Disease Control and Prevention. Mass casualty predictor. http://emergency.cdc.gov/masscasualties/predictor.asp.

Total expected casualties = Number of casualties arriving in 1 h × 2
- 1-h window begins when the first casualty arrives at the hospital.
- 50-85% of the acute casualties will arrive in the first 90 min.

Triage
Triage means "to sort."
- Sorting casualties allows medical personnel to identify the priorities of treatment and evacuation of the wounded or ill, given the limitations of the current situation.
- The highest priorities are to preserve life, limb, and eyesight.
- Triage is an ongoing process; it is repeated at each level of care and with each procedure.

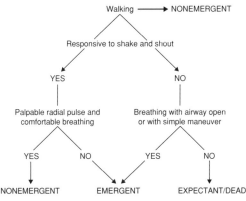

FIGURE 92   Example of rapid triage.

TABLE 4-2   Triage Levels

Triage Level	Examples of Interventions	Examples of Injuries	Examples from New York (September 11, 2001)*
Immediate (Red P1): These patients require life-saving attention within minutes to several hours of arriving at the point of care to avoid death or major disability.	The surgical procedures in this category should not be time-consuming and should concern only those patients with high chances of survival.	• Airway obstruction • Uncontrolled bleeding • Shock (SBP < 90 mm Hg) • Decreased mental status • Unstable head injury • Unstable penetrating or blunt injuries of the trunk, head, neck, or pelvis • Threatened loss of limb or eyesight • Multiple long-bone fractures • Unstable casualties with chest or abdominal injuries • Emergency amputation	• Airway compromise • Comatose • Penetrating torso trauma • Vascular trauma • Major limb deformity. • Second/third-degree burns
Delayed (Yellow P2): This group includes those wounded who are badly in need of time-consuming surgery, but whose general condition permits delay in surgical treatment without unduly endangering life.	Sustaining treatment will be required (e.g., stabilizing IV fluids, splinting, antibiotics, catheterization, gastric decompression, and relief of pain).	• Large muscle wounds • Fractures of major bones • Intra-abdominal and/or thoracic wounds • Burns covering less than 50% of total body surface area (TBSA)	• First/second-degree burns • Isolated trauma to extremity without vascular compromise or deformity • Stable post-chest tube
Minimal (Green)	Self-aid, buddy care	• Minor lacerations, abrasions • Fractures of small bones • Minor burns	• Psychological distress • Isolated auditory trauma • Minor wounds • All walking patients
Expectant (Black/Blue): Casualties in this category have wounds that are so extensive that even if they were the sole casualty and had the benefit of optimal medical resource application, their survival would be unlikely.	The expectant casualty should not be abandoned, but should be separated from the view of other casualties. Using a minimal but competent staff, provide comfort measures for these casualties.	• Unresponsive penetrating head wounds • Transcranial gunshot wound • High spinal cord injuries • Mutilating explosive wounds involving multiple anatomical sites and organs • Open pelvic injuries with uncontrolled bleeding; in shock, with decreased mental status • Second- and third-degree burns covering more than 60% TBSA • Profound shock with multiple injuries and agonal respiration	• Amputation with no signs of life • No respirations, pulse, and dilated pupils • NO CPR • NO open thoracotomy

*These are examples only; actual triage depends on the specifics of the situation.
Source: Triage. In *Emergency War Surgery, Third United States Edition Revision,* 2004. The Borden Institute. *Triage* (Chapter 3, 31-37).
http://www.brooksidepress.org/Products/Emergency_War_Surgery/Chp3Triage.pdf

TABLE 4-3   Immunizations for Individuals Displaced by a Disaster

Give the following immunizations if the individual's records are not available.

Children Younger Than 10 Years
Diphtheria, tetanus toxoids, acellular pertussis vaccine (DTaP)
Inactivated poliovirus
Haemophilus influenzae type B vaccine Influenza vaccine for all children 6-59 months of age, and all children 6 months through 10 years of age with an underlying medical condition that increases the risk for complications of influenza
Hepatitis B vaccine (Hep B)
Pneumococcal conjugate vaccine
Measles, mumps, rubella vaccine
Varicella vaccine unless reliable history of chickenpox
Hepatitis A (recommended for children > 1 year in the United States)
Children/Adolescents (11-18 Years)
Adult formulation tetanus and diphtheria toxoids and acellular pertussis vaccine (Tdap)
Meningococcal conjugate vaccine (ages 11-12 and 15 only)
Influenza vaccine for all children 6-59 months of age and all children 6 months through 10 years of age with an underlying medical condition that increases risk for complication of influenza
Adults (> 18 Years of Age)
Adult formulation tetanus and diphtheria toxoids (Td) if > 10 years since receipt of any tetanus toxoid-containing vaccine
Pneumococcal polysaccharide vaccine (PPV) for adults 65 years or older with a high-risk condition
Influenza vaccine
Crowded Group Settings
Influenza: Everyone ≥ 6 months of age should receive influenza vaccine. Children > 8 years of age should receive two doses, at least one month *apart, unless they have a documented record of a previous dose of influenza vaccine*, in which case they should receive one dose.
Varicella: Everyone 12 months of age or older should receive one dose of this vaccine unless they have a reliable history of chickenpox or a documented record of immunization.
MMR: Everyone 12 months of age or older and born during or after 1957 should receive one dose of this vaccine unless they have a documented record of two doses of MMR.

Immunocompromised individuals, such as HIV-infected persons, pregnant women, and those on systemic steroids, should not receive the live viral vaccines, varicella, and MMR. Screening should be performed by self-report.
Source: Centers for Disease Control and Prevention. Disaster recovery information: Interim immunization recommendations for individuals displaced by a disaster.

Tetanus Prophylaxis

- Clean the wound and debride it prn.
- Be aware that wounds associated with floods may be contaminated with waterborne organisms

Reference

Emergency wound management for healthcare professionals. http://emergency.cdc.gov/disasters/emergwoundhcp.asp

The decision to administer tetanus prophylaxis after trauma is based on the following factors:

- The patient's past vaccination history. All U.S. military personnel will have received at least a primary vaccination.

• Condition of the wound. Battlefield wounds are considered prone to develop tetanus.

TABLE A-4 Tetanus Prophylaxis

History of Vaccination	Non-Tetanus Prone Wound		Tetanus-Prone Wound*	
	Tetanus toxoid	Tetanus immunoglobulin	Tetanus toxoid	Tetanus immunoglobulin
Unknown or < 3 doses	0.5 mL IM	No	0.5 mL IM	250-500 units IM (separate syringe/site)
Three or more doses	Yes: 0.5 mL IM if < 10 years since last dose	No	Yes: 0.5 mL IM if < 5 years since last dose	No

*Tetanus-prone wounds include wounds that are oxygen deficient–those that are crushed, devitalized, contaminated with dirt, rust, feces, saliva, caused by missiles, burns, frostbite. Both minor and major wounds can cause tetanus.

References

Centers for Disease Control and Prevention. Tetanus prevention. http://emergency.cdc.gov/disasters/hurricanes/katrina/tetanus.asp

Diphtheria, tetanus, and pertussis: "Recommendations for vaccine use and other preventive measures." Recommendations of the Immunization Practices Advisory Committee (ACIP). MMWR 1991;40(RR10):1-28. www.cdc.gov/mmwr/preview/mmwrhtml/00041645.htm

Disaster Resources

• Centers for Disease Control and Prevention (see webpage for numerous resources):
  ◦ Training: "Radiological Terrorism: Medical response to mass casualties," http://emergency.cdc.gov/radiation/masscasualties/training.asp
  ◦ Information for Disaster Evacuation Centers: http://emergency.cdc.gov/disasters/evaccenters.asp
  ◦ Infection Control Recommendations for Prevention of Transmission of Respiratory Illnesses in Disaster Evacuation Centers: http://emergency.cdc.gov/disasters/disease/respiratoryic.asp
  ◦ Medical Care of III Disaster Evacuees: Additional Diagnoses to Consider: http://emergency.cdc.gov/disasters/medcare.asp
  ◦ Tsunami-Related Information for Clinicians: http://emergency.cdc.gov/disasters/tsunamis/clinicians.asp
  ◦ Bioterrorism: http://emergency.cdc.gov/bioterrorism/
  ◦ Chemical Emergencies http://emergency.cdc.gov/chemical/
• Nursing Emergency Preparedness Education Coalition: http://www.nursing.vanderbilt.edu/incmce/index.html
• American Nurses Association, Disaster Preparedness and Response: http://www.nursingworld.org/MainMenuCategories/Healthcareand-PolicyIssues/DPR.aspx
• U.S. Department of Health and Human Services, Disasters and Emergencies: http://www.hhs.gov/disasters/
• Pandemic influenza: PandemicFlu.gov
• American Red Cross, all disaster types: http://www.redcross.org/index.html

- Center of Excellence, Disaster Management and Humanitarian Assistance: www.coe-dmha.org
- American Medical Association, Center for Public Health Preparedness and Disaster Response (CPHPDR): www.ama-assn.org/ama/pub/category/6206.html
- Wynd CA. A proposed model for military disaster nursing. *Online J Iss Nursing* 2006;11(3). (See the entire edition for a discussion of disaster nursing issues.)

■ Iraq and Afghan Translations

Translation Guide

Source: Adapted from Defense Language Institute, Foreign Language Center. Field support modules: Iraqi medical language survival guide. http://fieldsupport.lingnet.org/index.aspx

TABLE 4-5 Iraqi Pronunciation and Medical Terms

PRONUNCIATION GUIDE FOR IRAQI SOUNDS UNFAMILIAR TO ENGLISH

H	as in	Hawil	or	ijrooHak
Kh	as in	Khamur	or	itKhaleena
Th	as in	haTha	or	naKhThak
S	as in	So'ooba	or	iSKhoona
Dh	as in	DhagheT	or	il maraDh
T	as in	Tila'	or	Tiflich
'	as in	'aTshaan	or	ju'aan
gh	as in	lughum	or	ghuma

We will try to contact someone from your group.	raH inHaawil nitiSil ibfad waHed min jamaa'tak	رَح نحاول نتّصل بفد واحد من جَماعتَك
Please.	raja-an	رَجاءً
Thank you.	shukran	شُكراً
You are welcome.	ahlan wa sahlan	اهلاً وسهلاً
Thank you for talking with me.	shukrun 'alamood Hecheet wiyaya	شُكراً علمود حچيت وِيَايَه
I will talk with you again.	raH aHchee wiyak mart luKh	رَح أحچي وياك مَرَة لُخ
Good-bye.	ma'a is salaama	مَعَ السلامة

(Continued)

TABLE 4-5 Iraqi Pronunciation and Medical Terms (*Continued*)

You have been hurt.	inta mit'awir	إنتَ مِتعوّر
We are all working to help you.	kulna raH insaa'dak	كُلنا رَح نساعدك
Help us take care of you.	saa'idna 'alamood indeer baalna 'alayk	ساعِدنا علمود ندير بالنا عليك
We have to remove your clothes.	laazim ninza' ihdoomak	لازِم ننزع هدومك

Are you having pain?	inta mitwaji'?	إنتَ متوجّع؟
Where are you having pain?	wayn yoj'ak?	وين يوجعك؟
Is the pain here?	il wija' ihnaa?	الوجَع هنا؟
Does anything make the pain better?	aku ay shee yKhalee il wija' yirooH?	أكو أي شي يخلي الوجَع يروح؟
Does anything make the pain worse?	aku ay shee yKhalee il wija' akthar?	أكو أي شي يخلي الوجَع أكثر؟
Did the pain start today?	bida il wija' il yom?	بِدا الوجَع اليوم؟

| 10 is the worst possible pain, and 1 is no pain at all. | 'ashra ma'naat-ha ihwaya wija' wo waaHid ma'naa maku wija' bil mara | عَشرَة معناتها هوايه وجع وواحد معناه ماكو وجع بالمره |
| Hold up the number of fingers. | 'ashir ib aSabee'ak | أشربأصابيعك |

| I need to clean your wounds. | laazim in naDhef ijrooHak | لازم إنظف جروحك |
| I am here to help you. | anee hna Hata asa'edak | آني هنا حتى أساعدك |

(*Continued*)

TABLE 4-5   Iraqi Pronunciation and Medical Terms (*Continued*)

Did you inhale any smoke or very hot air?	itnafasit duKhaan aw hawa Haar?	تنفِست دُخّان أو هوا حار؟
Do your lungs hurt?	'indak waja' bi ree-a?	عندك وجع بالرئة ؟
Are you having trouble breathing?	'indak Su'ooba min titnafas?	عندك صعوبة من تتنفّس؟
This will help avoid infection.	haTha raH yemna' il-iltihaab	هذا رَح يمنع الإلتهاب

TABLE 4-6   Translation Guide, Dari (Afghanistan)

PRONUNCIATION GUIDE FOR DARI SOUNDS UNFAMILIAR TO ENGLISH

Kh	as in meyKhaahee or Khuda
q	as in qaabale or maqsadet
gh	as in balghame or baghal
'	as in 'amaliyaat or 'azala

You have been injured.	zaKhmee shudayee	زخمی شده ای
You are ill.	mareez astee	مریض هستی
Lie still.	bey harakat daraaz bekash	بی حرکت دراز بکش
We will take care of you.	maa az shumaa moraaqebat meykuneem	ما از شما مراقبت می کنیم
Let us help you.	ijaaza bedey ke kumaket kuneem.	اجازه بده که کمک کنیم

Does this hurt?	aayaa eenja dard meykuna?	آیا اینجا درد میکنه؟
Move all of your fingers.	tamaame angusht haayet raa shor bedey	تمام انگشت ها یت را شور بده
Move all of your toes.	tamaame angusht haaye paayet raa shor bedey	تمام انگشت های پایت را شور بده
Open your eyes.	cheshm haayet raa waaz ko	چشم هایت را واز کو
Push against me.	tarafe ma teyla ko	طرف مه تیله کو

(Continued)

TABLE 4-6 Translation Guide, Dari (Afghanistan) *(Continued)*

Point to all the parts of your body that hurt.	har jaaye badanet ke dard meykunad neshaan bedey	هر جای بدنت که درد میکنه نشان بده
Does it hurt when I do this?	waqte ke man intoor meykunam dard meykuna?	وقتیکه من اینطور میکنم درد میکنه؟
Move this like this.	injay raa intoor shor bedey	این جای را اینطور شور بده
Turn over this way.	een taraf dawr beKhor	این طرف دور بخور
Did you inhale any smoke or very hot air?	aayaa dood wayaa hawaaye bisyaar garm tanafus kardeye?	آیا دود و یا هوای بسیار گرم تنفس کرده ای؟
Do your lungs hurt?	shush haayet dard meykuna?	شش هایت درد میکنه؟
Are you having trouble breathing?	dar nafas kasheedan mashkelaat daaree?	در نفس کشیدن مشکلات داری؟
This will help avoid infection.	ee az eltihaab jelaw geeree meykuna	ای از التهاب جلوگیری میکنه

Are you in pain?	dard daaree?	درد داری؟
Where is your pain?	kujaayet dard meykuna?	کجایت درد میکنه؟
Is the pain here?	dard dar eenjaa ast?	درد در اینجا است؟
Does anything make the pain better?	aayaa cheezey dard ra beytar mey saaza?	آیا چیزی درده بهتر می سازه؟
Does anything make the pain worse?	aayaa cheezey dard ra bad-tar mey saaza?	آیا چیزی درده بدتر می سازه؟
Did the pain start today?	dard imroz shuro' shud?	درد امروز شروع شد؟
How many days have you had the pain?	chand roz as ke dard daaree?	چند روز است که درد داری؟
Describe the pain on a scale from 1 to 10.	dardeta az darajey yak taa da bigo ke che andaaza ast	دردته از درجه یک تا ده بگو که چه اندازه است

10 is the worst possible pain, and 1 is no pain at all.	darajey da ya'ney shadeed tareen dard wa darajey yak ya'ney ke heych dard neyst	درجه ده یعنی شدیدترین درد و درجه یک یعنی که هیچ درد نیست
Hold up the number of fingers.	baa angusht haayet te'daad raa neshaan bedey	با انگشت هایت تعداد را نشان بده

(Continued)

TABLE 4-6   Translation Guide, Dari (Afghanistan) (Continued)

We will try to contact someone from your group.	maa koshish mey kuneem ke baa yak nafar az groope shumaa tamaas begireem	ما کوشش می کنیم که با یک نفر از گروپ شما تماس بگیریم
Please.	lutfan / bafarmaaye	لطفا / بفرمائید
Thank you.	tashakur	تشکر
You are welcome.	qaabale tashakur neyst	قابل تشکر نیست
Thank you for talking with me.	tashakur az eenke baa man gap zadee	تشکر از اینکه با من گپ زدی
I will talk with you again.	doobaara ba shumaa gap Khaahamzad	دوباره با شما گپ خواهم زد
Good-bye.	Khuda haafez	خدا حافظ

TABLE 4-7   Pashto (Afghanistan) Translations

PRONUNCIATION GUIDE FOR PASHTO SOUNDS UNFAMILIAR TO ENGLISH

Kh	as in	Khabare	or	maKhaa maKh
'	as in	maay'aat	or	saa'ta
gh	as in	ghwaret	or	balgham
q	as in	taqeeb	or	qaye

You have been injured.	ta ta pe sho we yeh	ته ټپي شوی يې
You are ill.	ta naarogha yeh	ته ناروغه يې
Lie still.	araam woghagaygah	ارام وغزېږه
We will take care of you.	moozh be staa sarana wokru	مور به ستا څارنه وکرو
Let us help you.	moozh ta ejaazah raaklaw che taa sarah kumak wokru	مور ته اجازه راکړه چه تاسره کومک وکړو

(Continued)

TABLE 4-7 Pashto (Afghanistan) Translations *(Continued)*

Does this hurt?	daa dard kawe?	دا درد کوي؟
Move all of your fingers.	Kh-pale toleh de las goteh wo Khorhavaa	خپلې ټولې د لاس ګوتې وښوروه
Move all of your toes.	Kh-pale toleh de pesheh goteh wo Khorhavaa	خپلې ټولې د پښې ګوتې وښوروه
Open your eyes.	sterge deh Khalasi kelah	سترګې دې خلاصي کړه
Push against me.	ze maa las taa feshar wokra	زما لاس ته فشار ورکړه
Does it hurt when I do this?	che ze daase kowom da dard kawe?	چې زه داسې کوم ، دا درد کوي؟
Move this like this.	daa ta daase harekat wokra?	دا ته داسې حرکت ورکړه
Turn over this way.	de Khuaa ta raataw sha	دې خوا ته راتاو شه
Did you inhale any smoke or very hot air?	taa dood ya dayrha garme hawaa tanafos kareda?	تا دود یا ډېره ګرمه هوا تنفس کړېده؟
Do your lungs hurt?	staa segeh dard larey?	تا سږي درد لري؟
Are you having trouble breathing?	ta tanafos kawaley shey?	ته تنفس کولای شې؟
This will help avoid infection.	daa bademe krob nowalo mahe wene sey	دا به د مکروب نیولو مخه ونیسي

Are you in pain?	dard larey?	درد لري؟
Where is your pain?	kum zaay ke dard larey?	کوم ځای کې درد لري؟
Is the pain here?	daa zaay dard kawe?	دا ځای درد کوي؟
Does anything make the pain better?	sa shey dard kamawe?	څه شي درد کموي؟
Does anything make the pain worse?	sa shey dard deyrawe?	څه شي درد ډېروي؟
Did the pain start today?	dard nen shuro sho?	درد نن شروع شو؟
How many days have you had the pain?	tsumra owrazeh da dard larey?	څومره ورځې دا درد لري؟

(Continued)

TABLE 4-7	Pashto (Afghanistan) Translations (Continued)	
Describe the pain on a scale from 1 to 10.	de dard andaazah de yaw ter las pure patanaasub wosheya1	د درد اندازه د ۱-۱۰ په تناسب ونښیه
10 is the worst possible pain, and 1 is no pain at all.	las beKhey der dard owyao hes dard mana larey	لس بيخي ډېر درد او يو هيڅ درد معنا لري
Hold up the number of fingers.	po goto nomrah wowaayah	په ګوتو نومره ووایه
Are you hungry?	doday ghware? / wogge yeh?	ډوډی غواړې؟ وږی يې؟
Do you need to urinate?	teshnaab ta ze?	تشناب ته ځې؟
Do you need to defecate?	teshnaab ta ze?	تشناب ته ځې؟
Do you want a cigarette?	seegret ghware?	سګرټ غواړې؟
I understand.	ze poheezhum	زه پوهېږم
I do not understand.	ze na poheezhum	زه نه پوهېږم
We will try to contact someone from your group.	mozh be kooshesh wokru che staase pe group ke dey yow cha sa ra Khabare wokru	موږ به کوښښ وکړو چې ستاسې په ګروپ کې د يو چا سره خبرې وکړو
Please.	lutfan	لطفاً
Thank you.	tashakor / manana	تشکر / مننه
You are welcome.	sha raaghlast	ښه راغلاست
Thank you for talking with me.	de Khabaro kowlo sa Khab manana	د خبرو کولو ځخه مننه
I will talk with you again.	ze be beyaa staa sa raa Khabare wokram	زه به بيا ستا سره خبرې وکم
Good-bye.	de Khudaay pa amaan	د خدا ی په امان

Other medical content is also available on the website:

- Registration
- Assessment
- Surgical consent
- Trauma
- Procedures
- Foley catheters
- Ophthalmology
- Surgery instruction
- Pain interview
- Medicine interview
- Orthopedics
- Obstetrics and gynecology
- Cardiology
- Neurology
- Exam commands
- Caregiver
- Postoperative care/prognosis
- Medical conditions
- Diseases

Medical Tools

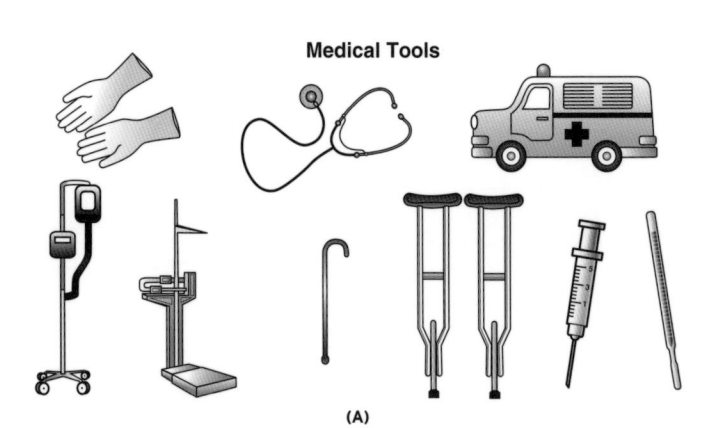

(A)

Medicine

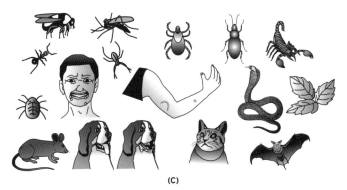

(B)

Bites

(C)

FIGURE 93A–C Graphics. A. Medical Tools. B. Medicine. C. Bites.
Source: Adapted from the Defense Language Institute Foreign Language Center.

■ Transport

Patient Transport

Refer to CENTCOM CPG Patient Transfer (July 2006) for specific details on patient transport. This section is meant as a guideline only; it is not a substitute for good clinical judgment.

TABLE 4-8 Parameters That Should Be Met Prior to Transfer of Any Patient

When any one or more of these criteria are not met, the treating physician should continue treatment at that facility or document the limitations at the current facility that compel urgent high-risk transfer.

Patients being transported with mechanical ventilation, vasopressors, ongoing resuscitation, or neurologic injury should be accompanied by appropriately trained personnel. Providers should include an RN (trained in critical care or emergency medicine) or paramedic and respiratory therapist in addition to the flight medic. On occasion, it may be appropriate to include an anesthesia provider or physician on the transport team.

Heart rate < 120 bpm	INR < 2.0
SBP >90 mm Hg	pH > 7.30
Hematocrit > 27%	Base deficit < 5
Platelet count < 50	Temperature > 35°C

TABLE 4-9 Joint Service Patient Movement Precedence and Description

Movement Precedence	Army, Navy, Marine MEDEVAC	Air Force Aeromedical Evacuation	Description
Urgent	Within 2 hours	ASAP	Immediate movement to save life, limb, or eyesight
			"Surgical" urgent = golden hour
Priority	Within 4 hours	Within 24 hours	Prompt medical care not available locally; condition may deteriorate and patient cannot wait for routine movement
Routine	Within 24 hours	Within 72 hours or next available mission	Condition is not expected to deteriorate while patient is awaiting movement

TABLE 4-10 Patient Movement Classifications

Psychiatric

1A: Severely ill psychiatric patient who requires close supervision and should arrive at the aircraft in hospital clothing, sedated, and restrained on a dressed litter.

1B: Moderate to severely ill psychiatric patient who is sedated, should wear hospital clothing, and should be transported on a litter. Restraints are not applied, but one set is secured to the litter or maintained by the patient's medical attendant.

1C: Cooperative, reliable, and moderately severe psychiatric inpatient traveling in ambulatory status, dressed in uniform or civilian clothes.

Notes:
- The medical attendant should be same sex and rank appropriate, if feasible.
- Use AF IMTS 3899F Physician Orders for Behavior Management and Restraints, 3899G Restraint Observation Flow Sheet.
- Use time-limited restraints.
- Conduct circulation checks every 15 minutes and keep the patient in line-of-sight observation.
- See the "Mental Health" section.

Litter

2A: Litter patient who may not or cannot ambulate, and may be unable to perform self-care. Requires assistance in the event of an emergency. Travels in hospital clothing and may sit in a seat.

2B: Litter patient, usually dressed in hospital clothing, able to ambulate and sit in a seat, and should be able to ambulate unassisted in an emergency.

(Continued)

TABLE 4-10 Patient Movement Classifications (Continued)

Notes: Consider the length of transport, the patient's medical condition (e.g., pain, fatigue, dependent edema/DVT risk), and en route care.

Ambulatory

3A: Nonpsychiatric, non-substance-abuse inpatient requiring medical treatment, assistance, or observation en route (usually minimal), or returning from an inpatient visit at a medical facility.
3B: Recovering inpatient, returning to home station, and requires no medical attention en route.
3C: Ambulatory drug or alcohol substance abuse inpatient going for treatment dressed in military or civilian clothing.

Notes: Consider the length of transport, the patient's medical condition (e.g., pain, fatigue, dependent edema), and en route care.

Infant

4A: Infant, younger than 3 years of age, occupying a seat and going for treatment.
4B: Infant, younger than 3 years of age, occupying a seat and returning from treatment.
4C: Infant requiring an airborne life support system (ALSS).
4D: Infant, younger than 3 years of age, on a litter.
4E: Outpatient, younger than 3 years of age, occupying a seat.

Notes:
· Use an FAA-approved car seat for children up to eight years old and/or 57 inches tall.
· The child may travel with a parent and/or medical attendant.

Outpatient

5A: Ambulatory outpatient going for treatment. Does not require a litter or medical assistance during flight.
5B: Ambulatory drug- or substance-abuse outpatient going for treatment.
5C: Psychiatric outpatient going for treatment.
5D: Outpatient on litter for comfort or safety going for treatment.
5E: Returning outpatient on a litter for comfort or safety.
5F: Returning outpatient.

Note: Unit Commander will need to approve patient movement.

Attendant

6A: Medical attendant (MA). A physician, nurse, or technician who is assigned to provide specialized medical/nursing treatment en route through to the patient's destination facility.
6B: Nonmedical attendant (NMA); spouse, parent, family member, military escort.

Notes:
· The attendant must carry deployment, NATO, and travel orders.
· Clothing, bags, and return travel must comply with IAW local policy.
· MAs are coordinated with the PMRC for patients whose care exceeds the capabilities of the medical crew or require special attention (e.g., 1A, ventilator).
· MAs are responsible for providing patient care, including coordinating and documenting care and medications.
· MAs will accompany the patient to the MTF or may be relieved by a same-level care provider.

Patient movement items (PMI) consist of medical equipment approved for flight needed to support the patient. Examples of PMI include ventilators, cardiac monitors, IV pumps, and pulse oximeters. Contact the supporting PMRC for the most current list.

Noncertified/nonstandard medical equipment required for en route care requires a waiver for AE missions. Contact the supporting PMRC.

Moving Patients and Equipment Safely

Follow local tactical procedures, and take the following steps to ensure safe transport:

- During ERO, wear gloves, earplugs, and goggles, and roll sleeves down. Ensure combat head gear is secure.
- Use at least four people of relatively equal strength when carrying litter patients and excessive weight over long distances, and while lifting a litter patient above the level of the waist.
- Switch to a two-person carry when walking on narrow ramps. See Figure 94.
- Ensure that all patient care equipment, medical records, supplies, and medications are present and safely secure.
- Provide patients with earplugs and protect them from extreme weather (e.g., heat, cold, rain). Keep blankets secure under the litter straps.
- Load patients only at the direction of the vehicle/helicopter/flight crew. See Figure 95.
- Rolling patients who are on gurneys and on other wheeled carriers up and down ramps is unsafe. Carry them only!

4 Man Litter Bearing: The Switch

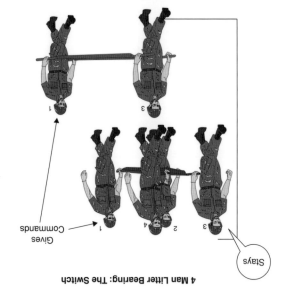

Gives Commands

Stays

FIGURE 94 Demonstration of how to switch from a four-man carry to a two-man carry. The person at the left-back position calls out the commands.
Source: U.S. Air Force. Aeromedical Contingency Operations (AFI 41-312).

Hand and Arm Signals

Assume Guidance   Move Forward   Move Back   Move Upward   Move Downward   Hover

Move Left   Move Right   Spot Turn Right   Spot Turn Left   Wave Off   Take Off

FIGURE 95   Vehicle/aircraft movement signaling.
Source: U.S. Air Force. Aeromedical Contingency Operations (AFI 41-312).

■ Patient Transfer Checklist

Patient identification band (Wrist)

Allergy band (Wrist)

Military identification card and dog tags (Note: These items may not be available; in such a case, you may need to use a permanent marker or tape to create an identification label.)

Passport, as required

Orders (military/NATO)

Medical records/X-rays

Medication, including an adequate supply for transport
- Level 3 to Level 4 (AOR to Germany): 1 day
- Level 4 to Level 5 (Germany to United States): 3 days

If patient is on a litter, litter mattress, clean sheets, blankets, and two litter straps

Thorough anti-hijacking search of person and bags, and written anti-hijacking certification complete

CASEVAC Documentation: IAW Local Directives

DD Form 1380, Field Medical Card
- U.S. and NATO documentation of DNBI, BI treatments, and death when medical records are unavailable
- SF 600, Standard Form: all-purpose medical record/clinical documentation

All Patients Using the Patient Movement System

AF IMT 3899: Patient Movement Record
Narrative summary
Allergies, Hgb/Hct, weight, vital signs, O_2 saturation, etc.
En route medical/special equipment approved for flight or waiver requested
Appropriate physician treatments/medications ordered/available

AF IMT 3899A: Patient Movement Progress Note
TBI screening
Risks en route for hypoxia (O_2 for ground/rotor transport, ventilator, suction)
Vital signs, temperature, O_2 saturation within normal limits
Pain assessment and adequate medications for duration of transport
Risk for skin breakdown (use litter mattress); turn every 2 h
Bowel/bladder toileting documented
Colostomy/ileostomy/urinary drainage bag clean/empty/totals documented
External fixator pin care within 2 hours of transport
Plaster casts–should be 48 hours old and bivalved if swelling is expected
Adequate circulation/neurologic status of all extremities and documented
Risks for DVT; prophylaxis considered
Dressing clean/dry/negative-pressure device
Dressings changed within 12 h of transport
IV catheter and tubing changed within 48 h of transport and patent
Fluids/meals as required; if NPO, IV maintenance ordered
Infection control precautions (contact precautions required for all combat wounds)
Hot/cold weather factors addressed, including appropriate footwear
Controlled drug accountability

AF IMT 3899I: Patient Movement Medication Record
Self-administration of medication (SAM): knows use and documented
Sufficient medication/IV solutions for the continuum, matches PMR/orders
IV medication labeled/timed/on pump
Plan for administering medications/drips ground/rotor transport

Patient's Property

Weapons, ammunition, explosives, lighters, matches identified/removed
Knives removed from patient's control and inventoried; use AF Form 3854, Receipt of Valuables, and AF Form 1053, Record of Patient Storing Valuables or Service Specific List
Items in excess of 60 pounds inventoried and transportation arranged by patient's service representative

Thorough anti-hijacking search of person and bags, and written anti-hijacking certification complete

Psychiatric Patients

(See the "Mental Health" section.)

Search all baggage and person for sharps, matches, lighters and cigarettes, and medication.

Items not allowed will be inventoried and accounted for as above

Litter (1A/1D) patients should travel in hospital clothing with a medical attendant; may carry eyeglasses, toothbrush, and a small amount of money (not to exceed $25.00), wedding band, rings, wristwatch, ID card, and wallet

1A: leather restraints; IAW AF IMT 3899F, Patient Movement Physician Orders for Behavior Management and Restraints, and start AF IMT 3899G, Patient Movement Restraint Observation Flow Sheet

- When leather restraints are on, restraints are not secured to litter.

Medical Attendant/Nonmedical Attendant

Appropriate skill-level healthcare provider; appropriate rank, same sex if accompanying psychiatric patients

Coordinated/approved by PMRC

TBI screening

Military ID

Original deployment, NATO, and travel orders to return to the AOR

Personal items/baggage compliant with IAW theater policy (carry-on, duffel)

Received point of contacts for arrival and departure, and planned itinerary back

No weapons, explosives, knifes/sharp objects, matches, or lighters

Thorough anti-hijacking search of person and bags, and written anti-hijacking certification complete

Patient Litters

NATO litter: Material is green canvas with wooden poles and lifting handles. Litter has not been tested for maximum patient weight. Do not exceed 250 lb.

Army DECON litter: Material is green or black polypropylene with aluminum poles and nylon (telescoping) handles. Maximum patient weight is 350 lb.

Some litter pole lengths can be adjusted from 90 to 94.4 inches to accommodate placement in a helicopter.

Raven litter: smaller; folds/mesh; for use in the field.

Overweight patient litter (OWL):

- Used to transport non-ambulatory patients weighing more than 250 lb
- Made of plywood secured to four standard NATO litter poles, and two litter poles with handles mounted at the normal width for securing in litter stanchions
- Use mattress pads, and include extra pillows and blankets to elevate the head.
- Use a minimum of 6 litter bearers and 3 litter straps to secure patient.

Warning: Nylon litters are not approved for AE missions owing to the slick surface and unsafe patient movement during take-off and landing.

FIGURE 96 NATO litter (canvas). Attachable 30° backrest is available. To obtain a 90° angle, remove the backrest and then rotate and reapply it. The litter seams at the feet and head and the cross-members increase skin interface pressure. Cross-members under the back (position under the sternum) may be used as a CPR backboard in an emergency.

Litter operation proceeds as follows:

- Open the litter and inspect it for damage; do not use the litter if material is torn greater than 1 inch. Ensure that the litter handles and spreader mechanisms are intact/engaged.
- Use a mattress pad with a clean sheet to prevent skin breakdown. Only use a Black DECON litter mattress with the DECON litter.
- CPR may be conducted on a non-DECON NATO litter when the shoulders are positioned above the cross-bars (backboard is preferable). A backboard is required when performing CPR on a DECON litter.
- Cover the patient with a clean sheet/blanket, and use a clean pillow and pillow case.
- Secure the patient to the litter with two litter straps over sheet/blanket at the mid-thigh and upper chest. Do not tie the excess strap in a knot.
- If not contraindicated, use a NATO backrest to elevate the patient's head to a 30° or 90° position. Clip the frame at the head of the litter inside the stirrups; reverse the frame to produce the other angle. Secure the backrest by threading the chest litter strap through both stirrups.
- Use a three- or four-person carry when using a backrest. Only use the 30° position for flight.

Pressure Ulcer Prevention During Patient Transport

Increased pressure over seams at the patient's head and heels and over the stabilizing straps of material on NATO litter may lead to pressure ulcers (generally under the shoulders and calves) during patient transport.

Consider the following points to avoid ulcer formation:

- Blankets do not decrease skin interface pressure and should not be used as padding to prevent pressure ulcers.
- A lateral turn decreases pressure minimally on the hip and may increase pressure on the heels. Consider use of pillows or blankets to provide a 10-20° lateral turn.
- An AE mattress effectively decreases pressure, but the patient still requires q 2 h repositioning.
- Elevate the heels at all times on pillows unless contraindicated,
- Pressure on the heels is increased with an increased HOB angle.
- Assess the patient's occiput and heels, and pay particular attention to prevention of excess pressure on these areas.

Transporting Patients to Ships

Patients may be transported to a ship using a rubber boat, lifeboat, or helicopter. The Stokes litter is used for helicopter-to-ship or ship-to-ship transport.

- The patient must be secured and have on a life jacket during ship-to-ship transport.
- If there is no flight deck on the ship, the Stokes litter and a cable are lowered and connected and the patient is moved in air.
- The Stokes litter is a different width/configuration from the NATO litter and requires modification of SMEED equipment transport sled.
- Padding should be applied between the patient and the litter if possible.

There is no medical equipment onboard lifeboats, so all necessary equipment/oxygen must be brought onboard with the patient. When loading a lifeboat, the most critically injured patients/medical team are loaded first, with the patients being placed in the lowest litter tiers. During helicopter MEDEVAC, the patient is transported on a NATO litter.

During such transports, patients may have increased exposure to environment. Ensure that steps are taken to prevent hypothermia.

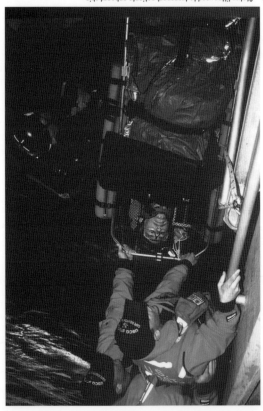

FIGURE 97A   Stokes litter used to transport patients onboard ship.
Source: Courtesy of PA2 Jacquelyn Zettles/U.S. Coast Guard.

FIGURE 97B Stokes litters positioned on a lifeboat aboard a USNS medical ship.
Source: Courtesy of Eddie Lopez, LCDR, NC, USN.

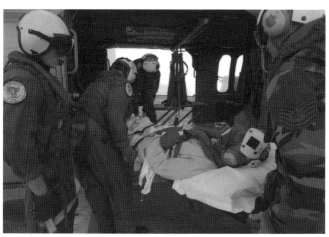

FIGURE 97C MEDEVAC from USNS Comfort; note that the patient is on a NATO litter.
Source: Courtesy of Mass Communication Specialist 3rd Class Kelly E. Barnes/U.S. Navy.

TABLE 4-11   Alphanumeric and Morse Code

Alphanumeric	Word	Pronunciation	Morse Code
A	Alpha	AL-FAH	• −
B	Bravo	BRAV-VOH	− • • •
C	Charlie	CHAR-LEE	− • − •
D	Delta	DELL-TAH	− • •
E	Echo	ECK-OH	•
F	Foxtrot	FOKS-TROT	• • − •
G	Golf	GOLF	− − •
H	Hotel	HOH-TEL	• • • •
I	India	IN-DEE-AH	• •
J	Juliet	JEW-LEE-ETT	• − − −
L	Lima	LEE-MAH	• − • •
M	Mike	MIKE	− −
N	November	NO-VEM-BER	− •
O	Oscar	OSS-CAH	− − −
P	Papa	PAH-PAH	• − − •
Q	Quebec	KEH-BECK	− − • −
R	Romeo	ROW-ME-OH	• − •
S	Sierra	SEE-AIR-RAH	• • •
T	Tango	TANG-GO	−
U	Uniform	YOU-NEE-FORM	• • −
V	Victor	VIC-TAH	• • • −
W	Whiskey	WISS-KEY	• − −
X	X-ray	ECKS-RAY	− • • −
Y	Yankee	YANG-KEY	− • − −
Z	Zulu	ZOO-LOO	− − • •
1	One	WUN	• − − − −
2	Two	TOO	• • − − −
3	Three	TREE	• • • − −
4	Four	FOW-ER	• • • • −
5	Five	FIFE	• • • • •
6	Six	SIX	− • • • •
7	Seven	SEV-EN	− − • • •
8	Eight	AIT	− − − • •
9	Nine	NIN-ER	− − − − •
0	Zero	ZEE-RO	− − − − −

TABLE 4-12   Radio Language

Over	I have finished talking and I am listening for your reply.
Out	I have finished talking to you and do not expect a reply.
Roger	Information received.
Copy	I understand what you said.
Wilco	Will comply.

Approach And Leave The Helicopter In A
Crouched Manner When Rotors Are Turning

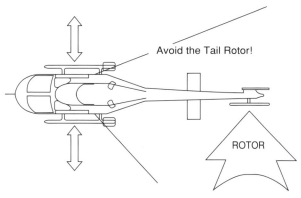

Avoid the Tail Rotor!

ROTOR

FIGURE 98 Helicopter operations.
Source: Federal Aviation Administration. Advisory Circular: Heliport Design (AC 150/5390-2B).
September 30, 2004.

Helicopter Operations/Loading

- Keep a low silhouette while in the circumference of the rotors; keep clear of the tail rotor.
- Do not approach the helicopter until the flight crew signals to do so.
- Approach at the 3 o'clock or 9 o'clock position off the nose so the pilot can view the loading activities. Warning: Follow specific aircraft and operational guidance.
- If landing zone is on a slope and if operationally feasible, approach from the downhill side.

FIGURE 99 Zulu time chart.

Location	GMT Offset																								
Kwajalein	−12	0500	0400	0300	0200	0100	2400	2300	2200	2100	2000	1900	1800	1700	1600	1500	1400	1300	1200	1100	1000	0900	0800	0700	0600
Midway Pago Pago	−11	0600	0500	0400	0300	0200	0100	2400	2300	2200	2100	2000	1900	1800	1700	1600	1500	1400	1300	1200	1100	1000	0900	0800	0700
Hawaii	−10	0700	0600	0500	0400	0300	0200	0100	2400	2300	2200	2100	2000	1900	1800	1700	1600	1500	1400	1300	1200	1100	1000	0900	0800
Elmendorf	−9	0800	0700	0600	0500	0400	0300	0200	0100	2400	2300	2200	2100	2000	1900	1800	1700	1600	1500	1400	1300	1200	1100	1000	0900
Pacific Time	−8	0900	0800	0700	0600	0500	0400	0300	0200	0100	2400	2300	2200	2100	2000	1900	1800	1700	1600	1500	1400	1300	1200	1100	1000
Mountain Time	−7	1000	0900	0800	0700	0600	0500	0400	0300	0200	0100	2400	2300	2200	2100	2000	1900	1800	1700	1600	1500	1400	1300	1200	1100
Central Time	−6	1100	1000	0900	0800	0700	0600	0500	0400	0300	0200	0100	2400	2300	2200	2100	2000	1900	1800	1700	1600	1500	1400	1300	1200
Eastern Time	−5	1200	1100	1000	0900	0800	0700	0600	0500	0400	0300	0200	0100	2400	2300	2200	2100	2000	1900	1800	1700	1600	1500	1400	1300
Bermuda Puerto Rico	−4	1300	1200	1100	1000	0900	0800	0700	0600	0500	0400	0300	0200	0100	2400	2300	2200	2100	2000	1900	1800	1700	1600	1500	1400
Azores	−1	1600	1500	1400	1300	1200	1100	1000	0900	0800	0700	0600	0500	0400	0300	0200	0100	2400	2300	2200	2100	2000	1900	1800	1700
England Ireland	GMT	1700	1600	1500	1400	1300	1200	1100	1000	0900	0800	0700	0600	0500	0400	0300	0200	0100	2400	2300	2200	2100	2000	1900	1800
Germany Italy	+1	1800	1700	1600	1500	1400	1300	1200	1100	1000	0900	0800	0700	0600	0500	0400	0300	0200	0100	2400	2300	2200	2100	2000	1900
Turkey Greece	+2	1900	1800	1700	1600	1500	1400	1300	1200	1100	1000	0900	0800	0700	0600	0500	0400	0300	0200	0100	2400	2300	2200	2100	2000
Riyadh	+3	2000	1900	1800	1700	1600	1500	1400	1300	1200	1100	1000	0900	0800	0700	0600	0500	0400	0300	0200	0100	2400	2300	2200	2100
Tehran	+4	2100	2000	1900	1800	1700	1600	1500	1400	1300	1200	1100	1000	0900	0800	0700	0600	0500	0400	0300	0200	0100	2400	2300	2200
Pakistan	+5	2200	2100	2000	1900	1800	1700	1600	1500	1400	1300	1200	1100	1000	0900	0800	0700	0600	0500	0400	0300	0200	0100	2400	2300
New Delhi	+5.5	2230	2130	2030	1930	1830	1730	1630	1530	1430	1330	1230	1130	1030	0930	0830	0730	0630	0530	0430	0330	0230	0130	0030	2330
Thailand	+7	2400	2300	2200	2100	2000	1900	1800	1700	1600	1500	1400	1300	1200	1100	1000	0900	0800	0700	0600	0500	0400	0300	0200	0100
Phillipines	+8	0100	2400	2300	2200	2100	2000	1900	1800	1700	1600	1500	1400	1300	1200	1100	1000	0900	0800	0700	0600	0500	0400	0300	0200
Okinawa Japan	+9	0200	0100	2400	2300	2200	2100	2000	1900	1800	1700	1600	1500	1400	1300	1200	1100	1000	0900	0800	0700	0600	0500	0400	0300
Alice Springs (AUS)	+9.5	0230	0130	0030	2330	2230	2130	2030	1930	1830	1730	1630	1530	1430	1330	1230	1130	1030	0930	0830	0730	0630	0530	0430	0330
Guam	+10	0300	0200	0100	2400	2300	2200	2100	2000	1900	1800	1700	1600	1500	1400	1300	1200	1100	1000	0900	0800	0700	0600	0500	0400
Wake New Zealand	+12	0500	0400	0300	0200	0100	2400	2300	2200	2100	2000	1900	1800	1700	1600	1500	1400	1300	1200	1100	1000	0900	0800	0700	0600

■ Zulu Time Chart

The "clock" at Greenwich, England, (Greenwich Mean Time [GMT]) is used as an international reference of time in military activities and patient care that cross time zones. The letter designator for this clock in Z. Baghdad (same time zone as Riyadh) is Z + 3 and Afghanistan is Z + 5. If you are in Baghdad, the local time is 2100 and the Zulu time is 1800; report both times to ensure clear communication of time across time zones. For those areas that practice Daylight Savings Time, add one hour (+1).